PLAYING POLITICS WITH HISTORY

Studies in Contemporary European History

Editors:

Konrad Jarausch, Lurcy Professor of European Civilization, University of North Carolina, Chapel Hill, and a Director of the Zentrum für Zeithistorische Studien, Potsdam, Germany

Henry Rousso, Senior Fellow at the Institut d'historie du temps present (Centre national de la recherché scientifique, Paris) and co-founder of the European network "EURHISTXX"

PLAYING POLITICS
WITH HISTORY

The Bundestag Inquiries into East Germany

Andrew H. Beattie

Berghahn Books

NEW YORK • OXFORD

First published in 2008 by
Berghahn Books

www.berghahnbooks.com

© 2008 Andrew H. Beattie

Library of Congress Cataloging-in-Publication Data

Playing Politics with History : The Bundestag Inquiries into East Germany /
Andrew H. Beattie. — 1st ed.
　　p. cm. — (Studies in contemporary European history ; v. 4)
　　Includes bibliographical references and index.
　　ISBN 978-1-84545-533-0
　　1. Germany—Politics and government—1990–. 2. Germany (East)—
Politics and government—1989–1990. 3. Governmental investigations—
Germany (East). 4. Governmental investigations—Germany. 5. Political
culture—Germany—History—20th century. I. Title.

DD290.29.B43 2008
943′.1087—dc22

2008026631

British Library Cataloguing in Publication Data

A catalogue record for this book is available from
the British Library.

Printed in the United States on acid-free paper

ISBN 978-1-84545-533-0 Hardback

To my parents, Margaret and James

CONTENTS

Preface

As an exchange student in Potsdam in the late 1990s, I was confronted for the first time with the complicated reality of postcommunist eastern Germany. The legacy of East German state socialism and the question of how to handle it were everywhere, not least in the presence of communist-era buildings and memorials, in the renovation boom transforming the city and particularly its patrician Wilhelmine villas after decades of neglect, or, more problematically, in a campaign to reconstruct the old Hohenzollern city palace, as also proposed in Berlin. The human and intellectual legacy left behind by the German Democratic Republic (GDR) was even more fascinating, especially as expressed in the complex identities and allegiances of my fellow students and new friends. Generally in their late teens during the upheaval of 1989–90, they were surely among the "winners" of the democratic transformation. Worlds had opened for them that had been denied their parents, not least in new opportunities to travel and to immerse themselves, for example, in Spanish, Irish, or even Australian language and culture. Yet they could not but be affected by the devastating collapse of the East German economy that cast many of their parents into premature retirement, work-creation schemes, or unemployment, and plunged many of their home towns into a deep and lasting crisis.

Above all, their political homelessness and their strident identification as *Ossies* (easterners) were striking. They were at once attracted and repelled by the Party of Democratic Socialism (PDS), as the former ruling Socialist Unity Party of Germany (SED) had remodeled itself in 1990; and they were generally left cold by the other parties, which they associated with the West. They were under no illusions about the political reality of the former regime, but clung firmly to memories and mementos of happy childhoods under state socialism, long before successful nostalgic films such as *Goodbye Lenin!* or *Sonnenallee*, and without the commoditization of East German identity in the form of the Berlin *Ampelmännchen* (pedestrian traffic-light figure) that had already become the stuff of souvenir shops. They displayed considerable discomfort under the dominant western gaze on the East German past and present; indeed, the uneven dynamics of the unification process appeared to be more important for their current identities than their actual experiences in the GDR.

One seemingly trivial episode alerted me particularly to the fragility, contestability, and potential, if unintended significance of every representation of the past in this highly charged context. In a casual conversation about eastern regions and regionalism, a friend told me that the eastern states (*Bundesländer*) had not existed in the GDR. The implication was that they were a western creation and lacked authenticity and legitimacy. Only later did I learn that the states had in fact been re-created after the Second World War, only to be dissolved in 1952 as part of the communist push toward centralization, and that in July 1990 the democratized East German parliament had voted for their reestablishment. My friend's statement was barely half true, but no less powerful for that.

This incident and the Potsdam experience more generally led me eventually to explore the postunification politics of Germany's postwar history. How did unified Germany handle the legacy of the East German regime? How and why did it attempt to develop a new understanding of its national past after the end of the Cold War? How did interpretations of history and the lessons drawn from the past inform approaches to contemporary politics, and vice versa? And how did the ongoing struggle to cope with the older, burdensome legacy of the Nazi regime and the crimes it committed inform, and how was it itself affected by, efforts to address a further difficult past?

In pursuing these questions and completing this book, I have incurred many debts that I gratefully acknowledge here. Particular thanks are due to Konrad Jarausch, who encouraged me to pursue not only the topic but also the publisher. Assistance in the research process was received from numerous quarters. Financial aid came in the form of an Australian Postgraduate Award and a grant from the German Academic Exchange Service. The bulk of archival research was conducted at the Deutscher Bundestag Parlamentsarchiv in Bonn, and the Matthias Domaschk Archiv (Robert Havemann Gesellschaft) in Berlin. My thanks are due to the dedicated staff at both archives, as well as at the Bundestag Press Office and the Archiv der sozialen Demokratie (Friedrich Ebert Stiftung) in Bonn, and the Archiv Demokratischer Sozialismus (Rosa Luxemburg Stiftung) and the Stiftung Aufarbeitung der SED-Diktatur in Berlin. My research benefited greatly from meeting and interviewing members of the commissions of inquiry. The encouragement they gave to my endeavors and their preparedness to discuss the inquiries and broader issues testify to the strength of their commitment to the inquiries' mission. They will undoubtedly disagree with some of my assessments, but I owe them particular thanks.

At the University of Sydney, I would like to thank the staff of the history and germanic studies departments, above all Dirk Moses, for encouragement, critique, and inspiration, and Ben Tipton. I am also grateful for the support of colleagues and friends at the Institute for International Studies at the University of Technology, Sydney. My thanks are also due to my friends in Potsdam, who opened my eyes to the experience of living in East Germany before and during unification, and to Marion Berghahn, Ann Przyzycki and Melissa Spinelli for their highly professional guidance. Lastly, I would like to thank my parents, who have been more than supportive at every step of the way, and my wife Melanie, to whom I owe a huge debt of gratitude for only occasionally doubting that the book would ever be finished.

The referencing conventions used in this book require a brief explanation. The main sources are the multivolume published materials of the Bundestag's two commissions of inquiry.[1] All references to the published materials of the first commission are given in the endnotes in the form: Roman numeral volume number: Arabic numeral page number. For example, I: 8ff. Subsequent references to the same volume within an endnote omit the volume number. References to the materials of the second inquiry use the same system, but are italicized. For example, *II: 230.*

Note

1. Deutscher Bundestag, ed., *Materialien der Enquete-Kommission "Aufarbeitung von Geschichte und Folgen der SED-Diktatur in Deutschland" (12. Wahlperiode des Deutschen Bundestages),* IX vols. (Frankfurt am Main, 1995); Deutscher Bundestag, ed., *Materialien der Enquete-Kommission "Überwindung der Folgen der SED-Diktatur im Prozess der deutschen Einheit" (13. Wahlperiode des Deutschen Bundestages),* VIII vols. (Frankfurt am Main, 1999).

LIST OF ABBREVIATIONS

B90   Alliance 90/The Greens (Bündnis 90/Die Grünen)

BZ   *Berliner Zeitung*

CDU   Christian Democratic Union (Christlich-Demokratische Union)

CDUD   Christian Democratic Union of Germany (Christlich-Demokratische Union Deutschlands)

CPSU   Communist Party of the Soviet Union

CSU   Christian-Social Union (Christlich-Soziale Union)

DBD   Democratic Farmers' Party of Germany (Demokratische Bauernpartei Deutschlands)

DBPa   Deutscher Bundestag Parlamentsarchiv

FAZ   *Frankfurter Allgemeine Zeitung*

FDP   Free Democratic Party (Freie Demokratische Partei)

FR   *Frankfurter Rundschau*

FRG   Federal Republic of Germany

GDR   German Democratic Republic

KPD   Communist Party of Germany (Kommunistische Partei Deutschlands)

LDPD   Liberal Democratic Party of Germany (Liberal-Demokratische Partei Deutschlands)

MDA   Matthias Domaschk Archiv

ND   *Neues Deutschland*

NDPD   National Democratic Party of Germany (Nationaldemokratische Partei Deutschlands)

NS   National Socialism; Nazism (National Sozialismus)

NSDAP Nazi Party (Nationalsozialistische Deutsche Arbeiter Partei)

PDS   Party of Democratic Socialism (Partei des Demokratischen Sozialismus)

SBZ   Soviet Occupation Zone (Sowjetische Besatzungszone)

SED   Socialist Unity Party of Germany (Sozialistische Einheitspartei Deutschlands)

SMAD   Soviet Military Administration in Germany (Sowjetische Militäradministration in Deutschland)

SPD   Social Democratic Party of Germany (Sozialdemokratische Partei Deutschlands)

SZ   *Süddeutsche Zeitung*

TAZ   *Die Tageszeitung*

USSR   Union of Soviet Socialist Republics

INTRODUCTION

At the final public hearing of the German Bundestag's first commission of inquiry into the East German past, held in the Reichstag building in Berlin in May 1994, East German author and dissident Jürgen Fuchs gave a bitter assessment of unified Germany's handling of East German history:

> When I heard the many clever thoughts here yesterday, which have been addressed in academic seminars for a long time already and definitely will continue to be with new diploma theses, doctoral dissertations, professorial dissertations and ground-breaking publications in reputable publishing houses and journals, progressive and critical, questioning and answering, provocative and explanatory, I suddenly realised that we are lost....
>
> Perhaps it is unavoidable that historians have the last word. But we are still here, we contemporaries. Just a little patience will be needed until the last dissection and last categorization, evaluation and disempowerment....
>
> Here today we all know what is to be done. We know it very well, so very well! And therefore my little polemic, in all modesty, my sadness, too, and also the certainty, which actually should only be said by-the-by, that we are lost in the moment—namely now—that things are getting better with us, apparently. Today, others are writing our biographies, relaxed and academically focused. That is good, but bitter as well.[1]

Fuchs's biting commentary on the emotionless and abstract scholarly handling of East German history reveals the central issues that dominated public debate after the collapse of the East German dictatorship in 1989–90: the questions of eastern autonomy and ownership of the East German past and its interpretation and historicization. Fuchs also railed against the West German left-liberal intelligentsia's alleged softness on communism and touched on the comparability of the German Democratic Republic and National Socialism and the place that antifascism and East German opposition hold in Germany's historical memory. Underlying his position on each of these issues was a desire not only that memory of the commu-

---

Notes for this section begin on page 14.

nist regime—its victims, supporters, and fellow travelers—be kept alive, but that it remain a source of moral outrage and political mobilization, that it not be left just to historians while others returned to "business as usual."

By no means can East German history be said to have been left to the historians. In fact, it is widely recognized that Germany made an exceptionally thorough attempt to come to terms with its communist past after 1989–90. It is also well known that the precedent of the Nazi legacy and the context of unification distinguished the German case from other post-authoritarian or postdictatorial settings.[2] Indeed, these two factors contributed to the thoroughness of the search for accountability for regime crimes in two powerful ways. First, in addition to a desire for justice, the reckoning with the GDR past was motivated to a considerable extent by the perceived inadequacies of the two postwar German states' handling of Nazism. To be sure, some liberals and socialists insisted that past omissions should not be used to justify a hypocritically tough reckoning with the GDR. Yet for many of the moderate Left, as well as for conservatives and eastern former dissidents, the relative lateness and half-heartedness in facing up to Nazism served as a warning against making similar errors in relation to communism.[3] Second, the extensive reckoning with East German communism was enabled in large part by the GDR's accession to the western Federal Republic of Germany (FRG). Unification completed the transition from dictatorship to democracy and created an extraordinary degree of political stability. The subsequent reckoning process could draw on an enormous range of institutional, material, and human resources provided, in essence, by the old Federal Republic.[4]

Yet the postunification and post-Nazi contexts also had other, less salubrious effects on the debate about the history and legacy of East Germany, which are less well understood. Crucially, both served to prevent a discussion of the GDR qua GDR.[5] Interpretations of previous efforts to "come to terms" with the Nazi past over-determined discussion about how to confront the communist legacy. Most commentators acknowledged the differences—which indeed perhaps outweighed the similarities—between the post-1945 and post-1989 situations, but basic affinities were frequently assumed.[6] The handling of the East German past was even more deeply intertwined with the older, yet ongoing process of dealing with Nazism. Indeed, the Nazi past was ever present in debates about the GDR, for instance in the revival of totalitarianist theories and in numerous postulated comparisons of, and continuities between the two regimes. A major aim of this book is to explore the interaction between these two pasts.[7]

The influence of unification was even greater than that of the Nazi legacy. For all the stability and resources unification provided, its effects were highly ambiguous. Superficially at least, it appeared to have created ideal preconditions for a reckoning with the GDR. One commentator even suggested that—given the ease with which discredited institutions and individuals could be replaced by untainted western substitutes—postcommunist transitional justice in Germany was being pursued in "laboratory conditions."[8] However, as A. James McAdams argues, "The matter of the FRG's competence to sit in judgment on the GDR's affairs" was "implicitly at the heart of nearly every controversy over the FRG's attempt to come to grips with the record of a second dictatorship in German history."[9] The problems included the question of whether Federal German or GDR legal standards should be applied when prosecuting crimes committed in the East, and the (for some grating) fact that in many instances western judges, employers, and bureaucrats were presiding over the fate of easterners.[10] Specifically eastern desires for a thorough accounting with past repression, complicity, accommodation, and responsibility, and for meaningful renewal of institutions, personnel, and political culture were confronted with a well-established institutional and procedural apparatus. Media sensationalism over Stasi collaborators in every sector of eastern society further contributed to the creation of an environment charged with moral superiority and seeming "colonization."[11]

In this context, it became easy for former representatives of the communist regime to claim that they were the victims of western "victor's justice."[12] Such claims were largely unfounded but had considerable influence. The latter is reflected in numerous scholarly portrayals of the reckoning with the East German past as a postunification or western-driven or -dominated phenomenon.[13] Yet the vigorous reckoning with the communist past should not be seen as the result of unification or as western victor's justice.[14] It had been a key preoccupation of eastern civil-rights movements and was on the political agenda since late 1989, when unification was still a hazy, distant prospect.[15] Moreover, the victors over the dictatorship of the Socialist Unity Party in Germany were primarily the GDR opposition and wider populace, and the West only at one remove. If one can speak of victor's justice at all, then it was the justice of those eastern victors as much as of western anticommunists. Thanks to their combined desire for accountability, unified Germany pursued an unrivalled and largely unwavering, if not uncontested, course of postdictatorial justice.[16] A second major aim of this book is to highlight the agency and examine the contributions of easterners—dissidents and others—to that process. They were no means merely "on the side-lines," and nor can one speak simplistically of the western "expropriation" of East German history.[17]

Unification's impact went far beyond providing stability and resources on the one hand and prompting pernicious claims of victor's justice on the other. It fundamentally altered the terms of debate and even the ostensible goals of the reckoning process (and consequently the expectations and evaluations of it). A sense of growing alienation between easterners and westerners following unification itself became a major preoccupation. To a considerable extent, the goal shifted from justice and accountability to the "inner unity" of the nation.[18] This was held to require, first, that East German history be placed in a national context and, second, that easterners and westerners develop a common understanding of their divided past and their difficult, if unified present. Like the Nazi legacy, unification thus hindered a discussion of the GDR qua GDR. Indeed, many debates that ostensibly addressed East Germany in fact revolved around multiple German pasts.

However, one should not exaggerate the significance of East-West issues. Much of the literature assumes that the geographical—formerly geopolitical—divide was of paramount importance.[19] To a considerable extent, this reflects the reality of postunification discourse: the East-West cleavage frequently obscured, or was conflated with intra-eastern and intra-western matters.[20] Yet internal eastern and western disagreements over various topics continued and should not be overlooked. A third goal of this study is to disentangle the various levels of debate and lines of division that rarely simply coincided with the former border. In addition to exploring the diverse roles and perspectives of easterners, as mentioned above, I also hope to provide a more differentiated picture of the roles and views of westerners, whose entrenched political divisions and ongoing ideological disputes had a major, but under-acknowledged impact on the handling of multiple German pasts after 1989–90.

While the exceptional vigor and propitious yet difficult circumstances of Germany's attempt to work through its postwar history are reasonably well known, its ideological and political aspects have been rather neglected.[21] Some commentators overlook the central role of western anticommunism or suggest overly hastily that Cold War-era politics and ideologies simply disappeared in 1989–90.[22] In part, such tendencies are due to the widespread use of the vocabulary of "working through" or "coming to terms with" the past, which obscures as much as it sheds light on the processes it describes. As has been remarked frequently, these terms are highly malleable, ambiguous, and loaded.[23] It is essential to examine how they are used, what assumptions they rest on, and what is at stake. The scholarly literature cannot afford to accept historical actors' language at face value, and must also look to the political motivations, intentions, and interests involved. It is not sufficient to consider or be satisfied that a discussion of the past took place or even to analyze how it was pursued; one must also ask to what ends.[24] This book seeks to keep that question in the foreground and thus to recognize that the postunification handling of the

East German past was never only about justice, truth, trust, or reconciliation, but also about power and ideology.

All of the above applies not just to the handling of postunification Germany's multiple pasts in general, but also to the two parliamentary inquiries that constitute the specific subject of this study. In March 1992, the German Federal Parliament, the Deutscher Bundestag, established a commission of inquiry (*Enquete-Kommission*) titled "Working through the History and Consequences of the SED Dictatorship in Germany." It was succeeded in 1995 by a second commission, "Overcoming the Consequences of the SED Dictatorship in the Process of German Unity" that ran until 1998. These inquiries are indicative not only of the thoroughness of Germany's reckoning with the GDR, but also of its many difficulties and complexities, including the fact that more was at issue than just the East German past, not least as a result of the superimposition of East-West issues on debates about the GDR.

This book is not the first study of the commissions, but it is the first based on extensive historical research. Some earlier analysts seem not even to have examined the inquiries' terms of reference or their findings, but rely exclusively on previous scholarship and isolated media reports.[25] Others draw on the commissions' terms of reference, prominent Bundestag debates, and/or the inquiries' reports.[26] Some authors draw on their impressions of individual commission hearings.[27] Other authors have gone to more effort still. Ralf K. Wüstenberg and A. James McAdams rely on interviews with commissioners and inquiry staff and consider the published protocols of some hearings.[28] This study is the first to draw on a wide range of all of these sources, as well as on the many expertise papers and reports the inquiries commissioned, their internal records such as minutes of in-camera meetings, and German press coverage. It is therefore in a position not only to correct a number of factual errors in sections of the literature, but also to offer new insights into the inquiries' aims, processes, and achievements.

In addition to limited primary research, another problem with some of the extant literature is its reliance upon, indeed its uncritical acceptance of, the selective or tendentious statements or literature produced by individual commissioners. Numerous authors fail to interrogate the relationship between participants' statements of intent or claims of achievement on the one hand and what was actually practiced or produced on the other.[29] The accounts of commissioners and inquiry staff, who dominate the German language literature, display varying degrees of detachment and divergent assessments. They range from uncritical endorsement of the inquiries' work,[30] across more reflective attempts to evaluate their achievements and shortcomings,[31] to complete condemnation.[32] Even authors in the second category lack sufficient distance to appraise critically their own role, and the assessments of each group are laced with self-justification or political or personal bias.[33] Precisely for that reason, they are an essential source of information and opinion about the inquiries, but must be treated with caution.

Whether due to limited research, uncritical acceptance of participants' statements, or the particular questions asked of the inquiries, much of the existing literature is selective in its presentation of the commissions. The second inquiry is often ignored altogether or no more than named.[34] Numerous authors declare what the (singular) goal of the first inquiry was or what its two goals were; others make similarly strong and inaccurate statements about what it never intended to do. Such claims frequently appear to read backwards from (interpretations of) the inquiry's approach, results, or reception, to its aims, the multiplicity of which goes unrecognized.[35] Indeed, there is a tendency in the literature to isolate particular parts of the inquiries' work and declare them to be the whole. Moreover, a rather static picture emerges that does not do justice to changing developments from the initial proposal for an inquiry in 1991 through to the end of the second commission's work in 1998, or even from the first inquiry's establishment through to the delivery of its 1994 report. As a result, the contingent, tentative, and rather experimental character of the endeavor has not been sufficiently captured, nor have important internal developments. I hope to offer a more comprehensive, historical account and to highlight the diversity, complexity, and the often contradictory nature of the inquiries' aims, work, and achievements.

The existing literature approaches the commissions from a number of different perspectives, each of which has merits and limitations. Not least among the latter is the application of evaluative criteria that are only partly applicable. A number of authors examine the commissions' handling of particular historical topics, such as the East German churches or state-society relations. They assess the inquiries' investigations and conclusions against scholarly criteria, but thus overlook the hybrid scholarly political nature of the enterprise.[36] Similarly, McAdams' approach of evaluating the inquiries' findings on the basis of the extent to which they took GDR history seriously is intuitively appealing and ostensibly convincing.[37] Yet it ignores the fact that—at least for the anticommunist majority on the commissions—the aim was never just to understand the GDR and its citizens, but to judge it against explicitly liberal-democratic criteria.[38] Substantively, too, such approaches generally overlook the extent to which both the Nazi past and West German history became implicated, the latter well beyond the reappraisal of *Deutschlandpolitik* (West German policy toward the GDR) that McAdams analyzes.[39]

Other scholars focus on the inquiries as instruments of reconciliation, often to the neglect of other issues. Jennifer Yoder, for example, considers the commissions' popular appeal and their contribution to Germany's "inner unity," but her analysis ignores the commissions' further goals.[40] Excessive attention to the East-West divide obscures other aspects of the commissions' work and leads, not infrequently, to their mutual conflation. Some commentators, for instance, fail to see a real or potential conflict between addressing the experiences of "ordinary" East Germans in the pursuit of national integration on the one hand and those of the immediate victims of the communist regime in the name of justice on the other; occasionally, emphasis on the need to integrate "ordinary" easterners leads to the virtual denial of the authentic eastern-ness of victims' or dissidents' experiences.[41] Much of the literature also—uncritically and misleadingly—perpetuates or remains excessively agnostic over claims of western victor's justice; it gives insufficient weight to the considerable eastern input into the inquiries and minimizes the difficulties they faced as Federal Republican institutions with western participation.[42] Inadequate complexity and inappropriate criteria also plague the few (rather unsystematic and often unsympathetic) comparisons of the inquiries with "truth commissions" established in other postauthoritarian settings.[43]

The Bundestag commissions are rightly seen as an instrument of transitional justice, yet their significance goes far beyond that. The inquiries have been characterized as "a form of didactic public history" (by Charles Maier), an official public "history lesson" (by Timothy Garton Ash), and an effort toward "moral justice" (by McAdams).[44] Such terms go some way to reflecting commissioners' desire to undertake a systematic, differentiated examination of the structures of power and oppression and thus to shift the focus of public discussion from the Stasi to the SED. Yet more was at issue than (just) factual or moral questions about easterners' behavior under (or western behavior toward) the communist regime.[45] Much of the literature accepts at face value the public-enlightenment aspect propagated by commissioners and the importance of moral values and notions of "truth" in working through the past.[46] The rhetoric (eastern) commissioners adopted reflected the language and the communicative style of politics developed in eastern bloc dissident milieus as a counterpoint to the communist regimes' complete domination and distortion of the language of power and interests.[47] However, a focus on questions of integrity, morality, and truth relating to individual or group behavior *within* (or toward) the GDR does not engage with the even more important question of the legitimacy *of* the GDR (or the FRG or unification).[48]

Indeed, fundamental questions about politics and power warrant more attention than they have received. The commissions provided a forum for the contestation of the legitimacy of the two postwar states and of unification and they made significant contributions to broader debates about the identity of unified Germany and its constituent political camps. The role of party politics and ideology and the historical narratives that supported these are surprisingly under examined. McAdams, to be sure, highlights the partisan nature of debate about *Deutschlandpolitik,* for example, but barely considers the ideological context of this dispute; similarly, his discussion of the first inquiry's treatment of the East German churches or the wider population does not reveal what was at stake politically or ideologically.[49] Neither he nor Anne Sa'adah considers competing historical narratives or how these related to wider discourses of German politics and identity.[50] Wüstenberg, in turn, is aware of issues of unification and national identity that were implicated in debates about the GDR, but his focus on reconciliation leads him away from considering partisan competition over the past.[51] Partisanship, however, was a central organizing feature of the historical narratives presented to and by the commissions, and not just an unwanted or inappropriate intrusion or shortcoming as depicted by some commentators and participants.[52] Broader issues of public memory and in particular the role of the Nazi past in the commissions' work similarly warrant more attention. The inquiries were influenced considerably by attitudes toward the past and present handling of the Nazi legacy. In turn, they had a not inconsiderable impact on the latter. While some of these various dimensions have been recognized by some scholars, they have not yet been synthesized into a coherent overall analysis.[53]

To do justice to the full scope of the inquiries' work and to better understand their historical development and overall significance, sharper analytical parameters are required than *Vergangenheitsbewältigung* (coming to terms with, overcoming, or mastering the past) and *Vergangenheitsaufarbeitung* (working through the past). In recent years, a shift in the direction of a more rigorous examination of the politics of dealing with the past has been evident in the literature on Germany's handling of the Nazi legacy. For too long debate largely exhausted itself in the competing claims of Left and Right over the insufficiencies or adequacy respectively of West Germany's efforts to face up to German complicity in Nazi crimes. Advocacy and critique largely substituted for analysis, and the debate was loaded with moral claims, emotional excitement, and psychoanalytic jargon.[54] Since the 1990s, however, alternatives have been put forward to the widely criticized vocabulary of coming to terms with and working through the past.[55] In an influential study of amnesty and integration in the Adenauer era, Norbert Frei introduced the concept of *Vergangenheitspolitik* that encompasses the set of state policies that address specific legacies of the past, including the punishment of (or granting of amnesties to) offenders through the criminal courts, the disqualification (or reintegration) of compromised representatives of the former regime, and the payment (or denial) of compensation to its victims and the restitution of their property (or rejection thereof).[56] While Frei's study is important above all for its empirical research and interpretative conclusions, his notion of *Vergangenheitspolitik* (policy toward the past) has been adopted by numerous researchers.[57]

Other terms have been put forward. Inspired by French research into collective memory, Peter Reichel introduced the notion of *Erinnerungspolitik* (memory politics) in his examination of controversies surrounding various "sites of memory" (both physical and immaterial) relating to the Nazi past.[58] Finally, in an examination of West German remembrance of the East German uprising on 17 June 1953 that the communist authorities put down with the help of Soviet tanks and that the Federal Republic subsequently established as the Day of German Unity, Edgar Wolfrum advocated the notion of *Geschichtspolitik* (history politics), which he applies to the study—in a democratic society—of the symbolic uses of history for the purpose of national identity formation.[59]

Rather than seeing them as rivals or focusing on their individual shortcomings, these concepts can—in modified form—complement each other to provide a multifaceted theoretical framework that encompasses judicial, legislative, and political measures as well as public debate, political rhetoric, and symbolic politics, thus allowing a more complete analysis of the handling of the East German past since 1990.[60] This study utilizes the notion of *policies for the past* to designate state policies of retribution, recompense, and reconciliation. *History politics*—or playing politics with history—is understood as the contestation of political legitimacy with respect to history. Finally, *commemorative politics* (which I prefer to the less precise "memory politics") refers more specifically to public ceremonies and memorials. All three played a role, albeit to varying degrees, in the Bundestag's commissions of inquiry.

These concepts are preferable to *Vergangenheitsbewältigung* and *Vergangenheitsaufarbeitung,* even as the latter have undergone more rigorous attempts at definition and elaboration. Their emphasis on politics and policies highlights the contingent nature of decisions about the handling of the legacy of the past and provokes questions about competing interests and positions. This is an important advance on the literature on *Vergangenheitsbewältigung* and indeed the burgeoning literature on "memory," which even at its most subtle frequently remains fixated on dichotomous questions of the success/failure, advantages/disadvantages, and pursuit/non-pursuit of certain strategies or indeed the entire endeavor.[61] A further reason for adopting the triumvirate is that they do not limit the past in question to dictatorial or negatively viewed pasts, as *Vergangenheitsbewäl-tigung* and *Vergangenheitsaufarbeitung* invariably are taken to. Numerous definitions of the latter terms assume that the past in question is regarded as a burden, and that the aim is to prevent its repetition.[62] Such an approach begs what surely should be one of the central questions to be pursued, namely, how the past is interpreted and assessed by different actors. After all, some people may not view it exclusively in negative terms and may even see positive elements that are worth maintaining. By defining *Vergangenheitsbewältigung* or *Vergangenheitsaufarbeitung* as dealing with a negatively viewed past, those who hold such views are either excluded from the picture or labeled a priori as being opposed to the enterprise. In postunification Germany, such an approach is unproductive, because no one opposed the goal of working through the East German past; even the Party of Democratic Socialism objected merely to how it was being pursued. Rather than focusing on a past that by definition is at best problematic, it should be recognized that it is possible to develop policies and to conduct politics with pasts—or aspects of the past—that are viewed positively, such as resistance to dictatorship.[63] In the postunification German case, this applied in the view of the majority not just to the anticommunist opposition, but also by and large to West German history; the PDS, on the other hand, saw positive dimensions to East German history. A genuinely analytical approach cannot itself define the past in negative terms; instead, it must keep open the central question of precisely how the past is evaluated by social actors.[64]

This book is divided into two parts. Chapters 1 and 2 address the establishment of the commission of inquiry and the subsequent development of the inquiries' work. They highlight the multiplicity of the aims of the enterprise and the varying extent to which those aims were pursued: initial plans for the development of policies for the past gave way to an almost exclusive concentration on a discursive elaboration of history. The latter is then examined in the subsequent chapters. As I argue in chapter 1, a sense in 1991 that the unification project and the reckoning with the communist regime were stalling led to the widespread belief—shared by eastern former dissidents and western politicians alike—that something more had to be done. Precisely what was unclear, but they hoped that a parliamentary inquiry would provide a systematic, critical, but differentiated examination of the GDR in contrast to the rather hysterical and haphazard public debate already underway. It was also widely felt that easterners and westerners would only achieve a happier union when they better understood each other's pasts. Indeed, working through the East German past was seen as an "all-German task" and an essential prerequisite for the "inner unity" of the nation, the promotion of which became one of the inquiries' major goals. Yet the commissions' work was marked by tensions over the extent to which West German history should be included in the examination, as well as by doubts about whether, as national bodies with western participants, they did not hinder autonomous eastern deliberation of the past.

In fact, the general desire for a thorough examination of the GDR and for practical responses to its legacy in the present merged with continuing ideological disputes between East and West but also within each of these. Chapter 2 shows how the politics of Germany's postwar history came to predominate, effectively marginalizing the search for practical responses to the consequences of the East German regime as well as efforts toward either intra-eastern or national reconciliation. In the end, the commissions had little direct impact on policies for the past, and engaged above all in the contestation of political legitimacy with reference to history. This contestation sought to delineate acceptable or legitimate interpretations of the past and political options in the present, and to develop the historical consciousness and national identity of the recently unified nation. I thus agree with the assessment of commissioner Manfred Wilke that the inquiries' primary significance was "as an instrument of the parliamentary history politics" of reunified Germany.[65]

The contestation of Germany's postwar history in and around the commissions of inquiry constituted the ideological continuation of the Cold War after its historical end, contrary to depictions of the latter's immediate obsolescence. Ostensibly, the foremost issues—discussed in chapter 3—were the questions of the legitimacy of the East German state and responsibility for the dictatorship. Here, as elsewhere, the East-West divide was less important than partisan divisions. An overwhelming majority— consisting of Christian Democrats, Free Democrats, Social Democrats, and members of Alliance 90/The Greens—insisted on the fundamental political illegitimacy of the GDR and advocated the commemoration of the victims of, and the opposition against the SED dictatorship. In contrast, Democratic Socialists defended the GDR's legitimacy even as they acknowledged its flaws. In a sense, anticommunists were writing victor's history or meting out victor's justice against communism and the PDS; but the victors, importantly, were easterners as well as westerners. Questions remain, however, over the extent to which eastern dissidents' legitimate desire for a moral and political accounting with the former regime was co-opted and instrumentalized by conservative western interests.[66] Irrespective of the answer, the commissions' central role in the posthumous delegitimization of the GDR must be emphasized.[67]

Yet even more was at stake than questions of responsibility for, and the political legitimacy of the GDR. As chapter 4 shows, the commissions were also a site of debate about the history and future of socialism, an aspect almost totally missing from previous accounts.[68] Western conservatives sought to discredit not only the former communist regime and its representatives, but also its ideological pillars. They used the inquiry to expound on the evils of socialist ideology generally, rather than merely its manifestation in the GDR. Their wide-ranging condemnation targeted not just the PDS, but also sections of the former East German opposition and the West German Left, whose traditions were to be tainted by association. There were thus "losers" on the western side as well. In response, Social Democrats and a number of eastern former dissidents felt compelled to defend themselves, revealing a lingering sympathy for socialist ideals and traditions. Together with Democratic Socialists, they urged differentiation in contrast with the conservative governing coalition's outright condemnation.[69]

Conservatives also sought to score ideological points with the postwar history of coming to terms with the Nazi past. Whereas antifascism had always been among the GDR's strongest sources of legitimacy and constituted its (and the PDS's) most powerful ideological weapon against the Federal Republic, chapter 5 shows how Christian Democrats and Free Democrats used the commissions to demolish the GDR's reputation as an antifascist state. Where possible, they also pointed to the FRG's relatively successful efforts to face up to the Nazi past. They thus sought not only to destroy any remaining legitimacy the GDR might possess, but also to neutralize antifascism as a source of critique of the Federal Republic, again not only from the eastern but also from the western Left.

Seeking to take their ideological victory one step further, conservatives and Cold War liberals attempted to reassert the totalitarian paradigm and reinstate an "antitotalitarian consensus" for reunified Germany, as discussed in chapter 6. They thus seemingly rejected the western Left's traditional insistence on the singularity of Nazi crimes and their centrality for contemporary German politics and identity. However, the German reckoning with communism did not lead to the Nazi past being forgotten or marginalized, as some feared in the wake of unification.[70] Indeed, a central aspect of that encounter—and of the work of the commissions of inquiry in particular—consisted precisely in condemning the GDR by association with Nazism or, from the standpoint of the PDS, in insisting on the noble antifascist foundation of the East German state. The Nazi past, and in particular the break with it, had been so central to the legitimation strategies of the two postwar states that discussing their legitimacy was seemingly impossible without referring to Nazism. The imputation of continuities with the Third Reich remained the most devastating argument against either state.[71]

Political, ideological, and identitarian questions were thus of central importance to the commissions of inquiry. The latter therefore need to be understood not just as instruments of transitional justice, but also in the context of wider debates about "what's left" after the collapse of communism and an even broader set of discussions about the renegotiation of German identities in the postunification era.[72] Alongside the debate about whether Bonn should remain, or Berlin should become the seat of the federal government and parliament, the inquiries provided a postunification substitute for a debate about the past and future of the country that had not occurred during the unification process itself.[73] It is therefore by no means true that "nothing was at stake," as one commentator has concluded from the fact that the inquiries did not offer amnesties to representatives of the communist regime.[74] In fact, a great deal was at stake: as Konrad H. Jarausch argues, the controversies over GDR history—to which one must also add other German pasts—constituted "an intellectual contest over the identity of the united Germany."[75] Commentators who express their disappointment about the lack of "surprises" generated by the commissions' investigation similarly overlook their role as a vehicle for the redefinition of the German polity and its constituent partisan traditions.[76] In such a process, a combination of continuity and change was always more likely than radical breaks.

How and to what ends unified Germany's political and intellectual elite evaluated and utilized its postwar history in the decade after unification are the central questions to be asked of the inquiries. Western conservatives used the GDR past as a political weapon against the eastern and western Left, while eastern dissidents continued a moralizing discourse about complicity and accommodation. In effect, both sought to delegitimize the entire history of the GDR (aside from the opposition to the regime, which they lionized) and its defenders in the present. In response, both the moderate and radical Left sought to defuse the communist past as a political and moral weapon through the historicization of the GDR; that is, by examining it on its own terms and contextualizing it historically. Where western and eastern anticommunists sought to maintain the rage against those who had supported or sympathized with communism, Social Democrats and Democratic Socialists called for differentiation and sobriety, and rejected the "overkill" of the dead GDR.[77] Yet they also played politics with history. For many liberals, Social Democrats, and some Democratic Socialists too, the victory of parliamentary democracy over single-party dictatorship was certainly to be celebrated; but they were also concerned to rescue progressive aspects of German political and intellectual traditions and to fight a rearguard action against conservatives' total condemnation. Conservatives and Cold War liberals, by contrast, sought to establish the inner unity of the nation on the basis of an antitotalitarian consensus founded on the complete rejection of everything for which the GDR had stood and on the acceptance of the Federal Republic as the only legitimate German state. The handling of the East German past thus both reflected and reinforced the fundamental asymmetries of unification as well as the inherited ideological positions of the Cold War era. It would be unrealistic to expect this to have been otherwise. Yet the choices and preferences of the diverse actors involved warrant detailed consideration. As ever, the historical process was more open, complex, and ambiguous than it often appears in retrospect.

Notes

1. I: 695, 696, 701.
2. See for instance Timothy Garton Ash, *History of the Present: Essays, Sketches and Despatches from Europe in the 1990s* (London, 2000), 294–314; A. James McAdams, *Judging the Past in Unified Germany* (Cambridge, 2001), 1–6; Noel Calhoun, *Dilemmas of Justice in Eastern Europe's Democratic Transitions* (New York, 2004), 51.
3. Cf. Jürgen K. A. Thomaneck and Bill Niven, *Dividing and Uniting Germany* (London, 2000), 86.
4. Cf. Charles S. Maier, *Dissolution: The Crisis of Communism and the End of East Germany* (Princeton, 1997), 312f.; Christoph Kleßmann, *Zeitgeschichte in Deutschland nach dem Ende des Ost-West-Konflikts* (Essen, 1998), 22; Anne Sa'adah, *Germany's Second Chance: Trust, Justice and Democratization* (Cambridge, MA, 1998), 8; Ulrich Herbert, "Drei deutsche Vergangenheiten: Über den Umgang mit der deutschen Zeitgeschichte," in *Doppelte Zeitgeschichte: Deutsch-deutsche Beziehungen 1945–1990*, eds. Arnd Bauerkämper, Martin Sabrow, and Bernd Stöver (Bonn, 1999), 386; Bernd Faulenbach, "Die Auseinandersetzung mit der kommunistischen Vergangenheit in vergleichender Perspektive," in *Auf den Kehrichthaufen der Geschichte? Der Umgang mit der sozialistischen Vergangenheit*, eds. Isabelle de Keghel and Robert Maier (Hannover, 1999), 23ff.; Jennifer A. Yoder, "Truth without Reconciliation: An Appraisal of the Enquete Commission on the SED Dictatorship in Germany," *German Politics* 8, no. 3 (1999): 64; Corey Ross, *The East German Dictatorship: Problems and Perspectives in the Interpretation of the GDR* (London, 2002), 183.
5. Cf. Konrad H. Jarausch, "Die DDR denken: Narrative Strukturen und analytische Strategien," *Berliner Debatte Initial* 4–5 (1995): 11f.; Herbert, "Drei deutsche Vergangenheiten," 387f.; Sa'adah, *Germany's Second Chance*, 107.
6. Cf. Friso Wielenga, "Schatten der deutschen Geschichte: Der Umgang mit der Nazi- und DDR-Vergangenheit in der Bundesrepublik Deutschland," *Deutschland Archiv* 27, no. 10 (1994): 1058–73; Claus Offe, *Varieties of Transition: The East European and East German Experience* (Cambridge, 1996); Bernd Faulenbach, "Die Auseinandersetzung mit der doppelten Vergangenheit im Deutschen Bundestag," in *Grenzen der Vereinigung: Die geteilte Vergangenheit im geeinten Deutschland*, ed. Martin Sabrow (Leipzig, 1999); Jeffrey K. Olick, *In the House of the Hangman: The Agonies of German Defeat, 1943–49* (Chicago, 2005).

7. For brief discussions on the connections between debates about the Nazi and GDR pasts, see Konrad H. Jarausch, "A Double Burden: The Politics of the Past and German Identity," in *Ten Years of German Unification: Transfer, Transformation, Incorporation?* eds. Jörn Leonhard and Lothar Funk (Birmingham, 2002); Bill Niven, *Facing the Nazi Past: United Germany and the Legacy of the Third Reich* (London, 2002), 2–7, 41–61.

8. Mary Albon, "Project on Justice in Times of Transition: Report of the Project's Inaugural Meeting," in *Transitional Justice: How Emerging Democracies Reckon with Former Regimes,* ed. Neil J. Kritz (Washington, 1995), vol. I, 48. Offe similarly—if hypothetically rather than empirically—suggests that Germany constitutes the "most favourable case" for a thorough or at least well-managed process of coming to terms with the past, *Varieties of Transition,* 86f.

9. McAdams, *Judging the Past,* 5f., 9.

10. See Inge Markovits, *Imperfect Justice: An East-West German Diary* (Oxford, 1995).

11. Cf. Edgar Wolfrum, *Geschichte als Waffe: Vom Kaiserreich bis zur Wiedervereinigung* (Göttingen, 2002), 136; Wolfgang Dümcke and Fritz Vilmar, *Kolonialisierung der DDR: Kritische Analysen und Alternativen des Einigungsprozesses* (Münster, 1996); Erhard Blankenburg, "The Purge of Lawyers after the Breakdown of the East German Communist Regime," *Law and Social Inquiry* 20, no. 1 (1995): 223–43; Paul Cooke, *Representing East Germany since Unification: From Colonization to Nostalgia* (Oxford, 2005), 1–20.

12. For a democratic-socialist rejection of the reckoning with the past as emanating from the West, see Ludwig Elm, *Nach Hitler, Nach Honecker: Zum Streit der Deutschen um die eigene Vergangenheit* (Berlin, 1991), 15.

13. Such erroneous portrayals are found throughout the literature. See Blankenburg, "The Purge of Lawyers," 243; Christhard Hoffmann, "One Nation—Which Past? Historiography and German Identities in the 1990s," *German Politics and Society* 15, no. 2 (1997): 4; Jonathan Grix, "1989 Revisited: Getting to the Bottom of the GDR's Demise," *German Politics* 6, no. 2 (1997): 193; Molly Andrews, "The Politics of Forgiveness," *International Journal of Politics, Culture and Society* 13, no. 1 (1999): 121; Daphne Berdahl, *Where the World Ended: Re-unification and Identity in the German Borderland* (Berkeley, 1999); Molly Andrews, "Grand National Narratives and the Project of Truth Commissions: A Comparative Analysis," *Media, Culture and Society* 25 (2003): 50ff.; Pol O'Dochartaigh, *Germany since 1945* (Basingstoke, 2004), 231ff.; Franz Oswald, "Negotiating Identities: The Party of Democratic Socialism between East German Regionalism, German National Identity and European Integration," *Australian Journal of Politics and History* 50, no. 1 (2004): 75–85; Geoff Eley, "The Unease of History: Settling Accounts with the East German Past," *History Workshop Journal* 57 (2004): 175–201.

14. Cf. Bernd Faulenbach, "Die Arbeit der Enquete-Kommissionen und die Geschichtsdebatte in Deutschland seit 1989," in *The GDR and its History: Rückblick und Revision, Die DDR im Spiegel der Enquete-Kommissionen* (*German Monitor* 49), ed. Peter Barker (Amsterdam, 2000); Thomaneck and Niven, *Dividing and Uniting Germany,* 85; Hasko Zimmer in collaboration with Katja Flesser and Julia Volmer, *Der Buchenwald-Konflikt: Zum Streit um Geschichte und Erinnerung im Kontext der deutschen Vereinigung* (Münster, 1999).

15. See Petra Bock, *Vergangenheitspolitik im Systemwechsel: Die Politik der Aufklärung, Strafverfolgung, Disqualifizierung und Wiedergutmachung im letzten Jahr der DDR* (Berlin, 2000).

16. Cf. McAdams, *Judging the Past,* 6; Sa'adah, *Germany's Second Chance,* 101. A discussion in 1994–95 about drawing a line under the past had little impact. See Sa'adah, *Germany's Second Chance,* 177. Serious wavering amongst the main political parties returned only in 2000 when the process began to affect western politicians. See McAdams, *Judging the Past,* 179–84; O'Dochartaigh, *Germany since 1945,* 231f.; Horst-Alfred Heinrich, "Geschichtspolitische Akteure im Umgang mit der Stasi: Eine Einleitung," in *Geschichts-*

politik: Wer sind ihre Akteure, wer ihre Rezipienten? eds. Claudia Fröhlich and Heinrich (Wiesbaden, 2004).

17. The former phrase is used by Yoder, "Truth without Reconciliation," 77. The latter by Amelie Kutter, "Geschichtspolitische Ausgrenzungen in der Vereinigungspolitik: Das Beispiel der Enquete-Kommission," in *Die DDR war anders: Eine kritische Würdigung ihrer sozialkulturellen Einrichtungen,* eds. Stefan Bollinger and Fritz Villmar (Berlin, 2002), 49. Cooke equivocates on the latter's appropriateness, *Representing East Germany,* 46.

18. Cf. Jutta Vergau, *Aufarbeitung von Vergangenheit vor und nach 1989: Eine Analyse des Umgangs mit den historischen Hypotheken totalitärer Diktaturen in Deutschland* (Marburg, 2000), 179f.; Helga A. Welsh, "When Discourse Trumps Policy: Transitional Justice in Unified Germany," *German Politics* 15, no. 2 (2006): 147f.

19. Yoder, "Truth without Reconciliation," esp. 73; Andrews, "The Politics of Forgiveness," 113, 121; Andrews, "Grand National Narratives," esp. 49.

20. Cf. Friso Wielenga, *Schatten deutscher Geschichte: Der Umgang mit dem Nationalsozialismus und der DDR-Vergangenheit in der Bundesrepublik* (Vierow bei Greifswald, 1995), 72f. Generally on the nature of the transition associated with unification, see Wade Jacoby, *Imitation and Politics: Redesigning Modern Germany* (Ithaca, 2000); Leonhard and Funk, *Ten Years of German Unification.* For an early example of intra-western discussion, see Cora Stephan, ed., *Wir Kollaborateure: Der Westen und die deutschen Vergangenheiten* (Reinbek bei Hamburg, 1992).

21. Ideology and symbolic politics are largely absent from Helmut König, Michael Kohlstruck, and Andreas Wöll, eds., *Vergangenheitsbewältigung am Ende des zwanzigsten Jahrhunderts (Leviathan* 18) (Opladen, 1998). Ideology and the politics of public memory are remarkably missing from McAdams, *Judging the Past.* Ralf K. Wüstenberg focuses more on efforts to prevent the "repression" and "distortion" of the past, than on the political contestation of historical interpretations and legitimacy, *Die politische Dimension der Versöhnung: Eine theologische Studie zum Umgang mit Schuld nach den Systemumbrüchen in Südafrika und Deutschland* (Gütersloh, 2004), 328. For a brief discussion of the ideological stakes of historical approaches to the GDR, see Konrad H. Jarausch, "The German Democratic Republic as History in United Germany: Reflections on Public Debate and Academic Controversy," *German Politics and Society* 15, no. 2 (1997): 33–48. Paul Cooke recognizes the importance of debates about the GDR for legitimizing unification, but treats official politics of memory merely as a source of perceptions of colonization and thus as a foil for exploring "postcolonial" cultural responses, *Representing East Germany,* 27–53.

22. See for example John Torpey, "Coming to Terms with the Communist Past: East Germany in Comparative Perspective," *German Politics* 2, no. 3 (1993): 425; Robert G. Moeller, "What Has 'Coming to Terms with the Past' Meant in Post-World War II Germany?" *Central European History* 35, no. 2 (2002): 230; Niven, *Facing the Nazi Past,* 6.

23. Theodor W. Adorno noted in the late 1950s that behind much talk about "working through the past" actually stood a desire to draw a final line under it, "Was bedeutet: Aufarbeitung der Vergangenheit," *Gesammelte Schriften* (Frankfurt am Main, 1977), vol. 10, no. 2, 555. Cf. A. Dirk Moses, "Coming to Terms with the Past in Comparative Perspective: Germany and Australia," *Aboriginal History* 25 (2001): 91–115; Peter Dudek, "'Vergangenheitsbewältigung': Zur Problematik eines umstrittenen Begriffs," *Aus Politik und Zeitgeschichte* 42, no. 1–2 (1992): 44–53.

24. Cf. Rudi G. Teitel, *Transitional Justice* (Oxford, 2000), 88; Lutz-Dieter Behrendt, "Mittel und Methoden der Vergangenheitsbewältigung," in *Auf den Kehrichthaufen der Geschichte?* eds. de Keghel and Maier.

25. Andrews, "The Politics of Forgiveness," 110; Maryam Kamali, "Accountability for

Human Rights Violations: A Comparison of Transitional Justice in East Germany and South Africa," *Columbia Journal of Transnational Law* 40 (2001): 116ff.

26. For instance, Calhoun, *Dilemmas of Justice;* Cooke, *Representing East Germany,* 34–41.
27. Sa'adah, *Germany's Second Chance,* 185; Yoder, "Truth without Reconciliation," 72; Wüstenberg, *Die politische Dimension,* 343.
28. See Wüstenberg, *Die politische Dimension,* 337–44, and especially the footnotes on 292ff., 325–47, 381–85, 390f., 403, 407, 410, 417f., 428; McAdams, *Judging the Past,* 96–101, 105–8, 110–14, 119–21, and the footnotes on 210ff.
29. Andrews, "Grand National Narratives," 50f.; Stefan Berger, *The Search for Normality: National Identity and Historical Consciousness in Germany since 1800* (Providence, 1997), 254f.; Paul Betts, "Germany, International Justice and the Twentieth Century," *History and Memory* 17 (2005): 67f.; Calhoun, *Dilemmas of Justice,* 88f.
30. In roughly chronological order: Rainer Eppelmann, "Fünf Jahre deutsche Einheit," *Deutschland Archiv* 28, no. 9 (1995): 897f.; Peter Maser, "Auf dem Weg zur deutschen Einheit: Anmerkungen zur neuen Enquete-Kommission des Deutschen Bundestages," in *Unrecht überwinden—SED-Diktatur und Widerstand,* Gerhard Finn, Frank Hagemann, Maser, Helmut Müller-Enbergs, Günther Wagenlehrer, and Hermann Wentker (Sankt Augustin, 1996); Marlies Jansen, "Enquete-Kommission," in *Handbuch zur deutschen Einheit,* eds. Werner Weidenfeld and Karl-Rudolf Korte (Frankfurt am Main, 1996); Marlies Jansen, "Enquete-Kommission," in *Handbuch zur deutschen Einheit 1949-1989-1999,* eds. Werner Weidenfeld and Karl-Rudolf Korte (Frankfurt am Main, 1999); Rita Süssmuth, "Auf dem Weg zur inneren Einheit Deutschlands—der Beitrag des Deutschen Bundestages," in *Eine deutsche Zwischenbilanz: Standpunkte zum Umgang mit unserer Vergangenheit,* eds. Süssmuth and Bernward Baule (Munich, 1997); Hermann Weber, "Rewriting the History of the German Democratic Republic: The Work of the Commission of Inquiry," in *Rewriting the German Past: History and Identity in the New Germany,* eds. Reinhard Alter and Peter Monteath (Atlantic Highlands, 1997); Hartmut Koschyk, "Die Beseitigung der Folgen der SED-Diktatur und die Frage der inneren Einheit," in *Wiedervereinigung Deutschlands: Festschrift zum 20jährigen Bestehen der Gesellschaft für Deutschlandforschung,* eds. Karl Eckart, Jens Hacker, and Siegfried Mampel (Berlin, 1998); Manfred Wilke, "Die deutsche Einheit und die Geschichtspolitik des Bundestages," in *Wiedervereinigung Deutschlands,* eds. Eckart, Hacker, and Mampel; Dirk Hansen, "Zur Arbeit der Enquetekommission des Deutschen Bundestages 'Überwindung der Folgen der SED-Diktatur im Prozess der deutschen Einheit,'" *Deutsche Studien* 139–40 (1998): 380–402; Dorothee Wilms, "Begründung, Entstehung und Zielsetzung der Enquete-Kommission 1992–1994 im Deutschen Bundestag," in *The GDR and its History,* ed. Barker; Rainer Eppelmann, "Die Enquete-Kommissionen zur Aufarbeitung der SED-Diktatur," in *Bilanz und Perspektiven der DDR-Forschung,* eds. Eppelmann, Bernd Faulenbach, and Ulrich Mählert (Paderborn, 2003).
31. Herbert Wolf, "Sine ira et studio??? Standpunkt zum Abschluß der Arbeit der Enquete-Kommission," in *Ansichten zur Geschichte der DDR* IV, eds. Dietmar Keller, Hans Modrow, and Wolf (Bonn, 1994); Dirk Hansen, "Befreiung durch Erinnerung: Zur Arbeit der Enquete-Kommission 'Aufarbeitung von Geschichte und Folgen der SED-Diktatur in Deutschland' des Deutschen Bundestages," *Deutsche Studien* 125 (1995): 71–81; Manfred Wilke, "Der Historiker und die Politik: Alexander Fischer als Sachverständiges Mitglied der Bundestags-Enquete-Kommission 'Aufarbeitung von Geschichte und Folgen der SED-Diktatur in Deutschland,'" in *Wandel durch Beständigkeit: Studien zur deutschen und internationalen Politik: Jens Hacker zum 65. Geburtstag,* eds. Karl G. Kick, Stephan Weingarz, and Ulrich Bartosch (Berlin, 1998); Faulenbach, "Die Auseinandersetzung mit der doppelten Vergangenheit"; Faulenbach, "Die Arbeit."

32. Ludwig Elm, "'Zwei Diktaturen'—'zwei totalitäre Regimes': Die Enquete-Kommissionen des Bundestages und der konservative Geschichtsrevisionismus der neunziger Jahre," in *Die selbstbewußte Nation und ihr Geschichtsbild: Geschichtslegenden der Neuen Rechten*, eds. Johannes Klotz and Ulrich Schneider (Cologne, 1997); Ludwig Elm, *Das verordnete Feindbild: Neue deutsche Geschichtsideologie und "antitotalitärer Konsens"* (Cologne, 2001).

33. For example, Bernd Faulenbach does not reflect on his own role as a key SPD ideologue or the rather tendentious nature of the distinctions he draws between various approaches represented in the commissions, "Die Auseinandersetzung mit der doppelten Vergangenheit," 42; "Die Arbeit," 27. Manfred Wilke overplays the role of the experts at the expense of partisan interests, and does not mention that he himself was a member, "Der Historiker und die Politik." Markus Meckel's early account does not hide his resentment at the conservative commission majority, "Demokratische Selbstbestimmung als Prozeß: Die Aufgabe der Politik bei der Aufarbeitung der DDR-Vergangenheit," in *Die Partei hatte immer recht—Aufarbeitung von Geschichte und Folgen der SED-Diktatur*, eds. Bernd Faulenbach, Meckel, and Hermann Weber (Essen, 1994), esp. 261f.

34. See for instance Mark Freeman, *Truth Commissions and Procedural Fairness* (Cambridge, 2006). In contrast, Jutta Vergau elides any distinctions between the two inquiries and ignores the considerably greater significance and resonance of the first commission and its report when she claims that it is too early to evaluate the commissions' work and their reception because its final report (i.e., that of the second inquiry) was published only in 1998, *Aufarbeitung von Vergangenheit*, 183f.; similarly, Kamali, "Accountability for Human Rights Violations," 117.

35. Kamali, "Accountability for Human Rights Violations," 117, 135; Yoder, "Truth without Reconciliation," 72, 75; Andrews, "Grand National Narratives," 50f.

36. Jonathon Grix, "The Enquete-Kommission's Contribution to Research on State-Society Relations in the GDR," and Stephen Brown, "'Angepasste Kirchenleitungen und aufmüpfige Basis'? Die Kirchen im Spiegel der Enquete-Kommissionen," in *The GDR and its History*, ed. Barker; Grix, "1989 Revisited." Commissioner Roswitha Wisniewski also discusses the first inquiry's work on the GDR education system, "Das Bildungssystem der DDR und sein Vermächtnis," in *The GDR and its History*, ed. Barker 129–43. Grix concludes from the inquiry's ostensible failure to engage with the broad public that it "has not had any wider impact outside the confines of academic research," which ignores its party-political and commemorative significance, "The Enquete-Kommission's Contribution," 63. On the tensions between scholarship and politics, see Robert Grünbaum, "Aufarbeitung der SED-Diktatur: Die Enquete-Kommission des Deutschen Bundestages zwischen Politik und Wissenschaft," *Deutsche Studien* 130 (1996): 111–22.

37. McAdams, *Judging the Past*, 92.

38. See Wilke, "Die deutsche Einheit," 470.

39. McAdams, *Judging the Past*, 101–9.

40. Yoder, "Truth without Reconciliation." Wüstenberg also focuses on reconciliation, albeit not just at the national level, *Die politische Dimension*, 240–431.

41. For the former tendency, see Andrews, "Grand National Narratives," 51f.; McAdams, *Judging the Past*, 122f. For the latter, see Yoder, 77; Andrews, "The Politics of Forgiveness," 121.

42. Yoder, "Truth without Reconciliation," 72f.; Andrews, "The Politics of Forgiveness," 121; Andrews, "Grand National Narratives," 51f.; Cooke, *Representing East Germany*, 28, 41f., 46, 52f.

43. See especially Andrews, "Grand National Narratives." For others who treat the inquiry as a truth commission, see Tina Rosenberg, "Overcoming the Legacies of Dictatorship,"

Foreign Affairs 74, no. 3 (1995): 148; Kritz, *Transitional Justice*, vol. 3, 216–19; Timothy Garton Ash, *The File: A Personal History* (London, 1997), 195; Garton Ash, *History of the Present*, 308; Jennifer A. Yoder, "Culprits, Culpability, and Corrective Justice," *Problems of Post-Communism* 45, no. 4 (1998): 14–21; Teitel, *Transitional Justice*, 95; Priscilla B. Hayner, *Unspeakable Truths: Confronting State Terror and Atrocity* (New York, 2001), 61f., 294, 319; Freeman, *Truth Commissions and Procedural Fairness*, 318–25.

44. Maier, *Dissolution*, 326; Garton Ash, *History of the Present*, 307; McAdams, *Judging the Past*, 88f.

45. I thus disagree with Yoder's description of it as a "fact-finding body free of emotionality," "Truth without Reconciliation," 77.

46. For example, Wüstenberg accepts as unproblematic the notion that reconciliation "is only possible in truth" or "through truth," *Die politische Dimension*, 294, 382f. He thus ignores the crucial question of "whose" truth and does not see such notions as (among other things) justificatory rhetoric for the condemnation of the communist regime.

47. See Helmut Fehr, "Öffentlicher Sprachwandel und Eliten-Konkurrenz: Zur Rolle politischer Semantik in den Dekommunisierungskampagnen post-kommunistischer Gesellschaften (Tschechische Republik, Polen und Ostdeutschland)," in *Eliten, politische Kultur und Privatisierung in Ostdeutschland, Tschechien und Mittelosteuropa*, ed. Ilja Srubar (Konstanz, 1998); Stefan Wolle, "Im Kleinhirn der Krake: Der Beginn der Stasi-Auflösung in Berlin im Januar 1990," in *Dem Zeitgeist geopfert: Die DDR in Wissenschaft, Publizistik und politischer Bildung*, ed. Peter Eisenmann and Gerhard Hirscher (Munich, 1992). Cf. Teitel, *Transitional Justice*, 70.

48. For example, McAdams sees the aim as uncovering "the truth about the moral choices that had been available in the GDR," *Judging the Past*, 92. See also Wielenga, *Schatten deutscher Geschichte*, 85. Cf. Sa'adah, *Germany's Second Chance*, 107ff.; Cooke, *Representing East Germany*, 39. Related to this common focus on behavior *in* the GDR is the frequent claim that the commission(s) examined the period from 1949 to 1989, McAdams, *Judging the Past*, 20; Hayner, *Unspeakable Truths*, 61; Freeman, *Truth Commissions and Procedural Fairness*, 32. This overlooks the extensive consideration of the 1945–49 period of Soviet occupation, and the less extensive attention to developments in 1989–90, both of which raised fundamental questions about the state's legitimacy, as discussed in chapters 3 and 4 below.

49. McAdams, *Judging the Past*, 92–116. See also his brief discussion in A. James McAdams, *Germany Divided: From the Wall to Reunification* (Princeton, 1993), 236–39.

50. Sa'adah, *Germany's Second Chance*.

51. Wüstenberg, *Die politische Dimension*.

52. Maier, *Dissolution*, 326; McAdams, *Judging the Past*, 117ff.; cf. Cooke, *Representing East Germany*, 35.

53. Marc Schulte examines references to the Nazi past in the Bundestag debate on the first commission's creation, "Die 'doppelte Vergangenheit' in der politischen Diskussion im Bundestag," *Geschichte—Erziehung—Politik* 4, no. 6 (1993): 361–68. Petra Haustein considers aspects of the inquiries' hearings on the commemoration of Germany's double dictatorial past, *Geschichte im Dissens: Die Auseinandersetzungen um die Gedenkstätte Sachsenhausen nach dem Ende der DDR* (Leipzig, 2006), 134–47, 173–84. Erik Meyer briefly considers the inquiries' role in the development of federal policy on memorials, "Erinnerungskultur als Politikfeld: Geschichtspolitische Deliberation und Dezision in der Berliner Republik," in *Die NS-Diktatur im deutschen Erinnerungsdiskurs*, ed. Wolfgang Bergem (Opladen, 2003), 125f. Cooke discusses problems relating to dictatorial comparison and totalitarianist approaches in relation to the first inquiry's report, *Representing East Germany*, 35ff., 39ff.

54. Cf. Bock, *Vergangenheitspolitik im Systemwechsel*, 4ff.; Vergau, *Aufarbeitung von Vergangenheit*, 167–78.

55. A first step in the direction of a sober political analysis was made by Peter Steinbach, *Nationalsozialistische Gewaltverbrechen in der deutschen Öffentlichkeit: Die Diskussion nach 1945* (West Berlin, 1981). Cf. Bock, *Vergangenheitspolitik im Systemwechsel*, 5. As Helmut König notes, for a long time authors restricted themselves to criticizing the term *Vergangenheitsbewältigung* without offering alternatives or subjecting it to rigorous examination, "Von der Diktatur zur Demokratie oder Was ist Vergangenheitsbewältigung," in *Vergangenheitsbewältigung*, eds. König, Kohlstruck, and Wöll, 378.

56. Norbert Frei, *Vergangenheitspolitik: Die Anfänge der Bundesrepublik und die NS-Vergangenheit* (Munich, 1996). For the English translation, see Frei, *Adenauer's Germany and the Nazi Past: The Politics of Amnesty and Integration*, trans. Joel Golb (New York, 2002).

57. See Ruth Fuchs and Detlef Nolte, "Politikfeld Vergangenheitspolitik: Zur Analyse der Aufarbeitung von Menschenrechtsverletzungen in Lateinamerika," *Lateinamerika Analysen* 9 (2004): 59–92.

58. Peter Reichel, *Politik mit der Erinnerung: Gedächtnisorte im Streit um die nationalsozialistische Vergangenheit*, rev. ed. (Frankfurt am Main, 1999). Reichel draws on Pierre Nora's "lieux de memoire," and sees the debates around them as part of the process of social or collective memory formation. See Nora, "Between Memory and History: Les Lieux de Mémoire," *Representations* 26 (1989): 7–25.

59. Edgar Wolfrum, *Geschichtspolitik in der Bundesrepublik Deutschland: Der Weg zur bundesrepublikanischen Erinnerung 1948–1990* (Darmstadt, 1999), 33; Edgar Wolfrum, "Geschichtspolitik in der Bundesrepublik Deutschland 1949–1989: Phasen und Kontroversen," in *Umkämpfte Vergangenheit: Geschichtsbilder, Erinnerung und Vergangenheitspolitik im internationalen Vergleich*, eds. Petra Bock and Wolfrum (Göttingen, 1999), 57f. The term "history politics" has been used pejoratively. According to Jürgen Habermas, history degenerates into history politics when the view of the analytical observer merges with that of participants in public debates about identity formation, "Vom öffentlichen Gebrauch der Historie: Warum ein 'Demokratiepreis' für Daniel Goldhagen," *Blätter für deutsche und internationale Politik* 42 (1997): 410. Others, like Peter Steinbach, seem ambivalent about the legitimacy of history politics and its status in democracies as opposed to dictatorships. Compare "Darf der pluralistische Staat 'Geschichtspolitik' betreiben? Zu einer Kontroverse der jüngsten Vergangenheit," in *Vergangenheitsbewältigung*, ed. Eckhard Jesse (Berlin, 1997), 85, with "Postdiktatorische Geschichtspolitik: Nationalsozialismus und Widerstand im deutschen Geschichtsbild nach 1945," in *Umkämpfte Vergangenheit*, eds. Bock and Wolfrum, 22, 25. Other authors use the notion of history politics without offering any conceptual discussion. See Aleida Assmann and Ute Frevert, *Geschichtsvergessenheit — Geschichtsversessenheit: Vom Umgang mit deutschen Vergangenheiten nach 1945* (Stuttgart, 1999), 13.

60. Of course, the sets of issues involved in each also merge. For instance, as Mitchell G. Ash argues, in the postunification East German "historians' dispute," questions about the future of academic careers and scholarly institutes were entangled with debate about the value and "symbolic capital" of East German historiography and the place of East Germany in German history more generally, Mitchell G. Ash, "Geschichtswissenschaft, Geschichtskultur und der ostdeutsche Historikerstreit," *Geschichte und Gesellschaft* 24, no. 2 (1998): 283f. Cf. Bock and Wolfrum, *Umkämpfte Vergangenheit*, 8f.; Bock, *Vergangenheitspolitik im Systemwechsel*, 10ff.

61. For example, König, who tries to avoid the tendency of analysis to merge with advocacy, seems caught between such a binary either-or approach on the one hand and analyzing how and to what ends certain policies are pursued on the other, "Von der Diktatur,"

380f. Even Frank Biess, in his excellent study of the POW issue in postwar Germany, falls into the trap of equating self-critical German approaches to the Nazi past with "more" memory, and more self-exonerating approaches with "less," *Homecomings: Returning POWs and the Legacies of Defeat in Postwar Germany* (Princeton, 2006), 46, 52, 58. For an example of a study that successfully avoids these pitfalls, see Robert G. Moeller, *War Stories: The Search for a Usable Past in the Federal Republic of Germany* (Berkeley, 2001). On the dichotomous nature of much writing on Geman memory, see A. Dirk Moses, "The Non-German German and the German German: Dilemmas of Identity after the Holocaust," *New German Critique* 34, no. 2 (2007): 45–50.

62. See Christa Hoffmann, "Aufklärung und Ahndung totalitären Unrechts: Die Zentralen Stellen in Ludwigsburg und in Salzgitter," *Aus Politik und Zeitgeschichte* 43, no. 4 (1993): 36; Eckhard Jesse, "Doppelte Vergangenheitsbewältigung in Deutschland: Ein Problem der Vergangenheit, Gegenwart und Zukunft," in *Vergangenheitsbewältigung,* ed. Jesse, 13; Offe, *Varieties of Transition;* Helmut Quaritsch, "Theorie der Vergangenheitsbewältigung," *Der Staat* 31 (1992): 519–51; Bernd Pampel, "Was bedeutet 'Aufarbeitung der Vergangenheit'? Kann man aus der 'Vergangenheitsbewältigung' nach 1945 für die 'Aufarbeitung' nach 1989 Lehren ziehen?" *Aus Politik und Zeitgeschichte* 45, no. 1–2 (1995): 31f.; König, "Von der Diktatur," 373, 375, 378, 381; Werner Bergmann, "Kommunikationslatenz und Vergangenheitsbewältigung," in *Vergangenheitsbewältigung,* ed. König, Kohlstruck, and Wöll, 399; John Torpey, ed., *Politics and the Past: On Repairing Historical Injustices* (Lanham, 2003); Teitel, *Transitional Justice;* Bock, *Vergangenheitspolitik im Systemwechsel,* 2.

63. Garton Ash, *History of the Present,* 294. Günther Sandner recognizes the need to include the handling of non-dictatorial pasts and proposes *Geschichtspolitik* as a superordinate notion encompassing "the political instrumentalization of history, the motives and modalities of its construction, the function of its presence and political virulence in the present"; he treats *Vergangenheitspolitik* as a subcategory relating to the handling of dictatorial pasts, "Hegemonie und Erinnerung: Zur Konzeption von Geschichts- und Vergangenheitspolitik," *Österreichische Zeitschrift für Politikwissenschaft* 30, no. 1 (2001): 7. Such a scheme has some merit, but loses the distinction between the policy and discursive components. On the other hand, recognizing the significance of positively viewed dimensions such as resistance can be taken too far, for example when Vergau effectively reduces the delegitimation of the old (in this case, the Nazi) regime to public commemoration of the resistance against it, *Aufarbeitung der Vergangenheit,* 31ff.; she also fails to see that resistance does not fit the category of a burden.

64. Related to the common foreclosure of the interpretation of the past through the definition of the terms as discussed thus far, *Vergangenheitsbewältigung* has been taken to constitute a process with the goal of removing the past's ability to constitute a "heavy burden for the formation of the present or a danger for internal peace," Peter Steinbach, "Vergangenheitsbewältigung in vergleichender Perspektive: Politische Säuberung, Wiedergutmachung, Integration," in *Geschichte und Transformation des SED-Staates: Beiträge und Analysen,* ed. Klaus Schroeder (Berlin, 1994), 398. This view overlooks the fact that the past is always used for the formation of the present, and the crucial task is to examine how this occurs. A further advantage of the notion of history politics is that it is open to eras even centuries old. See Heinrich August Winkler, ed., *Griff nach der Deutungsmacht: Zur Geschichte der Geschichtspolitik in Deutschland* (Göttingen, 2004).

65. Manfred Wilke, "Die deutsche Einheit und die Geschichtspolitik des Bundestages," *Deutschland Archiv* 30, no. 4 (1997): 607. Cf. Heinrich, "Geschichtspolitische Akteure," 20.

66. Cf. Cooke, *Representing East Germany,* 46. Some commentators go to the other extreme of ignoring the role of western anticommunists. See Petra Bock, "Von der Tribunal-Idee

zur Enquete-Kommission: Zur Vorgeschichte der Enquete-Kommission des Bundestages 'Aufarbeitung von Geschichte und Folgen der SED-Diktatur in Deutschland,'"
Deutschland Archiv 28, no. 1 (1995): 1183; Eckhard Jesse, "Die zweite deutsche Diktatur
auf dem Prüfstand: Materialien der Enquete-Kommission 'Aufarbeitung von Geschichte
und Folgen der SED-Diktatur in Deutschland,'" *Jahrbuch Extremismus und Demokratie* 8
(1996): 232. Cf. A. James McAdams, "Revisiting the *Ostpolitik* in the 1990s," *German
Politics and Society* 30 (1993): 56.

67. Cf. Cooke, *Representing East Germany*, 39. It is surprising that Vergau, who explicitly addresses regime delegitimization as a core component of working through the past, pays
so little attention to the inquiries' role in this regard, *Aufarbeitung von Vergangenheit*,
97–105.

68. For brief exceptions, see Jarausch, "The German Democratic Republic as History," 44;
Cooke, *Representing East Germany*, 38.

69. Cf. Jarausch, "The German Democratic Republic as History," 38ff.; Jarausch, "Die DDR
denken," 10ff.; Faulenbach, "Die Arbeit der Enquete-Kommissionen," 27; Faulenbach,
"Die Auseinandersetzung mit der doppelten Vergangenheit," 42.

70. For such fears, see Ian Kershaw, *Germany's Present, Germany's Past* (London, 1992), 12;
Wielenga, *Schatten deutscher Geschichte*, 13. Cf. Jarausch, "A Double Burden," 102f.; Andrew H. Beattie, "The Victims of Totalitarianism and the Centrality of Nazi Genocide:
Continuity and Change in German Commemorative Politics," in *Germans as Victims:
Contemporary Germany and the Third Reich*, ed. Bill Niven (Basingstoke, 2006). Other
analysts have noted that the feared displacement of Nazism did not occur, but do not
explain why. See Bergmann, "Kommunikationslatenz," 406.

71. See Antonia Grunenberg, "Antitotalitarianism versus Antifascism: Two Legacies of the
Past in Germany," *German Politics and Society* 15, no. 2 (1997): 76–90.

72. Cf. Ross, *The East German Dictatorship*, 176, 184–91; Sa'adah, *Germany's Second Chance*,
119–27. There are connections with the *Literaturstreit* (literature debate) and the East
German *Historikerstreit* (historians' dispute). On the former, see Thomas Anz, ed., *Es
geht nicht um Christa Wolf: Der Literaturstreit im vereinigten Deutschland* (Munich, 1991);
Bernd Wittek, *Der Literaturstreit im sich vereinigenden Deutschland: Eine Analyse des Streits
um Christa Wolf und die deutsch-deutsche Gegenwartsliteratur in Zeitungen und Zeitschriften*
(Marburg, 1997). On the latter, see Jürgen Danyel, "Die Historiker und die Moral: Anmerkungen zur Debatte über die Autorenrechte an der DDR-Geschichte," *Geschichte
und Gesellschaft* 21 (1995): 290–303; Ash, "Geschichtswissenschaft, Geschichtskultur und
der ostdeutsche Historikerstreit." More generally, see Antonia Grunenberg, ed., *Welche
Geschichte wählen wir?* (Hamburg, 1992); Andreas Huyssen, *Twilight Memories: Marking
Time in a Culture of Amnesia* (New York, 1995), 37–66; Anne-Marie Le Gloannec, "On German Identity," *Daedalus* 123, no. 1 (1994): 129–48; Konrad H. Jarausch, "Normalisierung
oder Re-Nationalisierung? Zur Umdeutung der deutschen Vergangenheit," *Geschichte
und Gesellschaft* 21 (1995): 571–84; Konrad H. Jarausch, ed., *After Unity: Reconfiguring
German Identities* (Providence, 1997); Alter and Monteath, *Rewriting the German Past*.

73. Cf. Dieter Dettke, ed., *The Spirit of the Berlin Republic* (New York, 2003), 3.

74. Jan-Werner Müller, "East Germany: Incorporation, Tainted Truth, and the Double Divi-
sion," in *The Politics of Memory and Democratization: Transitional Justice in Democratizing
Societies*, ed. Alexandra Barahona De Brito, Carmen Gonzalez Enriquez, and Paloma
Aguilar (Oxford, 2001), 268.

75. Jarausch, "The German Democratic Republic as History," 35. Cf. A. James McAdams
and John Torpey, "The Political Arsenal of the German Past," *German Politics Society* 30
(1993): 3.

76. Maier, *Dissolution*, 326. Peter Barker recognizes this function for the PDS, "'Geschichts-aufarbeitung' within the PDS and the Enquete-Kommissionen," in *The GDR and its History*, ed. Barker.

77. Faulenbach, "Die Arbeit der Enquete-Kommissionen," 30. Cf. Lothar Fritze, *Die Gegenwart des Vergangenen: Über das Weiterleben der DDR nach ihrem Ende* (Weimar, 1997); Jarausch, "The German Democratic Republic as History," 41; Konrad H. Jarausch, "Beyond Uniformity: The Challenge of Historicizing the GDR," in *Dictatorship as Experience: Towards a Socio-Cultural History of the GDR*, ed. Jarausch, trans. Eve Duffy (New York, 1999); Christoph Kleßmann, "Zwei Diktaturen in Deutschland: Was kann die künftige DDR-Forschung aus der Geschichtsschreibung zum Nationalsozialismus lernen?" *Deutschland Archiv* 25, no. 6 (1992): 601–6.

Chapter 1

ESTABLISHING THE COMMISSION OF INQUIRY

In hindsight, the creation of a parliamentary body to investigate the history and consequences of the East German dictatorship appears a logical and natural step along a coherent and well-planned path toward a thorough reckoning with the communist regime. Yet as A. James McAdams argues, political elites do not simply pick and choose from a menu of transitional-justice instruments, but face a range of competing needs, priorities, and constraints in real time and space.[1] Indeed, it is important to emphasize the contingency of the Bundestag inquiry's creation, which was by no means inevitable or preordained. Other aspects of postunification transitional justice—including the prosecution of governmental criminality, the resolution of the fate of the Stasi files, the compensation of victims, and the vetting of public-service personnel—were foreseen by the 1990 Unification Treaty; a parliamentary or other inquiry was not.[2] The proposal for such an institution came two years after the fall of the Berlin Wall and more than a year after German unification.

The timing and circumstances of the commission's creation warrant more sustained consideration than they generally receive, because they reveal a great deal about the motivations behind it and its multiple purposes. Far from being a component of a ready-made program of western victor's justice, the inquiry was an eastern initiative. Moreover, it was largely a reaction to the public discussion of the GDR and to the state of German (dis)unity in 1991–92. This reactive quality goes some way toward explaining the lack of clarity surrounding the commission's purpose, for many statements about its role were formulated in the negative. There was widespread agreement, for example, that discussion of the GDR should not be reduced to scandalous revelations about the East German secret police and spy agency, the Stasi. Similarly, the political parties agreed that the commission would not interfere with the criminal prosecution of offences committed in East Germany.

The initial lack of clarity was also due to the undertaking's unprecedented nature. This was the first inquiry of its kind in Germany to be devoted to historical and ideological questions. Precisely what a parliamentary body could, should, and would achieve—and how—were open questions. Reflecting a keen awareness of the novelty of the undertaking, proponents of the inquiry argued that it was essential to avoid repeating mistakes made in relation to the Nazi past. Indeed, a central, rather circular motivation was to prevent future accusations that unified Germany had similarly failed to deal with its communist past. To a considerable extent, the creation of the commission was therefore an end in itself.

Arguments in favor of an inquiry and positive goals for it to pursue were often formulated only vaguely. Everyone agreed that public deliberation of the past was necessary and that a parliamentary commission might participate in, foster, and lead such deliberation (although the PDS had reservations about the last aspect). Considerable symbolic value attached to the simple fact that the Bundestag considered the East German past worthy of its continuing attention, which indicated that the GDR's legacy was a national and not just an eastern problem. Frequent rhetoric about the importance to the unification process of working through the GDR past, however, hindered rather than aided the clarification of the commission's goals. Insistence on the need to avoid the mistake of neglecting to come to terms with the Nazi past similarly did little to explicate precisely what was intended.

One positive goal that was supported unanimously was to address the suffering of the victims of the communist regime, although precisely how remained unclear. A further, more or less, explicit aim was to focus attention on the old ruling party, the SED, rather than the Stasi, and to investigate the former's system of rule. These two goals—helping the victims and examining communist rule—indicate the bifurcated nature of the inquiry's intentions: it aimed both to address the ongoing legacies of the past through legislative and other practical measures (policies for the past), and to examine, interpret, and draw conclusions from the past (play politics with history). What this meant in detail is the subject of this chapter, which explores the motivations behind the inquiry, its aims, membership, and proposed methods.

The Path to Establishment

With the East German upheaval progressing in the winter of 1989–90, demands for the investigation of the regime's abuses formed an increasingly important aspect of the democratization process. Confronting the past was seen as essential for breaking the SED's monopoly on power and truth.[3] Specific calls to bring the regime's leadership and its repressive apparatus to account arose after police brutality and mass arrests of demonstrators by the Stasi on 7 October 1989, and as the result of ongoing revelations about the corruption and privileges of the ruling elite. Following the storming of regional and central Stasi headquarters in December and January 1990, the question of how to handle the legacy of the collapsing dictatorship became central. From then on, the newly established Round Table, the reinvigorated Volkskammer (the East German parliament), and central-government and municipal authorities debated how best to come to terms with the communist past. The prosecution of officials for corruption and abuse of power began, as did the rehabilitation of the victims of political persecution. The Volkskammer passed a law on the handling of Stasi records, and steps were taken to change communist street names, indicating a spontaneous desire to erase the communist past.[4]

With unification approaching, it was by no means inevitable that these early eastern efforts to bring the former regime to account would continue. After the breaching of the Berlin Wall on 9 November 1989, eastern dissidents were increasingly marginalized from political developments in the "rush to German unity."[5] They devoted correspondingly more attention to matters of dealing with the past, the one issue on which—at this early point—they were largely in agreement with the bulk of the population.[6] As unification loomed ever closer, some feared that their efforts toward a reckoning with the old regime would be endangered by western indifference or preference for stability. The West German government's agreements that the postunification Bundestag would consider the East German law on the Stasi records—that were to remain in the East—and that it would rehabilitate and compensate the victims were major victories for the dissidents and the democratically elected Volkskammer; indeed, working through the past was one of the few areas of noteworthy eastern influence on the Unification Treaty between the two German states.[7] After unification, western politicians remained concerned about the potential divisiveness of revelations about complicity with the SED regime and the Stasi in particular, but ultimately the western political establishment shared the desire of many easterners to bring those responsible to book.

By early autumn 1991, public prosecutors were investigating hundreds of cases relating to crimes committed by East German border guards, Stasi officers, and state and party officials, but there was continuing doubt about the possibilities and efficacy of prosecuting regime crimes. Former communist heavyweights denied publicly any responsibility for the regime, frequently blaming the Soviet Union and pointing to their own limited room for maneuver. Sensationalist revelations about individuals' involvement with the Stasi dominated the press, and questions over the fate of the Stasi records had yet to be resolved. Sensing the inadequacy of the reckoning with the communist regime, numerous eastern former dissidents put forward proposals for a "tribunal" to provide a public forum for discussion of the past. There was broad agreement among eastern dissidents and intellectuals on the desirability of public deliberation, but difficult questions remained about who would sit on such a tribunal, how it would work, and what legitimacy it would have. The name itself was enough to scare off some commentators, and many western politicians and intellectuals feared its disruptive and divisive potential.[8]

In this context in November 1991, two eastern former dissidents from protestant church circles, Markus Meckel and Martin Gutzeit, called for the creation of a parliamentary commission of inquiry (*Enquete-Kommission*).[9] Under paragraph fifty-six of the parliamentary standing orders, a commission of inquiry can be established for "the preparation of decisions on a substantial and important complex of matters." Unlike a parliamentary investigative committee, such commissions can include non-parliamentarians among their members, usually academics or other experts in the relevant field.[10]

The proposal for a parliamentary forum reflected its proponents' belief that the Bundestag had to assume responsibility for discussion of the past. Meckel and Gutzeit had supported representative parliamentary democracy and opposed the grassroots participatory democratic concepts of other civil-rights activists in 1989–90. They were among the cofounders of the East German Social Democratic Party in late 1989. Meckel had become the GDR's last foreign minister after the democratic elections to the Volkskammer in March 1990 and after unification was now a Bundestag deputy for the Social Democratic Party of Germany (SPD). Gutzeit had been leader of parliamentary business for the eastern Social Democrats in the Volkskammer, was briefly a member of the Bundestag in late 1990, and in autumn 1991 was conducting research into the GDR opposition; in 1993 he would become the Berlin State Commissioner for the Stasi Records.[11]

Their inquiry proposal did not create much media interest but did gain support within the Bundestag. The Alliance 90 parliamentary group was initially skeptical, fearing that a commission would fail to provide the public forum promised by a tribunal. Alliance 90 (B90)—originally an electoral alliance formed for the Volkskammer elections of March 1990—had constituted itself as a political party in September 1991 from remnants of numerous East German opposition groups, and merged with the western Greens in 1993.[12] It did not oppose the inquiry in principle; it simply wanted more, as did numerous former dissidents. It therefore called for federal financial support for additional, non-parliamentary initiatives.[13]

Former dissidents who had found their way into the major political parties meanwhile sought to convince their reluctant western parliamentary colleagues, and their cross-party networks proved to be crucial in this effort.[14] In December 1991, the Christian Democratic Union of Germany (CDU) accepted a recommendation from their new parliamentary leader Wolfgang Schäuble for an inquiry to address "forty years of German division and of the SED's unlawful state (*Unrechtsstaat*)."[15] Sharing the former dissidents' concerns about the stalling reckoning with communism and sensing the opportunity for a critical examination of the socialist past, CDU General Secretary Volker Rühe argued in February 1992 that dealing with the East German past was a "central political task" and a "challenge for all of Germany."[16]

Rainer Eppelmann was reported to be the commission's likely chairperson, and rapidly became its public face.[17] As the last GDR minister for defense, the pastor, civil-rights activist, and founder of the center-right citizens' group *Demokratischer Aufbruch* (Democratic Awakening) had suggested in 1990 that a general amnesty for offences other than murder, manslaughter, and wrongful detention should follow attempts to vet Volkskammer deputies for Stasi connections.[18] Yet as a CDU Bundestag deputy, Eppelmann became a vocal advocate of a vigorous anticommunist reckoning. In late 1991, he was defeated in elections to the post of CDU deputy leader in the eastern state of Brandenburg, having called on office bearers of the former eastern Christian Democratic Union of Germany (CDUD)—a member of the "democratic bloc" of parties previously allied with the SED—to abstain from party office.[19] He was also a protagonist in a fierce debate in 1991–92 about the Stasi connections of the premier of the eastern state of Brandenburg, Manfred Stolpe (SPD).[20] Eppelmann opposed a tribunal, believing that no one had the authority to sit in judgment over others: in the GDR, "we were all whores in one way or another."[21] In contrast, he supported a commission because there was "no compulsion in the end to pronounce a judgment."[22]

After much negotiation and the presentation of formal proposals by each parliamentary party, on 12 March 1992 the Bundestag voted, with only two abstentions, for the establishment of a commission of inquiry, "Working through the History and Consequences of the SED Dictatorship."[23] As the vote indicated, the PDS did not oppose the inquiry. It declared, "the necessity of an objective and differentiated confrontation with the history of the GDR is undisputed."[24] Not uncharacteristically, however, this position was qualified by an immediate objection to the one-sidedness of the inquiry's anticipated brief and an insistence that the GDR's positive sides be recognized: "At the same time, it is to be noted that the political stability of the GDR was not least the result of achievements and values in the GDR that found the approval of many citizens."[25] This "yes, but" stance was typical of the party's double strategy of formally supporting the inquiry while objecting to the content of its work and to the other parties' approaches to GDR history.[26]

Aims and Motivations

The parties agreed on the need for an investigation of the past, but precisely why it was necessary was often left unclear or expressed only in general terms. As became evident in the Bundestag debate preceding the 12 March vote, an important source of motivation was a widespread sense that the Germans had failed to come to terms with the Nazi past. Given traditional positions, it is hardly surprising that negative assessments were proffered particularly by members of the Left, whether easterners or westerners. Prominent eastern dissident Gerd Poppe (B90) argued explicitly that "the West and East Germans failed—admittedly in different ways—to deal with the Nazi past."[27] Yet members of the governing center-right coalition expressed remarkably similar views. Michael Stübgen (CDU), for instance, declared simply that the confrontation with the Nazi past had failed.[28] Dirk Hansen of the Free Democratic Party (FDP) claimed that West Germans had to ask themselves what they had achieved despite talking about it for decades, and he spoke critically of eastern antifascism and western anticommunism constituting "nothing other than foundational myths" of the two postwar states.[29] Hansen's evenhanded approach was applauded by Free Democrats, Christian Democrats, and Social Democrats, suggesting that a critical view of both western and eastern *Vergangenheitsbewältigung* was becoming increasingly consensual.

The more or less explicit implication of such critical views was that these past errors should not be allowed to recur. Rainer Eppelmann declared that one had to face up to the past because "our past catches up with us again and again," and "no one can sneak out of their history."[30] He argued further that the Germans had to learn from their past behavior in order to avoid "landing again in the stupid situation of a child who touches the hot oven door for a third time and once again gets its finger painfully burned."[31] Similarly, former West German Federal Chancellor and SPD Honorary Chairperson Willy Brandt insisted that—particularly after the experience with the Nazi dictatorship—he had no time for the "therapy of letting the grass grow."[32] More explicitly, Jürgen Schmude (SPD) argued: "The discussion over this Nazi period occurred hesitantly after the war, soon ground to a halt, and then continued with difficulties for decades. It had to take place—painful as it was, but much too late and with the price of grave disadvantages for the new beginning. As different as the eras and the circumstances were, the experience of the initially neglected and delayed confrontation teaches us that you cannot simply let things rest and that you cannot evade the truth."[33] Christian and Free Democrats drew similar conclusions.[34]

In addition to this apparently widely shared belief that facing up to the past was essential and unavoidable, a second lesson drawn from the post-Nazi experience was that it constituted an ongoing process that could not be completed quickly and then forgotten. This—as Dorothee Wilms (CDU) suggested in the Bundestag debate on the ratification of the inquiry's terms of reference on 20 May 1992—was a painfully gained insight that could now be applied to the GDR.[35] It found expression in the commission's preference for the notion of *Aufarbeitung* as opposed to *Bewältigung*, which is generally felt to suggest the prospect of eventual closure. There was no disagreement on this point, and the entire commission—including its more conservative members—accepted the lesson of dealing with the Nazi past: that such an enterprise is unending.[36] The contingency and radicalism of this development toward an enduring commitment is highlighted by a statement by Federal Chancellor Helmut Kohl (CDU) in the debate on the inquiry's establishment. Kohl reported that after 1945 many people had thought coming to terms with the Nazi past would be completed within a few years, but that he now believed it would continue (only) for as long as the victims were still alive.[37]

That the belief in the enduring nature of the process of facing up to a difficult past gained strength precisely when the opportunity for a reckoning with communism arose gives some grounds for skepticism.[38] Yet the inquiry was not motivated by a desire to end or replace the discussion of Nazism, or cover up its flaws. Instead, a double reckoning was deemed necessary. After 1989, it became common to speak of the need for a "second" or "double" coming to terms with Germany's dictatorial past(s). Such designations meant different things to different people, revealing divergent attitudes not only to the present reckoning with communism, but also to the older one with Nazism.[39] To some, a reckoning with a second German dictatorship was now necessary after the previous one with Nazism, a view that assumed that the latter could be regarded as completed.[40] For others, the call for a double reckoning meant that all Germans now needed to work through the communist past, while easterners also had to face up to the Nazi past. This position presumed that, unlike West Germany, East Germany had not mastered the Nazi past.[41] Still others believed that all Germans must continue to assume responsibility for Nazism, but that the East German past should be left primarily to easterners.[42]

All these views were evident to some extent in the commission of inquiry, but a fourth, according to which all of Germany now had an obligation to deal responsibly with the ongoing legacy of two dictatorships, predominated. It is unsurprising that parliamentarians who advocated the establishment of the inquiry and commissioners themselves regarded facing up to the communist past as a significant national responsibility; otherwise, they would not have been involved. The more interesting point was their consensual acceptance of the ongoing need to confront Nazi crimes and commemorate their victims. No one in the Bundestag debates or before the commission disputed this. As the commission's 1994 report would state, "The commission of inquiry is of the belief that working through the National Socialist era and honoring its victims is a constitutive part of the democratic historical culture of unified Germany."[43] In 1998, the successor commission reaffirmed Germany's "lasting obligation" to remember the Nazi past.[44] It seems that—for all the differences of the Historians' Dispute of the 1980s—a consensus had emerged in the political middle ground recognizing the profound, continuing consequences for German identity of the Nazis' unprecedented crimes.

This apparent consensus notwithstanding, the discrepancy between the eagerness with which the communist past was now being tackled and past hesitation over the Nazi past was open to interpretation. Some liberals and Democratic Socialists pointed to the hypocrisy of attempting to make up for insufficient denazification through a more rigorous process of decommunization, but others viewed the apparent inconsistency positively, as the outcome of a learning process. In the 12 March Bundestag debate, Markus Meckel (SPD) and Dietmar Keller (PDS) mentioned that the inquiry provided the first instance of a German parliament devoting itself to the country's past in such a fashion; they thus implicitly alluded to deficits on both sides of the Iron Curtain in relation to Nazism, but welcomed the present response.[45]

Assessments of eastern and western efforts at working through the Nazi past were by no means unanimously negative, and not every conservative who now subscribed to the continuing-obligation view necessarily welcomed criticism of the western record. But whether one held charges that the Federal Republic had failed to work through the Nazi past—or had been culpably late in doing so—to be justified or not, the aim now was to prevent similar accusations over the communist past.[46] During the inquiry's early stages and after the conclusion of its work, commissioners suggested that one of its main purposes was to show both the population and posterity that the postunification political establishment had not ignored the East German past. Dirk Hansen (FDP) went so far as to say that the point of the inquiry was to preempt allegations of a "third guilt," alluding to the "second guilt" of the repression of the Nazi past famously ascribed by Holocaust survivor and author Ralph Giordano. The inquiry was thus to a considerable extent an end in itself: its mere existence provided the German polity of the 1990s with immunity from future claims of inattention to the East German past.[47]

Beyond the provision of such an alibi and more general demands grounded in regret about omissions relating to the Nazi past, there was a strange reticence about why a parliamentary inquiry was necessary. That the Bundestag should be involved in dealing with the past was taken largely for granted. In light of the cross-party support for the inquiry, deputies perhaps felt little need to convince wavering colleagues that the initiative was worthwhile. Only the SPD made an explicit case, arguing that the parliament "as the highest elected body with deputies from the entire Federal Republic of Germany has a special responsibility for the political confrontation with this history"; this applied particularly because the Bundestag stood in legal succession to the democratically elected Volkskammer, "that was unable to devote itself in appropriate fashion to this task."[48] Yet even the SPD motion failed to formulate concretely the commission's purpose. As Rolf Schwanitz (SPD) acknowledged toward the end of the Bundestag debate, it was, for many, still rather unclear what the commission was supposed to achieve.[49]

Debate about the inquiry was marked by heady rhetoric, not least about the untreated wounds of the past contributing to the ills of the present. Dirk Hansen (FDP) described the inquiry as a "search for identity," and Gert Weisskirchen (SPD) spoke of a "search for truth."[50] For the SPD, the history of the GDR was an "unexamined" and "largely unknown" past that "weighs heavily upon people in the process of coming together" and "does not let us come to rest."[51] The SPD perceived the past as a history of "injustice and oppression," the experiences of which were "still alive," and whose "wounds cannot simply be washed away." At the same time, it was a history that touches millions of people, the history of everyone who lived in the GDR.[52] The governing coalition's justification contained even more pathos, but was just as vague about the inquiry's purpose. According to the motion of the CDU, the Bavarian Christian-Social Union (CSU), and the FDP: "The downfall of the GDR is not the end of its history. The past is all too clearly present; yesterday seems to shape tomorrow. ... Wounds rip open, old scars refuse to heal. Many people search for enlightenment, for orientation in dealing with their own responsibility and the guilt of others. ... The German Bundestag must and can not shut itself off from this discussion. On the contrary, its members are especially called upon now to provide answers to the question of the future of our past, to the question of the causes and effects of the SED's unlawful regime, of people's situation yesterday and today."[53] How the commission would contribute to these laudable goals was left unstated.

The inquiry's relationship with other actors and institutions address-ing the East German past required definition. To this end, there was con-siderable discussion about what the commission was *not* intended to do. The parties agreed that the Bundestag was not claiming a "monopoly" on working through the past.[54] According to Alliance 90, which was par-ticularly concerned about this: "Parliamentary initiatives for confronting the injustice in the GDR cannot replace the people affected by it and those involved in it dealing with it themselves. They can only complement and foster this. The Bundestag therefore welcomes the variety of social efforts and initiatives to research and deal with the injustice committed in the Soviet-occupied zone and the GDR (e.g., exhibitions, Round Tables, per-petrator-victim dialogues, regional-history workshops, 'tribunals,' etc.)."[55] In the Bundestag debate, many speakers called for the Stasi records to remain open and for greater assistance to the newly established Federal Commissioner for the Records of the State Security Service of the former German Democratic Republic.[56] The parties also insisted that the parlia-mentary commission would not interfere with or replace the judicial pros-ecution of GDR crimes, which in the words of the SPD "must remain the task of the courts alone."[57]

The parties were also concerned to dispel any fears that the inquiry was assuming the role of historians. In her opening remarks to the commis-sion's constitutive meeting on 19 March 1992, Bundestag President Rita Süssmuth (CDU) foresaw substantial difficulties in establishing the inqui-ry's relationship to historical scholarship, because its role was partly—but only partly—the writing of history.[58] Commissioners agreed that the in-quiry could not replace independent research on the GDR and would not proclaim an "official history," and its terms of reference included the disclaimer that it was "not to preempt or replace the necessary histori-cal research."[59] Agreeing on this minimal position functioned above all as a signal to skeptical historians, whose concerns that the commission might produce "a history legitimated by the state" had been noted.[60] Their fears were not surprising given comments such as Eppelmann's that the inquiry's tasks would include "research and analysis," and some press commentators saw them confirmed by the Bundestag debate.[61] The com-mission's relationship to historical scholarship would remain ambiguous.

Despite emphasis on what the commission was not intended to do and considerable lack of clarity about its purpose, it is still possible to discern a number of positive goals. The first was to improve the Bundestag's own ability to address the legacy of the past. By definition, commissions of inquiry are advisory bodies intended to aid the Bundestag in the preparation of legislation, and the SPD at least took this role seriously, arguing that the Bundestag needed to improve its capacity to act on the East German legacy.[62] Social Democrats repeatedly insisted on the inclusion of specific, practical goals and tangible, political outcomes, rather than concentrating on writing and evaluating history. They saw historical investigation primarily as a means to the end of better handling the past's legacy in the present.[63] Other parties, too, hoped the inquiry would provide the parliament with recommendations for action, where necessary. The commission was thus to be an instrument for addressing the material and personal legacy of the past through political means; that is, it was to develop policies for the past (*Vergangenheitspolitik*).

The practical measures envisaged focused on the victims, rather than the representatives of the regime. Numerous parliamentarians called both publicly and internally for victims' past suffering and continuing difficulties to be acknowledged and addressed.[64] What this involved and how the investigation should proceed were far from clear, as was exactly who was to be considered a victim. Nevertheless, many hoped that the inquiry would promote the politics of redress for the victims, and consider moral recognition as well as rehabilitation and financial compensation. In contrast, the perpetrators were absent from the goals of the commission.

Further positive goals were to foster and influence public debate about the past. The SPD stressed that the commission should fulfill a representative role: "With it the parliament would create for itself a site where, over years of continuous work, the necessity and the execution of the political working through will be maintained and repeatedly invoked."[65] Similarly, the CDU/CSU-FDP coalition wanted the commission "to foster discussion — that is to be held in many places — about working through the history and consequences of the SED dictatorship."[66] Here, too, the commission's aims were formulated above all in the negative. Many parliamentarians saw the commission as a "corrective" to both the style and focus of public discussion of the GDR as it was being conducted in 1991–92.[67] The often hysterical, inconsistent, and hypocritical style of debate — focusing on the moral failings of individual politicians like Manfred Stolpe or cultural figures like author Christa Wolf — was to be counteracted by a systematic approach. There were repeated calls for "differentiation" and greater objectivity, as well as objections to all-too-hasty judgments and black and white divisions into heroes and villains.[68] The commission was to develop clear, fair criteria for assessing the past and individuals' roles in it, in order to replace the party affiliation of the protagonists that seemed to be the sole criterion in the present.[69]

In addition to the style of public discussion, its focus was also to be shifted. Again, the regime's victims were to play a prominent role. CDU

General Secretary Rühe hoped that the victims would receive more attention in a media environment obsessed with the perpetrators, whether small-time unofficial Stasi collaborators or major espionage figures like Markus Wolf.[70] More importantly, the Bundestag debate demonstrated an inter-party consensus that the history of the GDR not be reduced to the Stasi. As Eppelmann put it: "We would fail in this working through if we limited ourselves ... only to the topic of the State Security. ... The experiences we have had in and with forty-five years of the GDR encompassed our whole life and every person and not just the possibly 500,000 official and unofficial employees of the State Security and their immediate victims." [71] Once again, the commission's focus was formulated ex negativo.

The positive corollary of this negative aim of shifting attention away from the Stasi was support for an investigation of the regime's functioning and for consideration of various levels of responsibility. With the exception of the PDS, all parties wanted the commission to undertake a structural, systematic investigation of oppression and of the regime's mechanisms of rule, to counteract media concentration on the top party and Stasi leadership, on scandals surrounding individual Stasi informers, and on particular abuses or instances of corruption. Revealing the extent and forms of oppression, persecution, and abuses of power and examining systematically the different levels of political responsibility would show that oppression and persecution were systemic and endemic, rather than incidental to the regime.[72]

The inquiry was thus never conceived as an open-ended, objective investigation of the entire history of the GDR. Instead, it was conducted with the stated purpose not only of focusing on repression, injustice, and control, but also of establishing the responsibility of the SED. Numerous parliamentarians demanded that the SED be the focus of attention, rather than its "Sword and Shield," the Stasi.[73] Eppelmann hoped to demonstrate that the SED leadership—rather than the policies of the FRG government or the machinations of the market economy—was responsible for the economic, social, and environmental malaise now facing eastern Germany.[74] The inclusion of the term "SED dictatorship" in the commission's name indicates the importance of this attribution of responsibility for the regime and its crimes to the ruling party (rather than the Stasi, or the Soviet Union). Although one might have expected its inclusion in the title to be controversial, it was never discussed in the commission's plenary meetings, and there seems to have been no reflection on its potentially tendentious or prejudicial nature.[75] PDS commissioner Dietmar Keller supported the title, but his party colleagues rejected it.[76]

In addition to highlighting SED responsibility, for conservatives in particular, but also for some members of Alliance 90 and the SPD, the commission was to serve the delegitimation of the GDR per se. The GDR was to be shown to be a thoroughly illegitimate state that had never constituted an alternative to the Federal Republic. All parties supported the investigation of the relationship between the party and the state. However, whereas the SPD and Alliance 90 addressed the GDR on its own terms and allowed for the possibility of distinguishing between the party system and the state itself, the coalition appeared to make its answer clear from the outset, referring to the "SED state" and the "SED's unlawful state."[77] Indeed, the coalition's proposal for the inquiry can be read as rejecting the existence of the GDR state as such, and its use of emotionally and morally loaded terms stood in contrast to the SPD's more neutral references to repression in the Soviet Occupation Zone (SBZ) and GDR.[78] As will be shown below, conservatives made few distinctions between the dictatorial regime *in* the GDR and the existence of the state per se, consistently denied the GDR any legitimacy, and sought to discredit all variants of socialism by association with the SED's state-socialist project.

While nominally supportive of the inquiry, Democratic Socialists had considerable reservations. In the Bundestag debate, Marxist Forum hardliner Uwe-Jens Heuer (PDS) argued with some justification that the inquiry's result was a foregone conclusion, as the other parties had already made up their minds about the GDR.[79] Heuer also objected to what he saw as the reduction of GDR history to repression, resistance, and conformity: "The big lie of the history of the GDR as a horror story of acts and mechanisms of repression."[80] He complained that such an approach left no room for "reformers" or for the question of "why so many people in all of Germany once actively supported the goal of socialism and saw an answer to the catastrophe of fascism precisely in this East German path."[81] Heuer's arguments were tendentious and provocative and served the legitimatory goals of the PDS, which sought to save the reputation of the GDR's antifascist beginning and its noble attempt at socialism. Yet they should not be dismissed out of hand. Heuer suggested with some justification that one could hardly expect a rational, scholarly discussion in an atmosphere in which "the enlarged Federal Republic has largely returned to the terminology of the Cold War."[82] Heuer himself did nothing to foster a more constructive environment, as his partially apt criticism was submerged amongst his wider railing (and the storm of protest it provoked) against the "final extermination" and "criminalization" of GDR history and the "campaign of revenge" against its supporters.[83] Such exaggerations indicated that Heuer himself was hardly interested in rational discussion, and he criticized the proposed commission on every possible ground, no matter how inconsistent. This uncompromising position of a few hard-line

PDS members would continue to undermine the constructive, self-critical participation of others.

Despite Heuer's assertions about the other parties' reduction of GDR history to persecution and resistance, numerous parliamentarians were at pains to distinguish between the reprehensible regime and the bulk of its citizens. In the Bundestag debate most speakers, although unsparing in their criticism of the SED and GDR, made a discernible effort to express their sympathetic understanding for the vast majority of the population. As far as the Christian Democrats and Free Democrats were concerned, the SED, the East German state, and the socialist project were to be discredited, but the general population was to be dissociated from the tyrannical regime and from the Stasi in particular. According to Eppelmann: "We will presumably establish that there were only very, very few heroes and unfortunately more guilty perpetrators and their henchmen. But we will also recognize that most people were neither heroes nor criminals, but simply tried to get through life with their small and large compromises, as uprightly, as honestly, and perhaps also as comfortably as possible—often enough hemmed in, tormented, broken."[84] Others similarly recognized a spectrum of culpability and compliance and insisted that one could not apply black and white categories of guilt and innocence to the whole population. Willy Brandt, for example, was at pains to insist that his respect for the vocal opposition did not diminish his understanding for the far greater number of GDR citizens who had simply sought to make the most of life for themselves and their families in their various "niches."[85] Jürgen Schmude (SPD) also argued that human-rights abuses, repression, and mismanagement of the economy were only part of the reality of life in the GDR.[86]

Such conciliatory efforts to demonstrate understanding for and thus integrate the more or less compromised population related directly to calls from all parties for "inner unity" between easterners and westerners. Brandt, for instance, saw a confrontation with the past as a contribution to national reconciliation and urged westerners to consider how they would have behaved had they lived in the GDR.[87] He objected to those in the West who poisoned the atmosphere in unified Germany by celebrating "retrospective triumphs" over their Cold War rivals and posing as "moral judges" over their eastern compatriots.[88] Angela Merkel (CDU)—who would become Germany's first female and eastern federal chancellor in 2005—argued, "If we are not capable of [great care of judgment] and do not find the courage to differentiate, we will not achieve inner unity."[89] Indeed, the topos of inner unity and the notion that working through the past could and should play a central role in overcoming the apparent alienation between East and West ran throughout the debate, and were repeated, mantra-like, throughout the inquiry's early discussions.

Characteristically, precisely what such statements meant and how national reconciliation could be achieved remained unclear. At times, commissioners declared that inner unity required both easterners and westerners to regard the history of the GDR as part of German national history. For example, Jürgen Schmieder (FDP) suggested, "It is our history, a component of the history of the German people."[90] Similarly, Eppelmann argued, "We all—that is, all eighty million Germans—are affected by this German history."[91] East German history was thus to be incorporated into the historical consciousness of the entire nation. At other times, parliamentarians declared merely that easterners should not be left alone with the task of working through their past. The often implicit suggestion was that, by working through the East German past together, easterners and westerners would "grow together," in Brandt's famous words.[92]

Not infrequently, the connection between inner unity and working through the past led to emphasis on the historical division of the nation. Whereas the SPD had proposed a straightforward examination of crimes and injustices committed in the GDR (thus an investigation of the GDR qua GDR), Christian Democrats wanted to illuminate the past in terms of the national question, emphasizing "the forty-year division of Germany."[93] Working through the past was thus not just to condemn the existence and abuses of the communist dictatorship and examine questions of responsibility and accommodation; it was also to reassert the national paradigm by highlighting the suffering of the national community through the crime of division, while also pointing to the lingering, popular desire for national unity prior to 1989. As the coalition put it, "The forced external division could not cut through our inner belonging together."[94] Wolfgang Schäuble (CDU) insisted that national division "was our common fate," and he referred repeatedly to the need to address it, and not just the history of the SED regime.[95] The implication was that Germans on either side of the East-West divide shared a divided past.[96]

Such stress on the history of division and the goal of national reconciliation did little to clarify the commission's specific aims. Frequent talk of the need for dialogue between easterners and westerners about their different experiences threatened to obscure the specificity of the GDR past—and the desire for analysis of the structures and mechanisms of the dictatorship and its consequences—amid the quest for East-West harmony and understanding. Particularly when the everyday experiences of "ordinary" people were emphasized, the whole venture threatened to degenerate into an ill-defined, cuddly getting-to-know-one-another session. The media picked up strongly on the anticipated inclusion of ordinary people. One press commentator seemed to think that the inquiry was to be a forum for easterners and westerners to tell each other about their lives.[97]

Moreover, affirming the national dimension and the shared history of division left the door open for the PDS to call for the inclusion in the investigation of West German history. The PDS insisted that the discussion should not concentrate on East Germany alone, as the GDR could not be isolated from the German-German or international Cold War context.[98] There was little prospect of the focus shifting away from the GDR, but the PDS hoped that certain "antidemocratic" aspects of the past-and-present Federal Republic would be scrutinized; it advocated, for example, comparisons of the handling of the "fascist" past and of crime rates in the two Germanys.[99] Such questions were legitimate, but the PDS sought comparisons only where—in the midst of the transformation crisis besetting unified Germany—it hoped to collect "nostalgia points."[100]

The commission, however, was not interested in examining West German history or comparing East and West. Eppelmann rejected a parallel examination of the two states, fearing this might suggest they were equally legitimate and their histories similarly problematic.[101] Yet appeals to a joint, national responsibility and to the Germans' common need to address their common past complicated the justification of an inquiry specifically into the GDR. Eppelmann, for example, stated that it had to pursue "questions about the very everyday behavior of the Germans, especially—but not only—in the GDR in the last forty-five years."[102] He did not explain the particular emphasis on East Germans. Indeed, the commission lacked a coherent strategy for justifying and achieving both an examination and delegitimation of the GDR on the one hand, and a project of national reconciliation between easterners and westerners on the other. This was not helped by the frequent elision of the separate questions of whether the western past should be addressed in the investigation and whether westerners should participate in the process.

If the commission was not interested in a balanced examination of both sides of the history of division, its deliberations were nevertheless to include the West to some extent. In fact, a further goal of the inquiry, and especially its conservative members, was an examination of the two German states' interaction and of West Germans' differing degrees of acceptance of the SED regime and national division. The earlier tribunal discussion and the original SPD proposal for a commission had focused on East Germany almost exclusively. The SPD worried that the inquiry would become "a parliamentary instrument for reciprocal reproaches" among the political parties over western *Deutschlandpolitik*.[103] After initial hesitation, Christian Democrats did indeed prove keen to address West German relations with, and attitudes toward, the GDR. Eppelmann, for example, wanted to examine "why West German politicians thought so late of talking to civil-rights activists and not just to the rulers."[104]

Such questions offered a welcome opportunity for conservatives to both attack the West German Left for what seemed in retrospect excessive accommodation with communism and acceptance of national division, and to praise those who had supposedly maintained their anticommunism and desire for unification through the long years of division. In contrast with the sympathetic understanding expressed for the East German population's varying degrees of complicity, anyone in the West who was seen as having accepted the GDR—let alone been a fellow traveler—was severely condemned, especially by Christian Democrats, but also by members of Alliance 90. "What discouragement," Schäuble said, "it must have meant back then for the people in the GDR ... that GDR socialism found so much sympathetic understanding in some political and in many so-called intellectual circles" in the West.[105] Similarly, at the commission's second meeting, CDU expert commissioner Alexander Fischer called on the inquiry to attempt to redress "the West German intelligentsia's view of the GDR as a socialist alternative."[106] As the SPD feared, disagreements and mutual reproaches over *Deutschlandpolitik* almost overwhelmed the debate on the inquiry's establishment, which was marked by partisan haggling and point scoring. Differences continued into the commission's term, with Social Democrats arguing that western attitudes and behavior were not central to the inquiry, and conservatives and eastern dissidents (outside the SPD) welcoming the opportunity to explore the western side of the history of division, at least to this limited extent.[107] That Christian Democrats wanted to claim the credit for unification is well known.[108] Their wider assault on the western Left is often overlooked.

The desire to open the discussion to westerners and to include aspects of the western past led to a change in the commission's title to "Working through the History and Consequences of the SED Dictatorship in Germany." The added phrase "in Germany" meant different things to different people. For some, it described where the working-through process was to occur, with the implication that westerners would also participate. For the majority, however, it referred to how the tentacles of the SED dictatorship had reached across the Wall into the West, and meant that inner-German relations and particularly the susceptibility of the West German Left to infiltration and manipulation by various organs of the SED regime were to be included in the inquiry's brief. As a result, much of the drama in the commission's work was associated with conservative efforts to condemn the Left on the basis of its relations with GDR communism, and the Left's resistance to this.[109]

Membership

The foregoing discussion has shown that the parties agreed that working through the past was an "all-German task" to be pursued by easterners and westerners alike. The very fact that the inquiry was an organ of the Bundestag meant that answers had been found to two central questions about the handling of the GDR past: whether it should be left to easterners themselves or also involve westerners, and in what forum debate should be carried out.[110] In contrast with the views of Wolfgang Thierse and others who pointed to the need for easterners to deal with their own past themselves, the establishment of a national parliamentary commission indicated the strength of the opposing position.[111] Eppelmann called for westerners to be included in order to avoid the "fatal impression" that dealing with the GDR past was not an all-German problem. However, he also hoped to avoid the impression that the West was sitting in judgment over the East, and it was agreed widely that at least half of the commission's membership should come from the eastern states.[112] Eppelmann and the commission as a whole thus sought a delicate balance between including westerners and avoiding the impression that easterners were not autonomously working through their own history.[113] Finding and maintaining this balance was to be perhaps the greatest challenge for the inquiry.

Calls for easterners to be represented beyond their numerical proportion in the Bundestag were answered: the majority of commissioners came from the GDR. The commission's membership consisted of sixteen parliamentarians (and sixteen alternates), and eleven outside experts. Of the thirty-two parliamentary members (both full members and alternates), twenty-one were from the GDR; even when the western-dominated expert members were included, 60 percent of the total membership at the start was from the East. The commission could therefore legitimately claim to have an "all-German" membership, and it did so repeatedly.[114] In further symbolic support for the project of national reconciliation, the commission was led by an eastern man and a western woman: Rainer Eppelmann was elected unanimously as the commission's chairperson and Margot von Renesse (SPD) as his deputy.[115]

Highlighting its mixed composition seemed necessary in order to defend the commission against misleading allegations by the PDS and others of western dominance and victor's justice. PDS representatives repeatedly sought to frame the debate in terms of East versus West, and cast themselves as the (sole) representative of the former. Uwe-Jens Heuer (PDS), for example, perceived in the commission "the morality and the authority of the victor."[116] They thus ignored the heterogeneity of the eastern population, the fact that the latter, and not the Federal Republic, had overthrown the SED regime, and the fact that easterners were amongst the most vigorous proponents of the reckoning process. It has been a remarkably successful strategy that has managed to convince many (particularly in the West) who, impressed, bewildered, or horrified by PDS electoral success in the eastern states, fail to see that most of the eastern population votes for parties other than the PDS.[117]

More surprisingly, PDS arguments about the western-dominated nature of the commission have found their way into several scholarly treatments of the inquiry. Jennifer Yoder, for example, argues that the past was "filtered and evaluated through western eyes and easterners were again subjects rather than participants."[118] As this book demonstrates, this is patently untrue. More specifically, Yoder is not alone in suggesting—also incorrectly—that all of the outside experts on the inquiry were from the West.[119] This not only overlooks several easterners among the experts, including Martin Gutzeit. It also relies on excessively categorical distinctions between easterners and westerners. The majority of the outside experts—all of whom were men, and most of whom had a professional academic background, mainly as historians—were certainly "westerners" at first glance. Yet a number of them had lived in the GDR for a time or had personal, often traumatic associations with the East German state. The CDU/CSU named as its outside experts historians Alexander Fischer and Manfred Wilke, legal scholar and historian Friedrich-Christian Schroeder, journalist and GDR scholar Karl Wilhelm Fricke, and Lutheran pastor Martin-Michael Passauer. Passauer was the only straightforward easterner, although both Fricke and Fischer had had grim personal experiences with the East German regime.[120] In addition to Gutzeit, the SPD nominated historians Bernd Faulenbach and Hermann Weber. The latter had been a member of the Communist Party of Germany (KPD) in his youth and worked as an SED-trained Free German Youth functionary in the Federal Republic before breaking with communism in 1953.[121] The FDP nominated the writer Walter Kempowski, who had lived in the SBZ/GDR and been imprisoned there before escaping to the West; but he was replaced before the end of 1992 by western historian and political scientist Hans-Adolf Jacobsen, having attended only a couple of meetings. Armin Mitter, an eastern historian who was close to the dissident milieu and had been active since 1990 in research on the Stasi and in the Independent Historians' Association, was the expert for Alliance 90.[122] East German political economist Herbert Wolf represented the PDS. Although the westerners dominated, there was a considerable amount of both professional and "biographical expertise" on the GDR among the experts, such that Yoder's claim that they "presumably did not experience life in the GDR" amounts to a false presumption.[123]

As this mixed membership and these complex biographies suggest, one should avoid the tendency to overemphasize both the East-West dichotomy and the inquiry's attempts to overcome it. The national paradigm served to obscure critical political and ideological issues. Inflated rhetoric about the achievement of inner unity (or colonization and victor's justice) distracted attention from important political and ideological cleavages on both sides. Geography—one's personal provenance in West or East—did not determine one's attitude to the GDR, and debates and disagreements in the commission rarely ran along East-West lines.[124] Pointing to a balance of eastern and western members, or to a majority of either, therefore says little about the inquiry or its members' views.

Political affiliation was more important. Crucially, the Christian Democrats nominated seven parliamentarian and five expert members, the Social Democrats five parliamentarian and three expert members, the Free Democrats two parliamentarians and one expert, and Alliance 90 and the PDS one parliamentarian and one expert each.[125] The experts were approached and nominated by the parliamentary parties, implying a basic political compatibility, but they were not necessarily members of that party. Wilke, for instance, was not a CDU member but was asked to work on the commission for the Christian Democrats because the party did not have enough GDR specialists in its ranks. Fricke was not a member of any party but was regarded across party lines as the Stasi expert, and would have been nominated by Alliance 90 had the Christian Democrats not proposed him. Mitter, though active in the Initiative for Peace and Human Rights in 1989–90, was not a member of Alliance 90, but knew Gerd Poppe and was approached by him on the basis of his work on the Stasi and his efforts in the Independent Historians' Association to renew the East German historical sciences. On the other hand, Jacobsen was a member of the FDP, and Faulenbach was a member of the SPD and its Historical Commission.[126]

As well as claiming to be an all-German body, the commission portrayed itself as broadly representative of eastern society.[127] There was a modicum of truth to this claim, as a range of political biographies was represented. With the exception of Eppelmann, most of the eastern Christian Democrats had been members of the CDUD bloc party, while the eastern FDP representatives had been members of its bloc counterpart, the Liberal Democratic Party of Germany (LDPD). The PDS representatives had belonged to the higher echelons of the SED or GDR state apparatus. In contrast, the eastern Social Democrats had been more or less prominently involved in oppositional activities in the GDR and the transitional phase in 1989–90, while the two parliamentary representatives of Alliance 90 were prominent dissidents. The commission thus included among its members individuals with various political records and affiliations, a diversity which has not been recognized by most commentators.[128]

However, although diverse, the inquiry's membership was hardly representative. In the first place, the various sectors of eastern society were represented in inverse proportion to their actual size in the population. The overwhelming majority of East Germans who had not been members of a political party or oppositional group was underrepresented, although several commissioners had become politically active or aligned only in, or subsequent to, the autumn and winter of 1989–90. The huge SED membership of 2.4 million in the mid to late 1980s was also underrepresented (with just three commissioners), while the large bloc parties with a combined membership of almost half a million were represented by a handful of commissioners. The relatively small opposition and church groups, on the other hand, were significantly overrepresented.[129] The commission's membership thus did not truly reflect the eastern population. What is more, easterners were more likely than westerners to leave the commission before the end of its term, and they were not always replaced by other easterners. More significant than the resultant fall over time in their numerical proportion—to just above 50 percent—was the reduction of their capacity for sustained contribution. This instability particularly affected former members of the bloc parties or those who had not been politically active or aligned in the GDR, whereas the dissidents comprised a stable cohort, whose influence increased commensurately.[130] If the inquiries constituted victor's justice, it was that of eastern as much as of western anti-communists, but the commissions' membership was more diverse than has generally been acknowledged. All of this applies also to the membership of the second commission of inquiry, which was slightly smaller but exhibited roughly the same characteristics.[131]

Methods

The methods the commission would use and how it would interact with the public and with other actors engaged in working through the East German past were initially far from clear. Early proposals were inconsistent, if they said anything at all about methods. On Eppelmann's suggestion, the commission's first meeting decided that public sessions would be arranged only for specific justified cases. Other commissioners, however, insisted that the inquiry not work behind closed doors, and that it needed to respond to, and take a leading role in, public debate.[132] Commissioners agreed that the inquiry had to engage in dialogue with other actors in the process of working through the GDR past, although the extent and form of this dialogue were not yet certain.[133] Christian Democrats were initially somewhat perturbed by oppositional and minor parties' suggestions for public hearings, but readily agreed when it became apparent that a format was needed for receiving oral rather than written statements from eye-witnesses and victims.[134] Eppelmann in particular quickly became a vocal advocate of "proximity to the citizens."[135] Although regular commission meetings were not open to the public, public hearings became a central component of proceedings, contrary to the erroneous depictions of some commentators.[136]

The commission clearly intended to engage to a considerable degree in the investigation, assessment, and production of history. Indeed, as the leftwing *Tageszeitung* newspaper noted, the parties' motions "read like vague proposals for a long-term historical research project."[137] Yet the inquiry's relationship to historical scholarship and its approach to history were far from unambiguous or undisputed. Two positions can be distinguished that reflected divergent understandings of the inquiry's purpose and its target audiences. The first view, evident mainly among Social Democrats, emphasized the political recommendations the commission would make and saw its investigation of the past largely as a means to that end. Bernd Faulenbach thus rejected the coalition's use of verbs like "depict" and "document," which he feared would lead to excessive concentration on writing history, rather than drawing consequences from it.[138] This approach assumed, and insisted upon, a separation between history and politics. It aimed at a scholarly and, as far as possible, objective and politically neutral understanding of GDR history, which could then serve as a basis for parliamentary decision making. The target audience was thus largely the Bundestag itself. Researching and writing history—to the extent that they were to be pursued at all—were one of a number of otherwise more overtly practical tasks, and were secondary to these.[139] Where the commission was to engage in research, those who subscribed to this view generally thought it should concentrate on areas neglected by academic scholarship thus far, rather than attempt to rewrite East German history.[140]

In contrast, the majority of the commission—western conservatives and numerous eastern dissidents—believed the inquiry should investigate and write GDR history on a considerable scale. The coalition was particularly keen to delve into the production of history, and its members' statements—including that of Rita Süssmuth (CDU), according to whom the writing of history was one of the commission's tasks—prompted Wolfgang Ullmann (B90) to express his concern that the inquiry saw itself as an historical commission.[141] Other eastern dissidents did not share Ullmann's concerns and themselves called for the investigation and writing of history. Angelika Barbe (SPD) and Poppe (B90) argued for the depiction of GDR history "from below" and "from the point of view of the citizens" rather than the rulers, and Armin Mitter called for an "inner history" of the GDR, rather than the western perspective that dominated the existing historiography.[142] On this view, the narration and interpretation of GDR history was perhaps the central purpose of the entire enterprise. It was seen as an end in itself and a highly political one, given that it entailed evaluation and the attribution of responsibility. Adherents to this second position did not insist on the separation between history and politics evident in the first position, and indeed regarded the rewriting of history as essentially political (generally with the intention of delegitimizing the GDR, but also in the minds of former dissidents with the hope of returning its history to the people). Mitter, for instance, argued explicitly that it was impossible to separate the historical and the political aspects of the commission's task.[143]

According to this second approach, the inquiry was to engage in history politics. The target audience was the German public at large, but the eastern public in particular. This approach perceived, perhaps more realistically than the first, that in a parliamentary commission a sharp distinction between history and politics was impossible to maintain, and that the autonomy of the former would always be secondary to the demands of the latter. The second approach prevailed, although both conceptions continued to exist side by side throughout work of the inquiries, and the tensions between them were never resolved.

Among other things, the dissonance over the commission's role in researching and rewriting East German history reflected differing assessments of pre-1989 western scholarship. The likes of SPD expert commissioner Hermann Weber, doyen of historical scholarship on the GDR, understandably saw it in a largely positive light, requiring only slight modification and enhancement. In contrast, Mitter at least initially dismissed it entirely, suggesting that a new beginning was needed based on research in recently opened state and party archives.[144] Both western conservatives and eastern dissidents were keen to use the inquiries to attack previous western GDR scholarship, and this formed part of the wider assault on the West German Left's purported softness on communism.[145]

Precisely how the investigation of the past would proceed still had to be resolved. Again, differing stances existed over whether the inquiry would rely primarily on its own expertise—particularly that of the expert members—or whether it would look to others for assistance. The commissioning of larger or smaller projects was widely supported, and a budget of two million Deutschmarks was available to fund research activities.[146] Western historians, again particularly Social Democrats, suggested that the inquiry commission large-scale research projects into historical questions such as the relationship between the leaderships of the SED and the Communist Party of the Soviet Union (CPSU).[147] There was considerable skepticism about the feasibility of such projects given that they would have to be completed in time for the commission's final report which had to be delivered before the end of the legislative period in 1994 (as well as concern about the production of official, politically sanctioned histories, and about commissioners' acquisition of public funds for their own research institutes).[148] Nevertheless, "expertise papers and research projects" were included among the inquiry's methods alongside public hearings and discussions with experts and citizens' groups.[149]

The Terms of Reference

After the official constitution of the commission by Bundestag President Süssmuth on 19 March 1992, its early meetings were occupied with discussing its tasks, determining its title, and developing its terms of reference.[150] As might be expected, the terms of reference, which were adopted unanimously at the commission's sixth meeting on 12 May, were the result of negotiation and compromise. The final document was more coherent than any of the parties' earlier proposals, but the practice of including rather than excluding suggestions had led to a daunting array of tasks. The commission's purpose was more clearly defined than previously, although much remained nebulous. The overriding goal was, "To contribute—in dialogue with the public—to the strengthening of democratic self-confidence and the further development of a common political culture in Germany."[151] The inquiry was to offer the German people, especially those in the eastern states, "assistance in the examination of the past and in the evaluation of personal responsibility," and "to serve an injured sense of justice by laying bare abuses and naming responsibilities." It was also to "contribute to reconciliation in society," although whether this meant East-West or intra-eastern reconciliation was left open; other references highlighted national reconciliation, expressed as "inner unification."[152]

The pursuit of these laudable aims entailed a number of specific activities. The commission was to "work on contributions to political-historical analysis and political-moral evaluation" of a variety of aspects of German history.[153] These included: "the structures, strategies, and instruments of the SED dictatorship, especially the question of responsibility"; "ideology, integrative factors, and disciplinary practices"; "the abuse of international human-rights conventions and norms as well as the forms of repression in different periods"; resistance and opposition to the regime; the churches;

and the international constellation and inner-German relationships.[154] The inquiry was also to consider "the question of continuities and analogies in the thought, behavior, and structures of German history in the twentieth century, especially the time of the National Socialist dictatorship."[155] In addition to these broad issues and themes, particular periods and events in East German history were to be investigated "by way of examples." The inquiry would examine the establishment of the dictatorship in 1945–49, the uprising of 17 June 1953, agricultural collectivization in the late 1950s, the building of the Berlin Wall in 1961, as well as the invasion of Czechoslovakia by Warsaw Pact troops in 1968, the transfer of power from Walter Ulbricht to Erich Honecker in 1971, and the peaceful revolution in autumn 1989 and German unification.[156] The terms of reference thus represented a compromise between those who wanted to investigate particular phases and events in GDR history and those who preferred to examine certain larger thematic issues throughout its history.

In addition to analyzing and evaluating the above, the commission resolved to work "primarily" toward a number of practical outcomes, relating to victims, archives, research conditions, questions about governmental criminality, and the "educational-psychological processing" of the past. Further, it had the general aim of providing "recommendations to the German Bundestag in relation to legislative measures and other political measures."[157] Social Democrats' insistence on practical outcomes thus bore fruit, although the ostensible primacy of these practical goals was reduced somewhat by their position in the terms of reference after the lists of issues, themes, periods, and events to be investigated.[158] Chapter 2 will show that this early deprioritization increased over time.

Ratification

The Bundestag considered the commission's terms of reference on 20 May 1992. The debate was shorter and less controversial than that on the inquiry's establishment two months previously, and most speakers expressed their satisfaction over the unanimous agreement on the inquiry's mandate. Markus Meckel recalled his skepticism six months earlier—when he had first called for an inquiry—about whether it would be established, as well as the widespread concerns upon its creation over whether the commission could agree to a mandate of any quality. In both cases, he argued, the doubts had not been vindicated; this seemed to indicate the political parties' substantial "will for consensus" and their preparedness to approach history in a differentiated and sensible manner, rather than as a weapon with which to attack each other.[159] Concerns nevertheless abounded about the size of the task at hand—Meckel spoke of a "potpourri of topics"—while uncertainties about its procedures lingered.[160]

Differences of opinion remained over the inquiry's goals, and commissioners tended to see what they wanted in the terms of reference, hoping to achieve their particular ends under its broad aegis. Meckel stressed the "fundamental" need for tangible results and recommendations to the Bundestag.[161] In contrast, Dirk Hansen (FDP), citing philosopher Jürgen Habermas, described the commission as part of a broad "ethical-political process of self-understanding."[162] According to Eppelmann, meanwhile, "We want to analyze politically, to determine, judge, and evaluate and then—where needed—suggest practical steps for action in this House."[163]

There was still more emphasis and clarity on what the commission should and could not do, than on what it could and would. On the positive side of the ledger things remained vague. For example, Hansen posed the crucial question of why the Bundestag should bother devoting itself to history, which he answered as follows: "Remembering liberates. It makes the future possible. It is part of reconciliation. It is the basis of democracy. To remember means to search for, and speak truths. This creates identity."[164] Such noble and elevated sentiments reflected a growing sense of the undertaking's significance. Meckel mentioned that the only precedent for the inquiry was a Reichstag committee in the Weimar Republic into the question of responsibility for the First World War, as no such body had been erected after the Second World War.[165] As it had in the first Bundestag debate, the motif of avoiding the mistakes made in facing up to the Nazi past thus recurred in the second debate.[166] The importance of reconciliation—generally meaning that between estranged easterners and westerners rather than between various elements of eastern society—featured prominently, although it had not been the focus of more than rhetorical invocation in the commission's internal deliberations thus far.[167] What was understood by reconciliation, and how and whether the commission could contribute to it, was still far from apparent. The primary focus remained a critical investigation of the East German past. Hartmut Soell (SPD) did not mince words, saying that the inquiry's purpose was "to delegitimize the SED and its leadership as the main bearers of responsibility for the leftwing variant of the totalitarian temptation in Germany's most recent history, and thus to contribute to the formation of a democratic consciousness."[168]

The apparently exclusive focus on repression and injustice in the GDR was the main justification provided by the PDS for voting against the resolution. Although he personally supported the terms of reference, Dietmar Keller had the unenviable task of indicating that his parliamentary colleagues did not.[169] In elaborating the PDS stance, Uwe-Jens Heuer and

Andrea Lederer argued that the commission's conclusions were predetermined and would not be "historically just" because it was one-sidedly interested in repression, neglected the "achievements and values that found the support of many citizens," and denied the legitimacy of the socialist "alternative to aggressive and antidemocratic traditions in Germany."[170] Heuer complained further that—in the current "social crisis" of mass unemployment—easterners were not helped by vengeful "condemnation and punishment" coming from outside, that is, the West.[171]

Such arguments carried no weight with the other parties and the commission of inquiry's establishment was completed with the Bundestag's ratification of its mandate by an overwhelming majority.[172] Many questions remained, however, about how it would proceed and about its ability to pursue and achieve the diverse tasks it had set itself. The answers to these questions are the focus of the next chapter.

Notes

1. A. James McAdams, "Vergangenheitsaufarbeitung nach 1989: Ein deutscher Sonderweg?" *Deutschland Archiv* 36, no. 5 (2003): 852.
2. Cf. Wüstenberg, *Die politische Dimension*, 250f.; McAdams, *Judging the Past*, 166.
3. See, for instance, the founding declaration of the eastern Social Democratic Party, reprinted in Carl-Christoph Schweitzer, Detlev Karsten, Robert Spencer, R. Taylor Cole, Donald P. Kommers, and Anthony J. Nicholls, eds., *Politics and Government in Germany, 1944–1994: Basic Documents* (Providence, 1995), 96. Cf. Ulrich Mählert and Manfred Wilke, "Die DDR-Forschung: ein Auslaufmodell? Die Auseinandersetzung mit der SED-Diktatur seit 1989," *Deutschland Archiv* 37, no. 3 (2004): 466; Hermann Weber, *Geschichte der DDR*, rev. ed. (Munich, 1999), 351; Bock, *Vergangenheitspolitik im Systemwechsel*, 60.
4. Bock, *Vergangenheitspolitik im Systemwechsel*; Wüstenberg, *Die politische Dimension*, 252, 257, 282, 290. On street names, see Rainer Eckert, "Straßenumbenennung und Revolution in Deutschland: Über die Beseitigung der Symbole und Benennungen der SED-Diktatur," in *Vergangenheitsbewältigung*, ed. Jesse. Cf. Calhoun, *Dilemmas of Justice*, 52.
5. Konrad H. Jarausch, *The Rush to German Unity* (Oxford, 1994). Cf. McAdams, *Judging the Past*, 89.
6. See Jürgen Leinemann, "'Schon wieder auf den Beinen,'" *Der Spiegel* 14 (1990), 23–27. Cf. Mark Thompson, "Reluctant Revolutionaries: Anti-Fascism and the East German Opposition," *German Politics* 8, no. 1 (1999): 55; Wielenga, *Schatten deutscher Geschichte*, 110; and, rather critically, Offe, *Varieties of Transition*, 23, 212 (fn. 20). On public attitudes, see Susanne Karstedt, "Coming to Terms with the Past in Germany after 1945 and 1989: Public Judgments on Procedures and Justice," *Law and Policy* 20, no. 1 (1998): 37.
7. Bock, *Vergangenheitspolitik im Systemwechsel*; Offe, *Varieties of Transition*, 23; Sa'adah, *Germany's Second Chance*, 100; Heinrich, "Geschichtspolitische Akteure," esp. 15–20.
8. See Albrecht Schönherr, ed., *Ein Volk am Pranger? Die Deutschen auf der Suche nach einer neuen politischen Kultur* (Berlin, n.d.); Joachim Gauck et al., "'Tribunal' als Forum der

Aufklärung," *Deutschland Archiv* 25, no. 2 (1992): 222–24. For a conservative western politician's account, see Wilms, "Begründung, Entstehung und Zielsetzung," 10ff.

9. "Presseerklärung vom 29. November 1991," reprinted in Markus Meckel, *Selbsbewußt in die deutsche Einheit: Rückblicke und Reflexionen* (Berlin, 2001), 159ff. Cf. Maier, *Dissolution,* 325. Kamali incorrectly states that Rainer Eppelmann first proposed a commission of inquiry, "Accountability for Human Rights Violations," 116 (fn. 103).

10. See Christian Heyer and Stephan Liening, *Enquete-Kommissionen des Deutschen Bundestages: Schnittstellen zwischen Politik und Wissenschaft* (Berlin, n.d.), 11; Frank Hampel, "Politikberatung in der Bundesrespublik: Überlegungen am Beispiel von Enquete-Kommissionen," *Zeitschrift für Parlamentsfragen* 22, no. 1 (1991): 111–33; Wolfgang Ismayr, "Enquete-Kommissionen des Deutschen Bundestages," *Aus Politik und Zeitgeschichte* 46, no. 27 (1996): 29–41. Generally on the organs of the Bundestag, see Wolfgang Ismayr, *Der Deutsche Bundestag: Funktionen, Willensbildung, Reformansätze* (Opladen, 1992).

11. Author's interview with Martin Gutzeit (Berlin, 22 August 2001). Cf. Bock, "Von der Tribunal-Idee," 1178; Cooke, *Representing East Germany,* 35.

12. The western Greens did not obtain 5 percent of the vote in the 1990 Bundestag election and were thus not represented in the 1990–94 legislative period, but a separate quota for the eastern states allowed B90 to be represented by eight parliamentarians. See Andrei S. Markovits and Philip S. Gorski, *The German Left: Red, Green and Beyond* (Cambridge, 1993); Geoffrey K. Roberts, *Party Politics in the New Germany* (London, 1997).

13. "Antrag der Gruppe Bündnis 90/Die Grünen (Drs. 12/2220 – neu) vom 9. März 1992: Einsetzung einer Enquete-Kommission 'Aufarbeitung der Geschichte und der Folgen der SED-Diktatur' und Förderung außerparlamentarischer Initiativen zum gleichen Thema," I: 8ff.

14. Author's interviews with Martin Gutzeit and Armin Mitter (Berlin, 20 September 2001).

15. "Schäuble schlägt Enquete-Kommission zur Aufarbeitung des SED-Unrechtsstaates vor," *Pressedienst der CDU/CSU Fraktion im Deutschen Bundestag,* 10 December 1991. The term *Rechtsstaat* means a constitutional state founded on the rule of law. An *Unrechtsstaat* is the opposite, a state *not* based on the rule of law. *Unrecht,* however, also indicates "wrong" and "injustice." *Unrechtsstaat* thus suggests not simply that the state does not operate according to the rule of law, but that it is fundamentally unjust, i.e., does not just commit, but is founded upon profound wrongs.

16. "CDU will Gerechtigkeit für DDR-Regimegegner," *Süddeutsche Zeitung* (*SZ*), 13 February 1992.

17. "Eppelmann soll Bonner 'DDR-Kommission' führen," *SZ*, 11 February 1992.

18. "'Wir haben Lynch-Stimmung': DDR-Minister Rainer Eppelmann über Stasi-Vergangenheit und Regierungsbildung," *Der Spiegel* 14 (1990), 21.

19. "Bitte prüfen," *Der Spiegel* 49 (1991), 22. On party development in the course and wake of unification, see Roberts, *Party Politics.*

20. On the Stolpe debate, see Sa'adah, *Germany's Second Chance,* 189–236; Barbara Miller, *Narratives of Guilt and Conformity in Unified Germany: Stasi Informers and their Impact on Society* (London, 1999), 75–84.

21. "Üblicher Heckmeck: Statt eines Tribunals soll eine Enquête-Kommission des Bundestages die DDR-Vergangenheit aufarbeiten," *Der Spiegel* 2 (1992), 25.

22. Ulrich Reitz, "Verlockung, Anpassung, Repression," *Die Welt,* 12 February 1992.

23. "Debatte des Deutschen Bundestages am 12. März 1992," I: 146.

24. "Antrag der Gruppe PDS/Linke Liste (Drs. 12/2226) vom 11. März 1992: Einsetzung einer Enquete-Kommission 'Politische Aufarbeitung der DDR-Geschichte,'" I: 12.

25. Ibid.

26. Cf. Bock, "Von der Tribunal-Idee," 1179; Barker, "'Geschichtsaufarbeitung' within the PDS," 84ff.; Cooke, *Representing East Germany,* 35.
27. I: 48.
28. I: 147.
29. I: 129.
30. I: 26, 28.
31. I: 27.
32. I: 31f.
33. I: 104.
34. I: 132, 140, 93.
35. "Debatte des Deutschen Bundestages am 20. Mai 1992," I: 159.
36. "Working through" was used in each party's motion. See I: 8, 11; "Antrag der SPD (Drs. 12/2152) vom 21. Februar 1992: Einsetzung einer Enquete-Kommission 'Politische Aufarbeitung von Unterdrückung in der SBZ/DDR,'" 3; "Antrag der Fraktionen der CDU/ CSU und der F.D.P. (Drs. 12/2229) vom 11. März 1992: Aufgaben der Enquete-Kommission 'Aufarbeitung der Geschichte und der Folgen der SED-Diktatur,'" 18. Meckel explicitly stated the SPD's preference. Deutscher Bundestag Parlamentsarchiv, Bonn (DBPa): Protokoll der zweiten Kommission der Enquete-Kommission "Aufarbeitung von Geschichte und Folgen der SED-Diktatur," 10. Subsequent references to the minutes of the internal meetings of the first commission are given as follows: DBPa: Protokoll meeting number: page number. Thus here: DBPa: Protokoll 2: 10. Cf. Schulte, "Die 'doppelte Vergangenheit.'" Here I disagree with Jutta Vergau, who suggests that *Aufarbeitung* was preferred because *Vergangenheitsbewältigung* was taken to imply a collective guilt (of East Germans), which was deemed undesirable, *Aufarbeitung von Vergangenheit,* 18. She offers no evidence for this contention, and it is inconsistent with the statements in the context of the Bundestag inquiry and elsewhere.
37. I: 39. Cf. Norbert Ommler, "Zweierlei 'Vergangenheitsbewältigung' ohne Tangieren des gemeinsamen Kerns?" *Geschichte—Erziehung—Politik* 4, no. 7–8 (1993): 438.
38. Cf. Kamali, "Accountability for Human Rights Violations," 131.
39. For a range of early 1990s views, see Eberhard Jäckel, "Die doppelte Vergangenheit," *Der Spiegel* 52 (1991), 39–43; Alexander von Plato, "Eine zweite 'Entnazifizierung'? Zur Verarbeitung politischer Umwälzungen in Deutschland 1945 und 1989," *Gewerkschaftliche Monatshefte* 42, no. 7 (1991): 415–28; Ludwig Elm, "Zweierlei Vergangenheitsbewältigung: Damals und heute," *Deutschland Archiv* 24, no. 7 (1991): 736f.; Christa Hoffmann, *Stunden Null? Vergangenheitsbewältigung in Deutschland 1945 und 1989* (Bonn, 1992); Gotthard Jasper, "'Vergangenheitsbewältigung': Historische Erfahrungen und politische Voraussetzungen," in *Ohne Erinnerung keine Zukunft!' Zur Aufarbeitung von Vergangenheit in einigen europäischen Gesellschaften unserer Tage,* eds. Clemens Burrichter and Günter Schödl (Cologne, 1992); Josef Isensee, *Vergangenheitsbewältigung durch Recht: Drei Abhandlungen zu einem deutschen Problem* (Berlin, 1992); Hoffmann, "Aufklärung und Ahndung"; Christa Hoffmann and Eckhard Jesse, "Die 'doppelte Vergangenheitsbewältigung' in Deutschland: Unterschiede und Gemeinsamkeiten," in *Deutschland: Eine Nation—doppelte Geschichte,* ed. Werner Weidenfeld (Cologne, 1993); Christoph Kleßmann, "Das Problem der doppelten 'Vergangenheitsbewältigung,'" *Die neue Gesellschaft/Frankfurter Hefte* 38, no. 12 (1993): 1099–105; Klaus Sühl, ed., *Vergangenheitsbewältigung 1945 und 1989: Ein unmöglicher Vergleich? Eine Diskussion* (Berlin, 1994). Only isolated voices considered other historical precedents. See Johann-Georg Schätzler, "Staatenfusion und Abrechnungsmentalität," *Deutschland Archiv* 30, no. 1 (1997): 105–15.
40. See Klaus Naumann, "Die geteilte Vergangenheit: Geschichte als Politik," *Blätter für deutsche und internationale Politik* 36, no. 11 (1991): 1398f.

41. See historian Karl Dietrich Bracher's comments before the inquiry, IX: 684; a statement by Alexander Fischer at its second meeting, DBPa: Protokoll 2: 21; and Michael Wolffsohn, "Doppelte Vergangenheitsbewältigung," in *Vergangenheitsbewältigung 1945 und 1989*, ed. Sühl. Cf. Karl Dietrich Bracher, "Vierzig Jahre Diktatur (SED-Unrecht): Herausforderung an den Rechtsstaat," *Recht und Politik* 27, no. 3 (1991): 137–41.

42. See the comments of Jürgen Habermas and Hans Misselwitz before the inquiry, IX: 691, 653; and Wolfgang Thierse, "Schuld sind immer die anderen: Ein Plädoyer für die selbstkritische Bewältigung der eigenen Geschichte," in *Ein Volk am Pranger?* ed. Schönherr.

43. "Bericht der Enquete-Kommission 'Aufarbeitung von Geschichte und Folgen der SED-Diktatur in Deutschland,'" I: 280.

44. "Schlußbericht der Enquete-Kommission 'Überwindung von Geschichte und Folgen der SED-Diktatur im Prozess der deutschen Einheit,'" *I: 599*.

45. I: 67, 114. Cf. Johannes L. Kuppe, "Was bei der Aufarbeitung zu bedenken ist," *Deutschland Archiv* 25, no. 9 (1992): 978–81; Schulte, "Die 'doppelte Vergangenheit.'" In fact, the first debate about the Nazi past in the Bundestag that was not connected with a piece of legislation took place in 1970. See Helmut Dubiel, *Niemand ist frei von der Geschichte: Die nationalsozialistische Herrschaft in den Debatten des Deutschen Bundestages* (Munich, 1999), 133f. For a more recent rehearsal of the left-wing critique, see Detlef Joseph, *Nazis in der DDR: Die deutschen Staatsdiener nach 1945—Woher kamen sie?* (Berlin, 2002), 89–96.

46. Even less critical assessments of the western reckoning with Nazism were used to justify a harsh reckoning with the GDR. Roswitha Wisniewski (CDU), hardly a critic of the West's confrontation with the Nazi past, argued merely that the Germans had a special obligation to deal with the dictatorial pasts and totalitarian ideologies, I: 149. Indeed, numerous conservative commentators rejected both old and new critical assessments of western *Vergangenheitsbewältigung*, claiming that the difficulties in dealing with the GDR past allowed the former to appear in a more favorable light. For many, see Hoffmann, "Aufklärung und Ahndung"; Eckhard Jesse, "Vergangenheitsbewältigung," in *Handwörterbuch zur deutschen Einheit*, eds. Werner Weidenfeld and Karl-Rudolf Korte (Frankfurt am Main, 1992); Jesse, *Vergangenheitsbewältigung*, 19. Cf. Andrew H. Beattie, "Die Delegitimierung von '1968' nach 1989/90: Das Beispiel der Enquete-Kommissionen des Deutschen Bundestages," in *Erinnerungsort 1968*, eds. Claudia Fröhlich and Andrea Genest (Berlin, forthcoming).

47. Author's interviews with Martin Gutzeit, Dirk Hansen (Lüneburg, 18 September 2001), Hans-Adolf Jacobsen (Bonn, 11 October 2001), and Markus Meckel (Berlin, 31 January 2002). See also the statement by Harmut Koschyk in the debate on the second inquiry's report, "Debatte des Deutschen Bundestages am 17. Juni 1998," *I: 843*. B90 expert commissioner on the second inquiry Ilko-Sascha Kowalczuk suggests that this was one reason for the lack of self-critical reflection at the beginning of the second commission: the very existence of the first was held to be sufficient in and of itself (author's interview, Berlin, 23 August 2001). Cf. Ralph Giordano, *Die zweite Schuld, oder Von der Last Deutscher zu sein*, new ed. (Cologne, 2000).

48. I: 7.

49. I: 96.

50. I: 130, 135.

51. I: 6.

52. Ibid.

53. I: 22f.

54. I: 43, 54, 69, 76, 105, 116, 132.

55. I: 9.

56. I: 50f., 70, 78, 104f., 132f., 146, 148. The Stasi records law had been passed on 20 December 1991, and citizens were able to apply to see their Stasi files from the beginning of 1992.

57. I: 6. Cf. Wüstenberg, *Die politische Dimension*, 325.

58. DBPa: Protokoll 1: 3.

59. DBPa: Protokoll 5: 5. I: 188. See also DBPa: Protokoll 2: 13, 22f.; Protokoll 3: 15. "Aufgabenstellung der Enquete-Kommission 'Aufarbeitung von Geschichte und Folgen der SED-Diktatur in Deutschland,'" I: 188. See Appendix A for a translation of the terms of reference. The word "official" was generally avoided, although Dirk Hansen describes the inquiry as an "official investigation," "Gemeinsame Aufarbeitung zweier Vergangenheiten in einem Land?" *Deutsche Studien* 141 (1999): 42. Cf. Vergau, *Aufarbeitung von Vergangenheit*, 184.

60. Markus Meckel, "Aufarbeitung der DDR-Geschichte als Aufgabe des Bundestages," in *Rück-Sicht auf Deutschland: Beiträge zur Geschichte der DDR und zur Deutschlandpolitik der SPD*, ed. SPD-Bundestagsfraktion (Bonn, 1993), 58. Cf. "Das demokratische Selbstbewußtsein festigen," *Woche im Bundestag*, 27 May 1992; Wilke, "Der Historiker und die Politik," 92f.; Markus Meckel, "Hilfe beim Verständnis der eigenen Vergangenheit: Hermann Weber zum Fünfundsiebzigsten," in *Bilanz und Perspektiven*, eds. Eppelmann, Faulenbach, and Mählert, 428.

61. "'Kein Tribunal des Hasses und der gegenseitigen Diskriminierung,'" *SZ*, 26 February 1992. For concerns following the debate, see "Keine Geschichtsstunde," *Frankfurter Rundschau (FR)*, 13 March 1992; Bettina Urbanski, "Nur keine Schlammschlacht," *Berliner Zeitung (BZ)*, 2 April 1992.

62. I: 7.

63. DBPa: Protokoll 2: 20; Protokoll 3: 13, 15, 19, 21, 41f. In an interview with the author, Meckel stressed how important he considered practical goals, as opposed to historical investigation. Cf. Meckel, "Aufarbeitung der DDR-Geschichte," 60; Meckel, "Demokratische Selbstbestimmung," 259ff. That said, the original SPD motion was itself replete with calls to "investigate," "reveal," and "depict" the past (I: 4f.). Unlike Faulenbach and Meckel, Hermann Weber described the main tasks of the commission as being, on the one hand, its investigation of East German history and, on the other, "to improve the preconditions for scholarly inquiry" into that history, "Rewriting the History," 203. He thus downplayed (other) practical outcomes, a position consistent with his desire to see support for historical research entrenched as the main focus of the Foundation for Working through the SED Dictatorship discussed below (author's interview with Weber, Mannheim, 10 October 2001).

64. I: 23, 28f., 42, 57, 66f., 68, 76, 97, 102, 112, 138, 149. DBPa: Protokoll 1: 8, 10; Protokoll 2: 9f., 14, 22f. Cf. Wüstenberg, *Die politische Dimension*, 293.

65. I: 7.

66. I: 18.

67. See I: 73. Cf. Meckel, "Demokratische Selbstbestimmung," 257; Jansen, "Enquete-Kommission," 266; Wielenga, *Schatten deutscher Geschichte*, 82.

68. I: 51, 58, 67, 70, 79, 95, 96f., 113, 116. Andrews' suggestion that the inquiry did not seek to promote or develop a differentiated view of the past and of individuals' biographies ignores these calls and the subsequent efforts in the same direction, "The Politics of Forgiveness," 120f.; "Grand National Narratives," esp. 52, 56f.

69. I: 19, 62, 66f., 76, 111.

70. "Rühe will DDR-Unrecht aufarbeiten," *Hamburger Morgenpost*, 12 February 1992. Cf. Fulbrook, "Heroes, Victims and Villains in the History of the GDR," in *Rewriting the German Past*, eds. Alter and Monteath, 182ff.; Wüstenberg, *Die politische Dimension*, 286.

Western media are often blamed for the excessive focus on the Stasi and the relative neglect of the SED, but as Petra Bock argues, the Stasi were consciously exposed by GDR authorities throughout the course of 1990 so that other governmental institutions could be salvaged and spared rigorous scrutiny and financial privations, *Vergangenheitspolitik im Systemwechsel*, 234, 277, 354, 406. Cf. Wüstenberg, *Die politische Dimension*, 315f., 319. The early focus on the Stasi applied not just to the media but also to historical publications. See Christa Hoffmann, "Deutsche Vergangenheitsbewältigung," *Jahrbuch Extremismus und Demokratie* 5 (1993): 196.

71. I: 26. Cf. Wilke, "Die deutsche Einheit," 463; Wilke, "Der Historiker und die Politik," 88; Bock, "Von der Tribunal-Idee," 1181.

72. I: 30, 32, 45f., 48, 49, 52, 69, 96, 111. Cf. Faulenbach, "Die Arbeit der Enquete-Kommissionen," 22f.; Wüstenberg, *Die politische Dimension*, 290.

73. I: 33, 45, 51f., 77f., 96f., 103, 109.

74. I: 27.

75. There is no evidence that the characterization of the SED regime in the title was discussed. In an interview with the author, Gutzeit appeared to consider the question of its tendentiousness for the first time, and claimed that it was a "hypothesis." If this were the case—and for this there is no evidence—it could, as he conceded, certainly have been formulated somewhat more hypothetically. Eppelmann said simply that it was an accurate description of the regime (author's interview, Berlin, 27 August 2001). On the other hand, Yoder exaggerates the extent to which it is controversial in eastern Germany, "Truth without Reconciliation," 70.

76. DBPa: Protokoll 3: 13.

77. I: 3f., 8, 19, 23.

78. I: 3.

79. I: 82. On different ideological strands within the PDS, see Jonathan Olsen, "Germany's PDS and Varieties of 'Post-Communist' Socialism," *Problems of Post-Communism* 45, no. 6 (1998): 42–52; Barker, "'Geschichtsaufarbeitung' within the PDS."

80. I: 87.

81. I: 81.

82. I: 80f.

83. I: 82, 88.

84. I: 30.

85. I: 34.

86. I: 104. See also 52f., 57, 79. Again, Andrews' depiction overlooks such differentiated positions, "The Politics of Forgiveness," esp. 116.

87. I: 32, 34.

88. I: 31, 34.

89. I: 113.

90. I: 47.

91. I: 28.

92. I: 33.

93. "Enquetekommission zum SED-Unrecht gefordert," *General-Anzeiger,* 11 December 1991.

94. I: 23.

95. I: 58. Schäuble hardly mentioned the East German regime or its history without also mentioning division, 57–67. On his understanding of the nation as a "community of fate," see Maria Zens, "Truism and Taboo: The Rhetoric of the Berlin Republic," in *Political Thought and German Reunification: The New German Ideology?* eds. Howard Williams, Colin Wight, and Norbert Kapferer (Basingstoke, 2000).

96. The German word *geteilt* expresses well the paradoxical nature of this past: in one sense it points to the fact that Germany had been "divided," but it also refers to the fact that this past was "shared." Cf. Christoph Kleßmann, Hans Misselwitz, and Günter Wichert, eds., *Deutsche Vergangenheiten—eine gemeinsame Herausforderung: Der schwierige Umgang mit der doppelten Nachkriegsgeschichte* (Berlin, 1999).

97. "Auf Schmerz gefaßt," *Hessische Allgemeine*, 13 March 1992. See also "Kommission will auch einfache Bürger hören," *Die Welt*, 23 March 1992; "Nicht nur Honecker und Bohley," *BZ*, 13 April 1992.

98. I: 11, 166, 176.

99. I: 12f., 17.

100. Bock, "Von der Tribunal-Idee," 1179. On the crisis of the early to mid 1990s, see Jürgen Kocka, *Vereinigungskrise: Zur Geschichte der Gegenwart* (Göttingen, 1995).

101. Author's interview.

102. I: 30.

103. "Kommission zur DDR-Geschichte," *Die Welt*, 20 December 1991.

104. "Rühe will DDR-Unrecht aufarbeiten," *Hamburger Morgenpost*, 12 February 1992. According to commissioner Manfred Wilke, inner-German relations and *Deutschlandpolitik* were the most important issues for the Christian Democrats (author's interview, Berlin, 1 August 2001).

105. I: 65.

106. DBPa: Protokoll 2: 21.

107. DBPa: Protokoll 1: 8; Protokoll 2: 13, 16, 19, 32. Former GDR opposition figures in the SPD did not join in the conservative attacks on the SPD for obvious reasons of party solidarity, but many were highly critical of the party's intimacy with the SED in the 1980s, which made them cautious about a union between the newly founded eastern SPD and its western sister party in 1990. See Roberts, *Party Politics*.

108. Cf. McAdams, *Judging the Past*, 106. For a critique of conservative myth-making on this point, see Lars-Broder Keil and Sven Feliz Kellerhoff, *Deutsche Legenden: Vom "Dolchstoß" und anderen Mythen der Geschichte* (Berlin, 2002), 229–51.

109. On *Deutschlandpolitik* specifically, see McAdams, *Judging the Past*, 101–9. More generally on debates about western attitudes toward the GDR, see Andrew H. Beattie, "A Fifties Revival? Cold War Culture in Re-unified Germany," in *European Cold War Cultures: Perspectives on Societies in the East and the West*, eds. Thomas Lindenberger, Marcus M. Payk, Bernd Stöver, and Annette Vowinckel (Providence, forthcoming).

110. Cf. Bock, "Von der Tribunal-Idee," 1171; Wüstenberg, *Die politische Dimension*, 257f.; Garton Ash, *History of the Present*, 294–314.

111. See Thierse, "Schuld sind immer die anderen."

112. "Westdeutsche sollen auch in Enquête-Gruppe," *BZ*, 12 February 1992.

113. See "'Kein Tribunal des Hasses und der gegenseitigen Diskriminierung,'" *SZ*, 26 February 1992. The commission's report referred to the inquiry as an "all-German pilot enterprise that was demanded particularly by deputies from Berlin, Brandenburg, Mecklenburg-West Pomerania, Saxony, Saxony-Anhalt und Thuringia," I: 191f.

114. See, for example, the commission's report, I: 192. Contrary to Helga Welsh, who argues that the majority of commissioners were westerners, "When Discourse Trumps Policy," 145.

115. Dorothee Wilms incorrectly states that Meckel was Eppelmann's deputy, "Begründung, Entstehung und Zielsetzung," 14. Petra Haustein incorrectly states that Siegfried Vergin—who was Eppelmann's deputy on the second inquiry—was the chairperson of both inquiries, *Geschichte im Dissens*, 118 (fn. 103).

116. I: 83. See also Werner Roß, "Kommt jetzt die Verklärung statt der Aufklärung?" *Neues Deutschland* (*ND*), 10 April 1992; Uwe-Jens Heuer, "Nein, ich schäme mich nicht!" *ND,* 8–9 August 1992. Cf. Barker, "'Geschichtsaufarbeitung' within the PDS," 86.

117. Witness the claims by SPD General Secretary Franz Münterfering in the lead up to the Berlin state election in October 2001 that an SPD-PDS coalition was justified and necessary because one could not continue to exclude East Berliners from representation in the city-state's government. See Jan Ross, "Rückzug mit Rückgrat: Richard Schröder fühlt sich wieder einmal nicht zu Hause in der SPD," *Die Zeit,* 2 August 2001; Richard Schröder, "'Egon, Du steckst im Kalten Krieg': Ist die PDS eine ganz normale Partei?" *Die Zeit,* 9 August 2001.

118. Yoder, "Truth without Reconciliation," 73.

119. Ibid.; Andrews, "Grand National Narratives," 51; Cooke, *Representing East Germany,* 36. Cf. Faulenbach, "Die Auseinandersetzung mit der doppelten Vergangenheit," 40; Faulenbach, "Die Arbeit der Enquete-Kommissionen," 24; Wilke, "Die deutsche Einheit," 610.

120. Fricke was abducted by the Stasi in West Berlin in 1955 and spent four years in Bautzen prison, becoming active as a journalist and scholar dealing with opposition, political persecution, and the Stasi after his release. See Karl Wilhelm Fricke, *Der Wahrheit verpflichtet: Texte aus fünf Jahrzehnten zur Geschichte der DDR* (Berlin, 2000). Fischer fled the GDR in connection with the SED campaign against the church youth organisation "die Junge Gemeinde." See Wilke, "Die deutsche Einheit," 467f.; "Der Historiker," 83, 98.

121. See "Die blaue Kolonne Ostberlins," *Die Zeit,* 21 June 2001; Hermann Weber (with Gerda Weber), *Damals, als ich Wunderlich hiess: Vom Parteihochschüler zum kritischen Sozialisten, Die SED-Parteihochschule Karl Marx bis 1949* (Berlin, 2002).

122. See Armin Mitter, "Angst und Hilflosigkeit in den Köpfen: Die DDR-Vergangenheit wird zum Problem der Zukunft," in *Krise—Umbruch—Neubeginn: Eine kritische und selbstkritische Dokumentation der DDR-Geschichtswissenschaft 1989/90,* eds. Rainer Eckert, Wolfgang Küttler, and Gustav Seeber (Stuttgart, 1992).

123. Yoder, "Truth without Reconciliation," 73. Cf. Wilke, "Die deutsche Einheit," 467; Jansen, "Enquete-Kommission," 265.

124. Cf. Faulenbach, "Die Auseinandersetzung mit der doppelten Vergangenheit," 40; Bock, "Von der Tribunal-Idee," 1182. Mitter argues that on issues relating to the internal history of the GDR there was virtually no East-West conflict; Gutzeit emphasizes there were often substantial differences between eastern opposition figures and westerners on *Deutschlandpolitik* (author's interviews).

125. I: 186. McAdams' suggestion that the commission had only sixteen members and that the experts were only "academic advisors" is incorrect, *Judging the Past,* 91. Freeman claims without any evidence that, despite the fact that the majority of commissioners were members of parliament, the independence of the inquiry was not diminished in the eyes of the public, *Truth Commissions and Procedural Fairness,* 133 (fn. 193). In the German context, however, concerns about independence of the state were less important than those about partisanship or bias related to eastern or western provenance.

126. Author's interviews with Armin Mitter, Ilko-Sascha Kowalczuk, Hans-Adolf Jacobsen, Manfred Wilke, and Bernd Faulenbach (Berlin, 30 August 2001).

127. Author's interview with Eppelmann. Similarly, Wilms, "Begründung, Entstehung und Zielsetzung," 15.

128. Yoder ignores the presence of the former bloc-party and SED members and incorrectly states that the "East German members ... were from the dissident milieu of the former GDR," "Truth without Reconciliation," 73. Andrews repeats this claim, "Grand

National Narratives," 51. Wüstenberg's claim that both major parties nominated mainly dissidents overlooks that Eppelmann was the only CDU member with such status, *Die politische Dimension*, 347.

129. Cf. Wolfgang Engler, "'Kommode Diktatur' oder 'totalitäres System'? Die DDR im Kreuzverhör der Enquete-Kommission," *Soziologische Revue* 19 (1996): 444; Wüstenberg, *Die politische Dimension*, 339, 347ff., 354.

130. See the dates of commissioners' participation, I: 195ff.

131. See *I: 156ff.* Cf. Yoder, "Truth without Reconciliation," 73. One difference was that the PDS did not have voting status on the second inquiry, a fact which inevitably aroused vociferous protest from the party and has attracted considerable attention from scholars, but which in fact signified little real change and had little real impact. See the discussion in chapter 2. Cf. McAdams, *Judging the Past*, 118; Barker, "'Geschichtsaufarbeitung' within the PDS," 91; Cooke, *Representing East Germany*, 53.

132. DBPa: Protokoll 1: 11, 9; Protokoll 2: 8, 12, 15, 21, 29.

133. DBPa: Protokoll 1: 9f.; Protokoll 2, 7f., 12.

134. DBPa: Protokoll 2: 19, 29. Author's interview with Mitter.

135. DBPa: Protokoll 3: 3.

136. Andrews states incorrectly that commission hearings "were not accessible to the public," "The Politics of Forgiveness," 110. Cf. Yoder, "Truth without Reconciliation," 72.

137. "Erinnerungsarbeit statt Tribunal," *Die Tageszeitung (TAZ)*, 24 March 1992.

138. DBPa: Protokoll 3: 13, 19, 21. That said, as mentioned above, the SPD motion also spoke of "depicting" the past.

139. DBPa: Protokoll 3: 19; Protokoll 4: 11.

140. DBPa: Protokoll 4: 19, 25, 29.

141. DBPa: Protokoll 2: 25; Protokoll 3: 16; Protokoll 4: 8. Hansen (FDP) wanted to examine the history of historiography on the GDR. DBPa: Protokoll 4: 36.

142. DBPa: Protokoll 4: 28; Protokoll 3: 21; Protokoll 4: 24.

143. DBPa: Protokoll 2: 19.

144. DBPa: Protokoll 2: 18f.

145. See Beattie, "A Fiftier Revival?"

146. DBPa: Protokoll 2: 18, 28; Protokoll 4: 5. "Kommission beginnt mit Detailarbeit," *Frankfurter Allgemeine Zeitung (FAZ)*, 7 November 1992.

147. DBPa: Protokoll 2: 19; Protokoll 5: 12f.

148. DBPa: Protokoll 5: 11; on the latter issue, Protokoll 4: 7, 20f., 24f., 29.

149. I: 191.

150. On 20 March the Bundestag had accepted a motion moved jointly by the SPD and the coalition calling for the inquiry to develop its own terms of reference not least on the basis of the parties' individual motions. "Antrag der Fraktionen der CDU/CSU, der SPD und der F.D.P. (Drs. 12/2230) vom 11. März 1992: Einsetzung einer Enquete-Komission 'Aufarbeitung der Geschichte und der Folgen der SED-Diktatur,'" I: 24.

151. References are to the version reprinted in the commission's report, I: 188ff. See Appendix A.

152. I: 188. Cf. Wüstenberg, *Die politische Dimension*, 331.

153. I: 188.

154. I: 188f.

155. I: 190.

156. Ibid.

157. I: 191.

158. Numerous commentators overlook all or most of the practical goals envisaged. See Andrews, "Grand National Narratives," 50; Wüstenberg, *Die politische Dimension*, 328, 335.

159. I: 161.
160. I: 162f., 164, 168, 171.
161. I: 162.
162. I: 164.
163. I: 168. These selective presentations have influenced some commentators. Andrews, for instance, quotes Hermann Weber and argues that, alongside the production of a judgment on communism, the inquiry's (only) other goal was to "improve the preconditions for scholarly inquiry" into GDR history, "Grand National Narratives," 50. She fails to recognize that his emphasis on the latter was the result of his personal preferences. Cf. note 63 above. If instead of Weber she had read Meckel, "Aufarbeitung der DDR-Geschichte," she would have come to a different conclusion about the inquiry's goals.
164. I: 165.
165. I: 162. See Ulrich Heinemann, *Die verdrängte Niederlage: Politische Öffentlichkeit und Kriegsschuldfrage in der Weimarer Republik* (Göttingen, 1983).
166. I: 165, 174, 159.
167. I: 161–71.
168. I: 173.
169. I: 165f.
170. I: 174, 176.
171. I: 174f.
172. I: 177.

Chapter 2

THE INQUIRIES AT WORK

The commission was saddled with considerable expectations and an enormous burden of responsibility. Its potential areas of activity and in particular its audiences and constituencies were legion. To begin with the largest audience: the commission was aware that world opinion was closely observing Germany subsequent to unification, particularly in relation to how it handled the Nazi and GDR pasts.[1] As a body of the national parliament, however, its main constituency was the German public as a whole, whose inner unity it hoped to promote. Yet its official raison d'être was to inform the Bundestag of pertinent matters requiring legislative action. As its tasks related specifically to East Germany, it also had to appeal particularly to the populations of the eastern states that were at least theoretically "existentially affected" by its work, and healing the wounds caused by the SED dictatorship was one of the inquiry's key goals.[2] Within eastern society, commissioners frequently spoke about addressing not only the leading figures of the opposition or of the party and state hierarchy, but also the experiences of "ordinary" people and their everyday lives. Yet they also felt particularly obligated to the victims of the regime, and hoped to give them a sense of justice for their past suffering. Further, the commission wanted to assist those it saw as its allies in working through the GDR past: the various civil-society groups that had established archives, museums, and memorials and pursued a wide variety of activities relating to the legacy of the past.

Satisfying these different groups' present needs and expectations, and addressing their various perspectives on the past was inherently challenging, a point that has not been sufficiently recognized in the scholarship to date. Concerns about the possibility of fulfilling all the tasks set out in the terms of reference were widespread. Commissioners therefore agreed that the inquiry could not deal in detail with every issue and spoke frequently of the need for *Mut zur Lücke* (courage to allow gaps) in its treatment.[3]

Notes for this chapter begin on page 84.

In assessing its approach and its achievements, it is important to bear in mind that the commission never claimed to give the final answer on any of the matters it addressed. Instead, it sought to make "contributions" and "strive toward" particular goals.[4] The commission thus immunized itself quite effectively—but not completely—from potential criticism that it failed to fulfill its objectives.[5] Moreover, to the extent that—as discussed in the previous chapter—the inquiry was designed to insulate the German political establishment from potential accusations of inaction over the communist past, its very existence was a success.

If not everything could be achieved by the end of the parliamentary period, what at least was to be attempted? Priorities had to be set. This chapter argues that a variety of factors—including the failure to reflect adequately on the commission's role and purpose in its initial stages, time constraints, its membership, and ideological interests—conspired to lead the inquiry away from consideration of practical political measures aimed at redressing the consequences of the past. Instead, it focused on the reconstruction and evaluation of recent German history. Moreover, the inquiry abandoned its early (limited) inclinations to open itself up to and foster public discussion and participation, and was content to become largely an elite-level enterprise of the cognoscenti. The result was that the commission's significance was largely discursive and ideological, and that—although it stimulated considerable media attention—its broader political and societal impact was less than it might have been. This assessment is largely consistent with those of other scholars, but in contrast to their rather static depictions, I insist on the need to see these characteristics not as inherent birth defects, but as the outcome of a historical process.[6]

In the end, the commission's efforts to speak to the various constituencies and audiences outlined above were highly variable. Despite the inclusive rhetoric of its terms of reference, the commission did not contribute to national reconciliation or the inner unity of the German nation, and did not foster widespread public discussion about German national identity in the wake of forty years of division and subsequent unification. It also did little to contribute to collective reconciliation between the various sectors of eastern society: regime representatives, victims, and those who fell somewhere in between. Similarly, it did not facilitate reconciliation between individual victims and those who were responsible for their suffering. Furthermore, individual commissioners' early populist ambitions soon waned, and the inquiry did not go to considerable lengths to include ordinary easterners (let alone westerners) in its work, or to make them feel included. Nevertheless, one cannot deny that these were among its initial goals as some commentators do, and the inquiry's work was more inclusive and less elitist than it is often given credit for.

As opposed to the general statements of intent in the prologue to the terms of reference, the commission's specific tasks focused on analysis and evaluation of East German history, and on helping the victims of the communist regime, and not on pursuing either national or intra-eastern reconciliation. Over the course of the inquiry's term, the analysis and evaluation—and in particular their distillation into the form of a final report—effectively came to dominate its work. The practical political outcomes that were the ostensible purpose of such commissions became increasingly marginal. Indeed, they served largely as an alibi that justified the exploration of history by a political body. To be sure, the commission gave numerous victims the invaluable opportunity to tell at least parts of their stories in a symbolic public forum, and it granted victims generally at least rhetorical, collective acknowledgment.[7] But surprisingly—given the extent to which this goal was emphasized and found early cross-party support—the commission had little discernible impact on legislative measures to help the victims, either materially or immaterially. Investigating, evaluating, and narrating the past became the commission's central concerns, and its work was largely discursive and symbolic, rather than policy oriented and practical. Playing politics with history came to dominate the development of policies for the past.

As noted in the introduction, the commission has been described with considerable justification as "a form of didactic public history" and an official, public "history lesson."[8] Yet such terms accept at face value the laudable aim of enlightenment for the public good that commissioners professed, and fail to capture sufficiently the inquiry's partisan nature and political function.[9] In fact, the commission produced a highly politicized analysis that was intended to delegitimize the GDR and support a renewed "antitotalitarian consensus," to which it hoped all Germans would subscribe. However, the commission was quite content to leave not inconsiderable sections of the population, such as anyone who thought there was anything positive about the GDR, and of the political spectrum, that is, the PDS, outside the consensus, and thus beyond the democratic pale. At the same time, the importance of the dialogic process of working through the past, with competing views of history being contested in an at least partially public forum, should not be underestimated.

The commission was thus both an instrument of and a site for conducting politics with history. It was a forum for the political parties and their allied scholars and intellectuals to proffer rival interpretations of recent German history and contest the legitimacy and illegitimacy of their political traditions. The opposition parties were all represented on the commission with speaking and (at least on the first inquiry) voting rights, and were able both to put forward their ideas about the commission's operation and to present their preferred version of the past. There was thus a considerable degree of debate and negotiation.[10] Yet as it relied on majority voting in the absence of consensus, the commission also constituted a tool for the governing coalition to promote its interpretation of history, which meant asserting the illegitimacy of the GDR and the responsibility of the SED, and highlighting the moral failings of the West German Left and the disastrous consequences of socialist ideology. Ultimately both the process and the final result—in the form of the commission's report—were aimed at discrediting the GDR and those who had sympathized with it or still did so, rather than at engaging in reconciliatory dialogue or incorporating a broad range of perspectives and experiences.

All of this applied also to the second inquiry that was established in June 1995 to continue the work of the first. Despite doubts in some quarters, most commissioners felt that further efforts were necessary in the following legislative period. This conviction reflected the belief, on the one hand, that the first commission had been unable to achieve all that it had wanted and, on the other, that working through the past was necessarily an ongoing enterprise. The second postunification Bundestag therefore supported the establishment of a new commission of inquiry, entitled "Overcoming the Consequences of the SED Dictatorship in the Process of German Unity," whose membership, aims, and methods displayed considerable continuity with its predecessor.[11] It is generally agreed that the second inquiry was politically less significant and received less media attention than the first. The following discussion therefore focuses primarily on the latter, but nevertheless addresses similarities and slight changes of emphasis between the two commissions; later chapters examine areas in which the second inquiry was of considerable significance.

Discursive Priorities

Political recommendations to the Bundestag are the raison d'être for commissions of inquiry generally and were ostensibly the primary goal of these commissions, yet ultimately they were a distant second priority behind the investigation of history. The first commission inevitably had to be selective in its pursuit of the aims listed in its mandate, but even before such priorities were established—indeed even before the terms of reference were adopted—crucial steps were already taken in setting the direction of its work. First, its style and tone were decidedly academic.[12] Secondly, the completion of a final report quickly became an objective in itself.[13] Thirdly, both the content of its deliberations and its internal organizational structure privileged examining and evaluating the past rather than addressing the latter's consequences in the present. The commission never lost sight of the present, but its main focus was a discursive analysis (and delegitimation) of the GDR, rather than the consideration of practical recommendations for the Bundestag.

Developing the first inquiry's mandate involved intense discussion of goals and methods, but these deliberations were far from exhaustive. The pressing need to formulate the terms of reference by the deadline of 20 May 1992 hindered far-reaching debate about exactly what the inquiry wanted to achieve and how it would proceed. Important issues—such as how the commission would pursue the broad goals expressed in the prologue to the terms of reference or the practical outcomes that were to be worked toward—were not resolved. Instead, such questions were frequently either left unanswered or became faits accomplis through apparently minor practical decisions or by deferral to various subcommittees. The lack of thorough debate about basic principles was an ongoing problem. The need to meet approaching deadlines and prepare upcoming events repeatedly hindered both substantial discussion of general questions and critical reflection on the commissions' proceedings. Indeed, time constraints were a continuing banal but significant factor in the commissions' work. But there was also a certain unwillingness to engage in critical introspection about the purpose, methods, and limits of the enterprise. Such reluctance was evident most saliently at the beginning of the second commission's term, where there was no evaluation of its predecessor's successes or failures.[14]

The first commission commenced its work without having engaged in exhaustive discussion about the general aims of working through the past, about the inquiry's own contribution to this wider process, or about basic principles of responsibility, guilt, or criteria for judgment. This was despite calls from various sides for the development of such criteria and for an early public discussion of what the commission might contribute. Christian Democrats were not interested in such a discussion of first principles, and suggestions from Markus Meckel for a public hearing to consider them were successively reduced to a narrow affair devoted to legal issues pertaining to the prosecution of GDR crimes, which was eventually held as the commission's first public hearing.[15]

In addition to time limitations and insufficient reflection, the commission's organizational structure contributed to the three developments mentioned above: the inquiry's scholarly approach, its focus on the report, and its concentration on the past. These developments were all reflected in, and reinforced by, the creation of subcommittees that were responsible for the six main historical topics gleaned from the terms of reference:

1. Power structures and decision-making mechanisms in the SED state and the question of responsibility
2. The role and significance of ideology, integrative factors, and disciplinary practices in GDR state and society
3. Law, justice, and police in the SED state
4. Inner-German relations and international conditions
5. The role of the churches and their conception of themselves in the different phases of the SED dictatorship
6. Possibilities and forms of deviant and resistant behavior and oppositional action, the peaceful revolution in autumn 1989, German unification, and the continuing effects of dictatorial structures and mechanisms[16]

These six macro topics formed—and their subcommittees performed—the core of the first commission's work, although smaller working parties were also formed to address other issues.

The absence of a subcommittee or working party on the situation of the victims of the regime is remarkable. It indicates that helping the victims—and indeed practical political outcomes generally—served primarily to justify the inquiry, rather than constituting one of its primary goals.[17] Only a few commissioners took literally the normal function of commissions of inquiry: to provide the Bundestag with information and develop recommendations for legislative action. Unsurprisingly, those who did were generally—although not exclusively—representatives of the opposition parties. Commissioners were certainly interested in helping the victims, and frequently called for legislative change, but the commission as a whole cannot be said to have made a significant contribution to the legislation of redress for regime victims.[18]

The commission's insignificance in this regard was due in part to the fact that the plight of the victims was being addressed elsewhere, but the inquiry failed even to develop a clear strategy for its interaction with political processes already in motion.[19] Significantly, Eppelmann's suggestion that the commission be permitted to participate in all parliamentary deliberations on measures affecting both victims and perpetrators was hosed down by his colleague and spokesperson of the CDU/CSU group, Dorothee Wilms.[20] This suggests another reason for the inquiry's ineffectiveness: the governing coalition had a majority on the commission and was hardly likely to embarrass the government by highlighting inadequacies in its policies or making extravagant demands. As a result, the commission's status was more that of interested observer than active participant. At best it could act as a lobby group, and throughout the life of both inquiries individual commissioners from various parties agitated within their parliamentary caucuses and standing committees for improvements to compensation and rehabilitation policies. Their efforts were no doubt strengthened by their participation in the inquiries, but the latter were unable to exert direct influence over legislation. The first commission's report called for improvements to existing and planned legislation and in particular for their speedy implementation, but the inquiry's focus was on listening to the victims' stories and seeking some sort of moral or histori- cal, rather than monetary or legal justice.[21]

The second commission addressed the consequences of the past in the present to a much greater extent than the first. In the Bundestag estab- lishment debate on 22 June 1995, Meckel claimed that the parties agreed that the first inquiry had neglected to develop political recommendations and that the new one would correct this omission.[22] Its terms of refer- ence foresaw the consideration of the adequacy and implementation of existing rehabilitation and compensation legislation.[23] The second inquiry was somewhat more successful than its predecessor, but the government continued to treat the inquiry as a passive observer, and again there was a palpable move to stress moral rehabilitation and public commemoration in lieu of financial compensation.[24]

In areas of policy for the past not relating to the victims, the first com- mission was either inactive, ineffective, or played at most a rhetorical supporting role. It informed itself about the activities of other state insti- tutions' efforts to work through the GDR past, but its own contribution was minimal. On Stasi questions, for example, the commission met with representatives of the Federal Commissioner for the Records of the State Security Service, and both individual commissioners and the inquiry as a whole frequently endorsed that institution's work and insisted that the Stasi files remain open.[25] Rather ironically, the only area of the federal com- missioner's activities about which they expressed concern was its research department, which inquiry members perceived not only as having unfair access to Stasi records, but also as constituting a questionable example of state-sponsored official history that lacked requisite scholarly accredita- tion and political independence.[26] Where the commission went beyond merely informing itself about other institutions' activities to explore top- ics itself, its efforts were directed—like the bulk of its work—at analysis and evaluation rather than action. Its handling of networks of old-regime insiders, for example, aimed not at concrete political outcomes let alone at investigating particular cases, but rather at raising as a public issue the presence of former SED members, Stasi operatives, and other former ap- paratchiks in the economy, the public service, and other social spheres.[27] The same was true of its handling of the Stasi and of its discussion of the "possibilities and limitations" of the judicial reckoning with GDR criminality.[28] One area in which the inquiry did undertake concerted efforts and developed numerous recommendations was in promoting access to regime archives, but here it had little impact, particularly on issues on which its views differed from the position of the federal government.[29]

Consistent with its greater focus on the consequences of the past, the second commission examined various aspects of unified Germany's efforts to work through the East German past. Rather than itself developing or pursuing policies for the past, in many areas it constituted a meta-institution, surveying and commenting on judicial, political, social, and international aspects of working through dictatorial legacies. It made numerous recommendations, many of which offered encouragement for other institutions' efforts, or called for the speedy implementation of existing policies and for more research into relevant issues. Other practical dimensions to the second commission's work—such as its development of commemorative policies or its deliberations on the appropriate institutional form to continue the process of working through the past (see below)—were clearly directed at concrete political recommendations. Yet here, too, the outcomes were discursive as much as policy related or practical, and the second inquiry continued its predecessor's investigation of the past and its interest in history politics. It explicitly endorsed the first inquiry's contribution to the latter and was itself charged with making "contributions to a political-historical analysis and a political-moral evaluation of the SED dictatorship" just as the first commission had been.[30] Both inquiries were thus significant above all for their discursive handling of the East German past, rather than for their efforts at developing policies to address its material or human legacy.

Simultaneous with this development from the practical to the discursive, the inquiry's plans also shifted from populist enterprises aimed at mass participation to a rather elite level of discussion. As the previous chapter showed, in its early meetings the need for the inquiry to open itself to the wider public—particularly in the East—was stressed repeatedly. The epitome of such inclinations was a suggestion by Rainer Eppelmann that the commission organize a bus to drive through the eastern states to receive documents, reports, and letters from citizens about their experiences in the GDR and to inform the public about the inquiry's work. He told *Newsweek* magazine: "I would like the commission to get information buses which drive through the new states for months at a time, equipped with photocopiers, tape recorders, cameras, so that people can come and tell about their lives."[31] One needed to make clear, Eppelmann said, that "the task of the commission of inquiry has to do with the citizens of the former GDR and that it is not only to be worked on in academic studies."[32] Like an earlier public appeal from Eppelmann that prompted a wave of letters to the inquiry and met with opprobrium from the commission secretariat and concerns from expert members about how such material could be incorporated into the inquiry's work, the bus tour idea was quickly shelved. While this has since been viewed with some regret, it did not find serious support at the time.[33] Similarly, a proposal for the commission to work toward "the facilitation of inner integration through dialogue with citizens of the former GDR and through making visible their particular life paths" was deleted from a draft terms of reference; and a suggestion from Dirk Hansen (FDP) to incorporate "dialogue with the citizens" in the inquiry's mandate was not accepted.[34] At the beginning of the second commission, there were renewed proposals to encourage easterners to write down and submit accounts of their life experiences in the GDR and the unification process, but these were abandoned just as quickly, again due to practical constraints and concerns about what to do with the material.[35] In the end, there was no large-scale gathering of testimony or submissions from the citizenry. Contrary to some scholars' depictions, however, it should be recognized, first, that such outreach measures were at least discussed and, second, that the institutional mechanism of the commission of inquiry did not necessarily prohibit them.[36] The failure to follow through on these populist proposals was due rather to practical constraints, methodological concerns, and without doubt also to elitist preferences.

At the other end of the methodological spectrum from such public ventures were proposals for substantial research projects into historical questions. Here, too, initial hopes were wound back, and smaller "expertise papers" were preferred to larger projects.[37] At the beginning of the second commission's term some western scholars again called for expansive research projects on topics such as the relationship between the leaderships of the SED and the CPSU. These suggestions were received fairly positively, but were eventually reduced to sizeable expertise papers. More ambitious proposals were rejected as impracticable and due to renewed concerns that the commission would be seen as inappropriately assuming the role of historical scholarship.[38] The adopted approach was nevertheless of a highly scholarly nature. The first inquiry commissioned almost 150 research papers, and the second almost 120, in addition to numerous reports from public institutions. As commissioner Dirk Hansen described it, the commissions constituted a "scholarly oriented political investigation."[39]

In lieu of more populist approaches, the commissions' most inclusive and open modus operandi proved to be the public hearing. These were held throughout the eastern states and at the seat of the parliament in Bonn on each of the first inquiry's six main historical topics as well as on a number of other more general or contemporary issues. The hearings helped to raise the public profile of the commissions and to encourage public dialogue about the past and the process of working through it.[40] The commissions stressed how many of their sessions were public hearings, but pointing out that approximately half of the inquiries' plenary meetings were public vastly overestimates their relative significance, because so much deliberation took place in subcommittee.[41] What is more, the public hearings were only one aspect of the inquiries' methods, an equally important one being the extensive collection of written material mentioned above, which came mainly from academic and governmental sources. Nevertheless, that so many public hearings were held—forty-four and twenty-five by the first and second inquiries respectively—is rightly regarded as among their most significant achievements, especially considering the amount of preparation, logistical organization, and expense involved.[42]

Yet as commissioner Peter Maser argued, the influence of the "wandering circus" of hearings in the eastern states must be seen in sober terms.[43] Most of the time, those who attended—and their numbers varied considerably—merely constituted an audience. Public hearing thus meant a hearing conducted *in* public, rather than a hearing *of* the public. Indeed, initial suggestions from Christian Democrats revealed their understanding of "public" as "open to the media" but not the broader public, although the latter, more generous understanding soon won out.[44] The remaining limitation to hearings in, rather than of the public was at least formally due to Bundestag standing orders, according to which non-commissioners could only speak if they had been invited formally to do so. On a limited number of occasions the standing orders were suspended so that members of the audience could participate more actively.[45] A desire to do this more often was not widely shared. A notorious incident at a hearing on "everyday life" held by the second inquiry in the eastern city of Eisenhüttenstadt in April 1997 only confirmed commissioners' reluctance about direct public participation: they were shocked by the positive views expressed about the GDR. At the end of a day-long hearing the commission held an *Erzählabend* (evening of stories) where audience members attacked the inquiry's negative focus on the GDR and insisted that not everything about the East German state was abominable, and that in many ways they had been happier then than they were now. Remarkably, the protocol of the discussion was deliberately excluded from that of the hearing, and the incident increased existing concerns about direct public participation.[46] Nevertheless, the myths perpetrated by some scholars about the absence of public participation—either active or passive—must be corrected.[47]

Although Eppelmann hoped that the first inquiry's efforts and its final report would not just be noted by historians but would be of benefit to as many as possible of Germany's eighty million citizens, the inquiries' work stayed largely at the level of experts and the political cognoscenti.[48] The commissions pointed rather self-satisfactorily to the considerable number of "experts and eyewitnesses" who appeared before them: 327 and 292 before the first and second inquiries respectively.[49] Yet a degree of skepticism about these numbers is warranted. Many of those who appeared were precisely experts rather than eyewitnesses (the totals did not distinguish between the two), and many of the latter were politicians or others who could hardly be considered to be without ready access to media or other avenues for the expression of their views. For instance, Federal Chancellor Helmut Kohl and other leading politicians appeared before the inquiry to discuss *Deutschlandpolitik;* and even on topics where "ordinary" people might have been heard, the commissions often found it easier to invite fellow politicians and even commissioners themselves.[50] Despite much rhetoric about listening to ordinary people's stories, the inquiries were if anything more interested in what historians and political and social scientists—who were often, but by no means always, westerners—had to say about the GDR than in hearing the tales of ordinary eastern citizens or the regime's victims. Even a so-called victim hearing was occupied to a large extent by discussion of research findings rather than the testimony of victims.[51] The limited opportunity for public input meant that even the hearings did little to counter the rather elitist, academic approach, as talks by commissioners or invited scholars featured alongside podium discussions of experts or prominent public figures, with a few "ordinary" eyewitnesses included for good measure. The claim by a critical reviewer of the first commission's work that it had "thoroughly missed" its aim of allowing typical representatives of the eastern population to speak thus had considerable justification.[52] On the other hand, one should not overlook the legitimacy of a representative institution such as the Bundestag pursuing representative (rather than comprehensive) work, not least through contacts with civil society (on which more below).[53]

Moreover, the hearings should not merely be assessed on the basis of who spoke before whom. A further crucial aspect—as commissioner Hermann Weber stressed—lay primarily in the fact that the public could see that the past was being contested; differing opinions may not have come to the fore to the extent that they did if the inquiries' deliberations had been held behind closed doors.[54] Indeed, the nature of the commissions' work as a dialogic process or a discussion in progress must be emphasized. As commissioners frequently remarked, "The path is the goal," or, as Gert Weisskirchen (SPD) put it, the investigation was "an end in itself."[55] Assessments therefore cannot focus exclusively on outcomes (such as legislative change) or findings (such as the reports), but must attempt to address the processual, indeed the performative nature of the inquiries' activities. For this reason, this study examines not just the views put forward in statements at hearings or in expertise papers, and certainly not just the final reports. It also considers the dialogic interplay between competing arguments and interpretations, as well as their development from the commissions' evidential basis in the hearings and papers to their distillation in the reports. The following sections of this chapter examine the commissions' handling of their various constituencies and consider the extent to which they pursued and met the various goals they had set themselves.

National Unity and Reconciliation

As we have seen, the first commission of inquiry emanated primarily from a set of East German problems, but these were immediately embedded in a national context. In the "rush to German unity," constitutional, legal, diplomatic, and other political questions were effectively settled, but social-psychological, cultural, and historical issues were largely neglected; what, if anything, was required to achieve "inner unity" was only considered after the achievement of formal, outward unity.[56] Then, it seemed, the two unequal halves of the once divided nation were not "growing together" as automatically or quickly as had been expected. Indeed, they seemed to be growing further apart, not least as a result of the Stasi debate in the early 1990s that created a climate of suspicion, with many westerners incorrectly regarding East Germany as a nation of spies, and many easterners viewing themselves as the victims of collective denigration by westerners and the unification process.[57]

As discussed in the previous chapter, the rhetoric of inner unity was prominent in both Bundestag debates about the first inquiry's establishment and featured equally saliently in the prologue of its terms of reference, so it is fair to conclude that the commission intended to contribute to national reconciliation.[58] The second inquiry was motivated to an even greater extent by the lingering, indeed increasing sense of alienation between easterners and westerners, and the rhetoric of inner unity and the conciliatory potential of easterners and westerners telling each other their stories accompanied this inquiry's establishment too.[59] Its name "Overcoming the Consequences of the SED Dictatorship in the Process of German Unity" and particularly its official parliamentary abbreviation, "German Unity," indicated that national reconciliation remained a key goal.[60] As mentioned above, many commissioners hoped to convince westerners that they, too, were affected by the history of division and that the GDR was part of their history. A further, often implicit strategy was the development of a common view of history that would be shared in East and West.[61]

The inquiries' specific tasks—the analysis and evaluation of historical questions and the consideration of practical outcomes—did not include particular items relating to the project of inner unity. To be sure, the mere fact that the Bundestag created inquiries into the divided postwar past carried considerable symbolic weight, the reconciliatory potential of which should not be dismissed out of hand.[62] Yet the commissions were beset by the very problems they hoped to overcome: the fundamental asymmetry of the unification process and the unequal standing of the eastern and western pasts in postunification Germany.[63] The western past was regarded largely as a success story—apart from the Left's excessive accommodation of the communist regime from the 1960s onward and some omissions in relation to the Nazi past—while the eastern past was seen as an unmitigated disaster that at best ended happily. West German policies and attitudes toward the GDR were to be investigated, as were the efforts of the SED and the Stasi to influence the West, but that was largely where consideration of the national dimension ended.[64] Moreover, the commissions' handling of these issues amounted less to the pursuit of East-West dialogue over the shared-but-divided national past, than to an intra-western dispute about which political parties and which sectors of society could be credited with upholding active support for unification, and which had given up on that goal and/or demonstrated themselves to be susceptible to communist manipulation.[65]

A slight change of emphasis occurred in the second inquiry, whose name—"in the *Process* of German Unity"—reflected the growing realization that inner unity was not a state that would be achieved in the short term.[66] The second commission devoted itself to a greater degree than the first to understanding the differences between easterners and westerners. Attention shifted significantly to the postunification consequences of division and communist rule, rather than examining merely that rule itself. Yet far from including the West to any considerable extent, the focus remained on the dictatorial system in the East and its consequences, while western ideological disputes over the national question and the western Left's softness on communism continued. At most the second inquiry can be said—unlike its predecessor—to have reflected on the apparent lack of national unity, its causes, and possible ways to overcome it; but the inquiry itself cannot be said to have worked actively toward national reconciliation.[67]

Neither commission attempted to bring the eastern and western populations together, or addressed itself to any considerable extent to the western population. For example, they did not hold public hearings in western cities, except—for the sake of convenience—in the parliamentary building in Bonn. It is thus hardly surprising that, as Dirk Hansen (FDP) lamented, much of the public was unaware of the "all-German" nature of the commissions' ambitions and, further, that the inquiries did not succeed in significantly raising western interest in the East German past or the history of division.[68]

Ultimately, the commissions' contribution to inner unity obtained largely in their attempt to develop—with eastern and western input—a common understanding of the divided past, particularly the history of the GDR, that might be shared by easterners and westerners.[69] Some critics see this notion of a common understanding of history as problematic, and there is certainly some justification to their concerns. Defining a politically and morally acceptable view of the past is a hazardous undertaking potentially inimical to diversity of opinion. On the other hand, the commissions can hardly be said to have been completely dogmatic or militant in their approach, and they incorporated a modicum of plurality.[70] Yet, particularly in the first inquiry, the goal was certainly a united view, and the not-infrequent failure to meet that goal—leading to the inclusion in the report of dissenting opinions—was generally viewed as precisely that: a failure, or a sign that partisan political interests had intervened and prevented a shared understanding.[71] That a common view of the past was desirable was taken for granted; the commissions barely considered whether it was achievable, or whether the interpretation they developed was acceptable to easterners or westerners. The last question was impossible to answer definitively, but recent scholarship suggests (as does much anecdotal evidence) that different understandings of the past still divide easterners and westerners, and that many of the former saw public depictions of the GDR as too negative.[72] For reasons elaborated below and in subsequent chapters, the commissions' approach—particularly that of the first inquiry—was bound if anything to reinforce rather than overcome that divided memory. Significantly, they did not reflect on the need to incorporate or address differing perspectives on the GDR in their final depictions, but aimed instead at consensus, albeit an exclusionary one.[73]

Intra-eastern Reconciliation and the Rehabilitation of Victims

Like national reconciliation, intra-eastern reconciliation—that is, reconciliation between perpetrators or former regime representatives and the regime's victims—was a rhetorical goal of the commissions, but was not an outcome that the inquiries actively pursued, at either a collective-symbolic or individual level. Discussions between perpetrators and victims—of which some had been organized in the GDR in 1989–90—were largely left to civil society after unification and did not form part of the German state's institutionalized mechanisms for working through the past. Catharsis was left to the judiciary and various forums of civil society.[74] A direct exchange between an individual perpetrator and his victim took place only on two occasions under the commissions' aegis, and these were not planned, and were certainly not integral to the inquiries' ambitions. It is therefore somewhat misplaced to criticize the inquiries for not generating "heat" or catharsis by confronting perpetrators and victims; this was not what they wanted.[75] Although representatives of the former regime were invited to appear as eyewitnesses on particular issues, they were hardly central to the inquiries' work, and the commissions were unapologetic about not inviting more. Moreover, they were invited in order to provide insights into the internal workings of the regime and not for the purpose of fostering reconciliatory dialogue. The second commission's explanation, according to which reconciliation between victims and perpetrators "cannot be forced by the state," is valid, but fails to answer the question of whether more could have been attempted.[76]

The commission cannot be said to have offered no prospect of reconciliation. It merely did little to encourage it. The participation of the PDS in the commissions should not be interpreted as evidence of a desire for reconciliation. The constructive contributions of Dietmar Keller (PDS) and PDS expert Herbert Wolf in the first inquiry certainly fostered a degree of understanding and empathy between these former representatives of the regime and some of its most determined critics. But this was more an unexpected, though welcome, byproduct of the commission's work than a conscious goal.[77] Keller was hardly representative of his party, and on occasion was critical of its approach to history.[78] Similarly, the conciliatory note he sounded in the Bundestag debate about the commission's report on 17 June 1994—where he offered a personal apology to the victims of the regime—has been hailed as a significant outcome of the commission. But this had more to do with Keller's individual effort to reflect critically on his role in the GDR than with the inquiry's goals, self-understanding, or achievements.[79] He spoke in a highly personal capacity rather than a representative one, and it was clear his views did not have the backing of his party.

PDS participation has been cited by sympathetic commentators—particularly with reference to the inclusion of its minority dissenting statement in the first commission's report—as indicating that the commission did not strive for a monolithic, homogeneous perspective on history, but allowed diversity of opinion.[80] However, once again the commissions can by no means be said to have engaged consciously and deliberately in dialogue with the PDS or to have sought to include Democratic Socialists in discussions of the past and present. That constructive engagement with the PDS was not at the forefront of the inquiries' objectives was indicated by the fact that the PDS representatives did not have voting status on the second inquiry, by a related controversy over precisely whom the party could send to the commission, as well as by other decisions about who would be allowed to participate in the inquiries' work or specific activities.[81] In the absence of consensus, speakers invited to public hearings or authors commissioned to write expertise papers were organized along party lines, but limited numbers generally meant that the CDU/CSU-FDP coalition and the SPD were represented, but the PDS was not.[82]

As Charles S. Maier argues, contestation of the past between former regime representatives and their opponents was not central to the inquiry's approach. Maier's argument that the commission instead "established an indictment for a trial that was not to take place" has considerable merit.[83] Yet it focuses on the inquiry as the instrument of the anticommunist majority and downplays its simultaneous function as a site of (asymmetrical) debate and (limited) dialogue. Although the indictment was overwhelmingly prioritized, the case for the defense was also presented: through PDS motions and speeches in the Bundestag, statements and questions by PDS commissioners at meetings, the dissenting reports, and the multi-volume PDS-sponsored publication *Ansichten zur Geschichte der DDR* (Views on the History of the GDR) that critically accompanied the inquiries' work. The present study incorporates these sources precisely to highlight the extant diversity of opinion and the dialogic nature of the renegotiation of the German past after unification.

The tenor of much of the commissions' work—including their final reports—was in fact directed rather at marginalizing and discrediting the PDS. Conservatives in particular referred regularly to the "democratic parties" from which the PDS was implicitly or explicitly distinguished.[84] In Rainer Eppelmann's summary of the goals of the first commission, the first was as follows: "Through the precise analysis of the totalitarian structures of rule of the SED dictatorship, the commission of inquiry was to contribute to the prevention of those forces that decisively organized the oppression of people in the GDR ever having a political chance in unified Germany again."[85] The creation of the second commission was in large part motivated by the continuing electoral success of the PDS in the eastern states.[86] Hostile, as opposed to constructive, engagement with the PDS was also indicated by the inclusion among the CDU experts on the second inquiry of Patrick Moreau, a leading expert on postcommunist politics and prominent scholarly critic of the PDS.[87] Indeed, the conservative majority was more than happy that the Democratic Socialists provided a target for their anticommunist rhetoric. Commissioners and other commentators frequently failed—it seems at times willfully—to distinguish between moderate, self-critical individuals (like Keller) and hardliners; they preferred to locate the entire party outside the democratic consensus, rather than recognize the diversity of opinion within the PDS and acknowledge that Keller and Wolf did not actually support its dissenting statement to the first commission's report.[88] In sum, the inquiries were not completely unforgiving or unwilling to admit to the possibility of reconciliatory dialogue with Democratic Socialists; they merely demanded of the latter that they unreservedly abandon any positive views about the GDR.

The commissions can be said to have provided to a limited degree a forum of personal rehabilitation for some victims who received the opportunity to tell their story before a public audience and an official institution.[89] The inquiries thus sought to respond to repeated complaints that no one wanted to hear about the regime's abuses and those who suffered them. The importance of appearing before an organ of the national parliament that granted the victims respect and accepted their story cannot be underestimated, and many victims expressed their thanks to the commissions for the opportunity afforded them.[90] Yet victims were only able to tell their stories at a small number of hearings and constituted only a proportion of the eyewitnesses who appeared. Even so, the victims who were granted the opportunity to speak represented many others who did not, as commissioners themselves stressed.[91] To criticize the inquiry for the limited numbers of victims heard in comparison, for example, with the South African Truth and Reconciliation Commission is to ignore this representative dimension and the very different functions of victim testimony in the two settings.[92] A more appropriate comparison is with the Bundestag commissions' own victim-centered rhetoric.

On the collective level, the commissions were no unqualified success for the victims, although they repeatedly invoked the latter's suffering to justify their own existence. The first inquiry's terms of reference included the task of "identifying groups of victims," and commissioners spoke of their desire to adopt the perspective of the victims in their investigation.[93] Yet the inquiry was strangely inactive in this regard. Its report included a list of "categories of victims" that remained very general and schematic, focusing largely on the acts of repression and persecution rather than the people who suffered them, and without making any attempt at quantification.[94] Indeed, this was not uncharacteristic of the inquiry's approach. Rather than addressing the victims' individual or collective experiences (more) directly, its primary focus was on the regime itself, while the victims' suffering was recognized almost implicitly. This focus was aptly illustrated by Eppelmann's summary of the first commission's goals: "The *discussion of the unlawful character of the SED regime* was to allow the victims—whose legal and material rehabilitation will only be possible within narrow limits—at least to experience historical justice."[95] It was safer to concentrate on the regime than to give victims a podium to express their views. Indeed, the failure of the first inquiry to make significant steps toward the victims' moral (or other) rehabilitation is demonstrated not least by the fact that its successor was charged with considering ways to accomplish this.[96]

The second commission achieved more than the first in relation to the victims' collective recognition, but again its success was not unqualified. Its terms of reference mentioned repeatedly the need for their public acknowledgment and stated that it would devote itself specifically to the "persecution of those who thought differently in the SBZ/GDR."[97] In addition to reviewing existing legislation, the second inquiry's victim-related efforts were again primarily historical and less than all-encompassing: its focus was on political prisoners, the use of the death penalty in the GDR, and the Stasi's use of the strategy of *Zersetzung* (disintegration) of perceived regime enemies. Victims of other abuses were not considered to any noteworthy degree, and again—and particularly in the report—the focus was as much on the regime's practices as on the victims themselves.[98]

Both commissions highlighted repeatedly the importance of acknowledgment, and must be credited with promoting the victims' collective moral rehabilitation and in particular their public commemoration (as later chapters will discuss in the context of the inquiries' work on commemorative policies). Nevertheless, their efforts and direct impact were less than they might have been. A revealing if perhaps unrepresentative example of the low priority accorded to the victims—as opposed to their constant rhetorical invocation—was provided by the second commission's organization of a ceremony in August 1996 to commemorate the thirty-fifth anniversary of the erection of the Berlin Wall. Only the vigorous protests and threats of an individual victim who had been paralyzed by a shooting at the Wall prevented the event from being dominated entirely by politicians' speeches and protocol. In the end, one "Wall victim" was added to the speaking list.[99] Despite such remarkable insensitivity, what the commissions did manage to achieve for the victims was certainly more than would have occurred without them. According to Martin Gutzeit, victims' organizations wanted a third inquiry, since the first two at least provided them with a public stage and advocate.[100] The Foundation for Working through the SED Dictatorship (see below) continues this role to a degree, although this is only one of its tasks.[101]

Promoting Civil-Society Initiatives

The victims' organizations comprised only some of the many civil-society groups engaged in working through the East German past that the commissions hoped to assist, and with which they wanted to cooperate. As the previous chapter demonstrated, the first commission readily acknowledged that it was not the only body engaged in examining the history and consequences of communist rule in East Germany, and commissioners emphasized repeatedly that, ideally, this process would involve the entire society. In particular, the inquiry wanted to establish contact with and promote the various *Aufarbeitungsinitiativen* (working-through initiatives) that had emerged mainly from opposition groups in the 1980s and citizens' committees during the upheaval of 1989–90. The former dissidents on the commissions regarded themselves as the natural allies of these independent historical groups, private archives, clubs, associations, and citizens' organizations, and wanted to draw them into the commissions' work or at least support them through it.[102] Among other things, they hoped, this would contribute to the commissions' goals of doing justice to the suffering of the victims and preserving the historical legacy of the GDR opposition, as these were among the groups' main fields of activity.[103]

The commissions are to be credited with some success in this regard. They consistently gave these groups encouragement, created a public forum for them on a number of occasions, and attempted to facilitate their mutual cooperation.[104] Despite early indifference from governing Christian Democrats, members of the opposition parties repeatedly raised the groups' need for financial support.[105] No significant developments occurred during the first inquiry's term, but it was widely recognized that something had to be done. The first commission's report called only generally for the continuation of the working-through process, while a minority vote of the SPD suggested specifically the establishment of a public foundation that would be responsible for fostering it.[106]

By the mid 1990s, the need for an enduring solution had become urgent, as many of the groups faced a gloomy financial future. One of the main tasks of the second commission, therefore, was to determine the most appropriate institutional arrangement for promoting the societal process of working through the East German past.[107] In April 1996, Alliance 90/The Greens proposed the creation of a public foundation, but it was not until October 1997 that the commission presented an interim report calling for the same. The proposal for a Foundation for Working through the SED Dictatorship was keenly supported by all parties except the PDS, which objected predictably to the prejudicial and tendentious nature of the terminology. In particular, the PDS advocated the replacement of "dictatorship" with "power structures," and complained about its own exclusion from discussions about and participation in the body.[108] The foundation was eventually established in 1998 and has become a central player in efforts to foster continuing research into and discussion of Germany's divided past. Supporting the various societal initiatives and helping the victims of the regime are among its central tasks. Nevertheless, concerns remained about certain centralizing tendencies (especially in relation to archival materials) of such a state-sponsored institution, while its limitation to granting funding to the initiatives for specific projects rather than to cover their institutional costs also attracted criticism.[109] The inquiries' attention to the working-through "scene" indicates that it was not as elitist, academic, and "top down" as some commentators portray it.[110]

Ordinary Easterners and Everyday Life

Closely related to early populist methodological suggestions—such as the bus tour through the eastern states—was a frequently stated desire to address the history of "ordinary" East Germans and "everyday life" in the GDR. Eppelmann emphasized repeatedly that the inquiry was interested in discussing not only prominent opposition figures such as Bärbel Bohley or SED functionaries such as Erich Honecker, but also the experiences of ordinary people. He insisted that they would have to "find themselves" in the commission's work and that it needed "proximity to the citizens."[111] Other commissioners (especially from the East) similarly argued that ordinary easterners had to see themselves as relevant to the inquiry's pursuits and "gain access" to their history.[112] In part, the inclusion of everyday life and ordinary people was intended to counter the rather more abstract and theoretical consideration of political structures, policies, and mechanisms to which—it was feared with some justification—many people might not relate. It also emanated from a desire to remedy public discussion of the GDR that focused on scandalous stories of spying, betrayal, shootings, and the like. According to Gerd Poppe (B90), the commission's work was to be less about spectacular events than about "the quiet repression in everyday life."[113]

As Poppe's statement suggests, only certain aspects of everyday life in the GDR concerned the commissions: not everyday life per se, but everyday repression. An early statement by the Christian Democrats that sought to demonstrate the first inquiry's interest in and relevance to easterners claimed that the CDU had "set itself the goal of putting everyday life in the SED dictatorship at the center of the commission's work" and that it wanted to investigate how people had responded "to the ever-present dictatorship."[114] Not uncharacteristically, Christian Democrat spokesperson Dorothee Wilms (CDU) argued that it had to be made clear "that the person who lived and suffered in the GDR is the starting and finishing point of the commission's work."[115] Eppelmann was also reported as saying that "above all we want to analyze the living circumstances of Joe Bloggs," by which he meant concretely that the inquiry would question people who had been forced out of their homes near the German-German border in 1952 and 1961, or small and large farmers who were victims of land reform and collectivization, or business owners who were dispossessed through nationalization.[116]

Such statements were founded in the perfectly legitimate desire to include ordinary people and not just prominent public figures in the inquiries' deliberations, but they begged a number of fundamental questions. Was the dictatorship "ever-present" as the CDU/CSU statement assumed? Did everyone or the majority of people in the GDR suffer, as Wilms implied? Were forced eviction, dispossession, etc., the experiences of Joe Bloggs, as Eppelmann seemed to suggest? Were they normal, typical, or characteristic of life in the GDR, or merely emblematic of selective understandings of it? Far too often, the commissions assumed the answer to, rather than posed, such questions. Indeed, as a newspaper headline's interpretation of the first inquiry's goals suggested, it was interested in a "search for the injustice in everyday life in the GDR."[117] It was certainly important to move beyond widespread understandings of repression that focused on blatant, direct, and brutal measures used by the Stasi and the GDR criminal justice system such as imprisonment, torture, and surveillance, and toward a more comprehensive understanding of repression that included more subtle and widespread forms. However, to investigate everyday life solely with a view to finding examples of injustice and repression, or to examine examples of injustice and repression and then equate them with everyday life was methodologically highly questionable. That experiences of injustice such as those mentioned above might not have been typical does not make them less insignificant, less terrible for the victims, or unworthy of the inquiry's attention. Yet they cannot simply be assumed to be representative and should not be equated from the outset with the everyday experiences of the wider population. There seems to have been a complete lack of awareness of such methodological concerns, which is symptomatic of the commissions' failure to reflect on their own presumptions, the frequently tendentious questions they posed, or the terminology they used.[118]

To a considerable degree, the problematic elision of quotidian repression and everyday life was due to the difficulty of appealing to differing constituencies. As we have seen, many commissioners saw themselves as

advocates for the victims of the regime, while the importance of addressing the experiences of ordinary GDR citizens was also stressed repeatedly. Occasionally, differences between the two perspectives were simply
ignored, for instance in Eppelmann's foreword to the published materials
of the second inquiry. Here he referred to the commission's efforts to help
people with differing biographies "find themselves" in the inquiry's work,
while in the next breath he moved on to speak of the inquiry's adoption
of the "perspective of the victims" which he equated with the "view from
below."[119] Doing justice to both groups' perspectives was inevitably difficult, but the first commission failed even to perceive a problem in this
regard, let alone consider how it could be overcome or how these two
(or other) perspectives could be combined (or kept distinct). This created
uncertainty and even confusion about the commissions' competing plans,
loyalties, and audiences.[120]

Notwithstanding the inquiries' rather confused efforts to address the
differing perspectives of ordinary easterners and outright victims, the
central component of their work lay in their investigation of the policies,
institutions, and mechanisms of SED rule. Compared to this focus, consideration of East German history per se or social or everyday history
was a marginal concern, particularly in the first inquiry. In part to address
this deficit, everyday life was once again promoted as a prominent topic
for the second inquiry. Indeed, it was a central justification for renewing
the inquiry's brief, and once again Eppelmann in particular had—and
raised—high hopes of the second commission's efforts in this area.[121] In
addition to appraising the process of working through the communist
past to date and promoting that project into the future, the main tasks of
the second inquiry were to examine topics such as the economy and social
and environmental policy that had been largely ignored by the first commission, and to explore in greater depth some topics that its predecessor
had addressed already to some extent.[122] Despite the fact that everyday
life had been so neglected by the first inquiry, it was not mentioned in
any of the parties' motions calling for a second commission. This repeated
absence suggests that the prominent talk about addressing everyday life
and exploring different biographies and personal experiences was largely
window dressing, while the real aim remained the delegitimation of the
communist regime in all its aspects.[123]

Everyday life was attended to nevertheless. Early proposals for a large-
scale oral-history research project foundered due to the longevity of such
undertakings, and initial enthusiasm waned. Work in this area was slow to
begin and remained limited. Its failure to meet expectations was due to a
combination of the inherent difficulty of the topic, underestimation of this
on the part of commissioners, and a lack of political will.[124] That everyday

life—indeed "life" in the GDR, rather than the regime and the opposition against it—could have been more central to the inquiry becomes evident through comparison of its work with the efforts of an inquiry established by the parliament of the eastern state of Mecklenburg Pommerania.[125]

In the end, the commission was not interested in everyday life or in hearing about people's different biographies beyond what they could reveal about the disastrous impact of the dictatorship and the lingering differences between easterners and westerners. The section on everyday life in the second commission's report justified the inquiry's interest in the topic primarily with reference to the consequences of the communist dictatorship for peoples' lives during and after the GDR.[126] Indeed, a key consideration was the attempt to explain differing eastern and western mentalities.[127] The report came to the welcome conclusion that such differences did not constitute a danger to democracy and that a pluralistic society should tolerate some diversity.[128] However, such a relaxed approach was inconsistent both with the tenor of other sections of the report and with many statements by commissioners which suggested, in contrast, that certain views of the past and present—such as a belief in (even partial, compromised) achievements of the GDR—were unacceptable and constituted a threat to democracy. Other aspects to this section of the report revealed a balanced approach and a conceptual sophistication that were often lacking in both inquiries' work. For instance, it discussed a number of scholarly approaches to the conceptualization of—indeed the question of the very existence of—"society" in the GDR; it also recognized that the reach of the regime into everyday life had varied and that the reality of life in the GDR cannot be understood entirely as the result of SED policy, for there were limitations to the realization of the party's totalitarian ambitions.[129] As discussed in subsequent chapters, all too often the inquiry overlooked such constraints on the regime. Even here, despite claiming to consciously avoid preferring a particular characterization of GDR society, the report continued to refer to it forthrightly as a *Mangelgesellschaft* (shortage society).[130]

The remainder of the second commission's limited activities on everyday life concentrated on leisure and on the situation of women, young people, and the elderly in the GDR and after unification. Not atypically, its attention to women focused on demolishing the notion that they were emancipated in the GDR. Here, as in other areas such as education and social policy where many easterners (and the PDS) have pointed to the GDR's positive features, the second commission sought explicitly to compare the regime's (positive sounding) aspirations with (the less impressive) reality.[131] In contrast with the regime's rhetoric of socialist female emancipation, the commission argued, women were professionally and economically disadvantaged, saddled with a double burden of paid and domestic labor, and rarely made it to the top of state and party organizations.[132] Not surprisingly, a PDS dissenting statement welcomed the commission's interest in everyday life but rejected much of its treatment, insisting on the existence of shared values, considerable popular identification, and the relative normality of life in the GDR. However tendentious, these were noteworthy points, but their credibility was undermined by some extraordinary minimizations about the mass exodus from the GDR in the 1980s and by glib criticisms of the "coldness of the market economy."[133] Tendentiousness and selectivity united both the anticommunist majority and the democratic-socialist minority.

Competing Perspectives and Expectations

Many of the characteristics of the dominant approach in the commissions discussed thus far emanated from the complexity of their various constituencies. The difficulties associated with investigating everyday life in particular revealed the diverging perspectives and experiences of easterners generally and victims more narrowly understood. The glossing over of crucial differences between these groups was evident in the imprecise use of the term *Betroffene* (persons affected), which was sometimes employed in a broad sense to include all easterners (or even westerners), and sometimes in a narrower sense as a synonym for victims.[134] Westerners aside, no easterner could be considered unaffected by the SED regime, but some were clearly more affected than others. Which group was meant in any particular instance was often unclear.[135] The problem was more than merely semantic. The tension between investigating everyday life in the GDR and the experiences of the majority of the population or of ordinary GDR citizens, on the one hand, and doing justice to the suffering of the regime's victims, on the other, proved an ongoing problem for the commissions. Remarkably, the two groups were frequently equated with one another.[136]

As this chapter has shown, the commissions were selective in the pursuit of the goals listed in their terms of reference. The ostensible overriding aims of fostering reconciliation within eastern society and between easterners and westerners were understood in rather narrow terms or simply were not prioritized or operationalized. The commissions paid considerably more attention to the victims of the SED regime, but here too their efforts were limited, focusing on public acknowledgment and moral rehabilitation. The inquiries were more interested in highlighting the victims' persecution and conducting a critical investigation of the regime responsible for it, than in hearing extensive testimony from victims themselves. Much the same can be said of their frequently expressed interest in the experiences of ordinary East Germans. The commissions' efforts to investigate everyday life in the GDR were indicative of their overall tendency to concentrate not on the history of the GDR per se, but on the negative sides of the SED regime. Further, the commissions refrained from populist approaches in favor of established parliamentary procedures and a rather elitist, academic approach. The latter, however, cannot be equated with methodological soundness or critical reflection. Ultimately, most commissioners were interested in elaborating the GDR's dictatorial and repressive nature and in delegitimizing the East German state. Precisely how the commissions went about this elaboration, how the majority interpretation of the past was pitted against and challenged by rival interpretations, and with what historical ammunition and political aims, are the subject of the following chapters.

Notes

1. See DBPa: Protokoll 2: 26.
2. Bernd Faulenbach, "Bewahrung der Erinnerung: Bedeutung und Probleme der 'Aufarbeitung' von Vergangenheit heute," in *Die Partei hatte immer recht*, eds. Faulenbach, Meckel, and Weber, 12. I thus disagree with Andrews' claim that the inquiry's audience was the Bundestag and not the East German people, "Grand National Narratives," 51; and with Yoder's claim that "healing was not the mission," "Truth without Reconciliation," 72.
3. DBPa: Protokoll 8: 17f.; Protokoll 19: 6f. Cf. Dirk Hansen, "Noch eine Vergangenheit, die nicht vergehen will," *Liberal* 35, no. 3 (1993): 17.
4. I: 188, 190. Cf. Wüstenberg, *Die politische Dimension*, 391.
5. In light of the self-consciously complementary nature of the inquiry's role as discussed in the previous chapter and of these limitations it placed on its objectives, Yoder's question of whether it constituted a "sufficient approach for working through the past and promoting reconciliation" is nonsensical, "Truth without Reconciliation," 71f. It never aimed at such sufficiency.
6. For similar if not unproblematic assessments, see Yoder, "Truth without Reconciliation"; Andrews, "Grand National Narratives"; Hayner, *Unspeakable Truths*, 61f.; Claus Leggewie and Erik Meyer, *"Ein Ort, an den man gerne geht": Das Holocaust-Mahnmal und die deutsche Geschichtspolitik nach 1989* (Munich, 2005), 73.
7. Cf. Wüstenberg, *Die politische Dimension*, 309, 343–53; Wielenga, *Schatten deutscher Geschichte*, 81.
8. Maier, *Dissolution*, 326; Garton Ash, *History of the Present*, 307.
9. See I: 32, 169, 187, 742.
10. Maier's argument that the inquiry failed to make contestation of rival views of the past central thus requires qualification, *Dissolution*, 326. Cf. Yoder, "Truth without Reconciliation," 72.

11. The aims and methods were set out in "Antrag der Fraktionen CDU/CSU, BÜNDNIS 90/DIE GRÜNEN und F.D.P. Einsetzung einer Enquete Kommission 'Überwindung von Geschichte und Folgen der SED-Diktatur im Prozess der deutschen Einheit,'" *I: 4–8*. See Appendix B for a translation. On the establishment of the second inquiry, see McAdams, *Judging the Past,* 116ff.

12. Cf. Yoder, "Truth without Reconciliation," 72; Hayner, *Unspeakable Truths,* 62; Wüstenberg, *Die politische Dimension,* 343.

13. See the revealingly titled "Beschluss: Gliederung der künftigen Kommissionsarbeit im Hinblick auf den zu erstellenden Bericht," DBPa: Protokoll 9: 19–24. This should not lead one to treat the report as the be-all and end-all of the inquiry, to the complete neglect of the preceding deliberations, as some authors do.

14. Author's interviews with Jacobsen and Kowalczuk.

15. DBPa: Protokoll 2: 29; Protokoll 4: 5, 7, 11; Protokoll 7: 3, 13; Protokoll 8: 18; Protokoll 9: 3, 6f. See the protocol of the hearing "Regierungskriminalität und justitielle Aufarbeitung—Möglichkeiten und Grenzen," IX: 4–119.

16. I: 191.

17. Author's interview with Hansen. Cf. Hansen, "Noch eine Vergangenheit," 17; Wilke, "Der Historiker und die Politik," 82.

18. See DBPa: Protokoll 2; Protokoll 3. Several commissioners agreed that little was achieved (author's interviews with Kowalczuk, Gutzeit, Meckel, Hansen, and Margot von Renesse [Berlin, 24 September 2001]). Only Eppelmann suggested that the inquiries influenced relevant legislation (author's interview).

19. The federal government had already presented its first bill by the time the first formal proposal for a commission was made; by June 1992, the opposition parties had presented their amendments; and the law was proclaimed on 29 October. Cf. Wüstenberg, *Die politische Dimension,* 294–301.

20. See DBPa: Protokoll 3: 22, 26, 29.

21. I: 645f. Even seeing it as a lobby for the interests of the victims is perhaps too generous. Jörg Siegmund barely mentions the inquiry in the context of victims' lobby groups and legislation, *Opfer ohne Lobby? Ziele, Strukturen und Arbeitsweise der Verbände der Opfer des DDR-Unrechts* (Berlin, 2003), 103, 115ff.

22. "Debatte des Deutschen Bundestages am 22. Juni 1995," *I: 50.*

23. I: 3.

24. These tendencies, as well as a proclivity to focus on the SED system and acts of repression rather than their victims, were evident in a statement to the inquiry by parliamentary State Secretary Eduard Lintner (CDU), for whom "moral acknowledgement" of the victims was synonymous with "comprehensive discussion and clarification of the totalitarian and unlawful character of the SED regime." Matthias-Domaschk-Archiv in der Robert-Havemann Gesellschaft, Berlin (MDA): Protokoll der achten Sitzung der Enquete-Kommission "Überwindung von Geschichte und Folgen der SED-Diktatur im Prozess der deutschen Einheit," Anlage, 2. Subsequent references are given in the form: MDA: Protokoll number: page number, or MDA: document title: page number.

25. DBPa: Protokoll 19: 11f. See VII: 371; I: 650; Angelika Barbe et al., "Thesen zur Aufklärung der Vergangenheit," *Deutschland Archiv* 25, no. 4 (1992): 446f. Cf. Heinrich, "Geschichtspolitische Akteure."

26. MDA: Protokoll 3: 17f.; Protokoll 8: 13. Cf. Anna-Sabine Ernst, "Zwischen eilfertiger Enthüllungshistorie und solider Quellenkritik: Die zeitgeschichtliche DDR-Forschung im Prozeß der Neuordnung," *Zeitgeschichte* 22, no. 7–8 (1995): 254f.

27. DBPa: Protokoll 16: 6f. See "Seilschaften in den neuen Bundesländern," VIII: 646–755.

28. See "Das ehemalige Ministerium für Staatssicherheit," VIII: 4–125; various expertise

papers commissioned on the Stasi, 126–643; and "Regierungskriminalität und justitielle Aufarbeitung."

29. See I: 651f., 678f. Cf. Hermann Weber, "Die Aufarbeitung der DDR-Geschichte und die Rolle der Archive," in *Die Partei hatte immer recht*, eds. Faulenbach, Meckel, and Weber; Matthias Buchholz, "Zur Problematik der 'DDR-Archive,'" in *Bilanz und Perspektiven*, eds. Eppelmann, Faulenbach, and Mählert.

30. *I: 4f.*

31. "Germany's Long Look Inward," *Newsweek*, 20 July 1992.

32. DBPa: Protokoll 3: 8.

33. DBPa: Protokoll 3: 3; Protokoll 4: 4. Author's interviews with Wilke and Eppelmann. A formal proposal was never put to the commission.

34. DBPa: Protokoll 5: 20, 5.

35. MDA: Protokoll 2: 21.

36. Yoder, "Truth without Reconciliation," 62, 75; Andrews, "Grand National Narratives," 51.

37. DBPa: Protokoll 7: 19.

38. MDA: Protokoll 2: 19, 22f.; Protokoll 4: 8; Protokoll 5: 11f.; Protokoll 18: 3.

39. I: 193; *I: 163.* Author's interview with Hansen. Cf. Hayner, *Unspeakable Truths*, 62.

40. Here the negative assessments of numerous commentators require qualification. Yoder overlooks the public hearings and the considerable coverage in the regional and local press when she argues that—apart from reading its final report or the national press—there was "no other way" to follow the commission's work, "Truth without Reconciliation," 76. Kamali argues incorrectly that the hearings did not get much coverage in Germany's "serious newspapers," "Accountability for Human Rights Violations," 118. The claim that "many" East Germans were unaware of the commission's existence is as plausible as it is imprecise, Kamali, ibid.; Andrews, "Grand National Narratives," 51. Such stress on the lack of public awareness and attention is somewhat inconsistent with claims by the same authors that "the East German public" reacted with skepticism at best and hostility at worst to the commission's efforts and its depiction of East German history, and with suggestions that the latter exacerbated the inner-German divide, ibid., 51, 60; Kamali, "Accountability for Human Rights Violations," 108ff. Grix also underestimates the degree of public reception, but at least this is consistent with his conclusion that the inquiry did not have any wide impact, "The Enquete-Kommission's Contribution." 62f.

41. I: 181, 193, 195; *I: iii, 164.* Cf. Wüstenberg, *Die politische Dimension*, 332.

42. I: 193; *I: 164.* Author's interviews with Hansen and Mitter. Cf. Wilms, "Begründung, Entstehung und Zielsetzung," 15.

43. Author's interview, Berlin, 28 September 2001. Maser worked on the secretariat of the first inquiry and was an expert commissioner for the CDU/CSU on the second.

44. DBPa: Protokoll 9: 6; Protokoll 12: 3. Cf. Friedrich-Christian Schroeder, "Die Enquetekommission des Deutschen Bundestages 'Aufarbeitung von Geschichte und von Folgen der SED-Diktatur in Deutschland,'" *Politische Studien* 324 (1992): 27; Weber, "Rewriting the History," 204f.

45. See, for example, II: 179–84, 197–204, 245–68; VII: 78–90. Eppelmann's depiction of the inquiries as an "open discursive process" with "the complete participation of the public" was thus overly generous, *I: v.* On the other hand, Yoder's claim of the absence of either passive or active participation as spectators or witnesses goes to the other extreme, "Truth without Reconciliation," 72.

46. See the protocol of the hearing "Alltag in der DDR zwischen Selbstbehauptung und Anpassung: Erfahrungen und Bewältigungsstrategien in der Mangelgesellschaft," *V:*

134; MDA: Ergebnisprotokoll des 29. Obleutegesprächs am 14.5.1997; author's interview with Faulenbach. For press coverage of the event including statements from the audience and commissioners' reactions, see "'Die Kommission will nicht beweisen, daß Ihr DDR-Leben nichts wert war,'" *Märkische Oderzeitung,* 30 April 1997; "'Wir hatten unseren kleinen Wohlstand,'" *BZ,* 30 April 1997; "'Wir waren in der DDR doch nicht alle bescheuert,'" *Der Tagesspiegel,* 30 April 1997; "Öffentliches Rühren im Kaffeesatz," *TAZ,* 30 April 1997; "Kaum Bananen, aber Arbeit für alle," *Mitteldeutsche Zeitung,* 30 April 1997; "Aus einer versunkenen Welt," *Berliner Morgenpost,* 2 May 1997; "Die Uhr ging früher langsamer," *SZ,* 3 May 1997; "Viele wollen die alte DDR wiederhaben," *FR,* 5 May 1997. Cf. Gisela Helwig, "Aufarbeitung ist Zukunftsgestaltung: Enquete-Kommission und Bundesstiftung," *Deutschland Archiv* 31, no. 5 (1998): 708; Koschyk, "Die Beseitigung der Folgen," 475; Stefan Wolle, "Herrschaft und Alltag: Die Zeitgeschichtsforschung auf der Suche nach der wahren DDR," *Aus Politik und Zeitgeschichte* 47, no. 26 (1997): 30–38.

47. See Yoder, "Truth without Reconciliation," 72; Andrews, "The Politics of Forgiveness," 110.

48. Author's interview with Wilke. Cf. Sa'adah, *Germany's Second Chance,* 185; Yoder, "Truth without Reconciliation," 75.

49. I: 181, 193; *I: iii, 164.*

50. See, for example, a "hearing of eyewitnesses" at a public hearing on Marxism-Leninism that involved the presentation of statements by three commissioners and by two further parliamentarians, III: 74–94. For lists of the experts and eyewitnesses heard, see I: 760–67; *I: 797–803.*

51. See "Die SED-Diktatur—politische, geistige und psychosoziale Unterdrückungsmechanismen/Erfahrungen im Alltag," II: 111–276.

52. Engler, "'Kommode Diktatur' oder 'totalitäres System'?" 444.

53. Scholars who stress the inquiries' elitist academic nature often overlook their contacts with civil-society groups. See, for example, Grix, "The Enquete-Kommissions' Contribution," 62f.

54. Author's interview. Cf. Maier, *Dissolution,* 326.

55. For the former expression, see *I: v;* Hansen, "Noch eine Vergangenheit," 17; Faulenbach, "Die Auseinandersetzung mit der doppelten Vergangenheit," 41; Jansen, "Enquete-Kommission," 269. Gert Weisskirchen used the latter phrase in an interview with the author (Berlin, 12 October 2001). Cf. Cooke, *Representing East Germany,* 47. Andrews fails to see that much of what she praises in relation to the South African Truth and Reconciliation Commission—in particular concerning the connection between process and product, but also more generally—also applies to the German inquiries, "Grand National Narratives," 62, 60.

56. Jarausch, *The Rush to German Unity.* Cf. Wüstenberg, *Die politische Dimension,* 254, 362, 365ff.; Wilke, "Der Historiker und die Politik," 85f.

57. Cf. Wüstenberg, *Die politische Dimension,* 319f.; Wilke, "Die deutsche Einheit," 457; Yoder, "Truth without Reconciliation," 65, 75.

58. Cf. Hansen, "Befreiung durch Erinnerung," 72f.; Wüstenberg, *Die politische Dimension,* 294.

59. See *I: 36, 43.*

60. MDA: Protokoll 3: 6.

61. Cf. Andrews, "Grand National Narratives," 52f.

62. Cf. Hansen, "Befreiung durch Erinnerung," 76; Christoph Kleßmann, "Eine Enquete-Kommission als historisches Gewissen der Nation? Das Parlament stimuliert die Aufarbeitung der jüngsten deutschen Geschichte," *Das Parlament,* 6–13 November 1998.

63. On the asymmetry of German division, unification, and the debate about the past, see Bauerkämper, Sabrow, and Stöver, *Doppelte Zeitgeschichte*, 12f.; Arnd Bauerkämper, "DDR-Vergangenheit zwischen Theologie, Strafjustiz und Geschichtswissenschaft: Umgang mit Schuld und Verantwortung im vereinten Deutschland," in *Verantwortung — Schuld — Vergebung* (*Loccumer Protokolle* 54), ed. Wolfgang Vögele (Rehburg-Loccum, 1999), 148; Faulenbach, "Die Auseinandersetzung mit der doppelten Vergangenheit," esp. 53; Wüstenberg, *Die politische Dimension*, 249, 362.

64. See Eppelmann's summary of the first commission's goals, I: 182; and the protocols of public hearings and the expertise papers commissioned on this topic, V: 1–2962.

65. Cf. McAdams, *Judging the Past*, 101–9; Wüstenberg, *Die politische Dimension*, 244. See Beattie, "Die Delegitimierung von '1968' nach 1989/90"; and "A Fifties Revival?"

66. Emphasis added. Cf. Wüstenberg, *Die politische Dimension*, 364ff.

67. See, for example, the hearing "Wechselseitige Wahrnehmungen und Reaktionen im geteilten Deutschland und ihre Nachwirkungen," *VIII: 9–119*.

68. Hansen, "Befreiung durch Erinnerung," 77.

69. See Wilke, "Die deutsche Einheit," 607.

70. Cf. Wüstenberg, *Die politische Dimension*, 368, 372.

71. Author's interviews with Jacobsen and Harmut Büttner (Berlin, 27 September 2001); Jansen, "Enquete-Kommission," 269; Hansen, "Befreiung durch Erinnerung," 78f. Both Faulenbach (interview with the author) and Wilms expressed their retrospective pleasure that dissenting reports displayed diversity of opinion, "Begründung, Entstehung und Zielsetzung," 18. In contrast, during early discussions of the possible publication of the first commission's materials, Wilms said that if numerous positions were put forward readers might ask themselves which was the right one. DBPa: Protokoll 74: 4. She clearly regarded such a possibility as undesirable.

72. Klaus Schroeder, *Die veränderte Republik: Deutschland nach der Wiedervereinigung* (Stamsried, 2006), 332; Charles S. Maier, "Geschichtswissenschaft und Ansteckungsstaat," *Geschichte und Gesellschaft* 20 (1994): 616–24; McAdams, *Judging the Past*, 13; Christoph Kleßmann, "Der schwierige gesamtdeutsche Umgang mit der DDR-Geschichte," *Aus Politik und Zeitgeschichte* 51, no. 30–31 (2001): 3ff.; Laurence H. McFalls, "Political Culture and Political Change in Eastern Germany," *German Politics and Society* 20, no. 2 (2002): 90; John S. Brady and Sarah Elise Wiliarty, "How Culture Matters: Culture and Social Change in the Federal Republic of Germany," *German Politics and Society* 20, no. 2 (2002): 4; Falk Pingel, "Vom Paradigma der Weltrevolution zur Unbestimmtheit der Postmoderne: Was heisst 'Zeitgeschichte' im Ost-West-Vergleich heute?" in *Doppelte Zeitgeschichte*, eds. Bauerkämper, Sabrow, and Stöver, 341f.; Dietrich Mühlberg, "Vom langsamen Wandel der Erinnerung an die DDR," in *Verletztes Gedächtnis: Erinnerungskultur und Zeitgeschichte im Konflikt*, eds. Konrad H. Jarausch and Martin Sabrow (Frankfurt am Main, 2002); Annette Leo, "Keine gemeinsame Erinnerung: Geschichtsbewusstsein in Ost und West," *Aus Politik und Zeitgeschichte* 53, no. 40–41 (2003): 27–32.

73. On the need to address diverging perspectives in a well-rounded account of GDR history, see Jarausch, "Beyond Uniformity," esp. 9. Cf. Yoder, "Truth without Reconciliation," 75.

74. Cf. Sa'adah, *Germany's Second Chance*, 71f.; Wüstenberg, *Die politische Dimension*, 294 (fn. 278), 284f., 291, 310; Hans Michael Kloth, "'Versorgungsfall' Vergangenheit? Stiftung zur Aufarbeitung der SED-Vergangenheit gegründet," *Deutschland Archiv* 31, no. 5 (1998): 865; Maier, *Dissolution*, 326; Katharina Gajdukowa, "Opfer-Täter-Gesprächskreise nach dem Ende der DDR," *Aus Politik und Zeitgeschichte* 54, no. 41–42 (2004): 23–27.

75. Betts, "Germany, International Justice," 71; Yoder, "Truth without Reconciliation," 71; Maier, *Dissolution*, 326.

76. *I: 249*. Cf. Wüstenberg, *Die politische Dimension*, 406ff.
77. See Rainer Eppelmann and Dietmar Keller, *Zwei deutsche Sichten: Ein Dialog auf gleicher Augenhöhe* (Bad Honnef, 2000).
78. See Barker, "'Geschichtsaufarbeitung' within the PDS."
79. See I: 813. Cf. Wüstenberg, *Die politische Dimension*, 344, 323f. Author's interviews with Weisskirchen, Gutzeit, Weber, and von Renesse.
80. Wüstenberg, *Die politische Dimension*, 347. Author's interview with Wilke.
81. See *I: 4, 19, 22f.* MDA: Protokoll 1: 8ff.; Protokoll 2: 7ff.; Protokoll 37: 17.
82. For instance, "double" expertise papers were requested only on issues that were fiercely disputed between the coalition and the SPD, such as *Deutschlandpolitik*, the bloc parties, and ideology.
83. Maier, *Dissolution*, 326.
84. *I: 121f., 843f.* See Koschyk, "Die Beseitigung der Folgen"; Maser, "Auf dem Weg zur deutschen Einheit," 72; Wilke, "Die deutsche Einheit," 609; Wilms, "Begründung, Entstehung und Zielsetzung," 16.
85. I: 182.
86. See *I: 45, 25*. Author's interview with Maser. Cf. McAdams, *Judging the Past*, 113; Welsh, "When Discourse Trumps Policy," 146.
87. *I: 159*. See Patrick Moreau, "Mit Lenin im Bauch...? Die PDS auf der Suche nach einer Berliner Republik von Links," *Politische Studien* 349 (1996): 27–42.
88. Keller and Wolf made their lack of support for the statement clear, but it had to bear Keller's name because he was the PDS representative on the commission. DBPa: Protokoll 78: 1. For commentators who fail to acknowledge this, see Hansen, "Befreiung durch Erinnerung," 78; Wolfgang Schuller, "Bericht der Enquete-Kommission 'Aufarbeitung von Geschichte und Folgen der SED-Diktatur in Deutschland,'" *Geschichte in Wissenschaft und Unterricht* 46, no. 12 (1995): 741; Jesse, "Die zweite deutsche Diktatur," 233f.; Beate Ihme-Tuchel, *Die DDR* (Darmstadt, 2002), 96. In contrast, see Barker's differentiated account, "'Geschichtsaufarbeitung' within the PDS."
89. Cf. Wüstenberg, *Die politische Dimension*, 332, 403; McAdams, *Judging the Past*, 91f.
90. VII: 429. Cf. Tina Rosenberg, *The Haunted Land: Facing Europe's Ghosts after Communism* (New York, 1995), 355; Charles S. Maier, "Overcoming the Past? Narrative and Negotiation, Remembering and Reparation: Issues at the Interface of History and Law," in *Politics and the Past*, ed. Torpey, 298; Wüstenberg, *Die politische Dimension*, 343; Garton Ash, *History of the Present*, 307.
91. Author's interview with Mitter. Cf. Wüstenberg, *Die politische Dimension*, 336, 403.
92. Andrews, "Grand National Narratives," 52.
93. I: 189; II: 268; *I: 25, 46*.
94. I: 639ff.
95. I: 182, emphasis added.
96. *I: 6, 11*. MDA: Protokoll 2: 22f.
97. *I: 6, 8*.
98. See the expertise papers on these topics, *II: 101–339*, and the report, *I: 171f.*
99. See "Öffentliche Gedenkveranstaltung aus Anlaß der 35. Jahrestages des Baus der Berliner Mauer am 13. August 1961," *I: 933–61*. For internal discussions of the event, see MDA: Protokoll 16: 7; Protokoll 18: 21ff.; Protokoll 20: 21f.
100. Author's interview. Cf. Sa'adah, *Germany's Second Chance*, 185.
101. "Gesetz über die Errichtung einer Stiftung zur Aufarbeitung der SED-Diktatur," *I: 137–41*. See the foundation's website <http://www.stiftung-aufarbeitung.de/> (22 April 2008).
102. Mitter, for example, believed it was important to help them gain access to official archives and to provide them with publicity. DBPa: Protokoll 2: 19.

103. On these groups' development, see Udo Baron, "Wege zur Aufarbeitung der SED-Diktatur: Unabhängige Aufarbeitungsinitiativen zur Geschichtsdebatte über die DDR," in *The GDR and its History,* ed. Barker; Tobias Hollitzer, "Die gesellschaftliche Aufarbeitung der SED-Diktatur," in *Bilanz und Perspektiven,* eds. Eppelmann, Faulenbach, and Mählert. For commissioners' intentions, see DBPa: Protokoll 1: 9f.; Protokoll 2: 8, 10, 19, 23; Protokoll 3: 3; Protokoll 4: 6; Protokoll 7: 7.

104. See "Erfahrungsaustausch mit Organisationen, die sich ebenfalls mit der Aufarbetung der SED-Diktatur befassen," IX: 120–220; and "Die Herausforderung des Aufarbeitungsprozesses und die Situation der Aufarbeitungsinitiativen sechs Jahre nach der Wiedervereinigung," *VII: 4–90.*

105. DBPa: Protokoll 15: 6, 9; Protokoll 17: 10ff.

106. I: 740f., 750. Cf. Meckel, "Demokratische Selbstbestimmung," 264.

107. *I: 5.*

108. See *I: 54–59, 60–75, 89–100, 117ff.*

109. See Hollitzer, "Die gesellschaftliche Aufarbeitung"; Rainer Eppelmann, "Die Stiftung zur Aufarbeitung der SED-Diktatur," in *Zehn Jahre Deutsche Einheit,* eds. Thierse, Spittmann-Rühle, and Kuppe; Jörg Siegmund, "Die Opferverbände des SBZ/DDR-Unrechts," in *Bilanz und Perspektiven,* eds. Eppelmann, Faulenbach, and Mählert.

110. See, for example, Andrews, "Grand National Narratives," 51; Yoder, "Truth without Reconciliation," 77 and passim.

111. DBPa: Protokoll 3: 3. See, for example, "DDR-Opfer in den Blick gerückt: Enquêtekommission setzt auf breite Bürgerbeteiligung," *FR,* 24 April 1992; "'Nicht nur über Honekker und Bärbel Bohley reden': Eppelmann um Bürgernähe bemüht—Meckel: Kein Monopol auf Geschichtsaufarbeitung," *Mitteldeutsche Zeitung,* 24 April 1992.

112. DBPa: Protokoll 3: 18, 21; Protokoll 4: 24f. Cf. "'Subjektive Erfahrungen in der Diktatur,'" *Woche im Bundestag,* 9 September 1992.

113. "Es geht um die 'leise Repression,'" *FAZ,* 24 April 1992.

114. Dorothee Wilms, "Bestandsaufnahme der DDR-Wirklichkeit—Arbeitsziele der Enquete-Kommission des Bundestages," *Deutschland-Union-Dienst,* 16 July 1992.

115. DBPa: Protokoll 3: 28.

116. "Ost und West aufarbeiten," *Junge Welt,* 23 March 1992.

117. "Suche nach dem Unrecht im DDR-Alltag," *BZ,* 2 April 1992. Cf. Grix, "The Enquete-Kommission's Contribution"; McAdams, *Judging the Past,* 111; Andrews, "Grand National Narratives," 52.

118. See the rather confused hearing "Die SED-Diktatur—politische, geistige und psychosoziale Unterdrückungsmechanismen/Erfahrungen im Alltag," I: 111–276.

119. *I: iv.*

120. See "Suche nach dem Unrecht im DDR-Alltag," *BZ,* 2 April 1992.

121. *I: ix.*

122. *I: 7f.*

123. Revealingly, particular attention—even in fields as diverse as those just mentioned—was to be paid to "the ideological bases and the repressive structure," *I: 7.*

124. See *I: 86, 130.* MDA: Protokoll 2: 21; Protokoll 4: 11; Protokoll 5: 11f., 18, Anlage 3, 1, Anlage 4; Protokoll 7: 10ff.; Protokoll 9: Anlage 1, 9; Protokoll 18: 19f.; Protokoll 26: 10; Protokoll 28: Anlage 2; Protokoll 50: 8f., 18f.; Protokoll des 2. Obleutegesprächs am 20. 9. 1995: 3; Protokoll der konstituierenden Sitzung der Projektgruppe F 1 (02) "Leben in der DDR" am 23. November 1995; Anlage 3 zur Tagesordnung des 11. Obleutegesprächs am 31.1.1996: 15. Author's interviews with Maser and Kowalczuk.

125. See Andreas Fraude, "'Leben in der DDR, Leben nach 1989—Aufarbeitung und Versöhnung': Enquete-Kommission in Mecklenburg-Vorpommern," *Deutschland Archiv* 28, no.

7 (1995): 681–82; Fraude, "Vergangenheitsaufarbeitung in Mecklenburg-Vorpommern: Zur bisherigen Tätigkeit der Enquete-Kommission," *Deutschland Archiv* 29, no. 5 (1996): 676–80; Fraude, "'Impulsgeber im Prozeß um Aufarbeitung und Versöhnung': Tätigkeitsbericht der Enquete-Kommission in Mecklenburg-Vorpommern," *Deutschland Archiv* 31, no. 1 (1998): 9–12. See Landtag Mecklenburg-Vorpommern, ed., *Leben in der DDR, Leben nach 1989: Aufarbeitung und Versöhnung, zur Arbeit der Enquete-Kommission* X vols. (Schwerin, 1996–1998).

126. *I: 522.*

127. See in particular the hearing "Generationen und Wertorientierungen in Ost und West," *V: 340–478.*

128. *I: 528.*

129. *I: 523.*

130. *I: 523, 528f.* This term featured prominently in the hearing in Eisenhüttenstadt mentioned above: "Alltag in der DDR."

131. See *I: 535, 7, 333f., 413; III: 111.* In other areas, where the "aspirations" were less positive or less frequently invoked by the PDS, the commission did not display the same level of interest in such comparisons or even consideration of the reality.

132. *I: 535f.*

133. *I: 547–52.*

134. See "'Subjektive Erfahrungen in der Diktatur,'" *Woche im Bundestag,* 9 September 1992; "Kommission beginnt mit Detailarbeit," *FAZ,* 7 November 1992.

135. For example, members of the first commission agreed on the need for cooperation with "those affected" and for a public hearing for them. It was not certain, however, whether the victims or the various historical groups and initiatives—or both—were meant, or even the population at large. DBPa: Protokoll 2: 9, 14, 19, 23.

136. This tendency to cast the entire population apart from the ruling elite as victims was not uncommon, as discussed in chapter 1 in relation to the Bundestag debate on the inquiry's terms of reference. Also, Eppelmann regarded all East Germans (outside the ruling elite) as having been imprisoned by the SED through the closing of the borders, a view sharply rejected by Keller, who said he had not lived in a prison, I: 793, 814. Cf. Eppelmann and Keller, *Zwei deutsche Sichten,* 17.

Chapter 3

THE SED'S DICTATORSHIP
FROM THE BEGINNING

For all the talk of doing justice to the victims, hearing ordinary East Germans' stories, and fostering inner unity, ultimately the focus of the commissions of inquiry was on the political history of the German Democratic Republic. Here two fundamental issues were at stake: the legitimacy of and responsibility for the GDR. These issues were more important than questions of truth, justice, trust, and reconciliation that dominate most accounts of the inquiries. The overwhelming majority on the commission—including Christian Democrats, Free Democrats, Social Democrats, and members of Alliance 90/The Greens—sought to establish the GDR's political illegitimacy, arguing that from the very beginning it had constituted a ruthless dictatorship that lacked popular support. The Party of Democratic Socialism, by contrast, was caught between acknowledging the GDR's dictatorial character and insisting on its legitimacy as a separate state and moral entity. The PDS suggested that the term *dictatorship* did not do justice to the complexities of East German history and that the GDR had constituted a legitimate alternative to the Federal Republic. As the commission's title clearly suggested, the majority attributed political responsibility for the dictatorship to the SED, although it also emphasized the latter's utter dependence on its Soviet protector. The PDS, by contrast, sought to exculpate much of the SED (and its own) membership, by suggesting that the GDR had been the dictatorship of the party leadership rather than the party as a whole, and by pointing to the constraints and distortions of the Cold War and to the role of the Soviet occupier to explain why a worthwhile attempt at socialism had ended, as it conceded, so abysmally.

In addition to these larger narratives of East German history, a number of smaller, supporting narratives attracted considerable attention, and the responsibility of non-communists was also vigorously contested. These secondary narratives warrant some attention, not least because they dem-

---

onstrate that debate did not just run along East-West lines or always pit the PDS against everyone else; in fact, all of the political parties were competing with all of their rivals for legitimation through history. The 1946 merger of the eastern SPD with the Communist Party of Germany (KPD) to form the SED and the role of the other "bloc" parties in the Unity Front of Antifascist-Democratic Parties in the SBZ and later the National Front in the GDR constituted particular challenges for the commission and its constituent party groupings, as they related directly to the non-communist parties' own histories and political heritage. Social Democrats and Democratic Socialists emphasized the co-responsibility of the bloc parties and pointed to the need of Christian Democrats and Free Democrats to come to terms with their bloc-party connections. In turn, members of the governing coalition stressed the willingness of Social Democrats in 1946 to support the union of the SPD and KPD. Unsurprisingly, commissioners tended to minimize their political forebears' willingness to cooperate with Communists, to play down the similarity of their political programs to that of the KPD/SED, and to magnify the level of their anticommunist resistance.[1] Yet given the potential to exploit these issues for political point scoring, the major parties ultimately accepted each other's depiction of themselves as resistors against, and victims of communist repression to a surprising extent. A concerted effort to delegitimize Communists and the state they were credited with erecting took precedence over infighting among the non-PDS parties. The master narrative was more powerful than the secondary narratives.

This chapter considers the first commission's handling of the two fundamental questions of legitimacy and responsibility. It analyzes the inquiry's investigation of Germany's postwar political history and examines the accounts that emerged and their political usefulness. I hope to demonstrate the central importance of partisan readings of history, which far outweighed any straightforward East-West cleavage. Nevertheless, the majority's effective refusal to examine critically West German history amounted to a double standard that could be exploited by those who sought to frame the debate in East-West terms. The first section discusses the commission's handling of calls from Democratic Socialists and others for a wide-ranging examination of German history that would address the postwar period or even the entire twentieth century. The commission was unwilling to examine West German developments in any depth, and preferred a selective, critical focus on the SBZ and the GDR. The second section discusses the commission's treatment of the union of the SPD and KPD to form the SED. This was marked at once by tension between conservative efforts to inculpate Social Democrats in this turning point on the road to communist dictatorship and Social Democrats' emphasis on resistance and repression, as well as by conflict between the PDS and SPD over the legitimacy of the merger. Similar tensions dominated the commission's handling of the legacy of the bloc parties that is the topic of the third section, although here the salient issue was co-responsibility rather than legitimacy. While the PDS and SPD highlighted the participation of the eastern Christian Democratic Union of Germany (CDUD) and Liberal Democratic Party of Germany (LDPD) in the East German political system, Christian and Free Democrats emphasized those bloc parties' resistance and repression, and the gap between their conformist leaderships and democratic memberships.[2] The fourth section explores the broader issue of the GDR's dictatorial character and the contested question of whether one can speak of democratic beginnings in East Germany. The fifth section examines the commission's response to the question of whose dictatorship the GDR had been, in particular looking at the existence and implementation of Communists' wartime plans for the postwar order, German Communists' dependence on the Soviet Union, and the putative distinction between the SED per se and its leadership.

On each of these issues, the commission as a whole and its conservative members in particular consistently pursued the argumentative strategy that best served the delegitimation of German communism and of political developments generally in the East, while minimizing the responsibility of their own political heritage. The commission denied any democratic beginnings in the SBZ and dismissed any appearances of pluralism as merely tactical. It stressed German Communists' utter dependence on the continuing Soviet presence in the SBZ/GDR. However, determined not to let them off the hook by locating power and responsibility in the USSR, conservatives also suggested that leading German Communists simply, but cunningly, put into practice plans they had drafted in wartime exile in Moscow. These arguments amounted to a total condemnation of the communist project in Germany's East, presenting it as a largely foreign import without domestic support that was only possible on the point of Soviet bayonets.

The PDS meanwhile sought to defend the legitimacy of the GDR against wholesale condemnation. It did not directly dispute the SED regime's dictatorial character, but insisted on democratic aspects to the "new start" made in the SBZ. Further, it argued that, later on, political power and responsibility lay in the hands of a tiny party elite, and that the vast majority of SED members were largely indistinguishable from non-members. While aware of the exculpatory implications of this argument for the PDS, the other parties were not unsympathetic to a narrative that implicated the top party leadership, even if it minimized the role of lower- and even higher-level functionaries, as long as the GDR was acknowledged as a dictatorship and responsibility was located in East Berlin rather than in Moscow alone. Similar narratives, after all, were supported by Christian Democrats and Free Democrats in relation to the bloc parties, and to a lesser extent by Social Democrats in relation to the SED's foundation. While the commission majority thus conceded some ground to PDS efforts to promote a narrower notion of responsibility, the majority was able to argue that the regime's dictatorial character was not disputed before the inquiry, and the commission continued to use its preferred designation for the GDR: the SED dictatorship.

Social Democrats and members of Alliance 90 frequently argued for differentiated, moderate positions between the extremes of conservative total condemnation and democratic-socialist defensiveness. On the questions of German as opposed to Soviet responsibility, the significance of communist wartime plans, and the "democratic beginnings" of political life in the SBZ, they pointed to the need to see the openness of historical moments, to take into account the complexities of historical reality, and to address individual and collective subjectivities as well as objective political developments, aspects often ignored by Christian and Free Democrats. Nevertheless, the similarities between the positions of these opposition parties and the governing coalition outweighed their differences on most of these issues.

For all the detailed debate about historical assessments, cause and effect, appropriate interpretations, and the co-responsibility of various political groupings, ultimately the fundamental legitimacy or illegitimacy of the GDR and the Federal Republic was at stake. The commission majority— including Social Democrats and Alliance 90—insisted on the GDR's lack of political legitimacy. Democratic Socialists meanwhile made numerous apparent concessions, and in particular did not question the GDR's dictatorial character and the responsibility of the SED. They continued, however, to insist on the historical and moral legitimacy of a socialist alternative to the Federal Republic, and on the equal legitimacy of the foundation of the two German states. The commission majority avoided tackling directly broader questions about responsibility for the two states' foundation and failed to address some of the points raised by the PDS, excluding the West and ignoring notions of moral and historical legitimacy. Instead, the commission was content to hammer home its messages of the political illegitimacy of the GDR and the responsibility of the SED.

The Limits of the Inquiry

Although the PDS called for the commission to examine the entirety of Germany's twentieth-century history was not supported by the other parties, and there was general agreement from the beginning that the commission's brief was to address the postwar period.[3] Yet it would have been highly questionable simply to investigate postwar developments without reference to the previous era; and the commission resisted the temptation to treat 1945 as a "Zero Hour" and sought to place postwar developments in their proper historical context by explaining how the occupation of the German territories had come about. In a paper that served as an introduction to the commission's discussion of GDR history generally and questions of responsibility in particular, historian and expert commissioner for the Christian Democrats Alexander Fischer emphasized that every discussion of postwar German communism must start from the premise that the Second World War—which Germany had unleashed—created the conditions for the USSR's position in, and hegemonic claims over German territory.[4] The commission firmly upheld this clear and emphatic attribution of ultimate German responsibility for defeat and occupation, and therefore at least for the preconditions of later division: if there had been no Third Reich, there would have been no German division and no GDR.[5]

After the emphasis placed on the national history of division during the commission's establishment, it would have been no surprise if the inquiry had investigated how Allied occupation and the Cold War had played out in both the East and the West. A comparative examination of the occupying powers' guidelines, their implementation, and the powers' interaction with German actors in the different zones might have sought to establish similarities and differences between East and West. Such an approach would have been particularly welcome given that comparative or synthetic historical studies of postwar developments were very much the exception, for the historiographies of West and East Germany had grown increasingly distinct during the years of division.[6] It might also have helped to engage with PDS arguments about the legitimacy of the East German path, as Democratic Socialists frequently argued that sociopolitical measures taken in the SBZ conformed to the Potsdam Agreement, and were thus legitimate.[7] However, PDS and others' calls for the commission to consider developments in eastern *and* western Germany fell on deaf ears.[8] The commission did not seek to explore or explain the creation of two separate states in a comprehensive fashion and did not consider the causes, course, or even consequences of the broader Cold War for German developments to any great extent, beyond inner-German relations.

The commission's focus—as its title and mandate indicated—was on the SBZ and GDR. When the inquiry did consider the western zones and the early Federal Republic, it did so superficially and uncritically, tendentiously seeking to portray the FRG in a positive light and the GDR in a negative one. It tended to see western developments as natural or necessary and therefore requiring no explanation, and did not interrogate either the role of the occupying powers or the contribution of West German actors. The development of a market economy and multiparty parliamentary democracy in the West—neither of which simply came into existence as ready-made entities in 1948 or 1949—was effectively ignored, and historical and historiographical conflicts were glossed over.[9] For the commission majority, the Federal Republic amounted to an automatic and almost flawless success story and the only legitimate answer to past Nazi and contemporary communist totalitarianism.[10]

The Foundation of the SED between Consensus and Force

This uncritical approach to the West and the asymmetrical approach to the frequently invoked "shared" history of division were eagerly exploited by the PDS and unwittingly strengthened impressions of victor's justice. Yet to suggest that the debate about East German history ran primarily along East-West lines is to ignore the central role of partisan disputes.[11] For example, the foundation of the Socialist Unity Party of Germany—brought about in the SBZ by the unification of the SPD and the KPD in April 1946—is one of the most interesting issues of debate about postwar German political history and constituted a recurring source of conflict in unified Germany.[12] The SED itself had cast the union of the two wings of the German workers' movement as a voluntary step and the historic solution to the fateful division of the Left that had resulted in the failure of the 1918–19 revolution and contributed to the Nazis' rise to power in 1933.[13] Such a positive assessment did not prevent the SED from pursuing a ruthless campaign from 1947 onward against *Sozialdemokratismus* (social-democratism), as the remnants of SPD mentalities and networks in the SED were derogatively termed.[14] In West Germany (and particularly among Social Democrats), the merger was generally regarded as amounting to a *Zwangsvereinigung* (forced unification), carried out against the will of the majority of Social Democrats. By the 1980s, however, the term *Zwangsvereinigung* had become somewhat unfashionable; using it was largely regarded as excessively anticommunist, although it still occurred.[15] After unification, the critical view regained its former prominence and the merger became regarded widely (outside the PDS) as one of a number of steps leading to the destruction of political opposition, the creation of a communist dictatorship, and the division of Germany. Within these general parameters, however, a range of interpretation existed.

How did the various political parties approach this complex and sensitive history, both in and around the commission of inquiry? Particularly given the subsequent marginalization and persecution of social-democratic elements in the SED, it is hardly surprising that Social Democrats tended to stress the undemocratic nature of the process, SPD opposition, KPD pressure and deceit, and coercion and persecution by the Soviet Military Administration in Germany (SMAD). Christian Democrats, Free Democrats, and Democratic Socialists, by contrast, emphasized SPD support for the merger, albeit for differing reasons. Christian and Free Democrats sought to inculpate the SPD in the formation of the SED and the establishment of its dictatorship, arguing that the fusion of the two parties weakened the position of the other bloc parties, the CDUD and LDPD. They pointed to the merger in order to distract from or relativize bloc-party complicity and sought to make political capital by highlighting the common ideological roots and political history of German social democracy and communism. The implication was that Social Democrats were at least co-responsible for the SED dictatorship. The PDS, meanwhile, sought to inculpate the SPD in order to legitimize the SED and the GDR by arguing that the merger indicated widespread support for antifascism and the socialist project in the SBZ and early GDR.[16]

The treatment of the SED's formation in the Bundestag debate on the inquiry's establishment highlighted the contrasting positions of the governing coalition and the SPD. In typical social-democrat fashion, Willy Brandt pointed to Social Democrats' struggle against the "forced unification" as evidence of their resistance against the communist regime and the severing of national unity.[17] Subsequently, Jürgen Schmieder (FDP) described the merger as one of the foundation stones of the Communists' monopoly on power and said that answers were needed to the question of whether it really had been forced.[18] Then—in addition to attacking the western SPD for its overly cozy relations with the SED in the 1980s—Wolfgang Schäuble (CDU) rejected SPD criticism of the bloc parties as hypocritical, and complained that Social Democrats never mentioned the role SPD members voluntarily played in the SED's foundation. Schäuble's broadside prompted an interjection from Peter Conradi (SPD), who, instead of addressing the substance of Schäuble's criticism, dismissed it out of hand as "an insult to the victims" of the forced merger.[19] Like Schäuble, Angela Merkel (CDU) also played off the "responsibility" of "large sections" of the SPD for the erection of the "socialist dictatorship" against that of bloc-party members who had failed to resist the pressure applied to them to conform.[20] These and other statements illustrated both the interest of the coalition in emphasizing Social Democrats' willing acceptance of the union and its wider consequences, and the interest of the SPD in playing down social-democratic support for it and drawing moral authority from reference to the victims. Although hardly discussed in the commission's early internal deliberations, the SED's foundation was included in the terms of reference, and the patterns of argumentation apparent in the Bundestag debate continued into the inquiry's work.

As the foregoing has already indicated, much of the debate between conservatives and Social Democrats focused on the term *Zwangsverei-nigung*. Indeed, the considerable dispute over this term was based less on substantial factual or interpretative disagreement—if one ignores the views of the PDS for the moment—than on political rhetoric.[21] For example, the authors of two expertise papers commissioned by the inquiry presented the foundation of the SED as a complex process relying on the interaction of numerous factors, including support and opposition in the SPD and coercion by the KPD and SMAD; they disagreed, however, on the appropriateness of the term. One author, Werner Müller, explicitly argued that the course of the merger and its accompanying phenomena justified the term, and he insisted that the union would never have been accepted in a process free from coercion and intimidation; the implication was that the vote for unification that had taken place was artificial and meaningless.[22] The other expert, Michael Richter, acknowledged that even the supporters of unity in the SPD had wanted a party that would uphold social-demo-cratic traditions and not the communist-dominated SED that eventuated, but he argued that the term *forced unification* was inappropriate because it both failed to take adequately into account the fact that many SPD members and functionaries had welcomed the parties' fusion, and ignored the "movement" from which the SED emerged. It was a forced unification, Richter insisted, only for those Social Democrats who opposed it; other Social Democrats who supported it themselves pressured their central committee and other party members.[23]

The dissonance over the merger—amongst scholars, but also between the SPD on the one hand and the CDU and FDP on the other—was thus one of differing emphasis reflected in rhetoric. Where Social Democrats referred to forced unification, conservative commentators tended simply to speak of the two parties' "unification" or "merger" (*Zusammenschluß*). The rhetorical nature of the terminological debate does not mean that it was insignificant, however, and on occasion the dispute became very heated. In 1995, CDU expert commissioner and historian-sociologist Man-fred Wilke coauthored an article in Germany's leading conservative news-paper, the *Frankfurter Allgemeine Zeitung*. He and coauthor Peter Erler rejected the view favored by Social Democrats and many historians that focused on the pressure applied to Social Democrats. Instead, they ar-gued, the merger must be seen as the *Unterwerfung im Einverständnis* (con-sensual submission) of the Social Democrats. Wilke and Erler concluded: "Without the socialist will for union and without the illusions over their own strength in the future unity party, the wild applause of the delegates of the 40th Party Conference of the SPD … cannot be explained." Wilke's and Erler's reasoning basically amounted to the familiar argument that it was "not only" the result of force, but also of "desires, illusions, and self-overestimations."[24] The article nevertheless provoked a number of very irritated letters to the editor, including one from the SPD party treasurer, who objected in particular to the term consensual submission, the only novelty in the article.[25]

Despite such controversies prompted by polemical attempts by conservatives to implicate Social Democrats in the erection of the communist dictatorship, the real conflict over the characterization of the SED's foundation, as might be expected, was between the two parties affected existentially by the issue: the SPD and the PDS. This conflict, too, played out both within and beyond the commission. At a public hearing on "The Transformation of the Party System" held in Bonn in November 1992, Dietmar Keller (PDS) asked Dieter Rieke, an eyewitness invited by the SPD, to estimate what proportion of Social Democrats and Communists had supported or opposed the parties' unification. The intention behind Keller's ostensibly reasonable question was clear from his prefatory comments, in which he implied that there was nothing unusual or illegitimate about what had occurred in the SBZ.[26] Rieke did not answer the question directly, saying only that two or three thousand of the ten or fifteen thousand Social Democrats in Magdeburg did not join the SED.[27] SPD expert commissioner Hermann Weber, however, did respond to Keller's question, insisting, rather nonsensically, that mere numbers of supporters and opponents were relatively insignificant, and, more plausibly, that something must have been terribly wrong with the merger because the KPD deceptively claimed to support parliamentary democracy but marginalized the Social Democrats within the new party.[28]

For all their differences over other issues and the rhetorical dissonance over the terms forced merger and consensual submission, a common front about the SED's foundation emerged between the governing coalition and the SPD, in opposition to the PDS. In a paper given at an internal commission meeting, Keller was highly critical of the SED but still upheld the rectitude of the party's foundation. He argued that the unification of the workers' parties was motivated and warranted by their shared experiences and traditions of antifascism dating from the Weimar Republic. Despite fears and tensions on both sides, he suggested, "The antifascist element was … so strong that it prevailed and led to the party."[29] Keller conceded that the unification of the democratic SPD and the undemocratic KPD in the Soviet-run SBZ could only ever have led to the dominance of hardened Moscow cadres and the marginalization not only of former Social Democrats but also of independent-thinking former KPD members.[30] He acknowledged that this outcome was lamentable, but still insisted that there had been nothing wrong with the attempt. The relative unanimity of the other parties when faced with divergent PDS views became clear in the subsequent discussion. A number of commissioners—including Christian Democrats—roundly rejected Keller's emphasis on and seemingly uncritical acceptance of antifascism as an explanatory factor, and instead highlighted the role of communist pressure.[31]

Ultimately, the merger of the SPD and the KPD could be seen as an example of coercion that fit into a larger picture of communist injustices and the establishment of the communist dictatorship, so that—with the exception of the PDS—the parties could largely agree on its interpretation. The commission's final report referred to the union as both merger and forced unification, without mentioning the debate over terminology.[32] The PDS dissenting report, on the other hand, avoided any mention of coercion, speaking merely of the two workers' parties being joined initially in "unity of action" and then merging in the SED.[33] The issue thus conformed to the increasingly familiar pattern of a mainstream anticommunist consensus standing in opposition to the lingering defensive antifascism of the PDS.

Dissonance over Bloc-Party Co-responsibility

The history of the parties that—together with the SED—had been members of the Unity Front of Antifascist-Democratic Parties in the SBZ and of the National Front in the GDR was expected to be one of the most contentious issues for the commission. The SPD, Alliance 90, and the PDS had every reason to highlight the compromised pasts of the eastern Christian Democratic Union of Germany (CDUD) and the Liberal Democratic Party of Germany (LDPD) and their continuities with the present-day CDU and FDP respectively. For the SPD, pointing to the bloc parties' responsibility could help distract from claims of social-democratic proximity to communism (whether in the context of the foundation of the SED, SPD-SED contacts in the 1980s, or SPD-PDS cooperation in the present). Alliance 90 and former members of the GDR opposition in other parties sought to highlight their own uncompromising opposition to the SED system, in contrast with the bloc parties' more ambiguous relationships. For the PDS, meanwhile, emphasis on the bloc parties' role was useful because it indicated that in the National Front the GDR had possessed a multiparty political system for which non-communists bore at least some responsibility.[34] The CDU and FDP, on the other hand, were naturally interested in an assessment of the bloc parties that, while critical of their role in the GDR, did not undermine the legitimacy of their fusion with their western counterparts in 1990.[35] The likelihood of conflict was thus substantial.

The few histories of the bloc parties that existed in the GDR had been published under the aegis of the parties themselves and were thus largely uncritical, shedding little light on their development over time or the influence of the SED and the SMAD. In GDR historiography there was a degree of ambivalence in the depiction of the Unity Front and later the National Front, as historians were torn between stressing the independence of the bourgeois parties (which in the early stages indicated the continuing class struggle, eventually won by the party of the working class, the SED), and emphasizing the degree of consensus within the bloc under communist "leadership" (thus granting it legitimacy). The few studies published in the Federal Republic made clear the role of two bloc parties in particular as "transmission parties" for the SED: the National Democratic Party of Germany (NDPD) and the Democratic Farmers' Party of Germany (DBD) had indeed been founded in 1948 on the initiative of the SMAD and were initially organized and run by former SED members delegated for that purpose. Whereas the history of the LDPD was relatively well researched in the FRG, the literature on the CDUD was comparatively sparse.[36]

With the unification of the bloc parties and their West German counterparts in 1990, the discussion of their past roles assumed new dimensions. Indeed, the varying degrees of responsibility of the bloc parties and the SED had been the topic of intense debate in the winter of 1989–90, when the SED-PDS accused leading bloc-party figures of unjustifiably passing sole responsibility for East Germany's dictatorial system to the SED.[37] The view expressed by prominent dissident Bärbel Bohley in 1989 that the bloc parties were "even worse" than the SED was hardly typical, but the derogatory term "bloc flutes" was used frequently to describe the parties' habit of playing along to the SED's tune.[38] As in other areas of GDR history, much attention has since been paid to the parties' resistance to SMAD and SED coercion, the persecution of their members, and their attitudes to the national question. The general scholarly consensus is that both the CDUD and the LDPD had been *gleichgeschaltet* (made completely conformist) by 1952 at the latest, and that subsequently they served as pliant transmission parties for the SED, as had been true of the NDPD and the DBD from the start.[39]

There was unanimity in the commission of inquiry that the bloc parties would be addressed, but this did not make their investigation any easier. The defensive and offensive intentions of the various parties were clear. On one side, former dissident Angelika Barbe (SPD) equated the bloc parties with the SED when she referred to "forty years of SED/bloc parties."[40] On the other side, Wolfgang Schäuble (CDU) rejected—to the applause of his coalition colleagues—the "bloc-flute discussion" since 1990 as "premature, supercilious, unjust," and he objected strenuously to the (nonexistent) impression that "only the so-called bloc parties were responsible for the injustice in the former GDR."[41]

To counter that (fictitious) impression, conservatives developed a narrative of CDUD history that sought to minimize the responsibility of Christian Democrats and that posited the party's early independence, its (resisted) transformation into a compliant source of support for the SED, and its ultimate retransformation into a democratic party in 1989–90.[42] At the commission's November 1992 hearing in Bonn on "The Transformation of the Party System 1945–1950," Konrad Adenauer Foundation representative Günter Buchstab sought to establish the CDUD's initial independence by differentiating three phases in its history: the "foundational phase" from 1945 until the end of 1947; the phase of its *Gleichschaltung* (being forced into line), beginning in 1946 and lasting until 1950–52; and its phase as a procommunist cadre party from the mid 1950s to the late 1980s.[43] Buchstab spoke further of the CDUD's "transformation" into a pliant party, a process that apparently had begun after the removal in late 1947 of noncompliant leaders Jakob Kaiser and Ernst Lemmer and their replacement with more communist-friendly apparatchiks.[44] As might be expected, such a narrative of transformation that presupposed an initial state of independence was strongly supported by conservative commissioners, who like Dorothee Wilms (CDU) insisted on the parties' "highly democratic origins."[45] In other statements, conservatives suggested that the parties had "reconnected" with these traditions in the late 1980s.[46]

While neither implausible nor completely inaccurate, this narrative of transformation and restoration was problematic on a number of counts, and was indicative of a widespread tendency amongst all parties, bar the PDS, to stress their rivals' and minimize their own past support for the GDR, socialism, and SED policy. First, it rested on a dubious premise, since it is debatable whether the bloc parties were ever completely independent. Buchstab himself indicated that the CDUD was at no stage able to implement an independent policy or question the framework prescribed by the SMAD, and other sympathetic experts highlighted the constraints imposed even at the parties' foundation.[47] In numerous accounts, the parties were depicted as having been "practically founded into the bloc" (*hineingegründet*), such that bloc membership was intrinsic to their very existence.[48] Secondly, there was a questionable conservative tendency to lengthen the supposed period of initial independence, which in some depictions lasted until 1950 or 1952.[49] Similarly, Buchstab's suggestion that the CDUD's transformation began only after the removal of Kaiser and Lemmer was illogical, for their removal—and indeed the earlier ousting of leaders Andreas Hermes and Walther Schreiber—should be seen as a central part of the transformation.

Thirdly, false premises for the narrative were also established when conservatives downplayed the commonalities between the various parties in the immediate postwar period. In particular, they minimized the antifascist and socialist dimensions to early Christian-democratic thought as well as bloc-party members' willingness to cooperate with German Communists and the Soviet authorities. When combined with a proclivity to magnify CDUD resistance and persecution, these tendencies created hard and fast distinctions between "democrats" in the CDUD on the one hand, and Communists on the other. Conservatives frequently failed to mention CDUD support for nationalization, and instead stressed (and on occasion distorted) the party's resistance to communist policies.[50] The CDUD's transformation into subservience was more complex than the narrative of heroic, albeit failed resistance of democrats allowed, since there was also a significant degree of cooperation between the bloc parties and Communists.[51] What is more, the suggested retransformation of the bloc parties into democratic parties in 1989–90 was also problematic.[52]

Many of the argumentative strategies employed here were reminiscent of the discussion of the SED's foundation, and a salient degree of hypocrisy was evident in the political parties' approaches to the two issues. Whereas Christian and Free Democrats emphasized the level of voluntary conformity and self-subjugation in the merger of the SPD and KPD, and Social Democrats stressed resistance and coercion, the emphasis was reversed when it came to the bloc parties. At a commission hearing, historian and SPD expert commissioner Bernd Faulenbach wondered to what extent the bloc parties' *Gleichschaltung* resulted from external pressure and to what extent they could be said to have conformed willingly.[53] CDU historian Fischer acknowledged that there was a degree of anticipation and acceptance of Soviet and communist power, but he stressed the differences between the party leadership—that initially resisted but eventually conformed—and the general membership that was more steadfast in its nonconformity.[54]

This distinction between the parties' corrupted, supplicant leaderships and their largely innocent broader memberships formed a key component of the narrative of transformation. It constituted an important argumentative strategy used by members of various parties to exonerate their memberships and their parties' historical legacies. Christian Democrats and Free Democrats made the distinction in relation to the bloc parties; Social Democrats drew it (albeit less frequently and forcefully) in relation to the foundation of the SED; and, as discussed below, the PDS pursued a similar strategy in relation to the SED. At the hearing on "The Transformation of the Party System," Christian Democrats immediately adopted Fischer's distinction between the leadership and the general membership. Buchstab emphasized its importance, while Reinhard Schorlemer (CDU) voiced his assumption that it would form the basis of the commission's further deliberations on the bloc parties.[55] This intimation proved to be accurate.

The distinction helped bridge the gap between those Christian Democrats who were highly critical of the bloc parties and those who were more sympathetic. As a genuine opponent of the SED system, Eppelmann detested the bloc parties' political and social function, seeing them as "fundamental prerequisites" of the SED dictatorship. He averred that, "After 1961 at the latest ... there was no longer a justifiable reason to join the bloc parties, as they had all agreed to the leading 'Party of the Working Class' ... condemning an entire people to life imprisonment on 13 August 1961 [with the Berlin Wall]."[56] Although Eppelmann had little time for the bloc parties, total condemnation would undermine the legitimacy of the 1990 amalgamation of the CDUD with Eppelmann's own Democratic Awakening and the western CDU. He therefore conceded that many party members and even officials at lower levels had tried to do their best under the circumstances, and acknowledged that the bloc parties had served as "niches" for people who did not want to be completely at the mercy of the SED but did not see "total refusal" as an option. Joining a bloc party thus constituted "a small compromise with the SED dictatorship," which relied on such "creeping minor corruption" of individuals.[57]

Related to the differentiation between the culpable party leadership and their innocent ordinary members was an unusual sensitivity among conservatives to the contingency of historical developments and in particular to individual and collective subjectivity. The discussion of the SED's foundation above showed that conservatives had little sympathy for the (unrealistic) optimism of Social Democrats, and subsequent sections and later chapters of this book will indicate that they frequently did not concern themselves with subjective hopes and expectations. Yet when discussing the bloc parties, conservatives displayed considerable readiness to acknowledge the impossibility of knowing what the future would hold, and they pointed frequently to hopes and optimism by way of mitigation. For example, in introducing the commission's hearing, "Encompassing and Binding People in the SED State: On the Role of Bloc Parties and Mass Organizations," held in Bonn in December 1992, Eppelmann referred to the "hope" of "many democrats" in 1945 that "a democratic new beginning" could be dared in Germany, a hope that led them to active engagement in the task of reconstruction.[58] Moreover, Eppelmann quite unusually qualified his highly critical characterization of the bloc parties as "offices of the SED only with their own company stamp," by stressing that this constituted his personal view alone and by acknowledging that it did not sufficiently capture the full extent of the phenomenon.[59] At the same hearing, invited expert Peter-Joachim Lapp emphasized that one had to understand that no one could predict the collapse of communism in 1989, and that in the mean time the bloc parties had offered their members "political niches for survival."[60]

Given the narrative of the bloc parties discussed so far, it is hardly surprising that conservatives saw their responsibility as minimal. According to Lapp, as non-communists, bloc-party members remained "clean and unburdened" of real responsibility and guilt.[61] Such argumentation inevitably drew the ire of the SPD and Alliance 90. Markus Meckel wondered whether Lapp's generous characterization did not also apply to a majority of the population and even to SED members.[62] Other commissioners objected to Lapp's designation of the CDUD as a *Stellvertreterpartei* (party of deputies), which they perceived as unacceptably minimizing its responsibility.[63] Gerd Poppe (B90) directly contradicted "the construction of a legend" since 1989, according to which bloc-party membership amounted to opposition.[64]

These heated discussions revealed a fundamental difference between the opposition parties and those in the governing coalition more sympathetic to the bloc parties: their point of comparison. Whereas the coalition sought to emphasize the bloc parties' differences from the SED, the opposition stressed their differences from the rest of the population and their similarities with the SED. Social Democrats and members of Alliance 90 pointed to the fact that the supposedly critical potential in the bloc parties was shared by the entire population and did not make the bloc parties special in any positive sense; indeed, they argued that the distinctiveness of the bloc parties was their greater complicity and responsibility than the general population, let alone genuine opposition groups. Where conservatives saw degrees of independence from the SED, their critics saw *vorauseilenden Gehorsam* (anticipatory obedience).[65]

While it could hardly be called a whitewash, the treatment of the bloc parties in the commission's final report can only be described as generous, as it tended to play down the parties' significance and effectiveness, while exculpating their memberships. The report emphasized that the parties were "dependent on the SED" and controlled by it, and were unable to "exert any independent influence" within the democratic bloc, a view that diminished their historical, political, and moral responsibility.[66] The report discussed at some length the parties' "stubbornness" and the maintenance of bourgeois "lines of tradition" and "values." It stressed, too, the differences between the CDUD and LDPD on the one hand and the NDPD and DBD on the other, seeing the latter as instruments of the SED against the former.[67] The CDUD and LDPD were thus cast in the role of victims of

SED policy. The report acknowledged that the parties' "societal function" was to transmit SED policy to various social groups in order to integrate them into the socialist state and social order; it also acknowledged that they served to control and limit potential sources of criticism.[68] According to the report, the parties' actual ideological influence was minimal, but they still worked to "stabilize" the system.[69]

Unsurprisingly, the report declared the difference between the general membership and the leaderships to be "of fundamental importance."[70] Membership of a bloc party indicated "formal evidence" of loyalty to the state, but should not be misconstrued as "real loyalty to the system of 'real existing socialism'"; instead, "distance from the system," it was suggested, correctly characterized "many members."[71] On the key question of political responsibility, the report maintained: "In evaluating the bloc parties, their completely different functions for the SED, for the functionaries of the bloc parties, and for the members must be considered. In assuming functions in subsectors and marginal areas of society they undoubtedly contributed to a certain stabilization of the political system of the GDR. However, on account of the factors discussed, one can talk only to a limited extent of responsibility for, and participation in the regime."[72] This assessment of the bloc parties' responsibility was generous, but still critical. Revealingly, the report immediately proceeded to stress that an "all-German identity" had existed in the LDPD and CDUD, as though continuing national sentiment was more important for an assessment of political responsibility than actual behavior in the GDR.[73]

Equally unsurprisingly, the SPD and Alliance 90/The Greens refused to accept this component of the report. Much of their dissenting minority vote did not directly contradict the majority view, but it set different emphases and used different yardsticks and more forceful language. Its main political thrust was the demand that the now unified CDU and FDP—like the PDS, and unlike the SPD and Alliance 90/The Greens —must confront and take seriously their shady East German histories and their financial, personnel, and other continuities with the old GDR parties.[74] The minority report contrasted the violent repression used during the "forced merger" of the SPD and KPD with the less violent installation of compliant leaders in the bloc parties.[75] It also questioned the parties' alleged "failure" to fulfill the functions allocated to them by the SED, arguing that they continued to perform important roles until 1989 by providing the regime with a democratic "alibi," facilitating the regime's contacts with the West, and "mobilizing" the population.[76] Again, the SPD and Alliance 90/The Greens compared bloc-party members unfavorably with those citizens who had belonged to no political party, and highlighted the similarities between the bloc-party and SED memberships.[77] The minority report's overall assessment was that the bloc parties had posed no danger to the SED and had done nothing to help overcome the dictatorship. The parties—and their functionaries in particular—therefore bore "co-responsibility for the injustices of forty years of GDR history."[78]

In its dissenting report, the PDS mentioned the bloc parties' "conscious support for the policy of the SED" and pointed to the legitimacy with which the bloc parties had endowed the GDR through their avowal of its independence and of the general goals of the construction of socialism and the preservation of peace.[79] The report stressed the antifascist commonalities among the programs of the various parties in 1945.[80] Even in 1989, the PDS insisted, the bloc parties were oriented toward socialism and the maintenance of a separate East German state. In contrast, the increasing involvement and eventual takeover of the eastern parties by their western counterparts was depicted as being unwanted and destructive of indigenous East German political activism, participatory democracy, and alternatives to capitalism.[81]

In conclusion, one can see that the political parties each sought to stress their rivals' past support for the GDR, socialism, and the policy of the SED. The PDS sought to lend retrospective legitimacy to the East German state and to SED policy by stressing Social Democrats' and the bloc parties' erstwhile support. The other parties, in contrast, hoped to discredit their rivals with the communist brush. Where conservative commissioners stressed Social Democrats' willingness to join the SED, Social Democrats stressed the bloc parties' contribution to the stability of the GDR. At the same time as pointing to their rivals' compliance, the CDU, FDP, and SPD sought to emphasize their own (or their predecessors') opposition to, and resistance against the SED, the GDR, and national division. The difference between the debate within the commission over the 1946 merger and that over the bloc parties—with more considerable disagreement and dissent over the latter—can be explained by the fact that the SPD's vulnerability on the former issue was limited. The event was long past and was mitigated by the marginalization and persecution of Social Democrats within the SED. In contrast, the bloc parties had proved to be increasingly compliant components of the dictatorial system over its entire duration, making the question of present-day continuities with the past more significant, and thus raising the political stakes of the debate.

A Dictatorship from the Very Beginning

In Germany after unification, there was little debate about whether the GDR constituted a dictatorship, since this characterization was held by most commentators to be beyond dispute. There was, however, consider-able disagreement about what sort of dictatorship, and precisely whose dictatorship it had been. Historians and social scientists vigorously dis-cussed whether the GDR is best described as a *totalitarian*, an *autalitar-ian* (a combination of totalitarian and authoritarian), a *post-totalitarian*, a *Stalinist*, a *modern*, or a *welfare* dictatorship, among others.[82] Isolated voices questioned how helpful such terms were, and the extent to which they captured the reality of life in East Germany, but did not dispute the re-gime's dictatorial character.[83] While debates in the political sphere were not as refined or subtle as these scholarly efforts to characterize the GDR, a similar pattern was evident here: there was almost complete consensus over the GDR's dictatorial character, but some disagreement about further qualifications or characterizations, or about the sufficiency of designat-ing the GDR a dictatorship. In both historiographical and public debates, another key question was whether the East German political system had constituted a dictatorship from the very beginning, or whether it is possi-ble to speak of democratic aspects and possibilities during the immediate postwar period. Official GDR historiography had emphasized the demo-cratic nature of this phase by referring to it as the "antifascist-democratic transformation."[84]

In the commission of inquiry, the dictatorial character of the GDR was not disputed. With the exception of the PDS, all of the parties referred to the GDR as a dictatorship in their motions for the creation of an inquiry.[85] In the Bundestag debate on the inquiry's establishment, members of every party—including the PDS—referred to the GDR as a dictatorship, albeit with various epithets and qualifiers attached; even PDS member Jutta Bra-band spoke of the "bureaucratic dictatorship."[86] The extent of the consen-sus surrounding the GDR's dictatorial character was further demonstrated by the fact that, as mentioned in chapter 1, there was no discussion within the inquiry about the appropriateness of including "SED dictatorship" in the commission's title, and the terms of reference repeated this designa-tion several times.[87] As Eppelmann argued, this was simply the conviction of those who formulated the document.[88]

Democratic Socialists did not question openly the GDR's characteriza-tion as a dictatorship, but they did object to what they perceived as the regime's criminalization and the reduction of the GDR past to the history of the dictatorial regime. During the Bundestag debate on the inquiry's establishment, Uwe-Jens Heuer (PDS) argued that focusing on the GDR qua dictatorship entailed reducing life in the GDR to "resistance, politi-cal persecution, church, going along, conformity, and lethargy," and in-sisted that "the very complex history of the GDR" was being limited from the start to one of injustice.[89] Such criticism exaggerated the extent of the problem, but was by no means entirely wide of the mark. Much scholarship on East German history since 1990 focused on political history, the workings of the regime, and its opponents, while the inclusion of social and cultural dimensions and everyday life has been a slow, difficult, and contested process.[90] Unsurprisingly, this applied even more to representations of the GDR in the political sphere. In the Bundestag debate on the inquiry's terms of reference, Heuer felt compelled to insist that "the GDR was state and society," and not just the former.[91]

More vigorous disagreement between the PDS and the other parties centered on the question of whether the GDR had constituted a dictatorship from the very beginning, or whether one could speak of "democratic elements" to political developments in the SBZ and the foundation of the GDR. This was a hotly contested issue after 1990. In the establishment debate, Angela Merkel (CDU) claimed that "most people experienced this state from the beginning onwards as that which it was: a dictatorship that rested on the use of violence."[92] By contrast, the PDS wondered whether there were not "positive experiences of a democratic renewal" between 1945 and 1949, including the first constitution of the GDR.[93] On this reading, a legitimate, auspicious beginning was deformed by the Cold War. Once again, the commission did not hesitate to assume a firm position in its terms of reference, which referred to the subjection of people living in East Germany to "almost six decades" of dictatorial rule.[94] This suggestion of an uninterrupted continuity from the Nazi to the communist dictatorship aroused the particular hostility of PDS members. In the Bundestag ratification debate in May 1992, Heuer and Andrea Lederer (PDS) explicitly rejected it, Lederer arguing that it "simply suppresses the democratic beginnings in the GDR [*sic*] after 1945."[95]

Most commissioners were averse to crediting either the "antifascist-democratic transformation" in the SBZ or the GDR itself with any democratic characteristics for fear of granting the socialist project in Germany's East some legitimacy. The famous statement attributed to Walter Ulbricht by communist renegade Wolfgang Leonhard—"It must look democratic, but we must have everything in hand"—was cited repeatedly at meetings and was included in the commission's report.[96] It succinctly summed up the coalition's interpretation of political developments in the SBZ as being directed by ruthless German Communists who had just arrived from Moscow to implement their plans to establish a communist dictatorship under the guise of an antifascist popular front. While there was certainly more than a degree of truth to this depiction, it was also overly simplistic, for it did not take into account the complex processes at work in the SBZ and the extent of conflict, and it ignored those socialists and Communists who had not been in exile, but had survived the Nazi regime in Germany (unlike Ulbricht and Leonhard).[97]

All too often, the commission concentrated on the plans of the communist leadership and on the ultimate form that political life in the GDR assumed, rather than on the *process* by which the latter was reached. Communist dictatorship thus appeared as the inevitable and desired outcome of communist planning, while wider national and international factors, historical contingencies, and the Cold War context retreated into the background. For example, CDU expert commissioner Manfred Wilke emphasized the importance of KPD plans for postwar Germany at a public hearing in November 1992. He cited comments from 1943–44 by leading communist functionary and later first President of the GDR Wilhelm Pieck, and quoted at length a talk given in Moscow in early 1944 by communist ideology expert Wilhelm Florin.[98] Wilke effectively portrayed the very formation of parties other than the KPD as nothing but a democratic fig leaf (a view that would seem to contradict the notion that the CDUD and LDPD were independent, democratic political parties between 1945 and 1947). Conservative commissioners clearly wanted the existence of communist plans to be seen as sinister and calculating, and they concentrated heavily on strategy and ideology to the neglect of other issues, including the actual realization of the intentions of communist leaders.[99]

The significance of these communist plans and the extent to which they determined what actually occurred in the SBZ/GDR are debatable. Whereas GDR historiography made a virtue of their existence, western historian Dietrich Staritz complained in 1985 that the GDR "still often appears as the product of a plan, as the result of an epochal calculation, that—drafted in Moscow as the war still continued—was unswervingly pursued, realized step by step."[100] In similar fashion, commissioners representing the SPD and PDS as well as numerous experts repeatedly cast doubt on conservatives' implicit equation of wartime or postwar plans with what actually happened in the SBZ/GDR, and insisted on the openness of developments, both objectively and, in particular, subjectively.[101]

Quite sophisticated views on the question of democracy in the SBZ were put forward for the commission to consider. According to an expertise paper on the party system in the SBZ by Michael Richter, democratic possibilities were heavily restricted from the beginning, subsequently reduced further, and only ever the result of the USSR's consideration of the western powers and its hopes to maintain influence over all of Germany.[102] This view was not incompatible with the strongly anticommunist view of the commission majority, but it was significantly more complex, because it addressed the tension between the establishment of the dictatorship and resistance against it. Hermann Weber also presented nuanced views that neither asserted that the SBZ was democratic, nor presupposed that the SBZ was a fully fledged dictatorship from the start.[103] Such a position more accurately reflected the prevailing scholarly consensus that dictatorial structures coexisted with democratic efforts in the early years, but that one could not speak of the GDR having a democratic "prehistory."[104]

Others sought to differentiate between objective realities and outcomes and the subjective meanings attributed to them by historical actors. Historian and expert commissioner for Alliance 90 Armin Mitter argued that "more consideration must be given to the independent weight [*Eigengewicht*] of political life in the SBZ." According to Mitter, there were genuine hopes for democratic development in the East, while democratic inadequacies in the western zones and later the FRG were exploited by the SED for its own purposes, until the reality of power in the East was brutally demonstrated in June 1953.[105] This view was entirely rejected by Fischer and Dorothee Wilms (CDU), who—in response to the figure mentioned by Mitter of thirty thousand westerners going to the GDR in its early years as a counterpoint to the tens of thousands of people who left for the West—claimed (a little like Weber in relation to SPD support for union with the KPD) that "statistics do not shed any light on the time back then."[106] Pointing to apparent deficiencies in the West and hopes invested in the East was rather unwelcome among the conservatives on the commission, even if it came from Alliance 90 rather than the PDS, and was intended for explanatory rather than polemical purposes.

The commission's overall approach effectively ignored the subjective question of what people other than leading Communists thought might happen or what they wanted to happen, and thus failed to do justice to the difficult matter, raised by Mitter, of hope. There is considerable evidence that optimism was widespread in 1945–46.[107] A range of views on this question was expressed before the commission. One witness spoke of his now seemingly illusionary beliefs that the SMAD would seek a good relationship with the population and not just rely on the SED, and that the LDPD could cooperate with the occupying authorities, beliefs that were finally shattered only with the GDR's foundation in October 1949, although the party had been "absolutely powerless" since 1946.[108] Another witness argued: "We should free ourselves today from the illusion that the beginnings in 1945 or 1946–47 allowed hope for democratic development. That was not the case."[109] Taken together these statements suggested that there were hopes, even though they were unrealistic. Yet the commission was not interested in discussing such hopes or the devastating effects of grasping that they were unrealistic, or in exploring the tension between the two witnesses' statements. It preferred, as shown below, to emphasize tales of repression and coercion, and Eppelmann suggested subsequently that examining GDR history in the commission during two legislative periods did not lead anyone to doubt the initial judgment that the GDR had been a dictatorship from the very beginning.[110]

The first inquiry's report did not address this question directly. It did not make clear from which historical point the commission would designate the regime in the SBZ a dictatorship. It referred only generally to the "establishment of the communist dictatorship in the Soviet Zone of Occupation" and to early SMAD and SED hegemony increasing successively.[111] The report certainly made no mention of democratic beginnings or hopes for democratic developments. Once again, the dissenting PDS minority report objected specifically to the depiction of a "seamless transition from one dictatorship to another," which it regarded as supported insufficiently by the evidence.[112] The PDS acknowledged, however, that by the time of the GDR's foundation, positive democratic tendencies had been abandoned, a view that represented a modest change from the defense of the 1949 constitution found in its 1992 motion.[113] But even this concession contained an insistence on democratic tendencies prior to October 1949 and—as the final section of this chapter shows—the PDS maintained its belief in the legitimacy not just of the "antifascist-democratic transformation" in the SBZ, but also of the GDR itself.

The SED's Dictatorship

The anticommunist interpretation of the East German regime, as a dictatorship from the very beginning that lacked any democratic possibilities, was thus pitted against the defensive position of the PDS that insisted precisely on democratic elements of the immediate postwar period and, somewhat waveringly, of the foundation of the GDR. Social Democrats and members of Alliance 90 sat somewhere between these two fronts. A further issue that was contested between the commission majority and the PDS was the question of whose dictatorship the GDR had been. After all, one of the commission's key goals was to establish responsibility for the dictatorship and its crimes.[114] Most commentators agree that—despite its Marxist-Leninist ideology and propaganda—the GDR never constituted the dictatorship of the proletariat or of the workers and peasants. The common view—and certainly that which dominated the commission and was shared by the SPD and Alliance 90 as well as the coalition—was expressed clearly in the inquiry's title: it had been the dictatorship of the SED.[115] The democratic-socialist minority, however, insisted that political power in fact had been held in the hands of a small leadership group within the SED and that therefore the GDR was much better characterized as the dictatorship of the Politburo. Democratic Socialists also emphasized the strictures of the Cold War and the role of the Soviet occupier, thus minimizing SED culpability. Like the notion of democratic beginnings, this fit into their overall rather apologetic interpretation that stressed the Stalinist deformation of a good start.[116]

The commission majority, in contrast, sought to emphasize the responsibility of German Communists in the KPD and then the SED. As discussed in the previous section, one central plank of the effort by conservative commissioners in particular to highlight the role of German Communists in establishing the dictatorship was to draw attention to the existence of plans developed by leading functionaries in exile in Moscow, the implication being that they had concocted the GDR even before war's end. Emphasizing these plans, however, ran the risk of minimizing the role of the USSR, underestimating the openness of Soviet thinking on the German question, and suggesting that the erection of a communist dictatorship had been a foregone conclusion. Such an approach was out of step with the overwhelming majority of research into the causes of the foundation of the GDR, according to which the foundation of a separate, socialist German state was not a long-standing goal of the Soviet leadership, but nevertheless a decision taken in Moscow, rather than East Berlin.[117]

The commission cannot be said to have minimized German Communists' dependence upon the Soviet Union. While there was substantial disagreement over the significance of wartime plans and over the conservative tendency to elide the distinction between their existence and what actually occurred in the SBZ, there was general agreement within the commission on the total dependence of the KPD/SED on the CPSU, at least until 1955, and its considerable dependence thereafter.[118] In internal introductory talks to the commission, both Fischer and Weber stressed this reliance. Fischer spoke of the German cadres' "utter dependency" on Stalin; he argued that their plans would have been inconsequential but for the Soviet leader's support and that they formed a "scruple-less power elite" on which Stalin could rely.[119] For its part, the PDS also acknowledged considerable dependency on Moscow.[120]

Interpretations and argumentative utilization of such dependency, however, differed widely according to political orientation.[121] Conservatives and Social Democrats stressed it in order to bring further into doubt the legitimacy of the unwanted foreign import of communism, and tended to portray the Communist leadership as national traitors performing the whim of a foreign imperial power. The PDS, on the other hand, questioned the far-reaching congruence of the interests of German and Soviet Communists as portrayed by others; instead they sought to exculpate the SED by emphasizing the Cold War context and the strictures of Soviet occupation, and by playing down the SED's room for maneuver.[122]

A further contentious issue concerning responsibility for the dictatorship in the GDR revolved around the distinction between the SED elite and the mass of the party membership. As already mentioned, Democratic Socialists distinguished repeatedly between the SED as a whole and the party leadership.[123] Dietmar Keller (PDS) ascribed to the party a "double character": it was simultaneously a mass party and a cadre party. On the one hand, he stressed its enormous membership, averaging two million members out of a total population of sixteen million. On the other, he emphasized that "in this party fewer and fewer people had more and more to say," and that a "hand-picked group" of less than one hundred people determined the party's fate.[124] Keller argued, too, that the Stasi was not—as propagated—the "Sword and Shield" of the party but that of the party leadership, which used it to control not just the state, but also the lower echelons of the party itself; and he stressed the extent of the diversity of views within the SED.[125] Although firm anticommunists themselves frequently also focused on the SED leadership and insisted on the distinction between leadership and membership in relation to the bloc parties, Keller's fellow commissioners from other parties expressed reservations about the exculpatory tendency of such arguments in relation to the SED.[126]

The first commission's final report did not mention explicitly the question of the realization of communist wartime plans for the postwar order, but it nevertheless adopted the rather reductive conservative approach. It cited Wilke's paper, but did not mention the caveats of other experts over the impossibility of drawing conclusions about postwar developments merely on the basis of wartime plans. Instead, it implicitly suggested that a direct correlation existed between the plans of the KPD leadership in Moscow exile and subsequent events in the SBZ/GDR.[127] It was clear, therefore, where responsibility was to be found.

The report also sought to emphasize the German Communists' dependence on Moscow without minimizing their culpability. Before stating that the SED dictatorship had only survived as long as it did "because the Soviet Union guaranteed its existence," the report claimed that the Soviet leadership "could rely on the German Communists of the Ulbricht leadership that actively participated in the continual extension of its hegemony. Even in the early years there was no sole responsibility of the Soviet Communists and certainly not in the later phases. The Soviet Union determined the general directions of policy, but their concrete development and execution were left to the GDR or SED leadership, whose responsibility is unambiguous."[128] This argument effectively countered the evasive PDS line and was generally supported by recent scholarship, although—as commissioners themselves repeatedly observed—precisely how the relationship between East Berlin and Moscow had functioned in specific cases still required further research.[129] The cited passage also indicated that the commission could not avoid making distinctions between the SED leadership and the mass of the party membership. At one point, the report stated that in reality the GDR had been ruled by a "dictatorship of the SED politbureaucracy" (*Politbürokratie*), which might suggest that PDS arguments had been successful.[130] Nevertheless, the commission continued to use "SED dictatorship" as its preferred and incessantly repeated designation for the GDR, and it was largely due to the Bundestag inquiry that this became a firmly established term in historical-political discourse in postunification Germany.[131] Whether the commission succeeded in its aim of shifting attention from the Stasi to the SED, however, is another question that is probably best answered negatively.[132]

Legitimacy and Illegitimacy in Postwar Germany

Throughout the 1990s, the PDS engaged in a difficult process of renegotiating its past and attempting to forge a political profile without abandoning its heritage, hence the ambivalence of its assessments of the GDR. Individual PDS representatives such as Dietmar Keller and Herbert Wolf assumed self-critical positions and expressed keen analytical views not too dissimilar from those of numerous Social Democrats, but the party as a whole clung uncritically to the legitimacy of the East German "attempt at socialism." Even those who—like Keller—accepted the regime's dictatorial character had reservations about the apparent reduction of the East German past to the history of the dictatorial regime. Keller insisted in the Bundestag debate on the commission's report that one could not simply dismiss the lives and hopes of those who had believed in and worked toward socialism as having lived in a prison, as Eppelmann was wont to do.[133] Other Democratic Socialists and the PDS minority report rejected the commission's finding that the SED had ruled for the length of its existence without the support of the majority of the population; instead, they pointed to popular support for the values and goals of the regime, thus countering the notion of fundamental political illegitimacy.[134]

Moreover, however critical they were of the GDR political system and however many apologies they made to the regime's victims—and Keller's in the final debate was the exception rather than the norm—even the more critical PDS representatives still insisted on the GDR's moral and, above all, its historical legitimacy, and occasionally also on its legal and political legitimacy.[135] The PDS minority report argued: "Both German developmental paths and the states that ensued were legitimate historically and in international law, morally, and politically," and that one cannot make one "sacrosanct" and "criminalize" the other.[136] Pointing in particular to the foundation of the two states, the PDS claimed, "It cannot be accepted that legitimacy is exclusively attributed to the parliamentary path into the Federal Republic of Germany, in which the crucial decisions could not however be made sovereignly by the population." For good measure, the party insisted again that both states had been founded legitimately, albeit not in self-determination, and that both were heavily influenced by their superpower patrons. The GDR had been politically and economically more dependent than the FRG, but both gained certain freedoms.[137]

The commission majority did not directly engage with PDS arguments about legitimacy. Indeed, as the commission had not examined the two states' foundation or their gradual acquisition of sovereignty and independence, it was in a poor position to do so. Yet in a final reflection on the inquiry's "Experiences, Insights, and Recommendations," the majority stressed that no one in the commission had questioned the application of the term dictatorship to the GDR and—with reference to the SED's failure to hold secret, direct elections according to proportional representation—it explicitly declared, "The GDR was—in all its phases of development until the fall of Erich Honecker—a state without democratic legitimation."[138] The report avowed that it was important to emphasize this fact precisely because the PDS dissenting vote pointed to the legitimacy of both postwar states.[139] Yet the majority report did not respond to the PDS notions of international, moral, or historical legitimacy, but contented itself with pointing to the GDR's lack of *democratic* legitimacy.[140]

A joint resolution in the Bundestag by the coalition parties, the SPD, and Alliance 90/The Greens to accept the commission's report again explicitly rejected the suggested equal legitimacy of the two German states and insisted, "Dictatorship is and remains illegitimate."[141] Going further than the report, the resolution declared, "The only legitimacy on which state order can rest is the constitutional provision, on the basis of human rights, of the liberal-democratic granting and control of state power."[142] This statement dismissed the possibility of other—moral or historical—sources of legitimacy, but again failed to engage specifically with the arguments of the PDS. Instead, the GDR was merely to be condemned as the illegitimate dictatorship of the SED. In his speech to the Bundestag on 17 June 1994, Keller responded by insisting again on the "historical legitimacy of a new beginning, of a different beginning after 1945" and "another alternative."[143] The commission's handling of the GDR's main source of historical and moral legitimation, antifascism, is the subject of chapter 5. For the moment, however, it is possible to conclude that, in the section of its work devoted to the functioning of and responsibility for the GDR political system, the commission majority was satisfied that it had deconstructed the GDR as the SED's illegitimate dictatorship. The only direct response to Keller in the remainder of the debate came from Konrad Elmer (SPD), who declared that it was important to recognize that the GDR did not have a free beginning, as Keller had suggested, and that a state with an unfree start was doomed to failure.[144] Elmer's statement neatly summed up the majority's position on East German political history.

Notes

1. Cf. Mählert and Wilke, "Die DDR-Forschung."
2. Here the abbreviation CDUD is used instead of the equally common CDU in order to distinguish the eastern from the western party of the same name. The original is maintained in quotations.
3. I: 12, 89.
4. Alexander Fischer, "Zwölf Thesen zur Geschichte der SBZ/DDR," II: 2994.
5. I: 208f.
6. Cf. Hermann Weber, *Die DDR 1945–1990*, rev., exp. ed. (Munich, 1999), 154.
7. Stefan Doernberg, "Zur Legitimät der beiden deutschen Wege nach 1945," in *Ansichten zur Geschichte der DDR* IV, eds. Dietmar Keller, Hans Modrow, and Herbert Wolf (Bonn, 1994), 125f.; Rolf Badstürmer, "DDR: zeitgeschichtlich erforschen oder 'aufarbeiten'?" in ibid., 99.
8. I: 13, 82f., 89, 115, 90, 129f.
9. To provide just one example, according to the commission's report, the eastern dictatorship "was erected," while the western democracy "emerged," I: 392.
10. On the western success story, see Axel Schildt, *Ankunft im Westen: Ein Essay zur Erfolgsgeschichte der Bundesrepublik* (Frankfurt am Main, 1999).
11. Yoder, "Truth without Reconciliation," 75; Andrews, "Grand National Narratives," 52.
12. Cf. Mary Fulbrook, *The Two Germanies, 1945–1990: Problems of Interpretation* (Basingstoke, 1992), 15. See Bernd Faulenbach and Heinrich Pothoff, *Sozialdemokraten und Kommunisten nach Nationalsozialismus und Krieg: Zur historischen Einordnung der Zwangsvereinigung* (Essen, 1998); Historische Kommission der PDS, "Zum Zusammenschluß von KPD und SPD 1946: Erklärung der Historischen Kommission vom Dezember 1995" (13 November 1995).
13. See Institut für Marxismus-Leninismus beim Zentralkomitee der SED, ed., *Die Vereinigung von KPD und SPD zur Sozialistischen Einheitspartei Deutschlands in Bildern und Dokumenten* ([East] Berlin, 1976); Weber, *Die DDR*, 179f. Cf. Andreas Dorpalen, *German History in Marxist Perspective: The East German Approach* (London, 1986), 477ff.; Wolfgang Leonhard, *Die Revolution entläßt ihre Kinder* (Cologne, 1955), 435f.; Raina Zimmering, *Mythen in der Politik der DDR: Ein Beitrag zur Erforschung politischer Mythen* (Opladen, 2000), 53; Heinrich August Winkler, "Kein Bruch mit Lenin: Die Weimarer Republik aus der Sicht von SED und PDS," in *Halbherziger Revisionismus: Zum post-kommunistischen Geschichtsbild*, eds. Rainer Eckert and Bernd Faulenbach (Munich, 1996), 11f., 17.

14. Cf. Weber, *Geschichte der DDR*, 83, 120; Beatrix W. Bouvier and Horst-Peter Schulz, "*...die SPD aber aufgehört hat zu existieren*": *Sozialdemokraten unter sowjetischer Besatzung* (Bonn, 1991).

15. See Reiner Pommerin, "Die Zwangsvereinigung von KPD und SPD zur SED: Eine britische Analyse vom April 1946," *Vierteljahreshefte für Zeitgeschichte* 36, no. 2 (1988): 319–25; Weber, *Die DDR*, 181f.; Peter Steinbach, "Die Erfahrungen der Arbeiterbewegung in Verfolgung, Widerstand und Exil," in *Sozialdemokraten und Kommunisten*, eds. Faulenbach and Pothoff, 41. More generally on changing attitudes within the SPD to postwar political resistance and persecution, see Friedhelm Boll, *Sprechen als Last und Befreiung: Holocaust-Überlebende und politisch Verfolgte zweier Diktaturen, Ein Beitrag zur deutsch-deutschen Erinnerungskultur* (Bonn, 2003), 274–334.

16. Cf. Hermann Weber, "'Hauptfeind Sozialdemokratie': Zur Politik der deutschen Kommunisten gegenüber den Sozialdemokraten zwischen 1930 und 1950," in *Halbherziger Revisionismus*, eds. Eckert and Faulenbach, 37f.; Weber, *Geschichte der DDR*, 71.

17. I: 36.

18. I: 45.

19. I: 65.

20. I: 110.

21. See Werner Müller, "SED-Gründung unter Zwang: Ein Streit ohne Ende? Plädoyer für den Begriff 'Zwangsvereinigung,'" *Deutschland Archiv* 42 (1991): 52–58.

22. Werner Müller, "Entstehung und Transformation des Parteiensystems 1945–1950," II: 2342, 2372.

23. Michael Richter, "Entstehung und Transformation des Parteiensystems 1945–1950," II: 2527.

24. Manfred Wilke and Peter Erler, "Grotewohl beschwor eine große und gewaltige Zukunft, Unterwerfung im Einverständnis: Die Vorgeschichte der Vereinigung von SPD und KPD in der Sowjetischen Besatzungszone," *FAZ*, 10 May 1995.

25. "'Zwangsvereinigung' ist die passende Bezeichnung," *FAZ*, 18 May 1995; "Nicht 'im Einverständnis,'" *FAZ*, 20 May 1995; "Von einvernehmlicher Unterwerfung der SPD keine Rede," *FAZ*, 14 June 1995.

26. "Die Veränderung des Parteiensystems," II: 71.

27. II: 74.

28. II: 81f.

29. Dietmar Keller, "Die Machthierarchie der SED-Diktatur," II: 3017.

30. II: 3014.

31. DBPa: Protokoll 24: 15. The debate about Keller's understanding of antifascism is discussed in chapter 5. Keller's talk—and particularly his claim that the SED lacked fundamental characteristics of "civilization" caused a storm of controversy within the PDS, II: 3013. See Dietmar Keller and Matthias Kirchner, eds., *Zwischen den Stühlen: Pro und Kontra SED* (Berlin, 1993). Wüstenberg incorrectly attributes the controversy to Keller's apology in the Bundestag debate on the commission's report, *Die politische Dimension*, 344 (fn. 463). As the publication date of Keller's book indicates, however, this would have the controversy preceding the statement that unleashed it. Cf. Barker, "'Geschichtsaufarbeitung' within the PDS," 86f.

32. I: 213.

33. I: 691.

34. Concerns that the bloc parties' assets provided them with financial and electoral advantage also prompted SPD calls for discussion of their role and of their unification with their western counterparts in 1990. See Bock, *Vergangenheitspolitik im Systemwechsel*, 389–97.

35. On the bloc parties' fusion with their western counterparts, see Roberts, *Party Politics*, 83–91; Alexander Thumfart, *Die politische Integration Ostdeutschlands* (Frankfurt am Main, 2002), 218–28, 236–43.

36. See Weber, *Die DDR*, 183ff.; Dorpalen, *German History*, 474ff.

37. Bock, *Vergangenheitspolitik im Systemwechsel*, 132.

38. Bohley cited by Michael Richter, "Rolle, Bedeutung und Wirkungsmöglichkeiten der Blockparteien—Die CDU," II: 2627. Cf. Christian von Ditfurth, *Blockflöten: Wie die CDU ihre realsozialistische Vergangenheit verdrängt* (Cologne, 1991).

39. Weber, *Die DDR*, 185f.

40. I: 127.

41. I: 65. Similarly, CDU expert Alexander Fischer insisted that the disparaging term "bloc flute" was inappropriate for the party, apparently at any stage of its history, II: 39. He even studiously avoided using the term bloc party.

42. The following analysis concentrates on the debate about the CDUD as the largest and most significant party, but the same also applies to the discussion of the LDPD. See Gerhard Papke, "Rolle, Bedeutung und Wirkungsmöglichkeiten der Blockparteien—Die LDPD," II: 2399–463.

43. II: 56f.

44. II: 57.

45. II: 334.

46. II: 327.

47. II: 56f.

48. II: 2519. According to Weber, even the notion of being "founded into the bloc" minimized CDUD freedom of action, responsibility, and closeness to the Communists, *Die DDR*, 169f. Cf. Klaus Schroeder, *Der SED-Staat: Partei, Staat und Gesellschaft 1949–1990* (Munich, 1998), 412.

49. See, for example, II: 2591, 2403.

50. See, for example, Fischer's magnification of CDUD opposition to land reform in 1945, "Der Einfluß der SMAD auf das Parteiensystem der SBZ am Beispiel der CDU," II: 37, which was contradicted at the same hearing by eyewitness and former CDUD member Erika Wolf, 42, 72.

51. See, for example, Rainer Eppelmann's reference to "the democrats" in the parties who were marginalized and persecuted, II: 279, or Fischer's stress on the (vain) efforts of liberal-democratic CDUD members to resist SMAD and KPD/SED pressure to conform, 33, 40.

52. According to Richter, in the late 1980s, the "Sleeping Beauty" of the CDUD awoke from her almost forty-year sleep, justifying the SED's long-held concerns about her, II: 2596. Richter acknowledged that the CDUD played no special role in the 1989 revolution, but argued that within weeks of the SED's repressive apparatus faltering, the CDUD *returned* to being an independent "people's party," 2631, 2638, 2604. Peter-Joachim Lapp argued that members remained orientated toward their democratic traditions, to which Mitter raised the objection that Lapp seemed to be depicting all members (including the leadership) as forming a niche and opposing the regime, 295, 298, 311.

53. II: 67f. Cf. Stephan Hilsberg, "Rolle und Funktion der Blockparteien und Massenorganisationen in der DDR," in *Die Partei hatte immer recht*, eds. Faulenbach, Meckel, and Weber.

54. II: 79.

55. II: 82, 71. Cf. Grünbaum, "Die Enquete-Kommission," 114.

56. II: 280f.

57. II: 280.
58. "Erfassung und Einbindung des Menschen im SED-Staat: Zur Rolle der Blockparteien und Massenorganisationen," II: 278f.
59. II: 279f.
60. II: 291.
61. II: 300.
62. II: 309.
63. II: 293, also 310f., 318.
64. II: 316.
65. Compare, for example, the views of Poppe and Siegfried Suckut, II: 332, 320f.
66. I: 233f., 236. Such argumentation was reminiscent of that used by Democratic Socialists about the SED's dependence on the CPSU to minimize their responsibility.
67. I: 233.
68. I: 235f.
69. I: 236, 234.
70. I: 237.
71. I: 238.
72. I: 239.
73. I: 239f. Cf. Schuller, "Bericht der Enquete-Kommission," 739f.
74. I: 247.
75. I: 241.
76. I: 242f.
77. I: 245f.
78. I: 246.
79. I: 704.
80. I: 688, 690.
81. I: 705.
82. See Ihme-Tuchel, *Die DDR*, 89–95; Ross, *The East German Dictatorship*, 19–44; Günter Heydemann and Christopher Beckmann, "Zwei Diktaturen in Deutschland: Möglichkeiten und Grenzen des historischen Diktaturenvergleichs," *Deutschland Archiv* 30, no. 1 (1997): 12–40. The notion of totalitarianism is discussed in chapter 6. For the other epithets, see, for example, Eckhard Jesse, "War die DDR totalitär?" *Aus Politik und Zeitgeschichte* 44, no. 40 (1994): 12–23; Jürgen Kocka, "The GDR: A Special Kind of Modern Dictatorship," and Konrad H. Jarausch, "Care and Coercion: The GDR as Welfare Dictatorship," both in *Dictatorship as Experience*, ed. Jarausch.
83. See Detlef Pollack, "Die konstitutive Widersprüchlichkeit der DDR, Oder: War die DDR-Gesellschaft homogen?" *Geschichte und Gesellschaft* 24, no. 1 (1997): 110–31.
84. Cf. Weber, *Die DDR*, 153; Ihme-Tuchel, *Die DDR*, 17 22.
85. I: 3f., 8, 18, 24.
86. I: 145, also 28f., 32, 44, 47, 88, 109, 118, 133f.
87. I: 154.
88. Author's interview.
89. I: 81f.
90. See Thomas Lindenberger, "Everyday History: New Approaches to the History of the Post-War Germanies," in *The Divided Past: Rewriting Post-War German History*, ed. Christoph Kleßmann (Oxford, 2001).
91. I: 174.
92. I: 110.
93. I: 13.

94. I: 154.
95. I: 174, 176. Cf. Gerhard Lozek, "Zum Diktaturvergleich von NS-Regime und SED-Staat: Zum Wesen der DDR im Spannungsfeld von autoritären und totalitären, aber auch demokratischen Strukturen und Praktiken," in *Ansichten* IV, eds. Keller, Modrow, and Wolf, 117f.
96. II: 3000; also 795, 368, 422, 2514; I: 211, 243. See Leonhard, *Die Revolution,* 365.
97. Cf. Norman N. Naimark, *The Russians in Germany: A History of the Soviet Zone of Occupation, 1945–1949* (Cambridge, MA, 1995), 11; Gareth Pritchard, *The Making of the GDR 1945–1953: From Antifascism to Stalinism* (Manchester, 2000).
98. Manfred Wilke, "Konzeptionen der KPD-Führung 1944/45 für das Parteiensystem in der SBZ und der Beginn ihrer Umsetzung," II: 14–22, esp. 17–21.
99. Wilke did not discuss the implementation of the KPD's plans as his paper's title suggested he would.
100. Dietrich Staritz, *Geschichte der DDR 1949–1985* (Frankfurt am Main, 1985), 10. Cf. Dorpalen, *German History,* 474; Weber, *Die DDR,* 169f., 174.
101. II: 67, 2328, 2510f., 2994, 3003f. DBPa: Protokoll 6: 16. Author's interview with Weber; Badstübner, "DDR: zeitgeschichtlich erforschen oder 'aufarbeiten'?" 89f.
102. Richter, "Entstehung und Transformation," II: 2510f., 2518, 2521.
103. See Hermann Weber, "Entwicklungsphasen der DDR-Geschichte," II: 3007. DBPa: Protokoll 6: 12; VII: 26. Weber's critical sensitivity derives in part from his personal experiences. See Weber, *Damals, als ich Wunderlich hiess.*
104. Cf. Ihme-Tuchel, *Die DDR,* 22; Hermann Weber, "Gab es eine demokratische Vorgeschichte der DDR?" *Gewerkschaftliche Monatshefte* 43, no. 4–5 (1992): 272–80.
105. DBPa: Protokoll 6: 10f.
106. DBPa: Protokoll 6: 11.
107. See, for example, Leonhard, *Die Revolution,* 388–97.
108. II: 50ff.
109. II: 74. See also 68f., 46; VII: 44, 114f., 74, 16f. Each of these statements suggested that, prior to the changes described, a democratic party system—or at least justified hopes for one—had existed.
110. Author's interview.
111. I: 208.
112. I: 682.
113. I: 719.
114. I: 155.
115. Cf. Ross, *The East German Dictatorship,* 20.
116. Author's interview with Wilke. Cf. Ross, *The East German Dictatorship,* 27; Cooke, *Representing East Germany,* 49.
117. See Ihme-Tuchel, *Die DDR,* 13–17.
118. Cf. Ihme-Tuchel, *Die DDR,* 4. Revealingly, the question of dependence is not regarded as a controversy worthy of inclusion in Ihme-Tuchel's account of historical controversies. That said, for Weber the extent of SED's room for maneuver was the most interesting question (author's interview).
119. II: 3002, 2999, 3001.
120. I: 14, 695.
121. Despite the apparent consensus over the importance of KPD/SED dependence on Moscow, when it came to naming the subcommittee to deal with the international constellation and inner-German relations, Wilms (CDU) rejected Meckel's proposal of "Soviet influence, international conditions, and inner-German relations," arguing that

it gave excessive prominence to Soviet influence. DBPa: Protokoll 9: 4. The CDU wanted "inner-German relations" to be the key phrase. Consequently, the shorthand term for this group (and the three volumes of materials it produced) was *Deutschlandpolitik.*

122. See I: 11, 13f. BDPa: Protokoll 3: 14. This was in marked contrast with East German historiography, which maintained that the transition from imperialist capitalism to socialism in the SBZ/GDR was largely the product of the struggle of the German working class and peasantry under the vanguard of the KPD/SED in *partnership* with the occupying power. Cf. Dorpalen, *German History,* 466f., 470. See also Ulrich Neuhäußer-Wespy, "Aspekte und Probleme der Umorientierung in der Geschichtswissenschaft der DDR von 1971/72," in *Geschichtswissenschaft in der DDR* I, eds. Alexander Fischer and Günther Heydemann ([West] Berlin, 1988), 82–88. By the same token, as Peter Thompson points out, the anticommunist position that now emphasized the role of the SED stood in contrast with previous (western) depictions that highlighted Moscow's responsibility, "The PDS: Marx's Baby or Stalin's Bathwater? or Vom Nutzen und Nachteil der Historie für das Leben der PDS," in *The GDR and its History,* ed. Barker, 104.

123. I: 15, 88f. DBPa: Protokoll 3: 14.

124. II: 3015.

125. II: 3030, 3022. DBPa: Protokoll 70: 9.

126. DBPa: Protokoll 24: 16. Author's interview with Martin Gutzeit.

127. I: 211.

128. I: 212f.

129. DBPa: Protokoll 6: 15; Protokoll 7: 19. Cf. "Der persönlichen Verantwortung nachspüren," *Woche im Bundestag,* 11 June 1992; Ihme-Tuchel, *Die DDR,* 4.

130. I: 740.

131. Author's interview with Kowalczuk. Cf. Maser, "Auf dem Weg zur deutschen Einheit," 71; Wilke, "Der Historiker und die Politik," 92.

132. Cf. Annette Weinke, "Der Umgang mit der Stasi und ihren Mitarbeitern," in *Vergangenheitsbewältigung,* eds. König, Kohlstruck, and Wöll; Ernst Wurl, "Die 'SED-Diktatur': Überlegungen im Kontext einer Kritik des Begriffs aus dem Bericht der Enquete-Kommission des Deutschen Bundestages," in *Ansichten zur Geschichte der DDR* V, eds. Jochen Černý, Dieter Lehmann, and Manfred Neuhaus (Bonn, 1994); Vergau, *Aufarbeitung von Vergangenheit,* 103, 179.

133. I: 814.

134. See the lengthy section in the dissenting report on the "acceptance" (note: not legitimacy) of the GDR in a variety of fields, I: 714-29. See also Walter Friedrich, "Regierte die SED ständig gegen die Mehrheit des Volkes?" and Stefan Bollinger, "'Geschichtsaufarbeitung': Machtinstrument oder Erkenntnishilfe? Einige Anmerkungen," both in *Ansichten* V, eds. Černý, Lehmann, and Neuhaus. Cf. Ross, *The East German Dictatorship,* 105f.

135. I: 813.

136. I: 692.

137. I: 691, 695. Cf. Badstübner, "DDR: zeitgeschichtlich erforschen oder 'aufarbeiten'?"; Doernberg, "Zur Legitimität"; Harald Neubert, "Die Vorgeschichte der deutschen Zweistaatlichkeit im internationalen Bedingungsgefüge (Thesen)," in *Ansichten* V, eds. Černý, Lehmann, and Neuhaus.

138. I: 738, 740.

139. I: 740.

140. Similarly, another brief discussion of the GDR's lack of legitimacy in the report's section on inner-German relations spoke of "inner legitimacy," understood basically as political legitimacy, I: 492.

141. "Entschliessungsantrag zum Bericht der Enquete-Kommission—Drucksache 12/7820," I: 783.
142. Ibid.
143. I: 814f.
144. I: 872.

Chapter 4

IMPLEMENTING AND RESISTING SOCIALISM IN THE GDR

The political parties did not just play politics with questions about the legitimacy of the GDR and responsibility for the dictatorship, but also with socialist ideology. The regime's ideological foundations occupied a central place in the commissions' deliberations, a dimension of their work—indeed of Germany's postcommunist transitional justice in general—that has not been properly appreciated.[1] Through the inquiries, Christian Democrats and Free Democrats sought not just to condemn the GDR as the illegitimate dictatorship of the SED, but also to discredit socialism generally. They argued that the GDR constituted the fulfillment of Marxist ideology, and that the disastrous results demonstrated that history had refuted Karl Marx and his followers. Their condemnation of socialism was directed not just historically at the GDR, but against anyone who adhered to the goal of socialism in the present, like the PDS, or had historical ties to Marxism, like the SPD. Conservatives thus sought to delegitimize any past, present, or future socialist alternative to or even critique of the prevailing "free, democratic basic order" of the Federal Republic. The PDS, by contrast, defended if not the reality of the East German political system then at least the legitimacy of the attempt to construct a socialist society, even if it had failed. The implication was that a future effort might one day succeed. The commissions thus by no means involved merely a retrospective examination of postwar history or a partisan competition over historical traditions—or, in the case of the PDS, a defense of East German biographies—but were intimately connected with ideological projects in the present.

The reappraisal of Germany's postwar history thus constituted an ideological battle, for which the parties' historical narratives provided ammunition. The political imperative frequently made for bad history. In its determination to claim final victory in the ideological contest between socialism and capitalism and seal the "end of history" in Francis Fuku-yama's sense, the conservative majority's staunch anticommunism trans-mogrified into a simplistic antimarxism with the help of some problematic argumentation whose political intent was all too apparent.[2] In response to conservative arguments that sought to discredit any variant of socialism, Democratic Socialists, Social Democrats, and, to a lesser extent, members of Alliance 90 insisted on the need for the observation of some basic meth-odological virtues that were often neglected by the conservatives' zealous antimarxism. Social Democrats themselves occasionally adopted rather defensive and inconsistent historical positions, while Democratic Social-ists simply asserted the legitimacy of the GDR's "attempt at socialism."

Competing understandings of ideology and socialism were also central to the inquiry's deliberations on resistance and opposition in the GDR. Like its anti-Nazi equivalent, the legacy of East German opposition and resistance were vigorously contested, since resisting dictatorship con-veyed legitimacy and demanded respect. Defining opposition, resistance, dissidence, and related phenomena is a difficult undertaking, which was instrumentalized frequently for political purposes. The various parties sought to maximize the extent of their own opposition. The previous chapter demonstrated this with regard to Social Democrats in the context of the "forced unification" of the SPD and the KPD, and Christian and Lib-eral Democrats in the context of the "forcing into line" of the bloc parties. This chapter shows that the PDS pointed in similar fashion to opposition circles and dissident thought within the ruling party. In addition to claim-ing the legacy of opposition for themselves, political actors also sought to restrict their rivals' access to the legitimatory power of opposition status. Conservatives in particular argued that only those who had opposed the GDR per se and who had favored national unification warranted accla-mation, whereas the parties of the Left insisted that much oppositional activity in the GDR had been directed at democratizing and reforming socialism, and that this, too, deserved recognition. This competition over the past represented the continuation into the postunification era of ideo-logical and political disputes that in some cases were decades old. It dem-onstrated again that the lines of division over the East German past did not run between easterners and westerners, but cut across the former German-German border.

A Socialist Dictatorship: Dictatorial Socialism?

Interpretations of the GDR's relationship with socialist ideology had direct implications for the legitimacy of the parties' political programs and identities in the present. As well as seeking to discredit the SBZ/GDR as an illegitimate dictatorship from the very beginning, for which the SED was responsible, the governing conservative parties had an ideological interest in condemning not just the former regime's practice but also its ideological underpinnings. In addition to the SED dictatorship itself, Marxism-Leninism, Marxism more broadly understood, and indeed the general goal of socialism were all to be excoriated. For the coalition parties, the historical narrative that supported such condemnation was self-evident: the GDR had constituted the authentic realization of socialist ideology, and its failure should therefore discredit completely the ideology in whose name it had been erected. As might be expected, Democratic Socialists saw things rather differently. They argued that what had been established in East Germany was a distortion, rather than the realization of socialism, and suggested that while this attempt had failed, others might succeed. They insisted on the legitimacy of hopes for a socialist alternative to capitalism, whether in the late 1940s, late 1980s, or early 1990s.

Social Democrats and members of Alliance 90 were caught in the middle of this ideological conflict between PDS defensiveness and conservative antimarxism: both parties sought to condemn the SED dictatorship as severely as the conservatives, but they also felt compelled to defend their own traditions and assert the legitimacy of past hopes for socialism. The SPD insisted on distinctions between GDR communism and Marxism-Leninism on the one hand, and Marxism understood more broadly on the other; Alliance 90 meanwhile defended the GDR opposition and its contribution to "1989" against conservative criticism that many dissidents had not broken with socialist dreams and only wanted a reformed but still socialist GDR.

The coalition parties called early on for the inquiry to analyze and evaluate not just the "historical causes and the surrounding conditions" of the East German dictatorship, but also its "ideological roots."[3] Western conservatives were particularly keen to include ideology in the inquiry's brief. CDU General Secretary Volker Rühe, for example, expressed his hope that the commission would demonstrate "why the ideology of socialism had to lead to a system that was so contemptuous of people."[4] In the Bundestag establishment debate, Roswitha Wisniewski (CDU) advocated an expansive "critique of Marxism," arguing that to understand a historical phenomenon "one has to try to recognize the roots and the goal out of which it arose, and in order to avoid similar negative developments for the future in this case the critical discussion of the ideology of the GDR is unavoidable."[5]

In comparison with such keen conservative interest, Social Democrats and members of Alliance 90 were reserved on the question of ideology, and sought to limit its anticipated discussion by the inquiry. Neither party's motions for the commission's establishment referred to the issue, although Gerd Poppe (B90) called for the investigation of ideology's particular role as an instrument of rule in the GDR.[6] Similarly, Hermann Weber insisted on behalf of the Social Democrats that one could not examine the whole complex of Marxism-Leninism (let alone Marxism more broadly), but only its role in the GDR.[7] The coalition parties accepted this position for the terms of reference, but conservatives still favored a wider discussion involving a broad "critique of ideology."[8]

The commission's handling of the topic revolved around two central questions: the possibility and/or necessity of differentiating between Marxism and Marxism-Leninism, and the extent to which either of these was put into practice in the GDR. The conservative position on these questions was unequivocal. First, conservatives either simply did not distinguish between socialism and communism, or between Marxism and Marxism-Leninism, or argued explicitly that it was impossible to establish clear-cut distinctions between them. Marx and Engels, after all, had been hostile to parliamentary democracy and advocated revolution and the dictatorship of the proletariat.[9] Second, conservatives suggested that Marxism had been implemented dutifully in the GDR, and they concluded that the practiced reality demonstrated that the ideological foundations were fundamentally flawed.

These arguments were directed at anyone claiming to be a socialist or Marxist, particularly the "democratic socialists" in the PDS, but also reform socialists amongst the GDR opposition. In light of conservatives' emphasis on the bloc parties' opposition to socialism and the GDR, they can be seen as an attempt to delegitimize leftist protest movements in the East and claim the moral high ground for the Right. As Wolfgang Mischnick (FDP) argued in the Bundestag debate on 12 March 1992, those who only wanted a better socialism had failed to recognize that "the whole system—its ideological basis—was wrong."[10]

Like their conservative opponents, Democratic Socialists spoke frequently of socialism rather than communism. However, where conservatives ignored or downplayed distinctions among socialism, Marxism, Marxism-Leninism, and Stalinism, Democratic Socialists insisted on these very distinctions. They criticized Stalinist "deformations" and even central tenets of Marxism-Leninism, yet defended the underlying "attempt at socialism." For example, the PDS motion for the establishment of an inquiry distanced itself from the SED's official Marxism-Leninism by placing it in quotation marks, but clung to the legitimacy of an indeterminate "socialist alternative" to Germany's disastrous history, and insisted on unspecified East German "achievements and values."[11] In the Bundestag debate, Uwe-Jens Heuer (PDS) and his party colleagues claimed that they had always been, and still were, in favor of a *democratic* socialism.[12]

Democratic Socialists also insisted on distinctions between ideology and practice in the GDR. The PDS motion alluded to a gap between Marxist-Leninist "aspirations" and East German "reality."[13] Heuer insisted that his political opponents did not criticize the SED and the PDS for real mistakes or actual injustices, "but for undertaking this attempt at all": "For the political forces that see in capitalism the end point of history, the conclusion from the attempt at socialism in the GDR stood and stands firm: There may never be such an attempt again, even one with a human and democratic face. Those involved in this attempt must be morally disqualified and punished."[14] The conclusion of socialists on the other hand, Heuer averred, was different: merely the concepts of the dictatorship of the proletariat and of the command economy were dead.[15] Heuer declared that—in the face of the "general condemnation of the GDR and the attempt at socialism made in it"—the PDS would continue to argue that "the efforts of millions of people for the construction of a different social order to overcome the fascist legacy require no apology."[16] Honorable hopes—whether past or future—should not be disqualified on the basis of problematic reality or faulty realization.

In contrast to conservatives' condemnatory and Democratic Socialists' defensive use of the terms socialism or socialist, Social Democrats and members of Alliance 90 generally avoided them. Neither party's motion for the establishment of an inquiry used them. In the Bundestag debate, again, the words socialism or socialist were not uttered by a single Social Democrat; Marx and Lenin were also hardly mentioned. Yet members of both parties—and in particular Social Democrats—soon felt compelled to respond to conservatives' expansive antisocialist rhetoric, not least because it was frequently directed explicitly against the West German Left, and not just the GDR.[17] Like the PDS, the SPD insisted on the distinction between Marx and Engels on the one hand and Lenin and Stalin on the other; it also argued that Marxist-Leninist ideology was not simply realized in the GDR, and that it served several purposes for the GDR's rulers. These questions remained the subject of an ongoing dispute between Christian Democrats on the one hand and Social Democrats (and Democratic Socialists) on the other. The contrasting positions were clearly drawn from the beginning of the inquiry's term and changed very little during its tenure.

Conservatives did not distinguish between various versions of socialist ideology and argued that Marxism had been realized in the GDR with disastrous consequences. In the Bundestag debate of 20 May 1992 on the ratification of the inquiry's mandate, Dorothee Wilms declared for the CDU that ideology constituted the "foundation stone … for everything that happened first in the SBZ and then in the GDR. That is why we will and we must discuss it. Theory and practice cannot be torn apart. The practice followed the prescribed theory."[18] At a commission hearing on "Marxism-Leninism and the Social Transformation in the SBZ/GDR," held in Bonn in February 1993, Commission Chair Rainer Eppelmann opened with a statement that, as usual, did not just introduce the topics and questions to be considered, but already proffered an answer. Eppelmann argued that Marxism and Marxism-Leninism were directed toward practice and not just theory, and suggested that the theory should therefore be judged to have failed because the practice had done so.[19] Roswitha Wisniewski (CDU) argued even more explicitly that "real existing" socialism in the GDR constituted the realization of Marxist theory and of Marxism-Leninism.[20] The implication was that these traditions were criminal and should be abhorred.

The comments by Eppelmann and Wisniewski and the latter's subsequent suggestion that history had refuted Marx's theories indicated that conservatives did not acknowledge distinctions between Marxism and Marxism-Leninism, and that in fact their main concern was a critique of Marx.[21] This became abundantly apparent at the same public hearing when expert witness and right-wing political scientist Konrad Löw pursued the question "Was the GDR Marxist?" by providing a string of quotations from Marx and Engels speaking favorably of the "dictatorship of the proletariat" and unfavorably of parliamentary and democratic institutions and states.[22] Löw did not address the question of whether their writings could be seen as the root cause of developments in the SBZ/GDR. Indeed, he said virtually nothing about the GDR, but merely implied that the theorists' antidemocratic and pro-dictatorial comments corresponded with the later GDR reality.[23] Rather than trying to explain the latter, Löw's main aim was to demonstrate that Marx was a *Vorkämpfer* (early activist) for totalitarianism, and that the only reason that he was still regarded positively by some was that he himself had never come to power; according to Löw, this constituted the fundamental reason for the difference in the historical evaluation of Marx and Adolf Hitler.[24] A report written by Wisniewski had much the same argumentative drive and methodological weaknesses.[25]

If conservative positions on the two central questions of differentiation and realization were intertwined closely, the counter positions of the moderate and radical Left were more distinctly delineated. Social Democrats and, to a lesser extent, members of the PDS and Alliance 90 advanced a range of arguments against conservative assumptions or assertions that the GDR had represented the realization of Marxism. At the Bonn hearing, Hermann Weber pointed out that the GDR's self-descriptions—as democratic or antifascist—were generally viewed with skepticism and that the same should apply to its Marxist-Leninist pretensions; that is, one should not accept at face value its claims of having realized Marxist-Leninist theory.[26] Furthermore, social reality in the GDR—a report that Weber coauthored with commission secretariat member Lydia Lange suggested—was "the result of an ensemble of conditions and political transformations."[27] It was far too complex to be simply predicted and shaped according to Marxist-Leninist ideology and could not be regarded as nothing more than the "result of the application of Marxism-Leninism" as conservatives claimed.[28] According to Weber at the Bonn hearing, theoretical ideological positions had been less important in the GDR than the "strict adherence" to the Stalinist system of power in which "ideological concepts were reduced to legitimation, [while] the main goal became gaining power and holding power enduringly."[29] Furthermore, he insisted, ideology was used retrospectively to justify policies that were already being or had already been pursued, while it also served to conceal the real power situation and provide motivation for socialist engagement.[30] Weber's emphasis on the various functions that ideology served for the regime was supported by numerous experts.[31]

As well as pointing to the need to examine the concrete historical functions of ideology in the SBZ and GDR, Social Democrats not surprisingly insisted on distinguishing between various versions of socialist and communist thought and practice. They argued that one could not simply draw a line from Marx via Lenin to GDR Marxism-Leninism as conservatives did. Historian and expert commissioner Bernd Faulenbach insisted that the reception of Marx also included figures such as Karl Kautsky who, unlike Lenin, did not adopt the notion of the dictatorship of the proletariat; Wolfgang Thierse (SPD) similarly objected to the practice of reading a single line of development back toward Marx.[32] Expert commissioner Martin Gutzeit pointed out that Marx's approach was above all a critical one, and that the enlightenment tradition for which he stood was later degraded to a "hermetically closed, circular self-justification of power," a development for which one could not simply blame Marx himself.[33]

There were blind spots and weaknesses in the arguments of both conservatives and Social Democrats, but the latter's case was stronger and had more substantial evidence on its side. The conservative position remained focused on Marxist ideas in general and suffered from an excessively monolithic, static, and undifferentiated approach to ideology. As Weber noted in response to Wisniewski, it was very easy to bring forward various quotations from Marx in support of all sorts of things that subsequently occurred in his name, but it was more important—and in the commission more appropriate—to examine the actual function(s) of ideology in the GDR.[34] This riposte could be applied to most conservative antimarxist contributions, for they hardly addressed the actual history of the GDR, but simply assumed, implied, or asserted that Marxist theory had been implemented completely and perfectly in the GDR.[35] Such an approach failed to address the specific question to which the commission purportedly sought an answer: how ideology had functioned in East Germany. It certainly failed to acknowledge that Marxism provided the basis of much opposition to, and criticism of communist regimes, and overlooked any emancipatory potential in Marx's ideas.[36]

Furthermore, conservative accounts lacked historical agency and tended to reify ideology.[37] Their analysis, too, did not explain why periods of relative ideological relaxation were interspersed with periods of heightened rigor, or why the 1949 constitution of the GDR was not socialist, let alone Marxist or Marxist-Leninist. If these facts were acknowledged, they were left either unexplained or attributed (not unreasonably) to tactical considerations, a problematic approach given that tactical and strategic considerations were otherwise absent from conservatives' analyses that gave the impression that Communists mechanically followed Marx's and Engels's (less than clear and consistent) directions.[38] When Wisniewski argued that the postwar socialist transformation—in particular the expropriations of landowners and capitalists—was "ultimately founded in Marxist philosophy and to be understood on this basis," she ignored not just Soviet power politics and drive for reparations, but also the role of antifascism.[39]

A further difficulty with the conservative approach was a substantial epistemological blind spot about ideology generally, and the contingent nature of conservative values more specifically. Wisniewski was not immune to the tendency to see ideologies as something peculiar to dictatorships, while regarding western democracies as being free of them.[40] The only apparent exceptions were misguided left-wing intellectuals who had fallen victim to socialist delusions, and Wisniewski attacked western intellectuals for their susceptibility to utopianism, again without admitting of any variations in socialist thought, and ignoring wider developments in Europe and beyond.[41] Conservatives were convinced that the "age of ideologies" had come to an end.[42] They failed to perceive the ideological nature of the belief systems such as liberalism and neoconservatism that were acceptable to them, and thus to see how highly ideological their own approach was. For instance, Wisniewski granted private property ontological status, claiming that the (Marxist) "prohibition on the right of disposal of private productive property was not merely a wrong economic decision, but beyond that a destructive intervention into human nature and its motivational forces."[43] The conservative desire to refute Marx and discredit any variants of socialism thus led to an overly simplistic, incomplete, and inconsistent approach.

The social-democratic position, in contrast, took more seriously the ostensible topic that the commission was pursuing and attempted to analyze the role of ideology in the GDR in its historical context and complexity.[44] Yet Social Democrats were so determined to focus on the various functions of ideology within the SED's system of rule that they often evaded the question of ideology's contribution toward motivating and guiding the socialist transformation. At the Bonn public hearing, Wilms (CDU) suggested with some justification that the SPD position implied that the GDR was "an ideology-free dictatorship," based purely on a notion of power that arose almost out of an intellectual vacuum.[45] Similarly, Dirk Hansen (FDP) wondered whether Weber's account—with its emphasis on power politics—did not ignore the importance of Marxism-Leninism as a world view that guided Communists' thought and behavior.[46] Weber did not disagree, but merely said that this was not the topic of the day, and that he was concerned to make the fundamental point of ideology's instrumentalization.[47] In making that point, however, he had come very close to arguing that the social transformation had nothing to do with ideology, and thus ironically depicted ideology in the GDR rather as the "smokescreen" for which Marx had held it in capitalist societies.[48]

The democratic-socialist approach was similar in significant ways to that of the Social Democrats, particularly in arguing against the construction of a straight line of responsibility from the GDR's failure back to Marx. PDS expert commissioner Herbert Wolf argued in similar terms to Weber and Faulenbach that real life in the GDR did not always conform to party resolutions, and that these may or may not have been formulated in accordance with Marx. He insisted that it was too simplistic to argue that Marxism was simply "practiced" in the GDR, and that in several important ways the SED in fact did exactly the opposite of what Marx had advised.[49] Similarly, in an article in the PDS-sponsored series *Ansichten zur Geschichte der DDR*, Erich Hahn argued that one had to acknowledge positive and negative discontinuities as well as continuities across Marxism, Leninism, and Marxism-Leninism. Not atypically for a Democratic Socialist, Hahn himself stressed the discontinuity of Stalinist deformations of existing models of socialism.[50] In the immediate postwar period, Hahn suggested, socialist ideas were initially widespread, but both socialist ideology and practice were influenced by the experiences of fascism and the Cold War. The (negative) influence of western reactions to communism should also not be ignored, he argued, and neither should the division of Germany that had important ramifications for all manner of ideological questions and led to complex changes in ideological line.[51] Hahn thus effectively blamed everyone but German Communists for the distortions of a good idea; but however tendentious his analysis, it was at least grounded in a historical context, unlike that of many conservatives. Both Wolf's and Hahn's writings indicated a critical stance on Stalinism, but the continuation of positive assessments not only of Marx but also of Lenin.[52]

Democratic-socialist positions differed from those of the SPD in their avowedly political purpose and their dogged optimism. Like Heuer in the Bundestag debate, Hahn stressed that the question of ideology was not just of historical interest but was also important for the present and future, and he pleaded for a neutral rather than a pejorative understanding of ideology.[53] Whereas Social Democrats' concerns about conservative intentionalism and reductionism were largely methodological and focused on socialism in historical perspective, Democratic Socialists unashamedly advocated socialist perspectives for the present and future as well.[54] At the Bonn ideology hearing, Dietmar Keller (PDS) spoke in general terms about the "social aspect" that he had found so fascinating in Marx, and repeated his point from the Bundestag debate that capitalism was not the final answer to human history.[55] Similarly, Wolf insisted that a utopian vision of an egalitarian society had existed for centuries and would not simply disappear with "real existing" socialism. He spelled out more clearly than any Social Democrat the possibility that Marx could still be rescued from the pile of historical rubble that bore his name; while the writings of Marx and Engels contained the seeds of their own dogmatization, this outcome was not inevitable.[56]

On one central issue, Democratic Socialists were slightly closer to the conservative position than were the Social Democrats: they readily acknowledged the role of ideology in motivating Communists in the GDR and in driving the social transformations there. For the SED, Hahn argued, genuinely Marxist insights were "present and effective," and Marxism-Leninism determined the overall "political-practical" development, while official ideological pronouncements depended on the *"influence of concrete situations and challenges."*[57] Again highlighting the mutability and contingency of ideological positions, Hahn also argued that the party's "leading role" had initially meant merely that it would offer "impulses," but that this justifiable goal was distorted into a desire for absolute rule, while Marxism's claim to insights into objective historical laws became a binding claim to party infallibility.[58]

Not surprisingly given the polarized views of conservatives and Social Democrats (not to mention the divergent political assessment of the PDS), the commission was unable to agree on a common position. The commission majority's stance in the final report—endorsed by the coalition and Alliance 90/The Greens—was by no means as strident as one might have expected, particularly from the heading "Marxism-Leninism as the Basis of the SED State." After declaring that "Marxism-Leninism formed the ideological basis for the political system in the GDR," much of the rest of its treatment was thoroughly compatible with the SPD view.[59] The majority did not enter into an exegesis of Marx and Engels or even Lenin or Stalin, and seemed to have accepted that this would be inappropriate for a report summarizing the work of an inquiry into the workings of the SED regime.

Yet the majority continued its push to blame Marx and Engels for the East German dictatorship and much more besides, and did not miss the opportunity for a general critique of socialism. It expressed concern that while Marxism-Leninism was largely "obsolete" in unified Germany, the same could not be said of all "Marxist ways of thinking," which—the report suggested regretfully—would probably continue to exist. It also declared that it was "urgently necessary" to confront the notion that "the political system of the GDR was not to be traced back to the theory of Marxism, but emerged through strict adherence to the prescriptions of the Stalinist system of power."[60] The report's apparent restraint thus did not indicate a retreat from conservative positions in the dispute with the SPD.

Here, as before, the case presented by the majority for arguing that ideology served as the basis for the regime's actions was not particularly strong, and in fact it was less confident than previously. Whereas Wisniewski had argued boldly that Marxism-Leninism had served as *Anleitung zum Handeln* (instructions for action), the report merely stated that the regime itself had "propagated" such a connection.[61] The report spoke of Engels's notion of "insight into necessity" being understood as the "conscious application" of Marxist-Leninist tenets, but said nothing about whether such an understanding was acted upon in the GDR. The point made by Weber and others about accepting uncritically the dictatorship's vainglorious pronouncements about itself was thus ignored, as was the possibility of a gap between pretensions and practice.[62]

The SPD dissenting report repeated its insistence that the inquiry was "not the place for an exegesis of Marx/Engels, Lenin or other 'classics' of Marxism-Leninism."[63] This was quite right per se but constituted a rather inappropriate response to the majority statement, for the latter did not in fact amount to an exegesis of communist classics. More apt was the SPD's insistence that the real task of the commission was to "determine the function of Marxism-Leninism in the GDR," and it attempted to do so with a sensitivity to the historical context that the majority report lacked, pointing to the crucial role of Soviet power politics and the need to justify the communist dictatorships that were established under its auspices.[64] Yet the dissenting statement skirted around key questions that had arisen during the commission's deliberations: it failed to address the social transformations that occurred in the GDR, stating that Marxism-Leninism was "declared to be the basis of politics, society, and culture" in East Germany, without discussing the extent to which such declarations were accurate.[65]

The PDS dissenting report similarly objected to the majority's depiction of "the entire social development in the SBZ/GDR from 1945 [as] nothing other than the practical implementation of an unrealistic Marxist theory."[66] According to the PDS, such a view was insufficiently supported by the evidence and—like Wolf's and Hahn's articles—the statement suggested that Marx's ideas had not actually been realized in the GDR.[67] In contrast to the conservative position, the PDS depicted developments in East Germany as an attempted "removal" of the societal foundations of the German *Sonderweg* (special path).[68] The Democratic Socialists insisted that one could not simply judge the socialist project from its end and that one had to remember that "real socialism" had appeared at various stages—especially in the 1950s and 1960s—to have good future prospects, which had less to do with official "Marxist-Leninist" self-understanding (from which the report's authors distanced themselves by using quotation marks), than with the notion of being a modern industrial society that was an alternative to "capitalism and bourgeois-pluralistic societies."[69] The PDS again stressed the widespread postwar desire—extending beyond the labor movement—to eclipse capitalism.[70]

Such democratic-socialist suggestions of a broad, even multiparty, postwar consensus behind a general—rather than Marxist-Leninist—attempt at socialism were undermined, however, by other statements in the minority report. These included repeated references to the divergent sociopolitical positions of the political parties and the occupying powers in the developing Cold War as well as to the KPD/SED's Marxism-Leninism and its orientation toward the October Revolution, the Soviet model, and "'revolutionary dictatorship' (Marx)."[71] In some degree of tension with such specificities, the minority report upheld the much more general legitimacy of a socialist alternative and of hopes for a more social, just, and "warmer" society, a tendency that downplayed the specific ideological nature of the regime and the society it had created in favor of an unspecific, vague belief in equality. The PDS's assessment of the Soviet model, Lenin, and revolution was thus ambivalent, but its defense of the societal changes that had occurred in the GDR and of the ultimate goal of socialism remained steadfast.

Opposing the SED Dictatorship: Opposing Socialism and Division?

The vigorous debate about ideology revolved fundamentally around the question of whether the GDR had constituted the realization of socialism, and the various answers to this question had direct implications for the legitimacy of the goal of socialism in past and present. The obverse question of whether opposition in East Germany had entailed opposition to socialism per se, to its "real existing" variety in the GDR, or merely to certain features or policies of the regime, was also fiercely contested. This question, too, had implications for the legitimacy of the GDR and the various political camps in the present. Conservative anticommunists made few distinctions in this regard and frequently interpreted any criticism of the regime (outside the SED) as hostility to the GDR's very existence, although they were also critical of those who had believed in the possibility of reforming socialism. The PDS, by contrast, insisted on the existence of criticism within the SED itself and argued that many—both within and outside the party—who were critical of the regime had nevertheless favored the continuation of the GDR as a separate state. Former opposition figures, meanwhile, displayed a range of views: some were defensive about implied criticism that they had only wanted to reform socialism, while others supported that very criticism. Once again, these questions did not first arise in the postunification era, and discussions about the rehabilitation of (generally communist or at least socialist) victims of communist persecution had been the topic of lively discussions in the autumn and winter of 1989–90.[72] Yet interpretations of opposition and of the views of regime opponents in that revolutionary period went to the heart of the legitimacy of German unification, and there was considerable competition over the "moral cachet" that oppositional status had come to confer in unified Germany.[73]

Opposition and resistance did not feature strongly in early debates about the inquiry, but it was soon agreed that the history and legacy of opposition in the GDR would be addressed. Various suggestions culminated in an SPD proposal for the inquiry to investigate the "possibilities of divergent and resistant behavior and oppositional action"; this topic—with the addition of "the peaceful revolution in autumn 1989 and the unification of Germany"—was included in the commission's mandate, and constituted one of the inquiry's six major topics for investigation.[74] Nevertheless, most Christian Democrats were much less interested in resistance and opposition than in condemning the ideological basis of the GDR or in demonstrating their own successful efforts in the area of *Deutschlandpolitik*.[75] Indeed, it is to this topic—along with that of the role of the churches in the GDR—that Margot von Renesse's (SPD) characterization of the commission as a "playground" for former East German dissidents applies most aptly.[76] Those most closely involved in this aspect of the commission's work had themselves opposed the East German regime more or less actively, and to a considerable extent they were writing their own history, although western sympathizers and historians also participated in discussions.[77] Suggestions of a general expropriation of easterners' history ignore such eastern agency. What is more, as the following discussion will show, dissidents were not the only easterners involved.

The central issues concerning opposition and resistance were the definition of these phenomena and the question of what should be included in a history of opposition and resistance in the GDR. The commission sought to learn and benefit from the lengthy scholarly debates about the nature and varying degrees of resistance, non-conformity, and immunity in Nazi Germany.[78] In particular, it sought to avoid some of the pitfalls, inconsistencies, and hypocrisy that had characterized the highly politicized reception of anti-Nazi resistance in the two postwar German states—a controversial history that had by no means ended with unification.[79] Apparently seeking to prevent a repetition of the unsightly battles that had raged between East and West Germany and within the latter over the significance, characterization, and legacy of conservative, working class, and—in particular—communist resistance against the Nazis, most members of the commission endorsed an inclusive approach that incorporated multiple actors and manifold forms of thought and behavior under the general rubric of resistance and opposition.[80]

Thus at the beginning of a two-day hearing on "Motivations, Possibilities, and Limits of Resistant and Oppositional Behavior" held in Jena in March 1994, Rainer Eppelmann staked out a wide ground. He declared, "In their historical diversity, the possibilities and forms of oppositional and resistant behavior in the GDR ranged from refusal to spontaneous protest, from conscious, demonstrative rebellion to internal party opposition, from the open formation of citizens' initiatives to resistance that met conspiratorially and operated actively."[81] The commission's report later echoed these inclusive sentiments and highlighted the usefulness of the debate over resistance against Nazism, all the while stressing the extent and diversity of criticism of the communist regime.[82]

However, the commission failed to do justice to the inclusive approach it espoused. Although it explicitly included a range of social behaviors in its understanding of resistance and opposition, its investigations and its report concentrated overwhelmingly on a fairly narrow band of political behavior, focusing on opposition qua dissent, as opposed to general or popular disaffection with the regime or refusal of its demands.[83] By no means atypical of the commission's work more generally, consideration of everyday oppositional and resistant behavior was anything but a priority. An entry on this topic at the end of the report's section on resistance and opposition reads much like an afterthought, however subtle its analysis.[84] Although this failing can be attributed in part to the inquiry's limited resources and insufficient time, it is revealing of the commission's interests in elites and its political focus.[85]

A more serious and less easily explained problem lay in the commission's handling of the political resistance and opposition to which it devoted more attention. Here—as in other areas—the commission's efforts did not live up to the forthright calls made at the beginning of its tenure to develop clear criteria for judging the past and people's past behavior. Given this frequently mentioned need—and the fact that the inquiry was charged expressly with establishing "the possibilities and forms of resistant and oppositional behavior in various areas, including the factors that influenced them"—its effective refusal to propose or utilize a transparent definition of resistance and opposition was striking.[86] This was especially the case because its report declared memory of opposition and resistance in the GDR to be part of the "historical inheritance" of unified Germany and expressed its hope that memory of "1989" would be a source of collective identity; and even more so because the work of the first inquiry formed the basis of its successor's deliberations on commemorative policies that were to include "resistance and courage in the dictatorships as well as the process of the dissolution of SED rule in 1989."[87] It was therefore unfortunate that the commission did not go to greater lengths to develop coherent definitions that could serve as the basis of discussion about commemoration.

The commission was aware of definitional difficulties, but it tried to avoid them by adopting the inclusive approach mentioned above. Eppelmann opened the Jena hearing by highlighting the vagueness of commonly used terms such as opposition, dissidence, immunity, and resistance, and he pointed to the difficulties inherent in their definition.[88] Rather than attempting to meet this challenge, however, he capitulated, claiming that opposition and resistance in the GDR were "largely beyond a general determination of terms."[89] Following Eppelmann, CDU expert commissioner Karl Wilhelm Fricke—the leading authority from the old Federal Republic on political persecution and opposition in the GDR—endorsed the broad understanding proposed by Eppelmann. He also quoted Peter Steinbach, a prominent historian of resistance in the Third Reich and proponent of an inclusive approach, to the effect that a "total history of resistance" was more important than "a historically informed theory of resistance," and that this history should be "as colorful as possible, differentiated in terms of content and historically."[90] But Fricke went beyond Steinbach's sensible endorsement of an inclusive history and not only declined to make any attempt at theorizing, but actually argued against concerted efforts to delineate the phenomena in question or to define key terms. "Definitional attempts," he suggested, are "questionable anyway," since historical phenomena such as opposition and resistance "in the end hardly allow themselves to be defined, let alone forced into the procrustean bed of a theory."[91]

Such rejection not only of theory but also of the possibility of—or need for—a definition might appear consistent with the inclusive approach the commission endorsed. It was also arguably an improvement on the restrictive position put by Fricke when he had first argued for the inclusion of opposition in the inquiry's mandate. Then he had favored a substantial limitation, saying that opposition should only be addressed "in so far as it called for free elections."[92] By the time of the Jena hearing, Fricke's approach was more relaxed. However, his explicit rejection of a definition was inconsistent with the commission's task of establishing the forms or the possibilities of opposition and resistance, which depended very much on how the phenomena were defined. Substantial differences and inconsistencies became evident during the commission's deliberations, due in part to this refusal to engage more directly with conceptual or definitional questions.[93]

Moreover, an inclusive approach that did not seek to differentiate between different behaviors as long as they were directed against the regime itself entailed (aspects of) a definition that required further elaboration. After all, the notion of being directed against the regime meant different things to different people. It could mean opposing particular policies at a particular time, or the general lack of human rights, or indeed the very existence of the GDR.[94] Unfortunately, these differences were not teased out either by Fricke or the commission as a whole.

Instead, there was a tendency in the commission to maximize the extent and degree of opposition by eliding precisely the distinctions among opposition to particular policies, opposition to the nature of SED rule, and opposition to the GDR's existence, at least when such elision seemed politically useful. Such inclusiveness increased the total amount of opposition to communism that could be registered, and thus aided the delegitimation of the GDR. Moreover, from the perspective of the 1990s, the more fundamental the opposition, the better, and—especially concerning the bloc parties—there were clear tendencies to maximize the degree of dissent. In an expertise paper on the CDUD, for example, historian Michael Richter argued that its members by definition comprised *Andersdenkende* (dissidents), and he equated criticism of SED policy and "distance" to the SED regime with opposition to the GDR per se.[95] Other experts similarly blurred distinctions between "reservations" about particular policies on the one hand, and opposition to the SED's leading role, to "communism," or to the GDR on the other, thus magnifying the extent of oppositional attitudes.[96] Conservatives tended to be rather inclusive toward non-communists who had opposed communist policy in one way or another, particularly in the SBZ and the early decades of the GDR. As a result, some behavior that had led to conflict with either the SMAD or the KPD/SED but that was not inherently of a political nature was included under the rubric of opposition; political motives were often asserted or implied where they were not necessarily or exclusively present.[97] Meanwhile, persecution—rather than opposition per se—frequently dominated discussions.[98]

These tendencies were evident in the commissions' handling of that most salient act of resistance against the SED regime prior to 1989: the uprising of 17 June 1953, which was among the central historical episodes to be addressed by the first inquiry.[99] The commissions tried to make the most of this event, consistently seeking to raise its profile in Germans' historical consciousness. Their final reports were debated in the Bundestag on 17 June in 1994 and 1998, and in other years the inquiries commemorated the anniversary with a hearing or a statement, with the exception of 1992 when the Bundestag itself promulgated an honorific declaration for the victims of communist tyranny.[100] The commissions hoped thereby to reverse the decline of the former Day of German Unity in the popular imagination, especially after it had lost this designation when it was replaced by 3 October as the Federal Republic's national day.[101] The first inquiry called explicitly for the strengthening of the day's significance in public awareness, a task with which the Foundation for Working through the SED Dictatorship was later charged.[102] In its recommendations, the second commission suggested that 17 June should serve as *the* day for commemorating opposition and resistance in the GDR, and called for the creation of memorials to the uprising in Berlin and other cities and municipalities throughout the eastern states.[103]

What was significant about the commissions' handling of the events of 1953—and indicative of their treatment of opposition and resistance more broadly—was, first, their designation of the uprising as a *Volksaufstand* (people's uprising) with highly political goals and, second, their attempt to place them in direct continuity with autumn 1989 and unification. These tendencies—that were consistent with the more general desire to maximize the extent of resistance for legitimatory purposes—became particularly salient at a public hearing on "The People's Uprising on 17 June 1953" held by the first commission in the Reichstag building in Berlin on the eve of the uprising's fortieth anniversary. After an introduction by Eppelmann, who spoke of the "patriots" involved, Bundestag President Rita Süssmuth (CDU) emphasized the connection between the 1953 *Volkserhebung* (people's revolt) and the breaching of the Berlin Wall on 9 November 1989, and stressed the popular desire for national unity.[104] She argued that the revolt had been more than a rejection of work norms and more than the "workers' uprising," as it was often designated. Instead, it was about a "political process of liberation, about free and secret elections, about the demand for the disappearance of the political system ... about German unity," and she thanked those who had stood up for the "democratic tradition."[105] Eppelmann, too, stressed that, although sparked by workers, it had quickly escalated into a "people's uprising, to a revolution" and become a "struggle for freedom and the reunification of Germany."[106] Alliance 90 expert commissioner Armin Mitter spoke of a "revolutionary uprising" that would have led to German unification had it not been forcibly repressed; he also termed it a "failed revolution."[107]

While there was undoubtedly some merit to these depictions, they were also rather tendentious. Local and economic goals had also been prominent; only a small proportion of the population had been involved; and not all participants were necessarily "pristine lovers of democracy."[108] At the hearing, numerous experts preferred the term workers' revolt; among them, Torsten Dietrich stressed that—although it was put down with military force—in many places the revolt simply dissolved due to its lack of leadership and clear goals, and that it had assumed explicitly political dimensions only in a few larger cities.[109] Historian Christoph Kleßmann expressed his doubts about an "all too hastily drawn line of continuity" between 1953 and 1989 and his concern that if one did not immediately subscribe to the "people's uprising" view, one was now regarded as being politically suspect; he also argued against the "inflationary use" of the term revolution.[110]

The commission's report was content to refer to the revolt as a people's uprising rather than a revolution, and to the political nature of the "demands of the rising masses."[111] In the Bundestag debate on the report on 17 June 1994, Süssmuth again commemorated the uprising, casting it as an attempt at "freedom, peace, and democracy" and placing it in direct continuity with 9 November 1989.[112] Similarly, Markus Meckel (SPD) called for memory of the revolt—which "symbolizes the Germans' will to freedom"—to be maintained; but in contrast with Süssmuth he associated it with 9 October 1989, the day of the largest mass demonstration against the SED regime, and thus with eastern self-democratization rather than the desire for national unity.[113] Dorothee Wilms (CDU) declared, "The people's uprising of 1953 belongs in the series of oppositional movements and currents that arose again and again over the decades in the GDR, but also in Poland, Hungary, and Czechoslovakia, which then contributed in 1989 to those peoples' liberation from communist dictatorship," and she insisted on the need to remember that such opposition and resistance belonged "to the tradition and to the democratic political culture of Germany and Europe."[114] The uprising of 1953 was thus deemed one of the very few positive features and legacies of East German history. Indeed, as discussed further below, it was viewed more positively than the ambiguous legacy of "1989."

Despite the proclaimed inclusiveness and the apparent unwillingness to develop definitions, discussions of resistance and opposition inevitably employed various criteria and were marked by selectivity in granting sought-after oppositional status to various historical actors and groups.[115] In particular, commissioners displayed greater enthusiasm for differentiating among varying degrees of distance to the regime when dealing with the question of the inclusion of SED members in the history of East German opposition. Conservatives and members of Alliance 90 were generally unsympathetic to SED members who had opposed SED policies, and dismissed conflicts with the ruling elite as mere "power struggles" rather than opposition. Fricke, for example, was notably more interested in definitional questions during discussions of opponents of current policy within the SED leadership, stating repeatedly that whether one characterized figures like Wilhelm Zaisser, Rudolf Herrnstadt, or Karl Schirdewan as belonging to an intra-party opposition depended on one's definition of opposition. He expressed his strong reservations about granting them oppositional status: "They definitely did not want to change the policy of the SED in principle. They sought new paths to the old goal."[116] Fricke's arguments were reasonable and largely supported by other scholars, but his position—that one's ultimate political and ideological goals mattered—amounted to the adoption of a definitional stance, such that mere criticism of current policy or direction did not qualify. Employing criteria in this way without discussing or presenting them explicitly was misleading and hypocritical and amounted to a rather blatant attempt to restrict access to coveted opposition status.[117] Not surprisingly, Social Democrats and Democratic Socialists were more insistent about including SED members and reform communists in any complete account of oppositional behavior and dissent.[118]

Intra-SED opposition was only one aspect of a broad range of critical or oppositional phenomena that were not necessarily directed against socialism or the GDR per se. Although the commission did not seek consciously to promote discussion about degrees of opposition, distinctions arose continually between those who had opposed specific aspects of the regime and those who had opposed socialism and the GDR in toto. After 1989, there was vigorous public debate about the reform-socialist or "Third Way" ideas of many intellectuals—in both East and West—as well as of many eastern dissidents. As chapter 1 and the first section of this chapter showed, some conservatives and liberals viewed the inquiries as a forum for reckoning with such views. At the Jena opposition hearing,

Hans-Adolf Jacobsen pointed to the need to differentiate between oppositional behavior "toward the reform of the system" and that "toward the overcoming of the system."[119] Former dissident Stephan Hilsberg (SPD), among others, sought to "energetically contradict" this point. He insisted that it was too intentionalist and that all opposition had amounted to fundamental opposition because it had demanded the right to speak for oneself, rather than be spoken for by the regime.[120] Numerous eyewitnesses testified to the compatibility of opposition to SED policies and rule on the one hand and the maintenance of socialist ideals on the other, as well as to the need to think and act within the parameters of the time, without the benefit of hindsight about the regime's eventual collapse.[121] Thus in contrast with conservatives' overly simplistic causational argumentation and their excessively monolithic approach—according to which support for socialism had equaled support for dictatorship—the Jena hearing also indicated the extent to which Marxist and socialist ideals had motivated criticism of the regime; opposition to dictatorship did not necessarily equate to opposition to socialism. That said, in contrast with the defensive position according to which it had been necessary to accept the tenets of the system in order to avoid criminalization, and that anticipating the regime's imminent demise had been impossible, some witnesses stressed that their demands had indeed implied the system's overthrow and the abolition of the East German state.[122]

As this discussion suggests, the question of precisely what had been opposed was intimately connected with the question of the positive political goals of the individuals and groups engaged in oppositional activities. Like the ongoing debate about anti-Nazi resistance, much of the discussion about the GDR centered on what the historical actors actually wanted, if their goal of overcoming the dictatorship was achieved. Fricke's sympathies clearly resided with the likes of the Eisenberg Circle of oppositional students in Jena, who "did not orientate themselves politically toward socialism" and who advocated a "thoroughly bourgeois alternative."[123] It was music to commissioners' ears to hear eyewitnesses report that the Federal Republic had constituted their political model and goal, or that free elections and unification were their aims. However, this was music only rarely heard.[124]

Some former dissidents from the opposition groups of the 1980s were particularly concerned to counter the notion that they had believed the GDR to be capable of reform and that all they had wanted was a more democratic brand of socialism. Key opposition figure and cofounder of the Initiative for Peace and Human Rights Gerd Poppe (B90) was at pains to stress that many opposition groups had not been interested in merely reforming state socialism.[125] According to Poppe, it was only possible to speak of "democratic opposition as opposed to the democratic socialists" after the mid 1970s, because only then was it realized that reform was not possible from within the SED, and that new "publics" had to be created.[126] From that point onward, Poppe insisted, one should not focus on whether opponents had wanted continuing, albeit reformed socialism, but on their support for democracy rather than dictatorship. In the concept of "democratic socialism," he argued, the emphasis lay on democracy, in opposition to the "real existing" variety of socialism. He suggested that the use of notions such as democratic socialism had been highly pragmatic: the expression of a more fundamental alternative had been impossible.[127]

While there was certainly a degree of truth to Poppe's view—and contemporary constraints and tactical considerations must be taken into account—he seemed to play down the socialist convictions of many regime critics by suggesting that (the majority of) dissidents in the 1980s had not been democratic socialists, but just democrats. This reflected a common tendency amongst former opposition figures.[128] Nevertheless, Poppe insisted quite rightly on more than one occasion that "to reject the GDR back then did not also automatically mean an unconditional agreement to the Federal Republic."[129] What was positively desired still remained rather inchoate, but Poppe's rejection of a black and white view that equated opposition to the SED dictatorship with support for the Federal Republic was well made.[130]

Others—particularly those who could hardly be accused of having favored a Third Way—were rightly skeptical of attempts to gloss over the socialist dimension of much oppositional thinking. The majority of dissidents had seemed to favor reformed socialism and to be interested in revisionism rather than more fundamental alternatives. Poppe's arguments prompted Martin Gutzeit to ask why other opposition groups had not adopted the vocabulary of non-socialist democracy or discussed the rule of law, parliamentary democracy, western democratic models, or capitalism. Gutzeit insisted that even in 1988 many dissidents had harbored considerable reservations about parliamentary democracy.[131] Gutzeit's fellow Social Democrat Markus Meckel likewise insisted that he and the few others who founded the party had been "fairly alone" with their demand for representative, parliamentary democracy.[132] Similarly, historian and eyewitness Hubertus Knabe argued that the continuation of Marxist thought and of reservations about parliamentary democracy had constituted a key intellectual failing.[133] However, even among these advocates of parliamentary democracy and critics of those who had held reservations about it, there was little discussion of abolishing the GDR or seeking unification. Indeed, attitudes to antifascism, national unity, or capitalism were remarkably absent from the commission's discussions of opposition, given their importance for understanding oppositional positions in the GDR.[134]

What critics specifically had opposed and what they had advocated were by no means the only issues of concern. At times, the potential or real effectiveness of oppositional activity seemed to be regarded as an important criterion, although it was not applied consistently. At one point, Fricke highlighted the small numbers of CDUD and LDPD delegates in the provisional Volkskammer in 1949 and declared, "Opposition in the Volkskammer was thus pointless from the very beginning."[135] His statement was repeated almost verbatim in the commission's report, despite its apologetic implication that opposition was only ever offered—or could only be expected—if it had good prospects of success, and that, when it lacked these, accommodation with the regime was perfectly acceptable. Fricke and his colleagues did not normally support such views. He also argued that as long as Soviet troops were stationed in the GDR one could not expect fundamental change or the collapse of the regime, and that to do so was unrealistic and an excessive demand of opposition and resistance.[136] This last statement failed to make clear whether he meant it was too much to expect opposition figures to call for fundamental change, or whether it was too much to expect them to achieve it. Fricke himself seemed unsure and inconsistent: in some cases he was satisfied with demands and was not concerned with their effectiveness (or prospects thereof), but here he seemed to give the latter greater weight.

Various forms of resistance and degrees of organization also constituted differential considerations. In their attempts to stress bloc-party members' opposition, conservatives occasionally insisted that, even if they had not acted as such, many members at least "thought like dissidents."[137] They begged the question of whether opposition or resistance had to be active. Questions of effectiveness and forms of behavior were also central to the debate over whether the flight and emigration of thousands of East German citizens between 1949 and 1989 had constituted oppositional behavior. Many who had sought to oppose the regime from within the GDR viewed emigration negatively, and tensions between those who left and those who stayed had been a crucial aspect of the upheaval of 1989 and continued to simmer thereafter.[138] Opposition groups' negative assessment of flight and emigration was itself viewed self-critically by some of their representatives, such as Social Democrat Stephan Hilsberg.[139] Others continued to display a proclivity to view leaving the GDR—as opposed to staying and fighting—as a soft option, whereas some who had stayed almost felt compelled to apologize for *not* having left, as staying in retrospect seemed to indicate socialist illusions.[140] Certainly, from Wolfgang Schäuble (CDU) to Gerd Poppe (B90), German politicians were quick to emphasize the historical importance of the waves of East German citizens who had fled the GDR, and Poppe insisted on the need to address their role in the commission's investigation of opposition.[141] Yet the question posed by Hilsberg at the Jena hearing remained: were those who emigrated oppositionists?[142]

In part to answer this question, the commission held a public hearing on the exit movement in Berlin in April 1994.[143] Once again, questions of definition arose, and the competition for the moral and political kudos associated with a radical break with communism was unmistakable. Those who were sympathetic to viewing emigration as opposition highlighted its destabilizing effects and its political motivation and (retrospective) justification. Günter Jeschonnek, for example, who had been active in organizing discussion circles for potential emigrants in East Berlin, stressed the political nature of the emigrants' demands, and that the desire and ability to emigrate were grounded in a belief in fundamental human rights, as opposed to mere material desires. He claimed, further, that opposition groups had been "insignificant" and "hardly played a role" in the regime's demise, whereas the issue of emigration had been of the highest political order.[144] Similarly, Werner Hilse, who had also helped organize mutual support for GDR citizens wanting to emigrate, suggested that they—unlike many opposition figures—had believed the GDR to be incapable of reform, and that history had shown their position to be "more radical and clearer."[145] In contrast, for CDU expert commissioner Martin Michael Passauer, it was less the (perhaps unintended) outcomes of their actions than their opinions and voice that were crucial, and he wondered about the lack of evidence for emigrants' protests once they arrived in the FRG.[146] Despite such doubts from some eyewitnesses and experts, considerable sympathy existed on the commission for the emigrants, who were generally free of suspicion of harboring socialist ideals and who were therefore somehow to be included in the pantheon of determined opponents of GDR socialism.[147]

A related controversial issue was the explanation of the demise of the SED dictatorship and the end of the GDR in 1989–90. This was vigorously contested in historical scholarship and public debate. The central questions were whether the popular uprising in autumn 1989 had constituted a revolution, and what role it had played in relation to other factors such as the regime's collapse or implosion, or Moscow's withdrawal of support for the SED.[148] There was (and is) no scholarly consensus on whether the mass protests in the GDR constituted a revolution, and the term *Wende* (turning point) undoubtedly became the most popular term for the 1989–90 upheaval in common parlance; yet the mainstream political parties generally designated the popular uprising and the collapse of the SED regime as a "revolution," with various qualifiers attached.[149] The Bundestag commission was no exception, and its mandate included the "peaceful revolution in autumn 1989" amongst the historical events to be examined.[150]

Remarkably, the commission did not address the revolution explicitly or seek directly to explain the SED regime's collapse. Many views were put forward in various hearings and expertise papers dealing with other topics, but no sessions, papers, or reports were devoted to explaining or interpreting 1989. Nevertheless, the commission's report referred to the "peaceful revolution 1989–90," and this became the standard term in political and commemorative usage.[151] Indeed, considerable emphasis was placed on the revolution as an East German contribution to unified Germany, with the intention of countering the asymmetrical nature of unification by creating a sense of pride in East German agency. Calls for autumn 1989 to be made a bedrock of postunification historical consciousness and identity (like 1953) were legion, and individual commissioners and the commission as an institution were at the forefront of this campaign.[152] Such emphasis on this (almost solitary) positive aspect of the East German past served generally as compensation for the otherwise total condemnation of everything East German. Unfortunately, it often constituted a mere afterthought, as the belated inclusion of Federal Commissioner for the Stasi Records Joachim Gauck in the official celebrations in 1999 to mark the tenth anniversary of the fall of the Berlin Wall indicated.[153] Claims that public memory of 1989 constitutes a central component of Germany's postunification identity thus approach wish fulfillment, as it has been continually necessary to point out that East Germany experienced liberalization and democratization before unification, not merely as a result of it.[154] One of the problems in establishing the centrality of 1989 lay precisely in the contested standing of the East German opposition and its diverse and ambiguous positive goals, which meant that straightforward praise for its contribution was not forthcoming. In contrast, 1953 proved to be relatively unproblematic, as not least demonstrated by the mass media furor accompanying its fiftieth anniversary.[155]

Perhaps the commission regarded the GDR's demise and the path to unification as too controversial to risk addressing head on. In the March 1992 establishment debate, Jürgen Schmieder (FDP) felt compelled to point out in response to Uwe-Jens Heuer (PDS) that the GDR's end was brought about not by the West, but by its own citizens.[156] Heuer countered that in autumn 1989 East Germans did not want the end of the GDR.[157] This, in turn, was rejected by Rolf Schwanitz (SPD), who argued that the "For Our Country" appeal by critical intellectuals in November 1989 calling for an independent, democratic GDR had received little support, and that people had wanted unity.[158] Angelika Barbe (SPD) also argued that from the beginning of November 1989—when Egon Krenz succeeded Honecker—reforms were no longer desired and that the opposition groups and the population wanted a change of constitution.[159] Again, however, this begged the question of whether a change of constitution was impossible within the confines of a continuing independent state. More forcefully and accurately, Heinz Eggert (CDU) insisted that people had wanted unity and "no second experiment" with socialism, although he conceded that not everyone regarded the political and social order of the FRG as the "best of all possible" worlds.[160] These differing views help explain why—despite the fact that the subcommittee on opposition and resistance was also charged with addressing the revolution and German unification—it singularly failed to do so, preferring instead to focus on those who had opposed the SED in one way or another before late 1989. The second commission, too, largely skirted the issue of unification as it related to opposition in the GDR and the latter's collapse.[161]

While they avoided unification and the vexed question of the possibility of separate statehood for a democratic East Germany, the examination of the history of opposition in the GDR offered conservatives another chance to reproach the western Left for having been too soft on communism. Questions of why SPD politicians and others had sought contacts with SED officials and not with opposition figures featured prominently in the Bundestag establishment debate in 1992.[162] At the Jena hearing in 1994, too, Manfred Wilke displayed a typically critical view of the western Left, wondering why the view of resistance as a fight for freedom had given way to seeing it as the activity of Cold Warriors that threatened détente.[163] Eyewitness Gerhard Finn suggested that opposition groups and individuals could have benefited from more support from the West.[164] At the Berlin emigration hearing, Wilke again suggested that the policy of détente pursued by the SPD-FDP governments of Willy Brandt and Helmut Schmidt had "systematically weakened the feeling for the nation in the Federal Republic, in part even killed it off among the younger generations."[165] Similar attacks sounded much less rehearsed and self-righteous when they came from former GDR citizens bewildered by the West German Left's apparent desire to see its "moral visions" realized safely across the border in the East, as eyewitness Andreas Eckert put it.[166]

The first commission's failure to establish definitional criteria relating to opposition and resistance led to inconsistencies in its treatment of the topic and left many open questions. Its report stressed that defining resistance and opposition was "problematic," and cannot be said to have presented clear criteria.[167] It did not attempt to explicate distinctions among differing degrees of opposition, differing sources of motivation, different forms or positive political goals, or to address the question of effectiveness. The report did not resolve or even seek to assess the diverse opinions on these matters.[168] It was ambivalent on whether only fundamental opposition qualified as such, or whether partial or particular opposition could also be included.[169] It referred to the fact that—even in autumn 1989—"Many still hoped for the possibility of a reform of the system," and quoted Rainer Eckert's expertise paper to the effect that criticism of the SED and GDR often went hand in hand with a "basic loyalty."[170] The report expressed a subtle preference for the view that one could not speak of an opposition movement in the GDR before late 1989 because opposition circles' criticism had remained system-immanent. However—apart from thus confusing organizational and ideological criteria—its argumentation begged the question that has run throughout this discussion of whether the object of that loyalty was the SED, the GDR, or socialism.[171] The commission did not tease out any differences here. This failure was consistent with its general reduction of East German history to that of the SED regime and its repeated equation of socialism with socialism in the colors of the GDR.

In contrast, the report had more sympathy with those to whom one could not attribute any loyalty to socialism, to the East German state, or to its ruling party. It cast emigration and flight from the GDR before the building of the Berlin Wall as forms of oppositional behavior. This applied even when "The motive for flight was not always political in the narrow sense," because it was always regarded—by whom was not stated—as "voting with one's feet."[172] Similarly, the report declared, "The application for emigration became a ballot paper against GDR socialism, such that it is unavoidable to see a new form of oppositional behavior in the mass efforts toward emigration" in the late 1970s and 1980s.[173] Precisely which criteria supported this assessment was unclear. The positive aims of oppositional activity were also not expressly discussed. The report stressed the departure from the goal of socialism and the advocacy of parliamentary democracy by the Eisenberg Circle and other groups in the 1950s, but an entry on "the struggle for free elections" presented very little concrete evidence of calls for such.[174] Demands for unification were noticeably absent from much of the section dealing with opposition and resistance, and the report conceded that with few exceptions the national question had not been "decisive" for the GDR citizens' movements.[175]

Meanwhile, the PDS emphasized the diversity of opinion within the SED. Its minority report pointed to the fact that—while reformers within the party were effectively stymied by the old guard—many party members had participated in protests in autumn 1989 when "oppositional forces outside the SED" gained the initiative for a short period.[176] The PDS did not provide a full account of the SED regime's demise. It avoided the term *revolution*, preferring to speak of the "collapse of the GDR" resulting from the leadership's inability to respond to a social crisis.[177] Moreover, it lamented the intervention of West German political parties and the FRG government in the internal affairs of the GDR, which had stifled the "grass-roots democratic impulse of GDR society of the year 1989–90 and the orientation toward an alternative to capitalism," that were apparently symbolized by the Round Table.[178] Here, the PDS turned an outgrowth of opposition against the SED against the West. In response, the Bundestag resolution on the commission's report supported by all parties except the PDS—which rejected the latter's minority vote in its entirety—specifically objected to the assumption that there had been a "majority of the population that fundamentally agreed with the SED state" even at the end of 1989, a claim that again relied on the elision of possible, indeed crucial, distinctions between the GDR qua SED state and qua East German alternative to the Federal Republic.[179]

The multiplicity and ambiguity of East Germans' views at various points in time thus constituted fertile ground for the post-facto contestation of the legitimacy of socialism, of the GDR, and of unification. The blurring of distinctions between support for and opposition against SED rule, socialism, and the East German state merely fertilized the parties' competing justifications and condemnations. As the next chapter shows, the maintenance or denial of such distinctions was also central to the debate about that other main source of the GDR's legitimacy: antifascism. Before moving on to discuss the commissions' handling of that topic, however, it is worth considering briefly the second inquiry's deliberations on the commemoration of resistance against Germany's two twentieth-century dictatorships, because they directly concerned definitional questions and the inclusive approach to opposition and resistance discussed above.

The second commission's mandate called for the development of "all-German forms of memory of the two dictatorships and their victims" and for the consideration, specifically, of the "different forms and content of honoring the resistance" against Nazism in the two Germanys.[180] Its report once again appeared to endorse an inclusive approach, suggesting that as long as people had opposed the dictatorial regimes or assisted their victims, the political order for which they had fought was irrelevant.[181] Yet in relation to commemorating communist resistance against Nazism, the report insisted, "In the democratic memory culture of the Germans it is necessary to commemorate above all those Communists who broke with their own movement, who provided resistance in both dictatorships and very often had to pay for that with their life or with renewed persecution."[182] An SPD minority report countered that all communist resistance had to be included in exhibitions at memorial sites, and that the subsequent fate of everyone who had resisted the Nazi regime—and not just the

Communists—should be addressed.[183] In reply, the coalition parties repeated that in honoring communist resistance, the extent to which its representatives "were otherwise active as Stalinist aids to Soviet foreign rule" had to be considered.[184] Clearly, conservatives were not as comfortable as they liked to pretend with an inclusive approach to anti-Nazi resistance. Revealingly, no such restriction or caveat was placed on commemorating the opponents and victims of communist dictatorship, who, irrespective of their positive goals or their earlier stance toward the Nazi regime, were deemed not merely to deserve a place for individual commemoration and mourning but also to have a right to "public memory and commemoration in a democracy."[185] Far from upholding a balanced inclusiveness, the inquiry's anticommunist bias thus led it to a highly inconsistent and selective approach to the commemoration of opposition and resistance—and not only them, as the next chapter will show.

Notes

1. For instance, Vergau argues that, unlike the regime itself, the GDR's ideological foundations were not subject to delegitimization after 1990, *Aufarbeitung von Vergangenheit*, 102. She ignores the commissions' efforts here. Cooke notes the inquiries' attention to ideology, but it barely features in his analysis; moreover, his not unreasonable claim that the first commission's report "paints the GDR as an aberration of history" overlooks conservatives' efforts—discussed in this chapter—to depict it as the historical realization of Marx's philosophy, and thus anything but an aberration, *Representing East Germany*, 38, 40.
2. Francis Fukuyama, *The End of History and the Last Man* (New York, 1992).
3. I: 19.
4. Alfred J. Gertler, "Gemeinsame Herausforderung: Bundestag will Enquete-Kommission über das DDR-Unrecht einsetzen," *Flensburger Tageblatt,* 13 February 1992.
5. I: 151, 149.
6. I: 52.
7. DBPa: Protokoll 4: 11.
8. DBPa: Protokoll 5: 5f. I: 170.
9. Conservatives frequently spoke generally about Marxism and socialism, rather than specifically about Marxism-Leninism, Stalinism, or communism. See I: 19, 29, 110, 57, 59f., 62, 67, 150f., 137f. If they did speak specifically about the GDR or Marxism-Leninism, they moved quickly from the specific to the general.
10. I: 92f.
11. I: 13, 12.
12. I: 93. See also 116, 146.
13. I: 15.
14. I: 85, 84.
15. I: 80, 84.
16. I: 85.

17. This was evident, for example, in Roswitha Wisniewski's claim that—in the entire western world—it was "above all" in the humanities disciplines at West German universities that Marxism "lingered," "Marxismus als Voraussetzung des politischen Systems der DDR," III: 2071.
18. I: 160.
19. "Marxismus-Leninismus und die soziale Umgestaltung in der SBZ/DDR," III: 12f.
20. III: 13.
21. III: 14f.
22. Konrad Löw, "War der SED-Staat marxistisch?" III: 22–29.
23. Löw's expertise paper, "Zur Funktion des Marxismus-Leninismus im SED-Staat," III: 1401–41, amounted again to a sustained attack on Marx and his sympathizers rather than an exploration of the indicated topic of ideology's function in the GDR. It contained significant slippage between analysis of what Marx said and the claim that Communists followed it. It also attempted to disprove those who claimed that Leninism, Stalinism, and communist regimes did not reflect accurately Marx's and Engels's thoughts and supported the opposite view: that Marx should be regarded as guilty in some way, and that democracies must ostentatiously disavow Marxism per se, 1437f., 1440f.
24. III: 70, 72.
25. Like Löw, Wisniewski focused on Marxist philosophy's "roots and traditions" rather than its role in the GDR, whose historical specificities and context she largely ignored, III: 2067. Indeed, she did little more than assert that the GDR represented the (necessary) consequence of Marxism, "an ideology that from its philosophical and general intellectual historical assumptions leads to revolutionary changes, as they occurred in the socialist states, and to totalitarianist political structures," 2068. Like Eppelmann at the public hearing, she assumed that, because Marx's writings constituted instructions for political action all later political action pursued in his name was not only consistent with his thinking, but also his fault, 2069 and passim. Characteristically, her report also contained considerable slippage between various versions of Marxism, 2069f.
26. III: 17.
27. Hermann Weber and Lydia Lange, "Zur Funktion des Marxismus-Leninismus," III: 2035.
28. Ibid.
29. III: 12.
30. III: 20.
31. See the comments of Fischer, II: 2994, 3002; Leonhard, III: 37, 42; and Horst Möller, IX: 636. See also Johannes L. Kuppe, "Zur Funktion des Marxismus-Leninismus," III: 1399f., 1381; Rüdiger Thomas, "Ursachen und Folgen der Gesellschaftspolitik im SED-Staat," 1851f. Cf. Alan Nothnagle, *Building the East German Myth: Historical Mythology and Youth Propaganda in the German Democratic Republic, 1945–1989* (Ann Arbor, 1999), 15.
32. III: 55, 77.
33. III: 61.
34. III: 18.
35. Wisniewski conceded that Marx's demands for the removal of certain social structures "could in the course of history only be partly realized," but she regarded it as more important to concentrate on his demands than on their later (incomplete) realization, III: 2084.
36. See, in contrast, II: 2036, 2050, 2057. Cf. Geoff Eley, *Forging Democracy: The History of the Left in Europe, 1850–2000* (Oxford, 2002).
37. See instances by Wisniewski, III: 2067, 2068, 2071.
38. III: 2066, 2063.

39. III: 2066. Her report mentioned expropriations of large landowners being "concealed as antifascist," 2091. In contrast, Thomas spoke of the "anticapitalist, antibourgeois, and antiliberal" characteristics of communist antifascism that enjoyed widespread support, 1846.

40. III: 2067. On differing conceptual approaches to ideology, see Michael Freeden, "Ideology and Political Theory," *Journal of Political Ideologies* 11, no. 1 (2006): 3–22.

41. III: 2066, 2071, 2090.

42. This was by no means a post-1990 phenomenon, but was reinforced strongly by communism's collapse. See Karl Dietrich Bracher, *The Age of Ideologies: A History of Political Thought in the Twentieth Century* (St. Martin's, 1984); Fukuyama, *The End of History.*

43. I: 151. See also III: 2094f.

44. See Weber and Lange, III: 2048–59.

45. III: 56.

46. III: 60.

47. III: 73.

48. Similarly, Leonhard accepted Hansen's point but insisted that he had concentrated on the function ascribed to the ideology by the SED, III: 67f. Weber's position appears to have become more one-sided in response to conservatives' reductiveness. At the inquiry's fourth meeting he had claimed that ideology served as *both* an instruction for action and an instrument of legitimation, and in an introductory paper he argued that developments in the SBZ/GDR were fundamentally determined by the Soviet occupier *and* the traditions and ideology of German communism. DBPa: Protokoll 4: 11. II: 3004. Cf. Beate Ihme-Tuchel, "Marxistische Ideologie: Herrschaftsinstrument und politische Heilslehre," in *Bilanz und Perspektiven,* eds. Eppelmann, Faulenbach, and Mählert. On Marx's notion of ideology and its often unconscious or implicit adoption by non-Marxists, see Freeden, "Ideology and Political Theory."

49. III: 58, 57. He expanded on these ideas in Herbert Wolf, "Einfluß und Elend der marxistischen Theorie im DDR-Sozialismus oder auch: Starb der Sozialismus an Marx oder Marx am 'realen Sozialismus,'" in *Ansichten zur Geschichte der DDR* III, eds. Dietmar Keller, Hans Modrow, and Wolf (Bonn, 1994).

50. Erich Hahn, "Zur Rolle der Ideologie," in *Ansichten zur Geschichte der DDR* I, eds. Dietmar Keller, Hans Modrow, and Herbert Wolf (Bonn, 1993), 217ff., 223.

51. Ibid., 222, 214f., 224.

52. The tenuousness of some Democratic Socialists' break with Marxism-Leninism was also evident when—in an angry exchange with conservative opponents in the establishment debate—Heuer defended Marxism-Leninism as "a good school" (which was met with the rebuke that it was "a very good school for mass murderers"), I: 84. Similarly, in the context of its rejection of the alleged equation of the GDR with the Third Reich, the PDS report defended "Marxism/Leninism" as being "connected with the rationalism and humanism of the enlightenment," as opposed to the "antihumane racial theory" of National Socialism, which was characterized by "mysticism and irrationalism," 711. Cf. Winkler, "Kein Bruch mit Lenin"; Thompson, "The PDS."

53. Hahn, "Zur Rolle der Ideologie," 211f.

54. For an exception from the SPD, see Wolfgang Thierse, "Oktober 1917—November 1989: Sozialismus zwischen Diktatur und Emanzipation," in *Diktatur und Emanzipation: Zur russischen und deutschen Entwicklung 1917–1991,* eds. Bernd Faulenbach and Martin Stadelmaier (Essen, 1993).

55. III: 89f.

56. Wolf, "Einfluß und Elend," 17, 28f.

57. Hahn, "Zur Rolle der Ideologie," 214ff., italics in original.

58. Ibid., 221, 233 (fn. 16), 223.
59. I: 268.
60. I: 277.
61. I: 269.
62. I: 269f.
63. I: 270.
64. Ibid.
65. I: 271.
66. I: 682.
67. Ibid.
68. I: 686.
69. I: 684.
70. I: 685, 688.
71. For the quotation, see I: 719.
72. See Bock, *Vergangenheitspolitik im Systemwechsel*, 213ff.
73. Ross, *The East German Dictatorship*, 104.
74. I: 155, 191. DBPa: Protokoll 3: 42, 11, 6; Protokoll 6: 24.
75. The coalition's draft terms of reference did not include resistance and opposition among the specific topics for investigation, although "analysis and documentation" of the "democratic revolution of autumn 1989" were mentioned. In contrast, the GDR's "ideological foundations" were mentioned not only among the specific topics, but also in the context of the inquiry's general tasks. DBPa: Protokoll 3: 38, 35f. That the subcommittee on opposition and resistance met sixteen times in contrast to twenty-five and twenty-seven meetings for those on ideology and *Deutschlandpolitik* respectively also indicates the topic's relative weighting, I: 195.
76. Author's interview.
77. Gerd Poppe was the chair of the subcommittee, which also included Armin Mitter, Martin Gutzeit, Jürgen Schmieder, Dietmar Keller, Karl Wilhelm Fricke, and Manfred Wilke, I: 199.
78. For historiographical efforts to benefit from research into anti-Nazi resistance, see, for example, Christoph Kleßmann, "Opposition und Resistenz in zwei Diktaturen in Deutschland," *Historische Zeitschrift* 262 (1996): 453–79.
79. See chapter 5 and J. David Case, "The Politics of Memorial Representation: The Controversy over the German Resistance Museum in 1994," *German Politics and Society* 16, no. 1 (1998): 58–81.
80. See VII: 54. On debates about anti-Nazi resistance and the development of an inclusive approach, see Ines Reich, "Geteilter Widerstand: Die Tradierung des deutschen Widerstands in der Bundesrepublik und der DDR," *Zeitschrift für Geschichtswissenschaft* 42, no. 7 (1994): 635–43; Steinbach, "Darf der pluralistische Staat 'Geschichtspolitik' betreiben?"; Steinbach, "Postdiktatorische Geschichtspolitik."
81. "Motivationen, Möglichkeiten und Grenzen widerständigen und oppositionellen Verhaltens," VII: 15.
82. I: 561ff.
83. The commission was by no means alone in this respect. See Erhard Neubert, *Geschichte der Opposition in der DDR 1949–1989* (Bonn, 1997), which similarly focuses primarily on political dissent, rather than societal opposition. See also Karl Wilhelm Fricke, Peter Steinbach, and Johannes Tuchel, eds., *Opposition und Widerstand in der DDR: Politische Lebensbilder* (Munich, 2002), 11, 23, which seeks to locate key elements of the GDR opposition in the context of various groups and individuals from the anti-Nazi resistance. A more genuinely inclusive approach is adopted by Ulrike Poppe, Rainer Eckert, and

Ilko-Sascha Kowalczuk, eds., *Zwischen Selbstbehauptung und Anpassung: Formen des Widerstands und der Opposition in der DDR* (Berlin, 1995). Cf. Ross, *The East German Dictatorship*, 99.

84. I: 606–10.
85. See the comments of Faulenbach, VII: 64, 122.
86. I: 155.
87. I: 745; *I: 6*.
88. VII: 13.
89. VII: 14.
90. Karl Wilhelm Fricke, "Widerstand und Opposition von 1945 bis Ende der fünfziger Jahre," VII: 15; I: 562.
91. VII: 15.
92. DBPa: Protokoll 2: 28.
93. At the Jena hearing, Hansen's (FDP) suggestion that it was necessary to differentiate among resistance, opposition, dissidence, *Resistenz*, and immunity revealed the extent to which such differentiations had *not* been pursued thus far, VII: 67. Quite divergent understandings of opposition were expressed by former dissidents and experts at the hearing; see 261ff., 122f. Cf. Ross, *The East German Dictatorship*, 107f., 110.
94. As Ross argues, "The partiality or generality of criticism seems crucially important to any evaluation of 'opposition,'" *The East German Dictatorship*, 112.
95. II: 2594, 2625, 2623f. This was despite also arguing that there was no evidence of anti-socialist goals in the reform movement in the CDUD even in 1989 and acknowledging that the party was no "hotbed of resistance," 2629, 2622.
96. See, for example, the comments of Lapp, II: 294ff., and Thomas Ammer, VII: 130.
97. See VII: 22; I: 609.
98. See VII: 17, 20f.; I: 571.
99. I: 156.
100. See "Der Volksaufstand am 17. Juni," II: 746–802 (1993); I: 790–874 (1994); *I: 24–53* (1995); "Die Herausforderung des Aufarbeitungsprozesses und die Situation der Aufarbeitungsinitiativen sechs Jahre nach der Wiedervereinigung," *VII: 4–90* (1996); MDA: Deutscher Bundestag, Pressemitteilung, Rainer Eppelmann, MdB, Vorsitzender der EK "Überwindung…" erklärt zum 17. Juni: "Der 17. Juni muss ein lebendiger Gedenktag in Deutschland sein!" (1997); *I: 807–49* (1998). For the 1992 declaration, see Deutscher Bundesrat, "Ehrenerklärung für die Opfer der kommunistischen Gewaltherrschaft," *Drucksache* 431/92 (1992).
101. From 1990, 17 June was no longer celebrated as the Day of German Unity and the 1953 law making it a public holiday was revoked. A 1953 proclamation by Federal President Heinrich Lübke according to which it became a National Day of Commemoration remained in place. See Wolfrum, *Geschichtspolitik*.
102. I: 753; *I: 73*.
103. See *I: ix, 631, 642f*.
104. "Der Volksaufstand am 17. Juni 1953," II: 747.
105. II: 748f.
106. II: 749f.
107. II: 767, 793.
108. Pritchard, *The Making of the GDR*, 210f. Unlike many commentators after 1989, Pritchard gives some credence to the official SED "fascist putsch" interpretation, arguing that former Nazis and ardent nationalists were involved, and that demonstrators painted Nazi slogans, ibid., 208f. He does not, however, suggest—as the putsch thesis had—that it was directed from the West. Cf. Ihme-Tuchel, *Die DDR*, 22–41, esp. 29–32.

109. II: 770–74.
110. II: 783, 792f.
111. I: 574. It consistently preferred the term "people's uprising," 204, 351 thrice, 356, 405, 492, 510, 574, to "workers' uprising," 413.
112. I: 790.
113. I: 799.
114. I: 838.
115. Fricke's paper at the Jena hearing was a conscious attempt to show what he thought should be included in a history of opposition and resistance in the SBZ and the early GDR, VII: 15f.
116. VII: 23.
117. Meckel asked Fricke for more criteria to distinguish between SED power struggles and democratic resistance. Fricke conceded that different political positions lay behind the former, but repeated his strong reservations against designating people who were co-responsible for the GDR's Stalinization as oppositional, VII: 54, 57f. His strong stance stood in contrast with his inclusion of 1950s "opposition in the leadership core of the SED" in his 1984 volume, *Opposition und Widerstand*, as cited in Eckhard Jesse, "Oppositionelle Bestrebungen in der DDR der achtziger Jahre: Dominanz des dritten Weges?" in *Wiedervereinigung Deutschlands*, eds. Eckart, Hacker, and Mampel, 92.
118. See the views of Meckel, Weber, and Ulrike Poppe, VII: 54, 58, 275. Democratic-socialist historians also emphasized the extent of critical, even oppositional thinking within the SED, often rather unconvincingly. See Wilfried Otto, "Widerspruch und Widerstand in der SED," in *Ansichten* I, eds. Keller, Modrow, and Wolf; Wilfried Otto, "Opposition und Widerstand zwischen Hoffnung und Enttäuschung," in *Ansichten* III, eds. Keller, Modrow, and Wolf. More critically, Thomas Klein points to the non-political nature of SED reformers, "Alternatives und oppositionelles Denken in der SED seit Mitte der 80er Jahre: Chance und Ausgang innerparteilicher Alternativbildung in der Endphase der DDR," in *Ansichten* IV, eds. Keller, Modrow, and Wolf. Neither Fricke nor the commission as a whole denied oppositional status to all SED members. At the Jena hearing, Fricke characterized intellectuals, scholars, and students (often SED members) who hoped to liberate Marxism-Leninism "from the chains of Stalinism and dogmatism" and wanted to humanize and democratize socialism as belonging to a "revisionist opposition," VII: 23f., a position endorsed by the report, I: 576f.
119. VII: 264, 304.
120. VII: 267. See the similar comments of Bärbel Bohley, 302.
121. See VII: 157, 162, 221, 112, 101, 110, 99.
122. See the comments by Ulrike Poppe, Gerd Poppe, and Angelika Barbe, VII: 262, 289, 308, 424, 373.
123. VII: 24.
124. Eyewitnesses offered vague and halting responses to a question from Hans-Adolf Jacobsen about what they had positively wanted, VII: 65, 70, 68, 49, 46f., 104f. See also Richter, II: 2622, 2624f.
125. VII: 424.
126. DBPa: Protokoll 6: 15f.
127. VII: 116f.
128. Cf. Jesse, "Oppositionelle Bestrebungen," 94, 98; Huyssen, *Twilight Memories*, 47.
129. VII: 370.
130. Poppe acknowledged that despite some calls for the rule of law, separation of powers, etc., skepticism about parliamentary democracy remained and, he added, had not disappeared by 1994, VII: 308. Similarly, Bärbel Bohley defended hopes for a "Third Way"

that she said was not necessarily a path to socialism, but a path between capitalism and socialism. She had learnt during her brief time in the FRG during the 1980s that there, too, people sought alternatives and thought that simply adopting the western model was not the only (or best) alternative, 302f.

131. VII: 121, 244, 236, 238. Despite highlighting the mental blinkeredness of many oppositionists, Gutzeit stressed that civil rights were central to the oppositional movements from their beginnings in the 1970s, 242.

132. VII: 295. Cf. Meckel, *Selbstbewußt in die deutsche Einheit*, 89–96.

133. VII: 121.

134. For rare exceptions, see VII: 238, 252f., 298. These issues feature more prominently in the often critical literature on the GDR opposition. See Thompson, "Reluctant Revolutionaries"; Christian Joppke, *East German Dissidents and the Revolution of 1989: Social Movement in a Leninist Regime* (New York, 1995). Cf. Neubert, *Geschichte der Opposition*, 27; Jesse, "Oppositionelle Bestrebungen," 98.

135. VII: 19.

136. VII: 25f.

137. See II: 2622, 324. See also VII: 38, 48, 60, 75, 121; I: 587f.

138. See Ross, *The East German Dictatorship*, 139; Albert O. Hirschmann, "Exit, Voice, and the Fate of the German Democratic Republic: An Essay in Conceptual History," *World Politics* 45, no. 2 (1993): 173–202; Steven Pfaff and Hyojoung Kim, "Exit-Voice Dynamics in Collective Action: An Analysis of Emigration and Protest in the East German Revolution," *American Journal of Sociology* 109, no. 2 (2003): 401–44. For the emotional debate amongst contemporaries, see Uwe Schwabe and Rainer Eckert, eds., *Von Deutschland Ost nach Deutschland West: Oppositionelle oder Verräter? "Haben die Ausreisewilligen der 80er Jahre den Prozess der friedlichen Revolution und das Ende der DDR eher beschleunigt oder gefährdet?"* (Leipzig, 2003). Bock recounts that many dissidents in 1990 opposed compensation for those who had left, even if they had done so for political reasons, *Vergangenheitspolitik im Systemwechsel*, 421f.

139. VII: 119.

140. See a tendentious question by Martin-Michael Passauer and a comment by Edelbert Richter, VII: 127, 98. Mitter publicly thanked those who stayed and expressed the sense that one sometimes felt the need to apologize for having done so, 278. Gutzeit argued similarly, 370.

141. I: 62, 50. DBPa: Protokoll 2: 30.

142. VII: 119.

143. See "Die Flucht- und Ausreisebewegung in verschiedenen Phasen der DDR-Geschichte," VII: 314–449.

144. Jeschonnek, "Die Selbstorganisation von Ausreiseantragstellern in den achtziger Jahren in der DDR," VII: 398, 405. Numerous commentators have emphasized the role, or radicalism, of "exit" over "voice." See Thompson, "Reluctant Revolutionaries"; Laurence H. McFalls, *Communism's Collapse, Democracy's Demise? The Cultural Context and Consequences of the East German Revolution* (New York, 1995), 64; Joppke, *East German Dissidents*. In contrast, Thomas A. Bayliss, "The *Wende* in GDR Research," *German Politics and Society* 21, no. 3 (2003): 114. Cf. Jarausch, *The Rush to German Unity*, 198.

145. VII: 394. In contrast, historian and eyewitness Rainer Eckert argued that staying in the GDR received "late justification" through the regime's collapse, 409.

146. VII: 52.

147. See the nuanced view of Knabe, VII: 85f., and Richard Hilmer, "Motive und Hintergründe von Flucht und Ausreise aus der DDR," 325. Cf. Thompson, "Reluctant Revolutionaries," 59.

148. Ross, *The East German Dictatorship*, 128. See Maier, *Dissolution;* Ludger Kühnhardt, "Umbruch—Wende—Revolution: Deutungsmuster des deutschen Herbstes 1989," *Aus Politik und Zeitgeschichte* 47, no. 40–41 (1997): 12–18; Konrad H. Jarausch and Martin Sabrow, eds., *Weg in den Untergang: Der innere Zerfall der DDR* (Göttingen, 1999); Jarausch, "Zehn Jahre danach: Die Revolution von 1989/90 in vergleichender Perspektive," *Zeitschrift für Zeitgeschichte* 48, no. 10 (2000): 909–24.

149. See I: 3, 19, 45, 50, 63, 100. Cf. Ross, *The East German Dictatorship*, 129; Jarausch, *The Rush to German Unity*, 71.

150. I: 156.

151. I: 597.

152. I: 745. See for example, Stephan Hilsberg, "Identitätsmuster in Ost und West: Zur Überwindung der inneren Teilung durch ihre Aufarbeitung," *Deutschland Archiv* 27, no. 3 (1994): 293; Pampel, "Was bedeutet 'Aufarbeitung,'" 37. Cf. Wüstenberg, *Die politische Dimension*, 253.

153. See Meckel, *Selbstbewußt in die deutsche Einheit*, 219–25. This episode of belatedness came even after Federal President Roman Herzog had insisted in 1995 that positive eastern contributions must be acknowledged in order for "inner unity" to be achieved. See A. James McAdams, "Germany after Unification: Normal at Last?" *World Politics* 49, no. 2 (1997): 307.

154. For such an optimistic claim, see Bernd Faulenbach, "Historical Foundations of the Berlin Republic," in *The Spirit of the Berlin Republic*, ed. Dettke, 23. For the insistence on eastern democratization, see Stephan Hilsberg, "Die innere Einheit Deutschlands: Eine brauchbare Vision?" *Deutschland Archiv* 29, no. 4 (1996): 607.

155. Edgar Wolfrum, "Neue Erinnerungskultur? Die Massenmedialisierung des 17. Juni 1953," *Aus Politik und Zeitgeschichte* 53, no. 40–41 (2003): 33–39.

156. I: 85.

157. I: 86.

158. I: 95f.

159. I: 124.

160. I: 74.

161. Secretariat member Thomas Ammer wrote a report, "Deutschlandpolitische Konzeptionen der Opposition in der DDR 1949–1961," *VIII: 291–510*, but there was no equivalent for the later period.

162. See I: 49, 122, 110f.

163. VII: 53.

164. VII: 69.

165. VII: 372.

166. VII: 382.

167. I: 561.

168. It regarded the departure of escapees and emigrants in the 1950s and early 1960s as oppositional, even though their exit had weakened the potential of opposition within the GDR, I: 572f. In contrast, it argued that the mass exodus of 1989 should be regarded as a form of "mass protest" precisely because of its effects, 609. It implicitly dismissed the suggestion that there were genuine reform elements within the SED in the 1970s and 1980s by asserting that "system-immanent" criticism was "hopeless," 586. For other areas, it did not discuss the questions of effectiveness or likelihood of success.

169. It endorsed Fricke's reservations about granting intra-communist power struggles oppositional status, but had no hesitation in pointing to CDUD opposition to the "procedure" of land reform as an example, I: 576, 565.

170. I: 601.

171. See its elision of organizational and ideological matters in its discussion of the historical point from which one could speak of a citizens' rights movement or active opposition, I: 593. Its tendency was to grant opposition status only to those who sought to overthrow not only SED rule but the GDR itself.
172. I: 572.
173. I: 582.
174. I: 577f., 570ff.
175. I: 589. The highlighted exception was Robert Havemann's "open letter" and the "Berlin Appeal" formulated by Havemann and Eppelmann. These would presumably have received even more attention if they had not also advocated a democratic version of socialism for a bloc-neutral Germany.
176. I: 701f.
177. I: 702.
178. I: 704.
179. I: 783.
180. *I: 6.*
181. *I: 588.*
182. *I: 598.*
183. *I: 601f.*
184. *I: 602.*
185. *I: 617.*

Chapter 5

VERGANGENHEITSBEWÄLTIGUNG
GOOD AND BAD

Memories of the experiences of dealing with the Nazi past (*Vergangenheits-bewältigung*) played an important role in discussions of the East German past. As chapter 1 demonstrated, a central motivation for a thorough reckoning with communism and in particular for the Bundestag's commission of inquiry lay in a widespread sense that the two postwar Germanys had each, in their different ways, failed to come to terms with the Nazi legacy. Indeed, one of the main justifications for the inquiry consisted precisely in the prevention of a repetition of past omissions, or future accusations thereof. A negative assessment of the handling of the Nazi past thus appeared to motivate and justify the present inquiry.

Yet dissonance soon emerged over its interpretation, such that it would be a mistake to argue that a consensus existed about previous, shared failings. Indeed, the East and West German records over the Nazi past became a major focus of the political battle over the past. Western conservatives painted a rather rosy picture of West German efforts, but portrayed East German antifascism as nothing but a doctrine imposed or prescribed from above, and instrumentalized by the SED for its own ends. In contrast, the PDS continued the former ruling party's double strategy of pointing to positive antifascist achievements in the GDR and unacceptable fascist continuities in the Federal Republic. These well-known Cold War–era arguments had lost little of their power in the early 1990s. Meanwhile, a number of Social Democrats and former eastern dissidents in Alliance 90 were highly critical of official GDR antifascism, but objected to conservatives' complete demolition of antifascism per se, seeing in it a set of beliefs that could usefully be drawn upon to foster democracy. At the same time, while far from demonizing it, they insisted on the problematic nature of the western handling of the Nazi past and sought to counter its whitewashing by conservatives. To some extent, they thus offered a mediating discourse between the Right and the far Left.

Assessments of East and West German approaches to the Nazi past thus went hand in hand with one another, yet despite calls from the Left for an examination of both states' responses to Nazism, the western record was not explored directly or thoroughly. The focus remained very much on East Germany, fueling suspicions of double standards and victor's justice. The fundamentally asymmetric nature of the status of Germany's postwar histories thus led to a missed opportunity for a sober, balanced consideration of the achievements and failures of the two states' records on the Nazi legacy.[1] Yet rather than lamenting this missed chance, it is important to recognize that many of the political actors involved simply did not desire such a reevaluation; their long-held views provided them not only with ideological certainty, but with useful political ammunition against their opponents.

This chapter highlights the (often dubious) argumentative strategies of (mainly western) anticommunists in their effort to delegitimize East German antifascism. This constituted a further, fundamental plank in their broader condemnation of the GDR. Three reasons made the discrediting of antifascism seem paramount. First, antifascism had been crucial to the SED's legitimation strategies. Second, it had been similarly central to the GDR's attempts to delegitimize the Federal Republic. And, third, many people in both parts of the divided country (and elsewhere) had accepted (and many continued to accept) both the GDR's self-depiction and its attacks on the FRG. The result was that East Germany had enjoyed an "antifascist bonus," which conservatives now hoped to destroy.[2] By implication, West German efforts to deal with the Nazi past were now—after all the caustic debate over the years—to be viewed more positively: as authentic and extensive, if delayed and controversial.[3] Such positions were of course anathema to the PDS. Meanwhile, Social Democrats and members of Alliance 90 had concerns about conservative overkill, but these were minor compared with their support for the delegitimation of the SED regime, and they were ultimately co-opted by the conservative majority, sharing its belief that the GDR had not faced up to Nazism in an honest, appropriate, or adequate fashion.

Attempts by Christian Democrats, Free Democrats, Social Democrats, and former dissidents in Alliance 90 to discredit the GDR were thus not exhausted in the effort to brand the GDR an illegitimate dictatorship from the very beginning or the realization of a criminal ideology. A key aspect of their retrospective deconstruction of East Germany consisted in the demolition of the GDR's reputation as a thoroughly antifascist state. The Nazi past thus not only provided motivation and justification for the reappraisal of the East German past, it was also vital to the substantive investigation and to the contestation of postwar history, in which the FRG was necessarily implicated in more or less positive contrast to the GDR. Yet far from being content with merely neutralizing the GDR's perceived bonus, conservatives used this topic to draw further parallels between the GDR and the Third Reich, just as they did between Marx and Hitler as seen in the previous chapter. I would therefore take Bill Niven's argument that the Nazi and GDR pasts could "only be effectively dovetailed by excluding from representations of the GDR the positive elements of anti-fascism and socialism" one step further.[4] Highlighting precisely the negative elements of antifascism and socialism was crucial to that dovetailing effort.

A Critical Consensus?

Chapter 1 demonstrated that negative assessments of East and West German approaches to the Nazi past were an important motivating factor for the commission of inquiry. This critical attitude might suggest that antifascist positions associated with the West German New Left were winning the day. After all, it had been highly critical of western *Vergangenheitsbewältigung* and had argued that more had to be done to face up to fascism, in contrast to the triumphalist antifascism of the SED which had declared that there was no ongoing need to assume responsibility for the past because fascism's social and economic basis had been destroyed in the East. A more self-critical view of the West's handling of Nazism was perhaps possible now that the antifascist GDR rival was no longer there to attack western continuities and shortcomings.

Certainly, cultural strategies were now widely seen to be necessary for both pasts, in addition to the establishment and defense of democratic institutions.[5] That this constituted a radical change in the conservative position became conspicuous at the commission's seventy-fifth meeting at the Reichstag in June 1994. Bernd Faulenbach asked conservative historian and expert witness Manfred Kittel whether he regarded historian Hermann Lübbe's view that a "communicative silence" (originally over the Nazi past) was necessary for the integration of a compromised population into a new democratic order as exemplary for working through the GDR past. Not surprisingly given the context, but very surprisingly given previous West German debates, Kittel said that he did not.[6] Contemporary Germany should not content itself merely with the formal existence of democratic institutions in the eastern states, but must engage in a more searching and introspective quest for accountability. It remains debatable whether this change of view reflected an opportunistic response to the present chance for a reckoning with communism, or a genuinely critical reassessment of earlier positions on the Nazi past. The current author's assessment is that both dimensions were present. While the statements accompanying the establishment of the inquiry were surely sincere, acceptance of continuing responsibility for the legacy of both GDR communism and Nazism into the present and future was not consistently accompanied by a critical approach to earlier efforts to face up to the Nazi past. For all appearances of a critical consensus, various assessments of the western and eastern records were evident, and they influenced and formed a key component of the wider debate about Germany's postwar history.

Of the four parliamentary motions calling for the creation of a commission of inquiry, only that of the PDS mentioned the history of coming to terms with the Nazi past. In its list of objections to and warnings about the proposed inquiry, the PDS impugned the western record, declaring, "The debate about the GDR cannot cover up the inadequate coming to terms with the fascist legacy and give nourishment to right-wing extremist tendencies." This was a concern that was widely held on the German Left and abroad.[7] What is more, the PDS went on the offensive, seeking to legitimize the GDR and delegitimize the FRG with reference to antifascism. It called on the commission to pursue the following questions:

> To what extent was the foundation of the GDR also the expression of a mass movement for an antifascist democratic development in Germany, for a socialist alternative? … To what extent were there positive experiences of democratic renewal in the antifascist-democratic phase in the SBZ until 1948–49 and with the first constitution of the GDR of 1949? … How did the discussion about the fascist past occur in the two German states? Which steps were taken toward "reeducation," denazification, and punishment of those responsible by the victorious powers, the newly formed parties, and the two German states?[8]

Far from merely being concerned that the reckoning with the GDR past might obscure the Nazi past, the Democratic Socialists still believed political points could be scored with the antifascist card.[9]

In the 12 March 1992 establishment debate, Uwe-Jens Heuer (PDS) restated his party's fear that the assault on the GDR was being used to conceal the inadequacies of the West's confrontation with Nazism. He claimed, too, that the parliamentary debate justified this fear, for only Gerd Poppe (B90) had said anything critical about National Socialism.[10] This was a facile criticism, as there was no evidence that any speakers felt anything but absolute loathing for Nazism; indeed, their assessments of the latter were hardly at issue. The debate concerned other questions: the significance of the Nazi past for postwar and contemporary Germany; Nazism's comparability with GDR communism; and the relevance of Nazi *Vergangenheitsbe-*

wältigung for working through the East German past. Yet Heuer also made a more substantial historical point—albeit with polemical intent—when he argued that adopting a view of the GDR that was limited to repression, resistance, and conformity made it impossible to answer the question of "why so many people in all of Germany once worked for the goal of socialism and saw an answer to the catastrophe of fascism precisely in this East German path." These goals had attracted him to Berlin in 1946, not least because he had seen "in West Germany a path toward the restoration of the old relations, largely with the old leadership personnel."[11]

Such Cold War–style attacks from the PDS prompted Cold War–style responses from its opponents. Whereas Dirk Hansen's evenhanded criticism of East and West (quoted in chapter 1) had received applause from the house, Heuer's simultaneous criticism of restorative tendencies in West Germany and his invocation of East Germany's antifascist credentials drew the ire of Christian and Free Democrats. They were more loathe than ever to accept the view that East Germany had dealt with the Nazi past more proficiently than West Germany, and objected directly to his broadside against the latter.[12] Indeed, many refused to accept any substantial or specific criticism of the western record and were keen merely to destroy the GDR's antifascist bonus. Günther Müller (CSU) questioned the antifascist credibility of the KPD by pointing to its cooperation with the Nazis at the end of the Weimar Republic, while Rudolf Karl Krause (CDU) argued that mass murder, expropriation, and other communist crimes—and not just antifascism—lay at the roots of the GDR.[13] Critical views of eastern antifascism thus appeared to unite all but the PDS, while western conservatives remained defensive about the FRG's record.

Deconstructing East German Antifascism

The first inquiry was not only motivated and justified by negative assessments of the East and West German records on the Nazi legacy; it also examined those records, albeit in a highly selective fashion. As we have seen, the PDS wanted an investigation of both postwar states' approaches to the Nazi legacy. Social Democrats also called for the consideration of western *Vergangenheitsbewältigung*, which they felt would provide an informed basis for tackling the communist past.[14] However, the governing coalition parties would have none of it; here, as elsewhere, the focus was to be virtually exclusively on the GDR, and not on both sides of the divided nation.[15] Old left-right ideological battles nevertheless reemerged, particularly regarding the question of the sufficiency of early efforts to face up to the Nazi past in the FRG. Conservatives sought to counter the widespread notion that West Germany had repressed the past until the 1960s, while liberals insisted that the 1950s could not be seen as a period of critical, open debate.[16] These familiar—largely intra-western—disagreements, however, were mere sideshows compared with the discussion of eastern antifascism, the investigation of which was an uncontroversial point of agreement.

In the Bundestag establishment debate and initial discussions within the commission, antifascism was situated in its historical context as one of a number of responses to Nazism. This is certainly how the PDS viewed it, and members of the SPD similarly favored a general historical approach, seeing antifascism as a variety of *Vergangenheitsbewältigung*. The SPD specifically proposed an investigation of antifascism's role among a number of "integrative factors and practices" in the GDR.[17] Such an approach recognized that antifascism had attracted numerous Germans to the SBZ and the nascent socialist republic in its early years, and that it continued to exert a certain moral and political appeal for the East German population, right through to the present.

When the center-right coalition parties agreed to the inclusion of the topic, however, a change in emphasis occurred that profoundly affected the modality of its treatment. A new draft terms of reference added "disciplinary practices" to the SPD's integrative factors, and increasingly the focus was on antifascism's function and its instrumentalization by the regime.[18] The terms of reference eventually listed antifascism alongside Marxism-Leninism as one of two aspects of GDR ideology to be examined.[19] This was characteristic of the narrowing and channeling of the questions the commission asked of East German history: rather than examine a phenomenon in its entirety, or pose questions about sources of support for the GDR or about its adherents' motivations, the inquiry focused on the mechanisms of SED rule, here specifically on the regime's use of antifascism as an ideological and political weapon. Despite all the rhetorical window dressing about addressing the experiences of "those affected," the focus was on the view from above.

Shifting and restricting the investigation's attention to this instrumental perspective had a clear argumentative thrust. The commission majority hoped to discredit antifascism by demonstrating that it had been a tool the regime used to legitimize itself internally and externally. Christian Democrats and Free Democrats—whether easterners or westerners—believed that the East German regime had not learnt any, let alone the right, lessons from Nazism. They upheld their decades-old rejection of East German antifascism, vehemently opposed the antifascist rhetoric of the PDS, and were infuriated by the latter's continuing attempts to claim the moral high ground. That many intellectuals and politicians on the West German Left had been sympathetic to East Germany's antifascist claims only height-ened the appeal of a concerted excoriation.[20]

There were several planks to the effort to discredit antifascism: it was to be depicted as prescribed from above and instrumentalized by the re-gime; the GDR's self-depiction as a state that had thoroughly purged Nazis from positions of power was to be shown to be untrue and its attacks on the FRG as hypocritical; the GDR's treatment of the victims of National Socialism—especially Jewish victims—was to be exposed as instrumen-tal, disrespectful, and inadequate, even persecutory; and antifascism was to be blamed for the explosion in xenophobic violence and right-wing radicalism that occurred in eastern Germany after unification. Running through all of this was conservatives' consistent reduction of antifascism to the SED's official version.

The primary avenue of the inquiry's exploration of the topic was a pub-lic hearing that, according to Eppelmann, occupied a "central place" in its work.[21] The structure and content of the hearing, held in Bonn in March 1993, was revealing. After Eppelmann's opening, Roswitha Wisniewski and Bernd Faulenbach gave introductory statements that concentrated on the regime's instrumental use of antifascism. They were followed by three further papers, the titles of which were indicative of the narrow focus: "An-tifascism as an Integrative Ideology and Instrument of Rule" by Günter Fippel; "The Instrumental Antifascism of the SED and the Legitimation of the GDR" by Manfred Wilke; and "Leading Nazis in the GDR" by Karl Wilhelm Fricke. The speakers also suggest both the considerable extent to which the commission relied on its own expertise and the narrow range of opinion on offer. PDS or Alliance 90 voices that might express different views were confined to question time.[22]

Christian Democrats repeatedly reduced GDR antifascism to the regime's instrumentalized doctrine. In his opening remarks, Eppelmann dismissed out of hand any suggestion that antifascism was not completely discred-ited by its manipulation by the SED. In particular, he rejected the views of those dissident intellectuals who—even during or after the dictatorship's collapse—had held on to antifascism as a "core of the GDR past that was to be maintained through every upheaval." "These people," he insisted, "had not yet been able to grasp the unscrupulous way in which the SED rulers also deployed and misused the ideal of antifascism only as an alibi of their own authoritarian rule."[23] On this view, antifascism consisted en-tirely in its instrumentalization by regime propagandists; this usage thank-fully had been brought to an end, and there were no alternative strands or facets beyond, or prior to its now obsolete propaganda value.

A more complex but still glaring example of reductionism was provided by Wisniewski who as usual addressed the etymological and ideological roots of SED doctrine. She recited official Marxist-Leninist definitions of fascism according to which it constituted the "dictatorship of capitalism" and the "most highly developed form of monopoly capitalism."[24] Repeating and ridiculing such authentic GDR-speak was a staple of conservative condemnations of antifascism, and it seemed to require little further comment.[25] In a manner familiar from the previous chapter, Wisniewski elided distinctions between Marxist and Marxist-Leninist understandings of fascism. More importantly—drawing on and overextending the findings of historian Günter Fippel—she focused on the rise of a "false" antifascism to the status of official doctrine, but completely ignored its "genuine" variant and the crucial question of how it had fared after 1945.[26] The predictable result was that antifascism in the GDR appeared to consist entirely of its utilization by the communist regime, and thus to be illegitimate.

No one before the commission disputed that antifascism had been an instrument of the regime, but there was disagreement over whether it had consisted of anything more than that, and thus about its ultimate legitimacy or criminality.[27] A lone voice questioning the otherwise standard implicit or explicit condemnation of regime instrumentalization was that of the inquiry's deputy chairperson, Margot von Renesse (SPD), who wondered how denouncing someone as a fascist in the GDR differed from labeling someone a communist in the early years of the FRG.[28] Such critical views of West German history and a preparedness to think outside the square of straightforward condemnation of eastern developments were all too rare in the commission, and her question was dismissed by her conservative colleagues.[29]

A related issue was the question of the extent to which GDR antifascism could be described as having been *verordnet* (prescribed) by the regime. This description had been popularized by Holocaust survivor Ralph Giordano in his book *Die zweite Schuld* (The Second Guilt) in the 1980s and was fiercely contested after unification.[30] A commonly drawn inference was that the GDR had been antifascist only by decree from above, whereas the FRG had gone through a more tortured, complex, and authentic process of facing up to its Nazi demons. Conservatives readily adopted the term and, in by now familiar fashion, eagerly equated prescribed antifascism with antifascism per se. At the Bonn hearing, Manfred Wilke referred to denazification in the SBZ as having been prescribed by the Soviet occupying power and claimed—much like Eppelmann in his opening remarks—that appeals to antifascist ideals by intellectuals in late 1989 indicated merely the latter's internalization of the regime's prescribed doctrine.[31] Evidently, there was no other antifascism in which they might have believed.

That the regime had officially ordained antifascism was not seriously questioned, but, as with the question of instrumentalization, there were disagreements about whether one could equate antifascism with the official version and whether its prescription necessarily condemned it.[32] Gerd Poppe was applauded at the Bonn hearing for rejecting the denunciation of "every form" of antifascism as prescribed. He further criticized directly Wilke's argument that antifascism's reclamation by intellectuals and dissidents in 1989 indicated the deep roots of official doctrine.[33] In fact, according to Poppe, it demonstrated precisely the opposite: "that there was also an antifascism that was not manipulated and instrumentalized"; and he defended the appeal to antifascist ideals in the Round Table's draft constitution of 1990.[34] Poppe was not alone. For Konrad Weiß—like Poppe, an East German dissident intellectual and Alliance 90 Bundestag deputy—the notion of prescribed antifascism was "stupid." Weiß insisted that there were different, non-prescribed strands—including a Christian antifascism that saw itself in opposition to the bloc parties and the SED regime—and he proudly declared that he continued to see himself as an antifascist to this very day.[35] Martin Gutzeit also argued that antifascism did not simply entail a negative opposition to fascism, but could produce a more positive stance in favor of democracy and the rule of law, and that this aspect had been prevalent in the thinking of opposition groups and intellectuals in autumn 1989.[36] In response to such views, Wilke reiterated that author Christa Wolf's and dissidents' continuing acceptance of antifascist goals that were "provided" (*vorgegeben*) by the SED was intimately related to their desire to "maintain the GDR," whereas he had wanted to abolish it.[37]

In defending antifascism from wholesale attack, left-wing representatives of the former GDR opposition movements found themselves in uncomfortable agreement with Democratic Socialists, and that is where Wilke's response intended to keep them. In terms quite similar to those used by Poppe, PDS expert commissioner Herbert Wolf criticized the Bonn speakers' lack of "requisite precision." He conceded that the GDR's "false presumptuous halo" must be abandoned, but insisted, "there simply was not just the prescribed, instrumentalized antifascism," and "you can only instrumentalize something that exists and is effectual."[38] Similarly, Dietmar Keller made a personal appeal:

> I think one will only understand the phenomenon of antifascism in the GDR if one does not just depict the misuse and instrumentalization—as was emphasized very strongly in the papers today—but if one also understands antifascism, at least for my generation, as an antiwar position, an antiwar movement or, positively expressed: "Antifascism as a profession of support for peace." I know about the misuse and instrumentalization and I don't want to disagree with everything that has been said here, but no one prescribed antifascism to me.... I would really like this side of antifascism that was not prescribed to be considered too.[39]

Both Keller and Wolf—like Weiß and Gutzeit—thus sought to rescue personal antifascist convictions from the demise of official doctrine.

Yet whereas the former dissidents were most concerned with the final phase of East German history, the Democratic Socialists were particularly preoccupied with its beginnings, as also seen in previous chapters. According to Wolf, personal experiences of war and fascism as well as more general political proclivities motivated people to go to the GDR in the early postwar period, and subsequently to identify with the East German state and even the SED to some extent.[40] In an internal paper mentioned already in chapter 3, Keller portrayed antifascism as the decisive element in the 1946 merger of the SPD and the KPD. He argued further, "This political moment of antifascism was a chance for the SED to survive, and even those generations that did not consciously experience fascism were confronted with this antifascist tradition from an early age and felt attracted to it."[41] Keller acknowledged that antifascism was used as a disciplinary device and he described how for many party members accusations of insufficient "antifascist spirit" were the worst criticism possible; yet for him this indicated not that antifascism was a mere tool of the dictatorship, but that "there was an ideological devoutness in the party that was veiled with antifascism."[42] Of all the views Keller expressed, it was his emphasis on antifascism that attracted most critical comment from his fellow commissioners.[43] Yet his defense was moderate and self-critical in comparison with other Democratic Socialists, who countered the conservative critique with a range of arguments, many of which amounted merely to familiar attacks on the FRG either for its insufficient reckoning with Nazism or for its overhasty demolition of eastern antifascism. Positive arguments of the sort Gutzeit made were rather rare, despite repeated insistence on the Stalinist betrayal of a putatively democratic antifascism.[44]

According to the inquiry's mandate, antifascism was to be examined from the perspective of both disciplinary practices and integrative factors. The SPD had initially proposed the latter, so it was only consistent that Faulenbach placed greater emphasis than conservatives on antifascism as a source of popular identification and integration. Indeed, he argued that it was "probably the most effective [integrative factor] on the ideological level."[45] Rather than being satisfied with dismissing East German antifascism as an instrument of legitimation that held some popular appeal, Faulenbach was interested in understanding how and why it worked as it did, and his approach was characterized by greater differentiation and historicity than that of numerous Christian Democrats. In large part, he agreed with their views on antifascism's functions: that it had been employed against political rivals and instrumentalized to facilitate the establishment of communist power, as well as to justify specific policies; that commemoration of communist anti-Nazi resistance had become a "quasi-religious antifascist state cult"; and that the regime had used antifascism to justify the otherwise unjustifiable, such as the suppression of the uprising in June 1953, the building of the Berlin Wall in 1961, and the Warsaw Pact countries' invasion of Czechoslovakia in 1968.[46] Faulenbach thus repeated the standard list of knockdown points against antifascism as an instrument of political legitimation and control; unlike Christian Democrats such as Wisniewski, however, he did not end his analysis there.[47]

Beyond trying to explain why certain people had identified with it, Faulenbach credited antifascism with "emancipatory potential" and an "inherent potential for resistance" against oppression. But why, he asked, did antifascist sentiment not prevent Stalinist mentalities and structures from developing and dominating the GDR? Why were (communist) antifascists not democratic?[48] Christian Democrats did not pose these questions because they did not credit antifascism with emancipatory potential as Faulenbach did, tending instead to see in any antifascist an undemocratic Communist or—at the very least—a deluded socialist. For Faulenbach, however, history was more complex and open: antifascism's emancipatory potential was paralyzed in the GDR through its particular communist influence, and remained for many Communists of secondary importance after their Marxist-Leninist convictions.[49] Faulenbach was thus highly critical of antifascism's historical function, but he saw this as contingent rather than necessary. Whereas Wisniewski elided the distinction between "genuine" and Marxist-Leninist varieties at the beginning of her discussion, Faulenbach maintained it to the end: "A *specific* antifascism was a constitutive element of the SED dictatorship."[50] On this view, antifascism did not obtain entirely in the official, instrumentalized version. While he acknowledged that it was now largely discredited, antifascism continued to hold positive meaning for people, representing a "last remnant of GDR identity."[51]

Although conservatives concentrated on antifascism as a tool of the regime, they did not ignore integration entirely. In his opening remarks at the Bonn hearing, Eppelmann acknowledged, "We all wanted to be antifascists," and that if ever the regime was at one with the population it was in proclaiming, "Never again fascism." Instead of exploring this idea, however, he claimed simply that as the regime collapsed, East Germans—with the exception of some deluded reform socialists—had come to realize, "Here, too, our government had lied to and manipulated us."[52] Wisniewski also acknowledged that East Germans' integration had been promoted by the justified rejection of National Socialism, through the demonization of the FRG as ridden with fascist continuities, through the worshipping of antifascist resistance fighters, but also through the fear of being labeled a fascist. She also stressed the exculpatory appeal of the Marxist definition of fascism that blamed abstract socioeconomic forces rather than individual culpability.[53] While thus making some effort to explain antifascism's attractiveness, Wisniewski still remained focused on the regime, and her discussion of integration was limited. Her approach excluded the oft-mentioned self censorship of many East Germans (like Christa Wolf or Dietmar Keller), who were insufficiently capable of criticizing the antifascist leadership. She also neglected the years 1945–49, when various political streams that could not have been brought together on the basis of shared, positive political goals were united under the antifascist banner, as Faulenbach pointed out; and she clearly did not want to acknowledge early Christian-democratic support for antifascist unity. Positive integrative aspects—such as contemporaries' hopes for a new, better, antifascist Germany—were ignored.

Nevertheless, much of the commission's discussion focused on what an antifascist position actually entailed: what did antifascists oppose and for what, if anything, did they positively stand? These questions had arisen in discussion of Keller's internal paper, where he was asked to explain what antifascism in fact meant to him, but failed to provide an answer to the satisfaction of his colleagues.[54] At the subsequent public hearing, Keller argued that it amounted above all to a commitment to peace, a response that again failed to satisfy his fellow commissioners, who sought their own conclusions.[55] Faulenbach suggested that "antifascism was somewhat clear only in the anti, but not at all in its positive aims, which were made concrete by communist interests."[56] Dirk Hansen (FDP) also wondered, "Where's the 'pro' if the 'anti' doesn't suffice?"[57] Noting the apparent absence of a clearly defined "pro," Wisniewski concluded: "A state cannot mentally exist in the long term only with the 'anti.' No one can do that, no state can do that. And thus the 'pro' is in reality the big task that we again have to complete, especially in relation to the new federal states" in the East.[58] Faulenbach's, Hansen's, and Wisniewski's points were all more or less valid, but one wonders whether any negatively defined consensus—including the antitotalitarian consensus that the commission was so eager to foster in unified Germany—was any different. Once again, the commission lacked a degree of introspection and criticized others for doing what it did itself.

A further significant component of postunification discussion of antifascism—and the conservative assault on it in particular—consisted of demonstrating that the GDR had not in fact dealt with the Nazi legacy satisfactorily, either on an absolute scale or in comparison with the Federal Republic. Wisniewski, for example, presented the Bonn hearing with a familiar litany of criticisms of the GDR: that genuine antifascists and victims of the Nazis had been subjected to renewed persecution by Communists; that former Nazis had assumed influential positions in the GDR; that there had been no objective research into Nazism; that daily life in the Third Reich had not been the object of interest because exposing the inner workings of dictatorships would have revealed dangerous similarities between the Nazi and communist regimes; that official antifascist rhetoric had become ritualized and meaningless; that the Holocaust had been largely absent from commemoration and research; and that official antifascism had failed to prevent and even fostered the development of right-wing extremism in East Germany.[59] Faulenbach, too, pointed to blind spots, inconsistencies, distortions, and falsifications in official GDR representations of fascism and antifascist resistance in particular, which had not only overstated communist heroism, but lost sight of Nazism's non-communist victims and its racial dimensions, almost completely ignored the perpetrators, and effectively exonerated the mass of the German population.[60]

In this context, postwar denazification, broadly understood, was inevitably a focus of attention, and assessments of its merits varied significantly.[61] Faulenbach argued for the Social Democrats that denazification had been carried out more rigorously in the SBZ than in the western zones, although not as completely as often claimed, since the SED was lenient toward "small" Nazis, while even some higher functionaries gained prominent positions. Nevertheless, he averred, the new political elite in the SBZ and GDR was thoroughly antifascist in composition.[62] He also mentioned the antifascist committees and the "antifascist consensus" of 1945 that saw widespread support across all the political parties for the denazification goals set out at the Potsdam Conference.[63] Democratic Socialists also frequently cited the fact that denazification was Allied policy. They pointed out that in the occupation period, political developments generally were ordered from above and from outside, and that not pursuing a thoroughly antifascist policy was not an option. They wondered, too, whether prescription was necessarily a bad thing, and argued that it was essential given the evident support for the Nazi regime even to the bitter end.[64]

Conservatives, not surprisingly, painted a more negative picture of eastern denazification, not infrequently with rather dubious argumentative strategies. In her Bonn talk, Wisniewski quoted Walter Ulbricht's declaration that the "roots of fascism—the rule of finance capitalism" needed to be removed. On Wisniewski's reading, this was to be achieved through "the purging of the administrative apparatus and scholarly institutions of all fascist elements; through the expropriation of the large land owners, the bank bosses, and large businesses; through the struggle against fascist ideology and against all ideologies that fascism might have been able to absorb."[65] Wisniewski made no further comment on this program, apparently believing that it spoke for itself and was clearly an abominable collection of goals. This ignored two crucial points. The first was that these goals had been widely supported in Germany in 1945–46, including by many Christian Democrats, such that Wisniewski's tacit condemnation of them was ahistorical. The second was that such demands constitute a fairly standard, if radical, plan for a transitional setting, even resembling in their extent, if not in their ideological direction, that which occurred in Germany following the demise of the SED regime. Indeed, the very hearing at which Wisniewski was speaking formed part of reunified Germany's struggle against socialist ideology and "all ideologies that [socialism] might have been able to absorb," such as antifascism. Citing such an agenda as a criminal abomination thus revealed a remarkable but not uncommon lack of self-awareness and a degree of hypocrisy that was unavoidable given the structure of the discourse according to which the FRG constituted an unquestioned norm and the GDR an unquestionable wrong.

At the Bonn hearing, Karl Wilhelm Fricke similarly sought to deconstruct the GDR's reputation as having been founded on thorough denazification. He referred, as had Faulenbach, to the SED's leniency toward ordinary Nazi Party (NSDAP) members and to the rehabilitation between 1949 and 1952 of those former Nazis and Wehrmacht soldiers and officers who had not been criminally prosecuted.[66] Fricke's main focus were former NSDAP members who had gone on to occupy prominent political and administrative positions in the GDR, including as Volkskammer deputies, leading figures in the NDPD, generals in the National People's Army as well as the Stasi, or as government ministers and even members of the SED's Central Committee.[67] It was a remarkable list for a state that claimed to have been thoroughly antifascist and that relentlessly attacked the FRG over former Nazis in leading positions. However, most of those for whom Fricke provided dates of entry into the NSDAP joined in or after the mid 1930s and—as Wolf and Meckel pointed out—many had been no more than ordinary party members.[68] Fricke's suggestion that these former Nazis in prominent positions in the GDR were equivalent to former *leading* Nazis in prominent positions in the FRG was thus rather misleading, but that mattered little compared to the overall thrust of his argument.

As this example indicates, despite the commission's refusal to undertake a comparative study of the handling of the Nazi legacy in East and West, comparative statements and arguments were never far from the surface. In addition to revising the picture of thorough denazification in the East, eastern and western images of the anti-Nazi resistance were the subject of some discussion. Early signs were that the inclusive approach to the resistance mentioned already in the previous chapter would be influential. Wilke claimed that political life in all four occupation zones had been initiated by "men and women of the German resistance."[69] Such a statement appeared to move beyond the disputes of the 1970s, 1980s, and indeed 1990s over whether Communists should be included in the resistance pantheon (given the conventional view of the Right that they be disqualified because they had only sought to replace one dictatorship with another). Significantly, Wilke explicitly included Wilhelm Pieck and Walter Ulbricht (both KPD, then SED) among those members of the anti-Nazi resistance who had assumed political responsibility after 1945. Rather oddly, however, he also included Konrad Adenauer alongside Kurt Schumacher and others in the West, even though Adenauer can hardly be said to have actively resisted Nazi rule, which Wilke later declared to be the key requirement for belonging to the resistance.[70] For all appearances of inclusiveness, Wilke's intent was to level the perceived differences between the more antifascist East and the less antifascist West. In the process, he glossed over the widespread popular sentiment toward resistors as national traitors in the early years of the FRG, and his approach was characteristic of the commission's tendency to criticize the GDR's exclusive focus on communist resistance while not mentioning the FRG's exclusive focus on the military plot of 20 July 1944. Wilke also revealed a remarkable inconsistency in his approach toward anti-Nazi and anticommunist resistance, demanding precise analysis of the function of individuals like Christa Wolf in opposing, supporting, or failing to criticize the communist regime, but being sloppy in relation to Adenauer and the Nazi regime.[71]

When conservatives discussed the SED regime's instrumentalization of antifascist rhetoric they regularly referred to East Berlin's attacks on the Federal Republic, and thus inevitably—if unintentionally—raised the question of how justified those claims of unacceptable continuities had been. Unsurprisingly, members of the Left tackled this question more directly. In his Bonn talk, Faulenbach pointed twice to the fact that East Germany's propagandistic assaults on the FRG as a post- or proto-fascist regime replete with former Nazis in leading positions were made easier and more powerful by the hesitant, scandal-ridden process of confronting the Nazi past in the FRG and by the presence of former Nazis such as Hans Globke in the Federal Chancellor's Office.[72] Alliance 90 expert Armin Mitter similarly argued that omissions in the West's handling of the Nazi past helped explain why antifascism had been instrumentalized by the SED so successfully; however hypocritical and tendentious, the SED's attacks had not been without foundation.[73]

That this was a sensitive point for western conservatives was indicated by their (over)reaction. Just as Uwe-Jens Heuer had been rounded on in the first Bundestag debate when he claimed that the GDR had dealt more thoroughly with the Nazi past than the FRG, Christian Democrats did not leave Mitter's statement unopposed. Dorothee Wilms responded vehemently to his comments, declaring that she would not let it be said that the Nazi era had not been addressed in the first decades of the Federal Republic's existence, and insisting that there had been a series of attempts in that direction, even before 1968.[74] Alexander Fischer also rejected Mitter's alleged claim that the West had not dealt with the Nazi past, and pointed to the research and education activities of historians, universities, schools, and the Federal Office for Political Education in the 1950s.[75] Yet Mitter had not said that nothing had been done to work through the Nazi past; he had merely stated that there had been omissions. Wilms's and Fischer's responses thus constituted misinterpretations or misrepresentations of what he had said, revealing a defensive overreaction to even slight criticism. Mitter repeated his main point: that the West's omissions had been exploited by the GDR.[76] Not wanting to let this stand, Wisniewski countered that the FRG had paid restitution and that scholarly examination had taken place there, whereas it had not been permitted in the GDR.[77]

This was not the only example of such a statement being met with an exaggerated, inappropriate response. In his internal talk about the SED referred to already, Dietmar Keller mentioned the image of the FRG with which his generation in the GDR had grown up: "We grew up with a *Feindbild* [concept of the enemy], with a classic *Feindbild*, meaning Globke, Oberländer, Filbinger, Kiesinger; we knew the biographies that we were taught almost by heart, and the Federal Republic of Germany was for us the legal continuation of the German Reich and thus also the continuation of a fascist past."[78] To this, Fricke reacted with forcefulness similar to that with which Wilms had criticized Mitter's comments. He rejected the supposed reduction of the FRG to the former Nazis in prominent positions whom Keller named, and insisted that "there was always more to the Federal Republic," such as a new democratic system of government.[79] Yet Keller had not proffered such a reduction, but was attempting to explain the *Feindbild* propagated—with some effect—in the GDR.

The conservative defense of the western record on the Nazi past—whether Fischer's and Wilms's insistence on scholarly examination, or Fricke's on the FRG's democratic institutions—sat uncomfortably alongside the view to which the commission generally subscribed, and of which it was a product: that coming to terms with a problematic past necessarily involved "a difficult, prolonged process of consciousness and public-opinion formation that in no way can be developed simply on the basis of files and archival materials," as the commission stated in its final report.[80] This insight did not go hand in hand with a preparedness to examine the process in the West, or to acknowledge the insufficiency of scholarly research not accompanied by a critical societal discourse and genuine political and judicial consequences, as Wisniewski's and Fischer's references to western scholarship on Nazism demonstrated. We thus see elements of a conspicuously uncritical, defensive attitude toward western *Vergangenheitsbewältigung* among western conservatives, who approached the issue as a zero-sum game in which no points could be conceded to the opposing side. They rejected any substantial criticism of the West that might even for a moment seem to allow East German antifascism to stand in a positive light.

The commission also chose to examine one area where it knew official GDR antifascism was particularly vulnerable, and where the Federal Republic had a comparatively strong record: the situation of Jews after 1945. Peter Maser, a theologian who was a member of the first inquiry's secretariat and became an expert member for the CDU on the second inquiry, wrote a report on SED attitudes toward Jews and Jewish communities in the GDR. Like much postunification criticism of the GDR's treatment of its Jewish citizens, the report focused on manifestations of Stalinist anti-Semitism, anti-Zionism, the failure to compensate the Nazis' Jewish victims, and the general "schizophrenia" that had characterized SED positions on Jewish matters.[81] Maser's report was not undifferentiated and acknowledged the considerable extent, for example, of treatments of the Holocaust in East German literature. Yet its argumentative drive was to reject any suggestion of responsible, adequate, or respectful treatment of Jews or the "legacy" of Judaism in the GDR. It amounted to a grab-bag of critical points, jumping for example from a critique of the GDR's propagandistic trials of Hans Globke to the "commemorative epidemic" of 1988.[82] In Maser's account, any ostensibly positive tendencies of the regime were dismissed as purely tactical, while the motives behind more honorable activities from below went unmentioned.[83] That tactical considerations had been central to western compensation policies was, not surprisingly, generally left unsaid.[84]

The main thrust of the inquiry's interest in this topic was unambiguous: to demonstrate that, for all its supposed antifascist virtue, the GDR had treated the Nazis' foremost victims with disregard at best, and contempt and renewed persecution at worst. In defending the inclusion in the report of a brief discussion of the topic against SPD criticism that the commission had not sufficiently deliberated it, Wisniewski argued that "the fate of the Jews in the SBZ/GDR makes alarmingly apparent that for some the transition from one totalitarian ideology and dictatorship to another was possible seemingly without large processes of rethinking."[85] However dubious the GDR's record, it was highly tendentious to draw such a line of continuity from Nazi policies and practices of persecution and genocide on the one hand to SED marginalization and paternalism on the other.

According to conservatives' anti-antifascism, East Germany had treated both Jewish and non-Jewish victims of the Nazis in an inadequate and even condemnable fashion. The Bonn hearing was presented with considerable evidence of communist persecution of people who previously had been victims of the Nazis. The focus of Günter Fippel's paper was that many victims—having survived the Nazis—were exposed to renewed persecution, whether by Soviet or German Communists. He reported that his personal archive included details of 3,721 inhabitants of the SBZ/GDR who were victims of Stalinism, 210 of whom had previously been victims of Nazism.[86] A quarter of these were Jews, and many had been accused by communist security organs of fascist or neofascist activities.[87] Karl Wilhelm Fricke also mentioned examples of victims of or resistors against fascism suffering anew at the hands of Communists.[88] With the exception of Renesse's comments cited above, no mention was made of the persecution of Communists in the FRG or of the denial of compensation to victims of the Nazis because they were Communists or otherwise viewed as unworthy.[89]

A further, related complaint about East German antifascism was that the communist theory of fascism played down the racial dimension of Nazism and overemphasized the class dimension, with the result that the Holocaust was inadequately addressed.[90] Both Faulenbach and Wisniewski pointed to the relative neglect of the Holocaust, and Hansen argued that the term "fascism" trivialized Nazism.[91] Wilms even claimed that it amounted to an insult to the Nazis' victims. Remarkably, too, given conservatives' proclivity for comparisons—especially those between the GDR and the Third Reich, as discussed in the next chapter—which they insisted did not necessarily result in equations, Wilms also argued that calling Nazism "fascism" was an insult to Italian and other fascisms that she believed were "not comparable" with National Socialism.[92] Moreover, Wisniewski asserted in the discussion that "reparations were rejected in the GDR," failing to mention either the intense postwar debate in the East about compensation for Jewish victims or negotiations with Jewish organizations in the 1970s and 1980s.[93] Her unqualified claim also overlooked reparations payments to the USSR.[94] More attuned to developments beyond SED officialdom, Markus Meckel argued that discussing either perpetrator guilt or German suffering had been almost impossible within the confines of official antifascism, but he pointed out that various community groups had undertaken reconciliatory activities with Jewish, Polish, and other groups of victims; this—like the arguments of Poppe, Weiß, and Keller discussed above—suggested that antifascism had various dimensions, a possibility generally ignored or denied by conservatives.[95]

The final plank in the commission's effort to discredit East German antifascism was its attempt to bring it into association with right-wing extremism. The Bonn hearing was revealingly titled "Antifascism and Right-wing Radicalism in the SBZ/GDR."[96] Referring to a brutal arson attack on a home for asylum seekers in the eastern city of Rostock in August 1992 and other horrific racist incidents after unification, Eppelmann's introduction posed the rhetorical question, "Was it the SED dictators' betrayal of the ideal of antifascism that sparked a right-wing radical scene, whose extent and dangerousness we have had to experience bitterly most recently?"[97] The intended answer was clear. Wisniewski asked again whether the decline of faith in antifascism was a reason for the rise of right-wing extremism, and Fippel argued that increasing neo-Nazi activity was "a logical consequence" of the diminishing integrative power of official antifascism.[98] While there are many reasons for believing that a connection exists, the links between antifascism and right-wing extremism—and indeed the causes of the latter generally—are by no means self-evident. Conservatives certainly laid emphasis on antifascism's causal role, whereas liberal and left-wing commentators pointed to other causes, both prior to and after unification. Unsurprisingly, Democratic Socialist Herbert Wolf rejected the tendency to see the GDR as a "breeding station of fascism."[99]

Given the discussion so far, it will come as no surprise that the relevant sections of the commission's report amounted to a sustained attack on GDR antifascism. The report—endorsed not only by the coalition but also by the SPD and Alliance 90/The Greens—listed almost all of the critical arguments discussed above, but failed to reflect the diversity of opinion or the complexity of the subject matter. The focus was very much on antifascism's political function and on its various flaws and shortcomings. The report acknowledged antifascism's integrative importance and its "certain emotional and political" appeal, but did not discuss these at any length.[100] The commission insisted that antifascism "repressed the co-responsibility of the eastern part of Germany for the National Socialist epoch" and resulted in a "certain feeling of moral superiority toward the Federal Republic," helped by the fact that "the considerable reparations payments of the Federal Republic of Germany—which had no equivalent on the side of the GDR—were not mentioned."[101] While admonishing GDR antifascism for not telling the whole story, the commission itself gave only a highly abbreviated and rather tendentious version both of the historical record and of its own discussions.

In contrast with the short shrift given to issues of integration and identification, the report elaborated on antifascism's instrumental political role at considerable length. In a brief section on "The Development of Antifascism," it referred to communist utilization of antifascism for purposes of legitimation, and its instrumentalization against opponents. Concomitant with antifascism, the report continued, was a *Feindbild* that encompassed both internal and external opponents and that could label as fascist any behavior the regime disliked. Inevitably, the examples cited included the regime's blaming of "fascist" forces for the June 1953 uprising and its justification of the Berlin Wall as an "antifascist protective rampart."[102] Further, the report claimed, "denazification occurred by no means as thoroughly as has often been maintained"; instead, "incriminated Nazis were even consciously employed, while on the other hand those persecuted by the Nazis were in no way safe from persecution in the SBZ/GDR."[103] In a further section on "The Function of Antifascism in the GDR," the commission discussed how antifascism had "served the legitimation of SED rule": the SED claimed to bear the legacy of the antifascist struggle, and leading positions "were for a long time filled by 'antifascists'" who possessed "a certain aura" and were "immune to attack."[104] Without mentioning Fippel's distinction between genuine and false antifascists, the report's use of quotation marks around the antifascists in leading positions suggested that their records were less than completely credible. The "myth" of antifascism—a term that had hardly been used, let alone discussed in the commission's deliberations—had developed into a "quasi-religious state cult" that "stimulated idealism and engagement in large sections of the population" but "ultimately stabilized SED rule."[105] Much of this was accurate, if rather one-sided.

The clearest example of imprecision and of a failure to do justice to the range of opinions expressed before the inquiry was the report's handling of the questions of the extent to which antifascism had been prescribed and whether there had been versions of antifascism beyond the official one. The following statement concluded the report's section on "The Function of Antifascism in the GDR": "Seen as a whole, antifascism clearly contributed in no small fashion to identification with the SED. This applies especially to intellectuals who—on the basis of 'prescribed antifascism'—first failed to recognize and correspondingly played down the true nature of the GDR regime. The extent to which it is possible to differentiate between a 'prescribed antifascism' and a democratic one still requires detailed scholarly discussion."[106] The acknowledgment of the possibility of an antifascism other than the official version indicated that the conservative majority had conceded some ground to those who did not simply equate antifascism with communist prescription, and the use of quotation marks also suggested that the notion of prescription was at least to some extent a matter of opinion. However, this statement hardly did justice to the complexity of the issue or the diversity of views expressed

before the inquiry. The report made no mention of the antifascist committees or the broad antifascist consensus of 1945, and the subjective positions
revealed by self-confessed antifascists at the commission's public hearing
were similarly ignored.[107]

Moreover, the report once again displayed a considerable degree of
slippage between the SED, its regime, and the GDR qua state. The first
sentence of the above quotation would be much more accurate—particularly in light of the second—if "SED" were replaced with "GDR." To be
sure, Keller had spoken to the inquiry of his own antifascist identification
with the communist cause and leadership, and a number of other commissioners had claimed that antifascist commemorations fostered such
identification with, or at least hindered criticism of the SED. Yet the discussion relating to intellectuals—both reform communists and democratic
socialists—had focused on identification not with the SED or the "GDR
regime," but with the GDR as a state. The likes of Poppe, Gutzeit, and
Weiß had if anything suggested that antifascism could be turned *against*
the SED in order to create a more democratic GDR, as did the examples
of Robert Havemann and Christa Wolf that had been cited repeatedly in
previous discussions. The commission's hearing had indicated that there
were multiple antifascisms and that subjectivity was crucial. Despite con-
ceding that the last word was not necessarily spoken on the topic, the report suggested unreasonably that anyone who subscribed to antifascism
had been loyal to the SED and was guilty of a lack of historical and political insight and of belittling communist crimes.

What is more, the commission continued its efforts to blame antifascism
for the development of right-wing extremism. In the process, it played
down social and political problems associated with the unification process, positing "genuine GDR-specific causes" rather than transitional, postunification ones. The report pointed to antifascism's failure to prevent the
development of right-wing extremism and suggested—again through the
posing of questions that it said the current state of research was unable to
answer—that a causal link existed between official antifascism and right-
wing extremism. Beyond doubt, in the commission's opinion, was that
"there were continuities of National Socialist thought in the SBZ/GDR."
These were demonstrated by "documentations such as the 'Brown Book
GDR,'" the report claimed with reference to Fricke's talk at the Bonn hearing.[108] This was an extraordinarily unqualified, poorly substantiated, and
hypocritical claim. The alleged continuities were not placed in any context, and it was not clear of what nature or extent they were, or how and
where they had manifested themselves. Moreover, aside from the fact that
Fricke had not actually referred to the *Braunbuch DDR* as claimed, to take
such a publication that sought to expose former Nazis in certain state and

party functions in the GDR as evidence of continuity of "thought" was problematic. It was deeply hypocritical, as any such suggestion that the GDR's own "Brown Book" against the FRG provided proof of continuities of Nazi thought in the Federal Republic would have been dismissed out of hand.[109] The commission's report thus failed to move beyond the self-serving mudslinging of the Cold War. Finally, to allude to such personal and intellectual continuities—that were strongest in the 1950s and 1960s—in the context of explaining the link between official antifascism and a right-wing extremist subculture that developed from the 1970s was more than a little specious, and the report provided no concrete evidence of a causal connection. While the GDR leadership should be taken to task for downplaying right-wing extremist developments, and "secondary values" advocated by neo-Nazis were indeed fostered by the regime, the report did little more than seek to tarnish antifascism by association with right-wing extremism.[110]

Further discrediting GDR antifascism and bemoaning its after effects, the report called for the "correction" of the distorted image it had propagated of Nazism, the Nazis' victims, and the anti-Nazi resistance, in particular at the former National Sites of Warning and Commemoration that had been established on the sites of major Nazi concentration camps. The report stated that the notion was common in the eastern states that the need to remember the Nazi era had become obsolete with the demise of SED antifascism. At the same time, it asserted the continuing significance of the antifascist claim that the GDR had learnt the lessons of fascism and that coming to terms with Nazism was something with which only West Germany need concern itself.[111] How these two consequences of antifascism (or its decline) could logically coexist is unclear. If good antifascist East Germans had really believed that remembering Nazi crimes and their victims was only the business of West Germans, one wonders why the obsolescence of SED antifascism or the GDR would have changed the situation in the eastern states for the worse.

Such flimsy argumentation was characteristic of the commission's tendency to list any negative points against the GDR—particularly in relation to the Nazi past, and especially in relation to the Holocaust and its victims—with little regard for context, sustained argument, or consistency. The main point, after all, was to demolish the GDR's antifascist bonus. Consistent with this aim, the commission majority—this time without the support of the SPD—included in the report a "short statement" on the SED's attitude toward Jews. This was despite acknowledging that the inquiry had not had time to consider "the entire problem of Jews and the Jewish communities" and that even the narrower topic of SED policy on Jewish matters required further research.[112] The report claimed that the survivors of the Holocaust who lived in the SBZ had been exposed to un-specified "new acts of repression"; that Jews had been regarded as passive "victims of fascism" and marginalized in antifascist commemorations; that they could only be admitted to the Committee of Antifascist Resistance Fighters if they had actively fought Nazism, while Jewish participation in the anti-Hitler resistance had gone unmentioned; and that Jews "gener-ally received no compensation in contrast with the Federal Republic." The report mentioned further: Stalin's anti-Zionism and the GDR's anti-Zionist positions even after his death; the strict control of Jewish communities, and Jews' inability to organize themselves politically; the assumption of leading positions in the only permitted Jewish organization by SED func-tionaries; and individual cases of Jewish communities being spied upon by the Stasi.[113] Most of this was true and reprehensible.[114]

Yet it amounted to a gratuitous collection of uncontextualized, selec-tive criticism. The nature and extent of the repression of Jews in the GDR was not made clear, and the implied parallels with Nazi persecution were not put into proper perspective.[115] The report also ignored the fact that some—albeit marginal and skewed—commemoration of Jewish suffering had occurred at the Sachsenhausen and Buchenwald concentration-camp memorials since the 1960s; and that in the 1980s there had been increasing concern in the GDR with Jewish history, the Holocaust, and its victims, some of which reflected an authentic commitment to justice and reconcili-ation from below, and some of which was born of the regime's blatant ef-forts to win perceived Jewish favor and influence in the USA. Continuing the now familiar pattern of skipping over the forgotten year of 1989–90 in the GDR, no mention was made of the fact that the democratically elected Volkskammer had accepted responsibility for the Nazi past and the Holo-caust to an extent that had never occurred under the SED, or that it had indicated a (rather inconsequential) preparedness to pay compensation for Nazi crimes.[116] Such developments suggested an authentic antifascism distinct from that of the regime, and therefore did not fit into the inquiry's desired picture.

Moreover, a set of parallel questions arises in relation to the more or less explicit point of comparison, the Federal Republic. There, too, Jewish resistance was not accorded the same significance as conservative military resistance. For decades, West Germany had exhibited a less than inclusive approach to the Nazis' victims, ignoring in particular communist victims, whether German or Soviet. In the West, too, Jews were for a long time regarded as passive victims and had to engage in a prolonged struggle for recognition and compensation, even after compensation for Israel, Jew-ish organizations, and individual survivors became government policy.[117] The report also ignored the fact that the highly controversial western restitution efforts were motivated not only by an upright sense of moral indebtedness but also by concrete political interests—and were thus instrumentalized—and that they were only possible thanks to the support of the opposition SPD, as the conservative governing parties under Adenauer had not supported them wholeheartedly.[118]

Not only was a very incomplete account given of the West in comparison with which the GDR was found wanting, but the GDR, including its early history, was being judged according to the standards of the 1980s and 1990s. Only then had groups of victims such as the Sinti and Roma, homosexuals, and slave laborers begun to receive substantial attention, having been ignored in both German states; so it was rather cheap to castigate the GDR for lack of inclusiveness. And only from the 1970s onward had either state move beyond its single-minded concentration on communist or conservative resistance.[119] Moreover, the condemnation of the GDR for not sufficiently addressing the Holocaust overlooked the fact that only over time had the Nazis' genocide of European Jews come to be seen internationally as the ultimate collective crime. Finally, conservatives' objections to the second-rate East German treatment of Jewish victims as opposed to communist resistance fighters amounted largely to crocodile tears; in 1992, rather than increasing compensation to the former, the payments offered to the latter were merely reduced to the same level.[120]

That the past should not be judged according to present-day criteria was one of the main arguments with which Democratic Socialists criticized the report. The PDS inevitably emphasized the fact that the Allies had imposed denazification and demilitarization measures on the whole of Germany and stressed that denazification was ratified by international agreements.[121] It also stressed the initial German consensus in favor of general antifascist goals in the early postwar period.[122] Thus both internationally and domestically, an alternative to the fascist German path was legitimate. In the East, the PDS argued, the destruction of what were perceived to be the social foundations of the German *Sonderweg* had proceeded apace.[123] Both power politics on the part of the "imperialist capitalist" forces and Stalinist hegemonic policies and practices on the part of the Soviet occupying power and some of their German supporters had prevented the realization of such an "epochal alternative" at national level.[124] In contrast to the East, West Germany saw the far-reaching continuity of structures and elites with "conservative authoritarian traits," while the "considerable deficits" of denazification constituted for "critical observers a birth defect that was never resolved."[125] The commission of inquiry, the PDS suggested with considerable justification, had "consciously excluded historical lines that lead from the Nazi era into the Federal Republic."[126] In contrast with the commission's simplistic demonization of the GDR, the PDS argued that the East German population had largely agreed with the basic principles of its antifascist and antiimperialist policies. The PDS conceded that antifascism had been interpreted one-sidedly and instrumentalized, but it defended antifascist positions of artists, intellectuals, and the East German education system against accusations that they had been merely affirmative and conformist.[127] Putting a different spin on the commission majority's view that antifascism had immunized the SED leadership from criticism, the PDS suggested that aversion to criticizing particular policies or the regime had arisen more from fear of playing into the hands of the Federal Republic "with its Globkes and Filbingers."[128] The PDS also highlighted the GDR's early acceptance of the loss of German territories in the East and its recognition of and reconciliation with eastern European victims of Nazi aggression.[129]

This, like the majority report it criticized, was a one-sided view, but acknowledging such issues would have given a more complete picture than that drawn by the commission. Yet expecting balance and completeness, it seems, was expecting too much. This was not just due to the approaching Bundestag elections; it also has to be seen in the context of a fierce, ongoing debate about the commemoration of anti-Nazi resistance.[130] Yet as the preceding discussion indicated, the positions in the commission of inquiry were polarized from the beginning. In his contribution to the Bundestag debate of 17 June 1994 on the commission's report, Rainer Eppelmann summarized the inquiry's major findings. They included, he averred, that the GDR had been "wrongly constructed at the foundations," not least because "it rested on an antifascism, of which many of its citizens honestly approved, but that was mendacious at its core because it was instrumentalized without reservation by the SED rulers for their own interests."[131] Over the vocal objections of critical Democratic Socialists and the less strident concerns of some former dissidents and Social Democrats, the chair of the commission of inquiry felt entitled to (continue to) dismiss GDR antifascism as an obsolete component of the SED's system of rule.

More practical matters concerning unified Germany's handling of the legacy of antifascist memorials and commemorative practices were left to the second commission of inquiry, but the first inquiry nevertheless laid some groundwork for its successor. The political tendency was clear from a list of questions developed for a joint hearing with the Bundestag Committee for Internal Affairs held in March 1994 at the Sachsenhausen memorial.[132] It included the following: "How should one handle the structuring of the memorials in the new states, influenced as they are by GDR antifascism? How can the reparations policy of the Federal Republic of Germany be made clear in contrast to the antifascism myth of the former GDR?"[133] Where it did not simply exclude western handling of the Nazi legacy entirely, the dominant conservative approach sought to position selected aspects of it as superior to GDR antifascism.[134]

As mentioned previously, the second inquiry was charged with the development of commemorative policies and specifically with considering the "different forms and content of honoring the resistance" against Nazism in the two Germanys.[135] This suggested greater readiness to include the West, but an uncritical, unbalanced approach continued: questions that dominated the analysis of the East were not asked of obvious West German parallels. To provide one example of the numerous inconsistencies in the second inquiry's report: it (again) criticized the SED's instrumental use of antifascism against the FRG, but praised western politicians in the 1950s for associating memory of the anti-Nazi resistance "with the current dispute with the SED"; such connections, it argued, "correspond[ed] to the self-understanding of militant democracy."[136] It seems the validity of instrumentalization depended merely on which side was doing it. The commission also adopted a rather self-satisfied position in relation to the level of research into and the financial state of western concentration-camp memorials, where, it seemed, everything was in order.[137] Discussion of the West, as the above quotations indicate, was generally limited to commemoration of anti-Nazi resistance, while commemoration and the more general treatment of the Nazis' victims were excluded or limited to continued uncritical praise for western compensation to Israel and Jewish victims. The commission glossed over the substantial hurdles with which those who had advocated more memory of Nazi crimes in the West were confronted, and its account amounted to a straightforward success story marked by the unfolding of an ever more honest and inclusive approach to the Nazis' victims and the resistance (but without open acknowledgement of the less honest and inclusive beginnings).[138] As an SPD minority vote insisted, however, there were also "shadowy sides" to the western story, which was by no means "free of scandals"; the PDS similarly objected with a degree of justification to the report's "historical misrepresentations."[139]

The second inquiry's treatment of GDR antifascism was thus largely consistent with that of its predecessor. The opposing positions of conservative anti-antifascism, tentative liberal historicization, and vocal democratic-socialist defense were still evident at a public hearing held at the Buchenwald memorial in October 1996.[140] The majority on the second commission was somewhat less condemnatory than it had been on the first, but there was certainly no revision of the latter's findings. The second inquiry's report conceded importantly that it was essential to distinguish between the regime's "ideological prescriptions" and the "preparedness of many people" in the GDR "to concern themselves honestly" with the Nazi past, and that even the official approach had increasingly included non-communist victims in the 1980s.[141] Nevertheless, the focus remained on the regime's monopolization, utilization, and "misuse" of antifascism.[142] The conclusion was unchanged: "Commemoration of the victims of the Nazi dictatorship was heavily burdened by the instrumental character of anti-fascism as a legitimation for the rule of the SED. The memorials in the GDR were deeply discredited as elements of communist antifascism."[143] This self-discrediting of official GDR antifascism, however, was not deemed sufficient. In the face of resistance from unspecified "political champions of SED antifascism," the report insisted that "the delegitimation of SED antifascism must belong to the basis of critical historical consciousness in unified Germany."[144] While this view again did not rule out the possibility of other antifascisms, the destruction of the GDR's antifascist bonus—to which the commissions had so eagerly devoted themselves—was to remain an ongoing project for contemporary Germany and a central feature of the broader delegitimation of the GDR and its defenders.

Notes

1. This was despite the obvious similarities on both sides. Cf. von Plato, "Eine zweite 'Entnazifizierung'?"
2. Lothar Probst, "Germany's Past, Germany's Future: Intellectual Controversies since Re-unification," *German Politics and Society* 30 (1993): 27. Cf. John Milfull, "What was Different about the German Democratic Republic?" *Australian Journal of Politics and History* 48, no. 1 (2002): 69.
3. See Naumann, "Die geteilte Vergangenheit."
4. Niven, *Facing the Nazi Past,* 58.
5. On the distinction between institutional and cultural strategies, see Sa'adah, *Germany's Second Chance.*
6. "Zur Auseinandersetzung mit den beiden Diktaturen in Deutschland in Vergangenheit und Gegenwart, 1. Teil," IX: 668, 670f. See Hermann Lübbe, "Der Nationalsozialismus im deutschen Nachkriegsbewußtsein," *Historische Zeitschrift* 236, no. 3 (1983): 579–99; Manfred Kittel, *Die Legende von der "zweiten Schuld": Vergangenheitsbewältigung in der Ära Adenauer* (Berlin, 1993).
7. I: 12.
8. I: 13.
9. See also Elm, *Nach Hitler, Nach Honecker;* Elm, "Zweierlei Vergangenheitsbewältigung"; Bernd Wittich, "Betrifft: Ludwig Elm, Zweierlei Vergangenheitsbewältigung: Damals und heute—DA 7/1991," *Deutschland Archiv* 25, no. 6 (1992): 625–29.
10. I: 89.
11. I: 81.
12. I: 81, 94. Schulte's claim that the treatment of the Nazi past was seen "unanimously" as a bad example is thus not entirely correct, "Die 'doppelte Vergangenheit,'" 363.
13. I: 118, 137.
14. See DBPa: Protokoll 2: 29, 33; Protokoll 4: 5, 9. Such calls were again made, but not met, in the second commission. MDA: Protokoll 13: 18f.

15. When Eppelmann as chair reminded commissioners of the SPD request, Wilms moved to defer the issue. DBPa: Protokoll 9: 6.
16. See Beattie, "Die Delegitimierung von '1968' nach 1989/90."
17. DBPa: Protokoll 3: 41.
18. DBPa: Protokoll 6: 24, 29f.
19. I: 155.
20. Cf. Hans-Helmuth Knütter, "Antifaschismus und politische Kultur in Deutschland nach der Wiedervereinigung," *Aus Politik und Zeitgeschichte* 43, no. 9 (1991): 17–28; Robert Erlinghagen, *Die Diskussion um den Begriff des Antifaschismus seit 1989/90* (Berlin, 1997); Zimmer, *Der Buchenwald-Konflikt*, 46.
21. "Antifaschismus und Rechtsradikalismus in der SBZ/DDR," III: 97.
22. The planners of the hearing had wanted to invite Annette Simon, a psychoanalyst who had published on GDR antifascism and "East German morality" and who would presumably have provided a more grassroots and sympathetic perspective, but she was unable to attend. They had also invited Günther Buch, who was also unable to attend at short notice. As a result, Fricke was called upon to speak, which he did very well given the short notice, but one wonders whether someone with a different perspective could not have been called upon, III: 98. See Annette Simon, *Versuch, mir und anderen die ostdeutsche Moral zu erklären* (Giessen, 1995).
23. III: 96.
24. III: 97.
25. See Manfred Agethen, Eckhard Jesse, and Ehrhard Neubert, *Der missbrauchte Antifaschismus: DDR-Staatsdoktrin und Lebenslüge der deutschen Linken* (Freiburg, 2002).
26. To use Fippel's terms to categorize the entirety of East German antifascism, as Wisniewski did, extended his analysis beyond his own empirical reach and applied it to fields (such as commemoration and education) where it was not necessarily appropriate. Fippel himself stated before the inquiry that his research did not reach beyond 1961, and he was at pains to uphold distinctions between various historical phases that Wisniewski ignored, III: 114f., 118f. For the original article, see Günter Fippel, "Der Mißbrauch des Faschismus-Begriffs in der SBZ/DDR," *Deutschland Archiv* 25, no. 10 (1992): 1055–65. See also Günter Fippel, *Antifaschisten in "antifaschistischer" Gewalt: Mittel- und ostdeutsche Schicksale in den Auseinandersetzungen zwischen Demokratie und Diktatur 1945 bis 1961* (Guben, 2003).
27. See Weber's statement to this effect, III: 145. Cf. Heinz Kühnrich, "'Verordnet'—und nichts weiter? Nachdenken über Antifaschismus in der DDR," *Zeitschrift für Geschichtswissenschaft* 40, no. 9 (1992): 819–33.
28. III: 156.
29. III: 157.
30. Giordano, *Die zweite Schuld*, 211. Cf. Kurt Pätzold, "Die Legende vom 'verordneten Antifaschismus,'" in *Ansichten* III, eds. Keller, Modrow, and Wolf, 111; Jürgen Danyel, "DDR-Antifaschismus: Rückblick auf zehn Jahre Diskussion, offene Fragen und Forschungsperspektiven," in *Vielstimmiges Schweigen: Neue Studien zum DDR-Antifaschismus*, eds. Annette Leo and Peter Reif-Spirek (Berlin, 2001), 9; Haustein, *Geschichte im Dissens*, 219f., 223. As Erlinghagen points out, Giordano was in fact more critical of western developments than eastern instrumentalization of antifascism, *Die Diskussion um den Begriff*, 77f.
31. III: 121.
32. Faulenbach also used the term, albeit in quotation marks, as did Fippel, albeit in more specific contexts, III: 109, 114f., 118.
33. III: 143f.

34. III: 144f.

35. III: 172.

36. III: 162.

37. III: 165.

38. III: 148f.

39. III: 155. The term "prescribed" infuriated democratic-socialist historians. Pätzold sees its "demagogic instrumentalization" as second in importance only to that of the term "unlawful state" for the "purpose of the falsification" of GDR history by Cold Warriors, "Die Legende vom 'verordneten Antifaschismus,'" 111. Cf. Wilfried Schulz, "Die PDS und der SED/DDR-Antifaschismus: Historischer Klärungsbedarf oder nur Nostalgie und neue Feindbilder," *Deutschland Archiv* 27, no. 4 (1994): 408–13.

40. III: 149.

41. Keller, "Die Machthierarchie der SED-Diktatur," II: 3017.

42. II: 3018.

43. See DBPa: Protokoll 24: 15f.

44. See, for example, the discussion of the commission's report in Hans Jürgen Friederici, "Das Thema 'Antifaschismus' im Enquete-Bericht: Kritische Anmerkungen," in *Ansichten* V, eds. Černý, Lehmann, and Neuhaus. See also Kurt Finker, "Faschismus, Antifaschismus und 'verordneter Antifaschismus,'" in *Ansichten zur Geschichte der DDR* XI, eds. Ludwig Elm, Dietmar Keller, and Reinhard Mocek (Bonn, 1998); Günter Benser, "Möglichkeiten und Grenzen einer antifaschistich-demokratischen Erneuerung in Deutschland nach dem zweiten Weltkrieg," in *Ansichten* IV, eds. Keller, Modrow, and Wolf; Pätzold, "Die Legende vom 'verordneten Antifaschismus,'" 121. Emphasis on antifascism is by no means limited to Democratic Socialists. See Michael Geyer, "Germany, or, The Twentieth Century as History," *South Atlantic Quarterly* 96, no. 4 (1997): 663–702.

45. III: 102f.

46. III: 104–8.

47. For other recitations of the litany, see III: 135, 143. The second commission's report referred repeatedly to the "antifascist protective rampart," I: 696, 934, 936, 943, 955f. See also Agethen, Jesse, and Neubert, *Der missbrauchte Antifaschismus*. Whereas conservatives were content with ridiculing the Wall's official designation, commentators on the Left have analyzed more productively how it located fascism beyond the GDR in the FRG. See Kühnrich, "'Verordnet'—und nichts weiter?" 822; Erlinghagen, *Die Diskussion um den Begriff*, 26.

48. III: 108f. Cf. Konrad H. Jarausch, "The Failure of East German Antifascism: Some Ironies of History as Politics," *German Studies Review* 14, no. 1 (1991): 85–101.

49. III: 109f.

50. III: 110, emphasis added.

51. III: 109.

52. III: 96.

53. III: 98.

54. DBPa: Protokoll 24: 15–19.

55. III: 157.

56. III: 108.

57. III: 159.

58. III: 171.

59. III: 98–101. For more complex assessments of GDR treatments of the Holocaust, see Olaf Groehler, "Der Holocaust in der Geschichtsschreibung der DDR," in *Zweierlei Bewältigung: Vier Beiträge über den Umgang mit der NS-Vergangenheit in den beiden deutschen*

Staaten, eds. Ulrich Herbert and Olaf Groehler (Hamburg, 1992); Joachim Käppner, *Erstarrte Geschichte: Faschismus und Holocaust im Spiegel der Geschichtswissenschaft und Geschichtspropaganda der DDR* (Hamburg, 1999); Thomas C. Fox, *Stated Memory: East Germany and the Holocaust* (Rochester, 1999).

60. III: 105ff.
61. For divergent views on denazification's relationship with the establishment of a dictatorship, see Jesse, "Vergangenheitsbewältigung," 717; Helga A. Welsh, "Entnazifizierung in der DDR und die 'Wende,'" in *Wendezeiten—Zeitenwände: Zur "Entnazifizierung" und "Entstalinisierung,"* eds. Rainer Eckert, Alexander von Plato, and Jörn Schütrumpf (Hamburg, 1991), 70.
62. III: 104, 107.
63. III: 104.
64. See Pätzold, "Die Legende vom 'verordneten Antifaschismus,'" 111–14; Doernberg, "Zur Legitimität der beiden deutschen Wege," 125f.; Benser, "Möglichkeiten und Grenzen," 137ff.; Kühnrich, "'Verordnet'—und nichts weiter?" 820f. Cf. Erlinghagen, *Die Diskussion um den Begriff*, 20f.; Zimmer, *Der Buchenwald-Konflikt*, 44; Thomaneck and Niven, *Dividing and Uniting Germany*, 79.
65. III: 98.
66. III: 141.
67. III: 141f.
68. III: 150, 154.
69. III: 123.
70. III: 133.
71. Perhaps feeling he was on thin ice, Wilke sought to support his claim by arguing that those Germans who were politically active during the occupation period at the very least came from parties that had been *suppressed* by the Nazis, a view that equated victims with resistors in a careless fashion, III: 124. Cf. Harmut Mehringer, "Sozialdemokratisches Exil und Nachkriegs-Sozialdemokratie: Lernprozesse auf dem Weg zum Godesberger Programm," in *"Ohne Erinnerung keine Zukunft!"* eds. Burrichter and Schödl; Werner Bramke, "Das Bild vom deutschen Widerstand gegen den Nationalsozialismus im Lichte unterschiedlicher Erfahrungen von Teilung und Umbruch," *Zeitschrift für Geschichtswissenschaft* 42, no. 7 (1994): 597–604; Bernd Faulenbach, "Auf dem Weg zu einer gemeinsamen Erinnerung? Das Bild vom deutschen Widerstand gegen den Nationalsozialismus nach den Erfahrungen von Teilung und Umbruch," *Zeitschrift für Geschichtswissenschaft* 42, no. 7 (1994): 589–96; Jürgen Danyel, ed., *Die geteilte Vergangenheit: Zum Umgang mit Nationalsozialismus und Widerstand in beiden deutschen Staaten* (Berlin, 1995); Case, "The Politics of Memorial Representation." Vergau completely ignores the continuing disputes about the inclusive approach to resistance when she claims that it had already won out by 1989, *Aufarbeitung von Vergangenheit*, 182.
72. III: 108, 110.
73. III: 152f. Cf. Kay Schiller, "The Presence of the Nazi Past in the Early Decades of the Bonn Republic," *Journal of Contemporary History* 39, no. 2 (2004): 285–94; Thomaneck and Niven, *Dividing and Uniting Germany*, 81.
74. III: 158f. For more on the significance of "1968" in this context, see Beattie, "Die Delegitimierung von '1968' nach 1989/90."
75. III: 161.
76. III: 168.
77. III: 170. For an account that similarly highlights scholarship's significance in lieu of a more thorough purge of elites, see Eckhard Jesse, "Vergangenheitsbewältigung im internationalen Vergleich: Die Reaktionen auf den Zusammenbruch des Nationalsozia-

lismus/Faschismus und des Kommunismus," in *Dem Zeitgeist geopfert*, eds. Eisenmann and Hirscher, 29.

78. II: 3019.
79. DBPa: Protokoll 24: 17.
80. I: 745.
81. Peter Maser, "Einstellung der SED gegenüber jüdischen Mitbürgern und zur national-sozialistischen Judenverfolgung," III: 1563.
82. III: 1585f.
83. III: 1587. For a more balanced account that encompasses tactical and more legitimate motives, see Peter Monteath, "The German Democratic Republic and the Jews," *German History* 22, no. 3 (2004): 448–68.
84. Unusually, at the commission's 75th meeting expert witness Eberhard Hubrich, who had been responsible for budgetary and compensation matters in the Ministry of Finance, said that Allied and Jewish World Congress pressure was paramount for the introduction of restitution and compensation policies in the West, IX: 656. Cf. Constantin Goschler, *Wiedergutmachung: Westdeutschland und die Verfolgten des Nationalsozialismus 1945–1954* (Munich, 1992), esp. 309–11; Hans Günter Hockerts, "Wiedergutmachung in Deutschland: Eine historische Bilanz," *Vierteljahreshefte für Zeitgeschichte* 49, no. 2 (2001): 167–214.
85. I: 873f.
86. III: 120.
87. III: 112.
88. III: 143.
89. Cf. Patrick Major, *The Death of the KPD: Communism and Anti-Communism in West Germany, 1945–1956* (Oxford, 1997); Goschler, *Wiedergutmachung*, 316f.
90. This was indeed the case. For a discussion of the "universalization" of National Socialism in the GDR see M. Rainer Lepsius, "Das Erbe des Nationalsozialismus und die politische Kultur der Nachfolgestaaten des 'Großdeutschen Reiches,'" in *Demokratie in Deutschland: Soziologisch-historische Konstellationsanalysen* (Göttingen, 1993).
91. III: 160.
92. III: 157.
93. III: 170
94. See Mike Dennis, *The Rise and Fall of the German Democratic Republic, 1945–1990* (Harlow, 2000), 42.
95. III: 154. Cf. Thomaneck and Niven, *Dividing and Uniting Germany*, 84; Niven, *Facing the Nazi Past*, 25.
96. III: 154. Both this topic and the GDR's treatment of Jews were addressed despite not being mentioned in the terms of reference. Compare I: 189 with 263.
97. III: 96.
98. III: 100, 119.
99. III: 150. See Wilfried Schubarth, Ronald Pschierer, and Thomas Schmidt, "Verordneter Antifaschismus und die Folgen: Das Dilemma antifaschistischer Erziehung am Ende der DDR," *Aus Politik und Zeitgeschichte* 41, no. 9 (1991): 3–16; Kühnrich, "'Verordnet' — und nichts weiter?" 826; Pätzold, "Die Legende vom 'verordneten Antifaschismus,'" 126; Patrice G. Poutrus, Jan C. Behrends, and Dennis Kuck, "Historische Ursachen der Fremdenfeindlichkeit in den neuen Bundesländern," *Aus Politik und Zeitgeschichte* 50, no. 39 (2000), 15–21.
100. I: 268, 278.
101. I: 279f.
102. I: 279.

103. I: 278.
104. I: 279.
105. Ibid.
106. I: 280.
107. See Jörn Schütrumpf, "Stalinismus und gescheiterte Entstalinisierung in der DDR," in *Wendezeiten—Zeitenwände*, eds. Eckert, von Plato, and Schütrumpf; Pritchard, *The Making of the GDR*.
108. I: 281.
109. See Olaf Kappelt, *Braunbuch DDR: Nazis in der DDR* ([West] Berlin, 1981); Nationalrat der Nationalen Front des demokratischen Deutschland, ed., *Braunbuch: Kriegs- und Naziverbrecher in der Bundesrepublik: Staat, Wirtschaft, Armee, Verwaltung, Justiz, Wissenschaft* ([East] Berlin, 1965).
110. I: 281.
111. I: 280.
112. I: 282.
113. Ibid.
114. Cf. Jürgen Danyel, "Bilder vom 'anderen Deutschland': Frühe Widerstandsrezeption nach 1945," *Zeitschrift für Geschichtswissenschaft* 42, no. 7 (1994): 611–21; Thomaneck and Niven, *Dividing and Uniting Germany*, 83.
115. Crucial questions such as whether such repression occurred because they were Jews, or whether they just happened to be Jews, were not posed, let alone answered. Similarly, Wilke had previously provided evidence that suggested that Communists emerging from concentration camps were not *exempt* from becoming the victims of Stalinist purges, III: 133f. He did not demonstrate a causal connection that might warrant the significance attached to "renewed" persecution.
116. See Angelika Timm, *Jewish Claims against East Germany: Moral Obligations and Pragmatic Policy* (Budapest, 1997); Käppner, *Erstarrte Geschichte*; Niven, *Facing the Nazi Past*, 23; Thomaneck and Niven, *Dividing and Uniting Germany*, 84; Herf, *Divided Memory*, 364f.; Monteath, "The German Democratic Republic and the Jews," 460.
117. See Moshe Zimmermann, "Die Erinnerung an Nationalsozialismus und Widerstand im Spannungsfeld deutscher Zweistaatlichkeit," in *Die geteilte Vergangenheit*, ed. Danyel; Herf, *Divided Memory*, 317–21; Niven, *Facing the Nazi Past*, 27; Eric Langenbacher, "Changing Memory Regimes in Contemporary Germany?" *German Politics and Society* 21, no. 2 (2003): 46–68; Robert G. Moeller, "Sinking Ships, the Lost *Heimat* and Broken Taboos: Günter Grass and the Politics of Memory in Contemporary Germany," *Contemporary European History* 12, no. 2 (2003): 147–81.
118. Cf. Christian Pross, *Paying for the Past: The Struggle over Reparations for Surviving Victims of the Nazi Terror*, trans. Belinda Cooper (Baltimore, 1998); Herf, *Divided Memory*, 280–88; Thomaneck and Niven, *Dividing and Uniting Germany*, 80f.
119. Cf. Reich, "Geteilter Widerstand"; Danyel, "Bilder vom 'anderen Deutschland,'" 611; Niven, *Facing the Nazi Past*, 3f.
120. See Jeffrey C. Alexander, "On the Social Construction of Moral Universals: The 'Holocaust' from War Crime to Trauma Drama," *European Journal of Social Theory* 5, no. 1 (2002): 5–85; "Gesetz über Entschädigungen für Opfer des Nationalsozialismus im Beitrittsgebiet," *Bundesgesetzblatt* I (1992), 906.
121. I: 685, 687f., 690. Cf. Pätzold, "Die Legende vom 'verordneten Antifaschismus,'" 112ff.
122. I: 685f., 690f.
123. I: 686.
124. I: 685.
125. I: 686, 689.

126. I: 708.
127. I: 714f., 723, 725.
128. I: 716.
129. Ibid.
130. See Case, "The Politics of Memorial Representation."
131. I: 795.
132. "Beteiligung des Bundes an Mahn- und Gedenkstätten," IX: 225.
133. Ibid.
134. Cf. Zimmer, *Der Buchenwald-Konflikt*, 34f.; Haustein, *Geschichte im Dissens*, 134ff.
135. I: 6.
136. I: 593f., 596, 590.
137. See Wilke's claim that western concentration camps were "well preserved." MDA: Protokoll der ersten Sitzung der Berichterstattergruppe Gedenkstätten: 2. Wilke's statement, like the inquiry's report, failed to acknowledge postwar utilization of former concentration camp sites in the West, again despite criticism of the GDR for its failure to preserve such sites in their "authentic" state, I: 595ff. The commission's greater concern for commemoration of the communist as opposed to the Nazi past at authentic sites was also clear from the relevant sections of the report, 608, 610, 612.
138. See MDA: Protokoll der ersten Sitzung der Berichterstattergruppe Gedenkstätten: 1, Anlage 1; Protokoll der dritten Sitzung der Berichterstattergruppe Gedenkstätten: 2. The report revealed many shared deficiencies, particularly in regard to various victim groups, yet only the GDR was taken to task for the one-sidedness of its commemorative practices until the 1980s. Compare I: 595 and 591; see also 589ff. Cf. Charles S. Maier, *The Unmasterable Past: History, Holocaust and German National Identity* (Cambridge, MA, 1988).
139. I: 600, 628.
140. See "Gedenkstättenarbeit für Nachgeborene," VI: 7–205.
141. I: 596, 595.
142. I: 598.
143. I: 596.
144. I: 598.

Chapter 6

THE DOUBLE TOTALITARIAN PAST

The three previous chapters examined the ideological content and implications of the Bundestag inquiries' work, aspects that have been rather
neglected in the extant literature. This chapter explores the areas in which
their ideological activity culminated, and in which their deliberations
assumed their greatest and probably most enduring public importance.
While the debates about issues such as the SED's foundation, Marxism-
Leninism, emigration from the GDR, or antifacscism were bitterly contested and had undeniable contemporary significance, the latter paled in
contrast with the inquiries' deliberations over the GDR's comparability
with the Third Reich, its putatively totalitarian character, and contemporary Germany's relationship with its double dictatorial past. These topics have received surprisingly little attention in most treatments, which
remain focused on issues of transitional justice, East-West reconciliation,
and individual morality and integrity.[1]

The anticommunist majority's cumulative condemnation of the GDR as
an illegitimate dictatorship based on evil Marxism and mendacious antifascism was radical, but far from complete. A further strategy of retrospective delegitimation of the East German state obtained in the propagation
of numerous similarities between it and Nazi Germany. While the 1990s
are often held to have witnessed the development of a liberal consensus in
Germany over the unrivalled centrality of the Nazi past and the unique-
ness of the Holocaust, the history of the Bundestag's commissions of inquiry tell another, more complicated and ambivalent story. Chancellor
Kohl's instigation of an undifferentiated commemoration of the victims of
war and tyranny at the Berlin *Neue Wache* in 1992–93 is well known, but it
was by no means an isolated incident. Bill Niven has noted that "the totalitarianist reading of the 1933–1989 period ... made inroads" into numerous museums and memorials in the eastern states in the 1990s. According
to Niven, however, "the totalitarianist theorists have found themselves

---

Notes for this chapter begin on page 219.

fighting an increasingly rearguard action."[2] This study, in contrast, shows them on the offensive and argues that it was their liberal and socialist opponents who were on the defensive.

Previous chapters have discussed how particular views about the reckoning with communism were justified with reference to the older reckoning with Nazism. The very fact that the two processes were seen as related indicates that a degree of similarity was posited between the two legacies. Frequently, double *Vergangenheitsbewältigung* was taken to imply a double *Vergangenheit*. But what was the connection between these pasts and the regimes that had dominated them? The answer for many in postunification Germany—especially on the Right but also for many on the center Left—was that both the Third Reich and the GDR had been totalitarian dictatorships. Conservatives eagerly reasserted the totalitarian paradigm that from their perspective had been unfairly maligned and marginalized in West Germany since the 1960s.[3] Unsurprisingly, Democratic Socialists rejected this assessment, and many Social Democrats and liberals also objected to the apparent equation of "red" and "brown" regimes.

Such diverging views assumed immediate relevance for questions about the commemoration of the two regimes and their victims. In 1990, mass graves were discovered of Germans who had died during Soviet internment in the postwar occupation period, while the extent of the persecution and mistreatment of GDR citizens by its security apparatus was also coming to light. These victims of communist regimes—whether the Soviet occupier or the SED dictatorship—called out for commemoration. Complicating matters and bringing issues of comparison and equivalence to a head, some of the sites of postwar injustice had also been sites of Nazi persecution. At several so-called special camps, the Soviets had interned Germans (as well as others, such as miscreant Red Army soldiers) in former Nazi concentration camps or prisons, and the GDR had also used as prisons buildings formerly utilized by Nazi security forces. Some locations— including the most prominent, Buchenwald and Sachsenhausen—had a threefold past: they had been Nazi concentration camps, Soviet special camps, and antifascist National Sites of Warning and Commemoration in the GDR.[4] Many of the issues discussed in the previous chapter relating to antifascism therefore featured in the debate about how to commemorate the various uses of, and abuses at, these sites of memory.

Such complex histories entailed a host of difficult questions. How could multiple pasts be remembered and the abuses and victims of the various regimes commemorated? Could or should commemoration occur collectively or separately? Was equal status to be accorded to the different epochs, regimes, crimes, and victims, or were some more significant than others? Was comparison possible, equation permissible, or were hierarchies necessary? These questions were bitterly contested in Germany after 1989, and they were the subject of intense discussion within and around the commissions of inquiry. Indeed, the inquiries were a central forum of Germany's commemorative politics, actively participating in the re-contestation of the West German Historians' Dispute of the 1980s.[5] On one level, the answers the commissions gave appeared clear: they stated explicitly that comparison of the Nazi and communist regimes was legitimate and necessary, but that such comparison should not entail equation, and that it was necessary to remember communist crimes without relativizing Nazi crimes. On the surface at least, this position represented a significant advance on similar debates in West Germany, where some on the Right had equated communism and Nazism, while some on the Left had rejected their comparison. A sensible—indeed the only sensible—compromise seemed to have been reached. Yet despite all protestations to the contrary, conservatives continued to object to what they saw as an ongoing hierarchy of memory and continued to make more or less explicit equations of the two regimes. It is therefore incorrect to suggest, as some have, that those who upheld the singularity of the Nazi past had an easy victory in Germany after unification.[6]

The Double Dictatorial Past

Despite the fact that the reckoning with communism was in part motivated by attitudes toward the reckoning with Nazism, discussing and discrediting the GDR did not necessarily entail comparing (or equating) it with the Nazi regime. Early debates in and around the Bundestag commission concerned primarily the workings and victims of the SED regime and postwar division and the present need for inner unity. The motions for the establishment of a commission of inquiry by the SPD, Alliance 90, and the governing coalition made no mention of Nazism. Moreover, the Bundestag establishment debate in March 1992 was dominated by conflict between Social and Christian Democrats over *Deutschlandpolitik* and bloc-party responsibility, and thus by allegations (and their rejection) of excessive softness on or collaboration with the SED.[7]

Yet there were early signs that the Nazi past would play an important role, above and beyond the lessons drawn from *Vergangenheitsbewältigung* discussed in chapter 1 and the competition over it discussed in the previous chapter. Echoing concerns that unified Germany might marginalize the Nazi past in its haste to work through East German history, a number of eastern and/or left-wing parliamentarians felt compelled in the Bundestag establishment debate to remind their conservative colleagues of the Nazi past, which the latter—in their zealous condemnation of communism and its fellow travelers—seemed disinclined to mention. For instance, after Wolfgang Schäuble described the GDR twice as a "totalitarian system" and referred to "totalitarian socialism" a further five times, Markus Meckel stressed that the GDR was not the first, but the second dictatorship in Germany.[8] It was in this context, too, that Uwe-Jens Heuer argued that the inquiry had to address Germany's twentieth-century history in its entirety and that one could not depict the GDR "as the continuation of the Nazi state" without saying anything further about the latter.[9] An interjection by Günther Müller (CSU) during Heuer's speech revealed the oft unstated views of conservatives: "Very true! Red and brown!"[10] Müller demonstrated the conservative predilection for equating communism with Nazism when talking directly about the latter was unavoidable.[11]

Not mentioning Nazism was impossible, and in fact bringing the GDR into immediate association with Nazism was a key goal for many commissioners. Numerous staunch anticommunists, whether western conservatives, Social Democrats, or eastern former dissidents, wanted the communist regime and communist ideology discredited as thoroughly as the Nazi regime and Nazi ideology. According to Manfred Wilke, for example, it was unacceptable to "allow the damning of the Nazi dictatorship for all eternity, but to allow the SED dictatorship to be justified on the basis of the happiness of the people." Wilke's specific objection to justifications or defenses of the GDR that played down the significance of its dictatorial nature and minimized its human rights abuses and systemic injustices was perfectly valid. Yet he revealed both a desire that the two regimes be regarded with equal abhorrence and some resentment that this was not the case.[12] The GDR, too, should be damned for all eternity.

Pursuing this goal amounted to a conscious attempt to reverse historical and cultural developments in West Germany since the late 1950s (and East Germany since 1945). Both German states had always defined themselves in opposition to each other, but also, in different ways, in opposition to the Nazi past as well as to various older strands of German history that were regarded as leading to the Third Reich. With each passing decade, however, the direct political significance of those older pasts had faded. In particular, with the decades-long stability of the Federal Republic, the trauma of the "Weimar syndrome"—the question of how Weimar democracy had allowed its own abolition—was effectively laid to rest.[13] In contrast, the significance of Nazi crimes for definitions of German identity and self- and external perception had only increased over time. The significance of the Third Reich qua dictatorship had receded, but in academic scholarship, cultural representations, political commemorations, and popular consciousness the question of how the genocide of the Jews could be perpetrated by a supposedly cultured and civilized people in the heart of Europe remained as burning as ever. West Germany's memory battles of the 1980s had not been fought over the dictatorial nature of the Third Reich, but over the Holocaust's implications for German politics and identity.[14] Moreover, it was generally felt that the Left had won those battles; that its objections to conservative equationist tendencies and its insistence that the Holocaust constituted a singular evil and a unique burden had carried the day. The postunification efforts of anticommunists to damn the GDR for all eternity thus required this outcome to be overturned. The fact that the East German regime had not committed genocide was not to be allowed to prevent it being condemned as vigorously as the Nazi regime. The parallels (discussed in the previous chapters) drawn between Marx and Hitler or between Nazi and East German treatment of Jews were just the start.

Although Wilke and other committed anticommunists had no objections to taking up the fight with the western Left, they were highly aware that the latter had much of world opinion on its side. Germany's neighbors and allies had suffered much more from National Socialism than from "real existing" socialism, and reactions to the prospect of German unification had revealed continuing fear in many quarters of resurgent German nationalism and power. Moreover, many of Germany's allies such as the USA and Israel had developed cultures of memory in which the Holocaust played an important, if not central role; from their perspective, Nazism constituted by far the greater evil.[15] As Dorothee Wilms stated at the commission's second meeting, "Overseas is watching how Germany is dealing with the second German dictatorship, which it believes does not have the same place in German history as Hitler's dictatorship." This awareness was one reason for conservatives' repeated denials of a desire to equate the two regimes and their frequent insistence that, "Comparison does not mean equation."[16]

Nevertheless, a number of strategies were employed to strengthen the association of the GDR and Nazism. That the history of coming to terms with the Nazi legacy was held to be relevant to the debate about working through the GDR ostensibly reflected the similarities between the post-1945 and post-1989–90 situations and the instruments of transitional justice available to democratic successor states. Yet the distinction between the handling of the two pasts and the pasts themselves was often overlooked and sometimes, it seems, deliberately elided.[17] Both before the commission of inquiry and beyond it, arguments for equal, comparable, or more rigorous treatment frequently presumed or asserted the basic equivalence of the Nazi and GDR regimes. The double reckoning was thus taken to assume and imply a double past.[18]

A more direct method of bringing the GDR into association with Nazism was through the application of similar vocabulary not to their legacies, but to the regimes themselves. This occurred with a series of terms, including "unlawful state" (*Unrechtsstaat*), "unlawful regime" (*Unrechtsregime*) and "rule of violence" (*Gewaltherrschaft*), but "dictatorship" was if anything more prominent and effective. As we have seen, it was in no small part due to the Bundestag's inquiry that "SED dictatorship" became such a common designation for the GDR after 1990. Importantly, the term allowed the connection of the Nazi and East German regimes, as exemplified by Rainer Eppelmann's statement in the debate on the commission's establishment: "Let us formulate the most important lesson of our century for us Germans: 'Never again dictatorship!' Whatever denotation it may have: national, religious, National Socialist, socialist, communist—never again dictatorship!"[19] The regimes' largely undisputed dictatorial nature was taken to constitute their primary commonality.[20]

Even more immediate associations were created by referring to the GDR, as commissioners and the commission often did, as the "second German dictatorship," or by talking of "two" or "both" dictatorships in Germany.[21] Considering how common the designation of the GDR as the second German *state* had been prior to unification—with the Federal Republic designated the first postwar German state—the new emphasis on its affinity with Nazism constituted a remarkable and deliberate change.[22] Designations such as the second German dictatorship, while factually uncontroversial, led to frequent banalities and imprecision, as the two regimes were lumped together with scant regard for their particularities. One example, which shall suffice for many, was Eppelmann's argument that understanding the reality and consequences of the two dictatorships required a European perspective, a claim he justified by arguing that "both dictatorships in Germany had effects on our neighbors, all of Europe, and the world."[23] He elaborated this inane claim by saying rightly that the peoples of the world had had to make great sacrifices to bring down the first dictatorship, and that Germans had the generosity and trust of their neighbors to thank for allowing unification after the end of the second dictatorship.[24] Such statements—that in fact indicated less that both dictatorships had an impact on all of Europe (let alone the world), than that the latter had affected the outcomes of the two German regimes—exemplified the platitudes and inaccuracies that arose from careless talk about what united the two German dictatorships.[25]

Similarly problematic was the notion of continuous dictatorship from 1933 to 1989. In the Bundestag establishment debate, Gerd Poppe spoke of the East German population's resistance to indoctrination even "after a total of fifty-six years of dictatorship."[26] This motif was taken up in drafting the inquiry's terms of reference whose preamble stated, as previously quoted, that East Germans "had been subjugated to dictatorial forms of government over a period of almost six decades," a formulation Eppelmann highlighted positively in the ratification debate.[27] Not surprisingly, Democratic Socialists vigorously rejected it as an unacceptable insinuation. In addition to ignoring the "democratic beginnings" in the East after 1945, Andrea Lederer claimed that it perpetuated the Historians' Dispute by denying fascism's "singularity."[28]

The Double Totalitarian Past

Casting the GDR as Germany's second dictatorship and placing it in direct association and continuity with the Third Reich did not go far enough for some. During the commission's early deliberations, Christian Democrats, Free Democrats, and some more anticommunist Social Democrats referred repeatedly to the GDR as a totalitarian regime or called explicitly for it to be addressed with the concept of totalitarianism. As we have seen, Wolfgang Schäuble vigorously employed the notion in the Bundestag debate, where Angela Merkel also stated, "For the second time we Germans stand before the difficult question of how we should deal with a totalitarian past."[29] Dirk Hansen suggested that totalitarianism was a concept that could be usefully applied, despite the Historians' Dispute having shown that one had to avoid relativizing the Nazi past.[30] Less hesitantly, Hartmut Soell (SPD) declared that the inquiry's mission was to discredit "the left-wing variant of the totalitarian temptation," and Alexander Fischer called directly for the commission to make a "statement" early on in its term "about a certain continuity of totalitarian structures in the German history of the twentieth century."[31]

As with the topic of antifascism, the SPD made the first concrete proposal to examine "the question of continuities of thought, behavior, and structures in twentieth-century German history," and this, too, was greeted with general enthusiasm.[32] The formulation was soon incorporated into the inquiry's mandate, following changes suggested by Jürgen Schmieder. Schmieder reported the desire of the Federal Ministry for Justice, led by his FDP colleague Klaus Kinkel, "to touch upon and allow certain analogies and comparisons between the Nazi regime and the repressive apparatus of the Stasi."[33] "Analogies" were therefore added to the SPD's continuities, as was an explicit statement that those with "the era of the National Socialist dictatorship" were of particular interest.[34] The gate was thus open for extensive comparative and analogous discussion of the GDR and Nazi Germany.

It would be misleading to suggest that exploring continuities and analogies was one of the first inquiry's major tasks, but they nevertheless played a significant role in its work, as did the notion of totalitarianism.[35] Frequently, they crept in almost unnoticed. Indeed, as one observer-participant noted, the inquiry used the concept of totalitarianism "almost self-evidently."[36] Yet there were also more explicit discussions. The main focus of the first commission's deliberations on analogies, continuities, and comparisons was a two-day public hearing "On the Confrontation with the Two Dictatorships in Germany in Past and Present," that was held in the Reichstag building in Berlin on 3–4 May 1994. It was the first inquiry's final public hearing and the commission regarded it as a central event, even the culmination of its work. Commissioners referred to the event as a "totalitarianism hearing" and subsequently stressed that it had affirmed the legitimacy not just of the comparison of the two dictatorships, but also of the totalitarian paradigm.[37]

Far from resolving the longstanding debate over the usefulness of the notion of totalitarianism and its application to the GDR, however, the inquiry actually perpetuated many of the paradigm's flaws and limitations. Indeed, the commission's approach to GDR history typified them in a number of ways. First, like totalitarianist approaches, the commission concentrated on power structures, mechanisms of rule, oppression, and repression and did not address the entire social reality of life in the GDR. As we have seen throughout this study, for all its desire to include ordinary people and in particular the victims of the regime in its deliberations, the inquiry's primary interest lay not in East German history per se, but, as its title indicated, in the SED dictatorship. This was evident in the topics investigated and the mode of investigation. Antifascism, for example, was of interest only insofar as it had been instrumentalized by the regime, while everyday life was investigated with a view to finding examples of everyday repression and material shortage. Historical explanation, social experience, and subjective questions of individual motivation, loyalties, and beliefs took second place to the search for examples of communist brutality, hypocrisy, and failure.

This was particularly true of the commission's explicit deliberations on the totalitarian paradigm and the comparability of Nazi Germany and the GDR. Here, life in the two states was not at issue; the focus was on a comparison of the two dictatorships' systems of rule and their crimes and abuses. The first session of the May 1994 Reichstag hearing was nominally devoted to "National Socialism and SED Dictatorship in Comparative Perspective." Here, conservative historian Horst Möller pursued a "structural analysis" of the two regimes, listing "comparable techniques of power" and providing a very incomplete comparative discussion of various crimes and groups of victims, on which more below.[38] The inability of the totalitarian paradigm to capture more than the structures of rule and oppression and to adopt a perspective other than the view from above was also evident in a treatise on totalitarianism by commission secretariat member Bernhard Marquardt. Like Möller, Marquardt discussed political structures to the virtual exclusion of other questions, justifying this by claiming that "the content and the goal of the politics of a state reveal themselves" in its "structure of rule."[39]

Social Democrats and liberals objected to such concentration on the regime, with little impact. At the Berlin hearing, historian Jürgen Kocka insisted that "the many layered historical reality can only be partially decoded as an object of dictatorial state rule alone," and that the notion of totalitarianism forced one to look "from above, from the system onto the society," and ignored "many aspects of life, of everyday life, of sociability."[40] In the subsequent discussion, Bernd Faulenbach called for the inclusion of popular experiences to complement the examination of the regime.[41] Such exhortations came too late for the first commission, which did not provide a more complete picture of historical reality but was content to deconstruct the dictatorial political system. The brief justification of the use of the concept of totalitarianism in its final report listed a series of commonalities relating to the political structures and crimes of the regimes.[42] In response, an SPD minority report referred to (possibly divergent) "experiences" of totalitarian rule, while the PDS dissenting report insisted more forthrightly that the complex social reality of the GDR could not be embraced by biased totalitarian theories.[43]

A second, related deficiency in the commission's method that also reflected more general problems of totalitarianist approaches was its focus on the regime's goal of total societal domination to the neglect of the realization of its ambitions. The inquiry frequently either elided the difference between the regime's claims and their execution, or simply emphasized the former. Apart from when used either merely attributively to denounce the party or the political system, or in the context of explicit calls for the application of the totalitarian paradigm, most instances of the utilization of the notion of totalitarianism in the commission's hearings, expertise papers, and final report referred to the SED's totalitarian claims, rather than to their achievement or effectiveness. For example, the first sentence of the historical substance of the report declared, "The fundamental basis of the more than forty-year long SED dictatorship was the totalitarian claim to power of the Soviet and German Communists," and the report went on to list a "series of elements of totalitarian rule" through which the SED had ensured its monopoly on power, including the "as-far-as-possible total coverage of people" through mass organizations, mobilization, militarization, ideological education, etc.[44] The question of what had been possible was glossed over. Significantly, too, the report's justification of the use of totalitarianism declared, "The dictatorship of the SED, like the Nazi dictatorship, corresponded to a system that subjected the individual and the society ideologically, politically, and organizationally to the monopoly claim of a party" and stated that "both systems wanted to reorganize society and create a 'new person'—admittedly with very different goals, methods, and consequences."[45] The extent to which either had succeeded was left open, and the consequences were not elaborated.[46]

Conservatives were not unaware of these problems. At the Berlin hearing, Möller noted the common objection that the totalitarianism model does not allow for resistance, opposition, and accommodation, or for niches of relative freedom from the state's clutches. He countered such criticisms by claiming that these phenomena do not alter the party's "totalitarian claim," and by insisting that distinctions between ambitions and their realization were "marginal, not central for the question of the applicability of the term"[47] On this view, rule by a totalitarian party rather than the totalitarian rule of the party was crucial. This was by no means an untenable position, but it rested on a particular definition of totalitarianism that was not explicated clearly or applied consistently.[48] Moreover, as Kocka suggested, rather than altering one's definition in order to make it fit the GDR, one might investigate the "limits of the achievement of dictatorial rule."[49] Indeed, the extent of such limits remains a central issue in the ongoing scholarly debate about the GDR. Few doubt that the SED made encompassing, even total claims over individuals, groups, and society as a whole, but there has been vigorous discussion about the extent to which it was able to achieve its aims and whether one can equate its claims with historical reality. One might expect that the inquiry's discussion would have commenced, rather than been broken off at this point, but the desire to cast the GDR as a totalitarian state meant that such questions were rarely posed, let alone answered in its deliberations.[50]

The third major problem with totalitarianist approaches—including that of the inquiry—was their ultimately phenomenological rather than analytical or explanatory character and their insufficient openness to historical subtleties, nuances, and changes over time. As liberal sociologist Sigrid Meuschel argued at the Reichstag hearing, totalitarianism is "actually no theory" but an "accumulation of characteristics" that neither offers an explanation for their interconnection nor suggests a social or political dynamic.[51] Instead, it presents certain criteria against which regimes are judged to be totalitarian or non-totalitarian, or somewhere in between.[52]

Secretariat member Marquardt conceded that totalitarian theories had failed to deal adequately with the "historical-genetic dimension," but ultimately for Marquardt totalitarianism was a "typology."[53]

Clearly, typologies have limitations. One of this typology's limitations, as it was applied by the inquiry, was that many of its components—the purported similarities between the regimes—were superficial or banal. This was aptly demonstrated when Möller accepted a series of qualifications and objections to his claim that the NSDAP and SED were fundamentally similar totalitarian parties, but insisted nevertheless that they were identical instances of a "mass organization that is thoroughly hierarchically structured and whose task is the execution of rule."[54] Such a superficial statement—valid, but almost meaningless—indicated the limited explanatory and analytical power produced by a dogged determination to highlight similarities. The commission report's elaboration on the applicability of the concept of totalitarianism to the SED dictatorship was similarly general, consisting, as mentioned above, of a list of characteristics and abuses that united the two German dictatorships.[55] Such generality was a favorite method for circumventing the problem—pointed out by Kocka at the Berlin hearing—that the closer one looked, the more apparent the differences between the regimes and their histories became.[56]

The fourth problem with the commission's use of the totalitarian paradigm was related to the third, but derived its particular significance from the specific context of the discussion of Germany's double past. Commissioners and experts appearing before the inquiry frequently equated the Nazi and GDR regimes implicitly, or glossed over substantial differences, and concentrated on often partial, tenuous, or superficial similarities and parallels. This was despite their regular protestations that comparison did not mean equation and that the inquiry was interested in differences as well as commonalities. Such equationist tendencies were fostered by the application of totalitarianism as a tool for comparisons of dictatorships, which amounted to the confusion of two distinct sets of assumptions, perspectives, and questions. Comparison of dictatorships, its proponents and critics agree, should entail the balanced examination of similarities and differences between dictatorships. In contrast, the notion of totalitarianism helps to elucidate differences between putatively totalitarian dictatorships on the one hand and other systems of rule—primarily authoritarian regimes or democracies—on the other. Its practitioners therefore posit similarities, rather than differences among "totalitarian" regimes.[57] This commonplace but fundamental distinction was (and is) frequently overlooked. The two sets of questions were conflated, leading to misunderstandings and problematic results that might otherwise have been avoided despite the undeniable diversity of opinion on these complex matters. Many positions were not absolutely irreconcilable, but the blurring of the debate about totalitarianism on the one hand and the comparison of dictatorships on the other and the failure to recognize their divergent comparative parameters led to considerable confusion and mutual suspicion, creating rather more heat than light.[58] This point requires some elaboration.

Strongly anticommunist Christian and Free Democrats advocated both the comparison of dictatorships as well as the use of the totalitarian paradigm. They perceived fundamental affinities between the SED and Nazi regimes, which they regarded, rightly, as having had more in common with one another than they had with democracies. Yet while they professed to be interested and engaged in balanced comparison, they were actually more interested in what the regimes shared, than in what separated them.[59] This was made abundantly clear by Horst Möller, who explained to the commission that it was impossible to undertake a detailed comparison of the two political systems in half an hour: "That's why I will try to reflect—on the basis of structural *similarities*—on the question of comparability or non-comparability."[60] Similarly, for Rainer Eppelmann differences seemed merely to obstruct comparison. He opened the Berlin hearing by declaring that every comparison of the two dictatorships had to bear in mind "the three fundamental differences that *limited* the comparative perspective on National Socialism and real socialism," namely, the former's "crimes of racism, genocide, and the unleashing of a war." "Only when that is stated quite clearly," he continued, "can we think and speak about what makes the dictatorships comparable." For Eppelmann then, "comparable" meant not similar in some respects and different in others, but only similar. The outcome of the "comparative" discussion was thus clear from the start: "Both dictatorships were comparable in that—that's my opinion—they were totalitarian dictatorships."[61] In other instances, such as Alexander Fischer's statement that undertaking the comparison is a "method, to be sure, but also a substantial statement," the result of comparison was revealed to be of secondary importance; here, the mere act of comparison indicated basic affinity.[62] These strident anticommunists were not interested in the differences between the dictatorships; they treated their comparison primarily as an avenue for highlighting what they had in common.

They thus did not seek a balanced comparison of dictatorships, but a search, above all, for what united totalitarian dictatorships and, secondarily, what distinguished them from other regimes, especially democracies. Expert witness and right-wing political scientist Klaus Hornung made this explicit. He argued before the commission that totalitarianism was a designation of a certain type of regime, indeed a "counter type to the liberal-democratic constitutional state," and that the notion "makes clear that the systems in question display more commonalities and similarities amongst themselves, than they possess in comparison to the liberal-democratic counter type."[63] While this constituted a perfectly reasonable summary of totalitarianist approaches, Horst Möller's comments revealed the frequent (con)fusion of dictatorial comparison and totalitarianism: "Let me come to the main point: In what then does such a comparison obtain? … We start from and must start from the political-ideological opposition of *all* totalitarian ideologies of the twentieth century to the liberal-democratic state ruled by law. And this means that with the early totalitarianism theorists, beginning with C. J. Friedrich, we have a series of defining characteristics of totalitarian systems … that in my view apply to the Nazi dictatorship as well as to the GDR dictatorship."[64] On this analysis, underlying any comparison of the two German dictatorships was their fundamental difference from, and opposition to, liberal democracy and their fundamental similarity with one another.

With this approach, any differences between the dictatorships were only of tertiary importance. To be sure, Möller insisted that "comparison does not mean equation," and that it was "a political distortion of scholarly discussion" to maintain "nonsensically" that any comparison was aimed at equation. Such protestations were logically true and presumably also honestly intended. Yet they were practically irrelevant if one then put the differences to one side or if one assumed that the notion of totalitarianism and the "fundamental opposition between democracy and dictatorship" were essential for the comparison.[65] Such an assumption was neither necessary nor self-evident, but it was central to the thinking of Möller, Eppelmann, and other conservatives, who conflated the totalitarianism debate with the comparative discussion of dictatorships.[66]

Conservatives' desire to focus on similarities between totalitarian regimes led to problematic approaches to the regimes' crimes. In comparing the GDR and the Third Reich, they often placed Nazi crimes to one side, all the better to focus on the similarities between the regimes' political systems. Eppelmann, as we have seen, saw Nazi crimes as "limiting" the comparison of the two dictatorships.[67] Möller also seemed to suggest that crimes should be external to the comparison of political systems and structures, to which the former were apparently not intrinsic. The exceptional nature of the Nazis' crimes and the fact that the GDR had not committed genocide or waged war were thus regarded as irrelevant, or at least far from central to the comparison.[68] This was clearly a problematic approach, both from a scholarly perspective and in relation to public memory in contemporary Germany.

When they were not extricating crimes from regime comparisons, conservatives sought to establish direct parallels between GDR and Nazi persecution and inhumanity or to qualify or ignore the considerable differences between them. Eppelmann, for instance, spoke of the two regimes' fundamental "disregard for people."[69] Marquardt listed among numerous similarities the "systematic abuse of human and civil rights" and the persecution of dissidents, concluding, "In such features both systems were alike."[70] Möller argued that "all totalitarian systems are characterized by the *marginalization* and repression, in part extending to murder, of large groups of the population that are defined as political enemies."[71] Aside from the absence of any quantitative detail and the lack of specificity in relation to the nature of such marginalization, one wonders whether its different forms warranted more attention than Möller gave them, and whether without such attention his statement reached a dubious level of abstraction.[72] Even the GDR's "failure" to launch a war was qualified in the conservative effort to draw parallels between it and the Third Reich.[73] With considerable justification, Kocka responded: "It is not right to equate the two German dictatorships according to the degree of their criminal inhumanity. Such an equation also easily contains a certain belittlement of Nazi crimes."[74]

Another common conservative approach lay in shifting between the GDR specifically and communism more generally. Möller, for example, conceded that "in communism" there was "no 'racial murder' of millions." But he insisted that there was "murder of millions out of different ideological motives, a class murder, as in the Stalinist system," and that terror and political murder began with Lenin and not Stalin.[75] This was perfectly correct, but had little directly to do with the GDR. Alluding to mass murders in the USSR in the 1920s—as CDU expert commissioner Friedrich-Christian Schroeder also did—amounted to condemning the GDR by association.[76] Members of the moderate Left complained repeatedly that National Socialism and Soviet Stalinism were being compared (or equated), whereas the GDR was supposed to be at issue.[77] Conservatives generally ignored such objections, although Wilms and Gerd Poppe made the valid point that one could not understand the GDR without reference to the USSR.[78] In similar fashion, distinctions between the SBZ and the GDR were frequently ignored, for example when the second commission's report referred to "the communist dictatorship," the "double past," and the "dual dictatorial past of the Germans."[79] The use of these terms for pre-1945 Nazism and post-1945 communism persisted at the expense of the more accurate differentiation of three pasts: the Nazi era, the period of Soviet occupation, and the years of the GDR itself.

In contrast with—indeed as a conscious correction of—the conservative tendency to focus on the similarities and gloss over or qualify the differences, Social Democrats and liberals took literally the ostensible topic of discussion: the comparison of the GDR and the Third Reich. They insisted on addressing the GDR rather than Stalinism or communism more broadly, and were more open than conservatives to the differences between the regimes. In deliberate contrast with Möller and Eppelmann, Kocka insisted, "We should not necessarily lead this comparative discussion with the goal of stressing the similarities in the two systems," and that "there were countless considerable, weighty differences between Nazi Germany and the GDR."[80] For Kocka, these differences arose from closely examining "the system of rule, social and legal policy, minorities policy, social history, economic history, daily life, culture," and not just the structures of rule or the political system as emphasized by Möller, Marquardt, and other conservatives.[81]

Social Democrats, liberals, and Democratic Socialists were much less inclined to remove Nazi genocide and war crimes from the comparison, or to minimize differences between Nazi and communist crimes. Eppelmann, Möller, and Marquardt tended to put differences in this area to one side, or like Möller to minimize them. Yet for Kocka they were crucial: "Grave differences ... become apparent precisely in those areas in which the inhumanity of the National Socialist system developed particularly crassly.... Thus precisely that which even after fifty years makes the National Socialist dictatorship such an enormous burden for the following generations, a past that will not pass—these unprecedented, state-initiated and -directed mass murders and the war, which Germany began, with its millions of victims above all outside Germany—precisely that did not occur in the GDR."[82] Again in direct contrast with Möller, Kocka insisted that this distinction was due not just to the GDR's lack of autonomy in foreign policy, but also to "internal reasons."[83] Similarly, Meuschel took issue with Möller's claim that ideological differences were irrelevant because the systems of rule had been the same, and objected in particular to the notion that the reason for victims' persecution was unimportant. She insisted that it made a difference whether one was persecuted for what one did—such as oppose a regime—or on the grounds of ascribed characteristics such as racial identity.[84] Herbert Wolf also wondered whether one could really compare "the politically or ideologically tolerated killing of people" with "the directed murder, in the sense of a willfully brought-about killing with the aim of the eradication of whole groups, hundreds of thousands, millions of people."[85] He thus seemed to suggest that Stalinist mass murder had occurred accidentally and without human agency, but at least he did not seek to remove either regime's mass crimes from the discussion.

The differences between the Right and the Left should not be overemphasized. Moderate left-wing scholars, intellectuals, and politicians—mainly

Social Democrats but also moderate Democratic Socialists such as Keller and Wolf—regarded the GDR as a dictatorship and recognized the legitimacy and utility of its comparison with other dictatorships. They did not doubt the fundamental difference between dictatorship and democracy, and accepted the legitimacy of the notion of totalitarianism.[86] Some more vigorously anticommunist Social Democrats like Hartmut Soell and Gert Weisskirchen not only acknowledged the legitimacy of the notion of totalitarianism, but also regarded it is as useful and thoroughly applicable to the GDR.

On the other hand, other Social Democrats, Democratic Socialists, and liberals had reservations about the ways in which the comparison of dictatorships was being used. They feared, with considerable justification, that similarities between the GDR and Nazi Germany were stressed at the expense of crucial differences. Jürgen Kocka noted at the Berlin hearing: "Very different use is currently made of the Nazi-GDR comparison in public. The spectrum ranges from the improper knockdown argument of equation—equally criminal, both belonging to the 'Evil Empire'—to the subtle analysis of similarities and differences with the goal of better recognizing what was particular about the GDR system or what was particular about the Nazi dictatorship too."[87] Kocka's emphasis on the use of comparisons highlights an important, but frequently overlooked distinction between the principle and the practice of comparison.[88] Anticipating Alexander Fischer's comment quoted above, Kocka also perceived, "Already the choice of the comparative partner is a value-laden decision." He also indicated that he believed there were important "limits" to the comparison, and that "the comparison of the dictatorships throws light on individual areas of GDR reality, but not others."[89]

While critical of the totalitarian paradigm—particularly of its analytical and explanatory power—the likes of Kocka and Sigrid Meuschel did not abandon it entirely. Instead of being content with a list of unspecific features that totalitarian regimes shared, they sought to develop ways in which the notion could be applied to a genuine comparison of the histories of various regimes. Kocka wanted to explore the "degree of totality" of various modern dictatorships, and Meuschel advocated developing an "ideal type of totalitarianism" for assessing "the respective degree, the direction, and the duration of the totalization."[90] Such applications of the notions of totality and totalitarianism were open to differences, historical context, and developments over time, rather than just ticking off criteria developed in static contrast to liberal democracies.[91]

Such objections from the Left did not go down well with staunch anticommunists, whether Christian Democrats, Free Democrats, or members of Alliance 90. Frequently, the latter (mis)read them as being indicative of a refusal either to acknowledge the extent of the GDR's crimes or to accept the comparison of dictatorships, or of an insufficiently normative and pro-democratic stance (or indeed of a combination of these). For example, Armin Mitter suggested that Kocka's concept of "modern dictatorships" was "more bland" (*verwaschener*) than totalitarianism and accused him of "playing down the SED dictatorship," to which Kocka responded that finding similarities and differences did not amount to minimizing anything.[92] Möller also insisted in response to Meuschel and Kocka that the GDR's "innocence was not so large," to which Kocka replied accurately that he had said nothing about the GDR being innocent.[93] Similarly, Gerd Poppe took Meuschel's insistence on the notion of post-Stalinism to mean that she thought the GDR after 1956 was "post-totalitarian" and thus civilized; he rejected such a notion, which she in fact had not suggested; she again insisted that addressing the differences required multiple forms or notions of totalitarianism.[94] Finally, Kocka's citation and qualified endorsement of the view that many East Germans were offended by the comparison of dictatorships was taken by some of his collocutors to mean that he felt such offence was justified or that he himself objected to the comparison.[95]

Accusations that the Left was minimizing the GDR's crimes or that it accepted the dictatorships' comparability less than halfheartedly were hardly justified.[96] There was more justification to conservatives' claim that the moderate left-wing position insufficiently addressed what the SED and Nazi dictatorships had in common with each other vis-à-vis democratic states. Yet for the Left this latter distinction was not a central issue. For them, the question at hand was the comparison of two dictatorships, not what distinguished them from democracies. By the same token, left-wing criticism of conservative concentration on the commonalities between dictatorships was also somewhat misplaced, for it failed to recognize that for conservatives the comparative field included democracies, even when the ostensible focus of discussion was the comparison of GDR communism and Nazism.

Unsurprisingly, the commission's final report largely reflected the fiercely anticommunist position. It utilized the notion of totalitarianism extensively to describe and condemn the GDR political system, and it overlooked distinctions between totalitarian claims and totalitarian practice.[97] It was particularly disappointing that it did so without defining the concept or discussing various totalitarianist theories or objections to them. The report's crucial Section E—which addressed broad issues relating to memory, politics, and the self-understanding of unified Germany—affirmed that comparison of dictatorships was admissible and that it did not entail equation.[98] It also insisted that a differentiated use of the notion of totalitarianism "does not aim for the equation of National Socialism with 'real existing socialism.'"[99] Nevertheless, following Marquardt's formulations, it went on to speak of totalitarianism constituting "a certain type of political rule," and listed a series of shared characteristics in its justification of the term.[100]

Despite the commission's apparent endorsement of the conservative approach, some liberal influence was also apparent. The report affirmed "fundamental differences" between the regimes, primarily in relation to the degree of their criminality. Echoing Kocka's powerful insistence at the Berlin hearing, it claimed, "That which makes the Nazi dictatorship an unresolved burden even for generations to come did not exist in the SED dictatorship."[101] However, this recognition of significant differences was not allowed to obstruct the affirmation of totalitarianism. The report immediately continued, "At the same time the concept of totalitarianism . . . is also thoroughly useful for the present—and not just as a theoretical instrument for gaining insight, but also as a critical measure against 'totalitarian temptations' to which even a stabile democracy is not immediately immune."[102] Only the "confrontation with the two dictatorships on German soil" could provide such immunity by "sharpening the understanding of the superiority of the liberal-democratic state ruled by law."[103] To this end, the commission called for an "antitotalitarian consensus," citing, without naming him, liberal philosopher Jürgen Habermas's endorsement of such a consensus at the commission's last public hearing.[104] It did not mention his qualification that the consensus would only deserve this name if it were not "selective."[105] As one commentator has argued, the insistence on such a consensus "created a unique political investment in a debatable category produced by a hardly infallible academic discipline."[106]

The politically highly charged atmosphere of the commission's final deliberations spilt over into the report, exacerbating existing disagreements rather than fostering emphasis on common ground. In a minority statement complaining about the haste with which the commission's work and the report had been finalized, the SPD did not take issue explicitly with the majority report in relation to the present topic. However, it avoided the term totalitarian and insisted: "The necessary confrontation with the GDR past cannot be allowed to lead to the horrors of the Nazi era being relativized in contemporary consciousness; the comparison, but not the equation of the Nazi and SED dictatorships is legitimate. The question of continuities and discontinuities of structures and modes of thinking and behaving still poses itself to the Germans."[107] The SPD clearly believed political mileage could be gained by sticking reasonably closely to traditional leftist positions familiar from the Historians' Dispute. Moreover, this brief statement highlighted the fact that consideration of twentieth-century historical continuities and analogies had been reduced to those between Nazism and the GDR, to the exclusion of others.

Meanwhile, in its extensive minority report the PDS rejected the notion of totalitarianism completely and insisted, rather ludicrously, that the two regimes were so different that no term could possibly unite them.[108] The statement revealed that critical Democratic Socialists like Dietmar Keller and Herbert Wolf had been effectively marginalized by hardliners in the PDS who insisted on the GDR's historical, moral, and even political legitimacy, were ambivalent about acknowledging the GDR's dictatorial nature, and rejected firmly its comparison with the Third Reich, let alone its purported totalitarian character.[109]

In the majority report, the PDS dissenting statement, and, to a lesser extent, the SPD minority vote, we see a general problem inherent in the commissions of inquiry: however subtle, refined, and encompassing the inquiries' deliberations were, the reports had to be selective. Complex theoretical, historiographical, and methodological questions were discussed by the commissions, but subtleties and nuances of interpretation, to say nothing of consistency or completeness, tended to be lost in the final analysis. The latter was dominated by the desire for a firm political judgment and for sharp partisan contours. In part this was due to the mixed parliamentary-scholarly nature of the commissions, but in part also to the inevitable need for selectivity in any process of research and writing. Many important differentiations and qualifications discussed in internal debates fell by the wayside; this was by no means due just to the influence of pending Bundestag elections, but was inherent in the parliamentary nature of the institution.

The further removed from the detailed and often, but by no means always, sophisticated internal deliberations, the more frequent and loose the use of the notion of totalitarianism became. On the basis of the report's affirmation of totalitarianism, conservative politicians felt free to apply the term with abandon. Here again, a result of the commissions' parliamentary nature was apparent. The commissions were bodies of the Bundestag, and it was therefore parliamentarians—naturally inclined to firm judgments rather than scholarly uncertainties—who were responsible for public representations of their work, particularly after the formal end of their deliberations. The Bundestag resolution that accepted the first inquiry's report and sought to summarize its key findings had little hesitation in positing basic continuities and similarities between the Nazi and GDR regimes: "Eastern Germans had the misfortune of again becoming subjects of a dictatorship and having to live in a totalitarian system."[110] It reaffirmed that the SED state remained a totalitarian system in which the SED's claims to leadership were "achieved" (*durchgesetzt*).[111] Moreover, it repeated the demand for an "antitotalitarian consensus" based on the rejection of "every form of totalitarian ideology, program, party, and movement."[112] Similarly, in his foreword to the report, Eppelmann spoke of the process of coming to terms with "totalitarian pasts" and of the SED's "totalitarian structures of rule," while in his foreword to the commission's published materials he pointed to the SED's responsibility for its forty-year "totalitarian rule."[113]

Commemorating the Double Past

The rather abstract issues of the comparability and similarity of dictatorships and the concept of totalitarianism assumed greater practical relevance and political immediacy when it came to public commemoration of the two regimes. This was particularly the case at locations where the regimes had committed grave abuses and where mass deaths had occurred. In the winter of 1989–90, mass graves were discovered near the National Sites of Warning and Commemoration at both Buchenwald and Sachsenhausen. They were the graves of Germans and others interned by the Soviet occupiers in "special camps" between 1945 and 1950. As has been emphasized throughout, the reckoning with the East German past began in the GDR and was not an invention of West Germans. This applied to the discussion of antifascism, and it also applied to the debate about these physical sites. Indeed, the two issues were closely linked, because the revision of official antifascist memorial sites was driven not least by the rediscovery of additional layers to the history of the former concentration camps, layers that represented communist abuses.[114] Nevertheless, even before unification West Germans were involved in these debates. For example, in her capacity as West German minister for inner-German relations, Dorothee Wilms demanded as early as July 1990 Buchenwald's transformation into a memorial "for the victims of arbitrariness and persecution."[115] The "double past" of these places was taken by many as confirmation of the totalitarian character of the Nazi and communist regimes, and they were thus predestined to assume a prominent role in public and political debate.

Beyond the specific sites with multiple pasts, broader questions about the relative weight that unified Germany should attribute to various periods were debated vigorously, and these debates must be seen in large part as the continuation of longstanding western disputes. The central questions in postunification Germany were whether communist crimes could be remembered without displacing or equating them with Nazi crimes, and whether the singularity of the latter could be maintained without relegating the victims of the former to "second-class" status. As Wilms's statement suggested, conservatives sought to commemorate the Nazi and communist dictatorships and their victims together.[116] This approach was pursued further in 1992–93 by Federal Chancellor Helmut Kohl's establishment of the *Neue Wache* on Unter den Linden in Berlin as a new Central Memorial Site for the unified nation. There were several controversial aspects to this move, but most important for the present discussion was the dedication of the memorial "To the victims of war and the rule of violence," which for many critics failed to distinguish adequately among perpetrators, victims, and bystanders.[117]

Meanwhile, debate raged at the former National Sites of Warning and Commemoration about the revision of the memorials' one-sided antifascist exhibitions and commemorative elements and the inclusion of the special-camp histories. Two commissions of experts established by the state governments in Thuringia and Brandenburg to develop new conceptions for the memorials gave clear priority to the Nazi past. In its recommendations of January 1992, the Brandenburg commission—under the leadership of Bernd Faulenbach—called for a documentary exhibition on the special camp at Sachsenhausen, but the memorial's emphasis was to remain on the Nazi concentration camp. The commission made no reference to commemoration, as opposed to documentation, of the special-camp inmates.[118] The report insisted that tendencies to equate the two camps or set them off against one another had to be countered, and that, "The NS crimes must not be relativized by the crimes of Stalinism, nor must the crimes of Stalinism be trivialized with reference to the NS crimes."[119] In contrast, the Thuringian commission spoke of commemorating as well as documenting the special-camp history, but it argued that such commemoration had to be "subordinate" to, and spatially separate from that of the Nazi concentration camp. This constituted an explicit call for what Bill Niven has called a "hierarchical system of memory."[120] Such recommendations failed to satisfy victims' groups on both sides.[121]

While debate continued at the local and regional level, the issues were caught up with more mundane questions about federal financing of memorials. In line with cultural policy in the Federal Republic generally, memorials were constitutionally a matter for the individual states. Yet with the huge tasks of reforming the memorial sites in eastern Germany and the insecure financial status of the eastern state governments, federal involvement appeared necessary. Despite the federal government's initial hesitancy, a consensus emerged rather quickly that federal support for eastern memorials was essential, at least in the short to medium term, and the government co-funded a growing number of memorials from 1991 onward.[122] Inevitably, questions arose about which memorials would benefit, how they would be determined, whether funding should extend beyond the original plan of ten years, and whether it should be restricted to eastern memorials. The first commission of inquiry did not play an active role in these debates and its report barely touched on issues of commemoration and memorials.[123] As with questions of rehabilitation and compensation, the federal government did not wait for the commission's input and the Bundestag's deliberations proceeded irrespective of the inquiry. While some memorial sites were already benefiting from federal funding, by the end of the parliamentary term in 1994 no detailed or systematic concept for federal support had been developed.[124]

The second commission of inquiry became a major player in Germany's postunification commemorative politics because it was charged with developing recommendations for such a concept.[125] This was in itself a rather bizarre eventuality: a body otherwise devoted explicitly to working through the history of communist rule, crimes, and injustice would develop a concept for memorials generally, including those related to historical eras and events that were otherwise beyond its brief and its expertise. Did this suggest a desire to shift the focus of the German memorial landscape away from Nazi crimes to communist ones? Such an understanding would support Bill Niven's not unreasonable interpretation of federal government preference (and funding) for sites of memory with a double past, compared with the purely regional support for Nazi concentration-camp memorials in the western states.[126]

The commission certainly saw itself, and its conservative members in particular saw themselves, as advocates of anticommunist memory of communist crimes, often in quite explicit opposition to those who insisted on the centrality of Nazi crimes. For example, at a public hearing with victims' groups and memorial experts, Karl Wilhelm Fricke referred to the organizations of the victims of Nazi concentration camps as the "other side."[127] The implication was that the commission was on the side of the victims of communism. Such advocacy could be justified as a counterweight to the predominance of experts in, and advocates of Nazi memory in other fora, such as the commissions in Brandenburg and Thuringia, but it was problematic nevertheless.[128] There had never been such explicit political advocacy and high level parliamentary consideration of appropriate and desirable efforts to remember the Nazi past. Only in the context of discussing the communist and the double past did either the Bundestag's Internal Affairs Committee or an institution such as a commission of inquiry assume responsibility for or hold debates about memorials to the Nazi past, and only in this context did the prospect of ongoing federal funding arise.[129] Commemoration of Nazi crimes had never received the same level of political and scholarly support.

The commission devoted considerable attention to the analysis and characterization of the special camps, and sought to bring the rival victims' organizations together, albeit with little success. At a public hearing held at the Buchenwald memorial in October 1996, the International Buchenwald Committee staged a walkout after reading a statement declaring its refusal to sit at a table with the "defenders of our executioners," by which it meant the organized victims of Stalinism.[130] In contrast with this extreme view, much of the debate revealed considerable agreement, on the one hand, that the special camps had not been full of Nazi criminals and, on the other, that not every internee had an uncompromised past. There was also widespread agreement on the appalling treatment of the internees. Importantly, Ignatz Bubis of the Central Council of Jews in Germany accepted that even those who had been Nazi perpetrators became victims because they were punished according to Stalinist methods.[131] Within the commission there was some resistance to seeing the camps as comparable with the western occupiers' internment camps, and much more willingness to place them in the context, on the one hand, of the establishment of a communist dictatorship and of the Soviet Gulag and, on the other, of Nazi concentration camps.[132]

The commission can by no means be said to have equated the special camps with the latter, although it saw strong affinities. Its report declared: "The comparison of special camps and concentration camps at the authentic site should also be seen in the larger context of the comparison of dictatorships, of the comparison between Stalinist Gulag system and National Socialist concentration-camp system, as part of a Europe-wide camp experience of the twentieth century."[133] The report made little effort to offer figures on the various reasons for internees' internment, and declared—quite inconsistently with much expert opinion expressed before both the first and the second inquiry—that the camps "did not serve denazification."[134] It gave more attention to internees' unjust treatment, appalling conditions, and general suffering.

These questions of historical interpretation were inevitably caught up in debates over value-laden remembrance, despite frequent calls to uphold or at least consider the distinction between documentation and research on the one hand and commemoration on the other.[135] The distinction between individual mourning and public, collective commemoration was also frequently elided.[136] For many strongly anticommunist commissioners and witnesses, the lack of due process associated with internment meant that, Nazis or not, the internees were victims of communist oppression who warranted commemoration. Indeed, some argued that the repressive, unjust use of camps—not least those that previously had been used by the Nazis—constituted a substantial continuity or similarity with the Nazi regime, such that remembrance of communist oppression and its victims should be accorded equal status with that of Nazi persecution and its victims. Some advocated joint commemoration, or rejected the separate commemoration proposed at Buchenwald and Sachsenhausen.[137] Some conservatives called explicitly for the use of the totalitarian paradigm in this context.[138]

On the other hand, many experts and a number of social-democrat commissioners agreed that the inmates had suffered gross violations of due process and human rights, but insisted that they should not necessarily be viewed or mourned as victims. They argued that only innocent victims should be commemorated, that is, those who had not previously compromised themselves under the Nazi regime. On this view, the whole biography, including its possible dubious pre-1945 components, had to be considered when commemorating those who suffered after 1945.[139] Others argued that commemoration was appropriate, but that it had to occur separately from and cede priority to remembrance of Nazi crimes. This hierarchy was deemed necessary either because the latter were prior to and partially causative of the communist crimes, or because the Nazis' victims came from so many different countries and the Germans could not just focus on narrow national commemoration.[140] Numerous experts and commissioners directly rejected calls for the utilization of the totalitarian paradigm in this context.[141]

Despite these concerns, the second commission's report endorsed a full program of unqualified commemoration for the victims of communist injustice and persecution, including the special-camp internees. It acknowledged that one had to see the entirety of individuals' biographies, both before and after their imprisonment. Yet it made no specific reference to Nazi perpetrators becoming victims of communism and thus did not adopt the suggestion that only innocent victims be commemorated.[142] Indeed, it went beyond supporting the right of individuals or victims' groups to private mourning, declaring that all victims of "inhumanity, injustice, and terror" also had a right to "public remembrance and commemoration in a democracy."[143] The report also expressly forbade a "hierarchization" of victims.[144] What is more, in the context of discussing Berlin memorial sites, it called directly for "common offerings of the memorial sites for the memory of the NS dictatorship and the SED dictatorship," which it believed would help foster an antitotalitarian consensus.[145] The inquiry was thus much more equationist and closer in its approach to the positions of the more anticommunist organized victims' of Stalinism than numerous scholars have appreciated.[146]

As we have seen, the commissions' preferred terms of double dictatorial past and two dictatorships in Germany and their endorsement of totalitarianism made precious little distinction between the significance of the East German and Nazi pasts. The same can be said of their suggested elevation of 17 June to a national day of commemoration for the victims of (and opposition against) communism, equivalent to the recently created national day of commemoration for the victims of National Socialism on 27 January.[147] The second inquiry's report also reaffirmed the first inquiry's commitment to the antitotalitarian consensus. It stated: "The double dictatorial experience in Germany, the twofold experience of the admittedly differently justified enmity toward the open society and parliamentary liberal democracy strengthens the commitment of the Germans to immutable and inviolable human rights as the basis of every human community, to liberty and democracy as the basis of every state order. This is the core of the antitotalitarian consensus and the democratic culture of memory in Germany."[148] Characteristically, differences between the two pasts were relegated to a sub clause (relating to ideological justification) while the focus remained on their equivalence. Differences in the outcomes or the scale of criminality were apparently irrelevant. The identity-creating political-moral conclusion (that was at the same time the starting point and purpose) of the comparative approach to the two dictatorships was bound to concentrate on the common elements and to minimize the differences.

The majority report insisted, however, that differences between the different regimes and their camps must be made apparent. It acknowledged that the special camps would never have existed in Germany without the Second World War and that they should not be removed from their larger historical context.[149] It also endorsed the position of the Brandenburg commission: "National Socialist crimes must not be relativized by the confrontation with the crimes of Stalinism. Stalinist crimes must not be trivialized through reference to the National Socialist crimes."[150] The PDS claim that the second commission's report amounted to a "permanent equation of Nazi Germany and the GDR" was thus an overstatement, but by no means a complete distortion.[151] Inevitably, the prospect of former Nazis among the internees receiving public commemoration provoked a specific objection from the PDS.[152]

As the foregoing discussion has suggested, both commissions' handling of Germany's multiple pasts was highly ambivalent. On the one hand, the inquiries seemed to recognize the singular importance of Nazi crimes and warned against neglecting differences and equating the regimes and their crimes. On the other, they used the terminology of the double past, two dictatorships in Germany, and totalitarianism to emphasize commonalities at the expense of particularities. This ambivalence of both the commissions' position and their role was evident in the second inquiry's recommendations for the development of a concept for federal funding of memorial sites. Not surprisingly, it argued that commemoration was due to both dictatorships and their victims. Yet it also recommended that funding be extended to memorials in the West as well as the East.[153] That is, it was not just interested in supporting sites with a double past, but also sites relating exclusively to Nazi crimes, such as Dachau or Bergen Belsen.

This recommendation neatly captures the ironies and ambiguities of Germany's handling of its "double past" in the 1990s. There is no denying the apparent inconsistency of the Federal Republic undertaking a more rigorous reckoning with the communist past in shorter time than it had with the Nazi past. Yet the delegitimation of the communist past and the enhancement of the status of communism's victims and the anticommunist resistance occurred not through forgetting the Nazi past but by drawing parallels between the two regimes, their crimes, and their legacies. Such parallels and frequently posited equivalences, while often dubious, ultimately benefited, rather than damaged the cause of remembering the Nazi past.[154] While genocide and war crimes could be marginalized in conservative comparisons of totalitarian structures of rule, they could not be forgotten. For all the vetoes the commission and others sought to place on hierarchies of memory, they could not assail the precedence and preeminence of National Socialism, as the construction, with federal support, of a Memorial to the Murdered Jews of Europe in the heart of Berlin indicated. The fear, felt by many and expressed by Jürgen Habermas before the first commission in its final hearing in May 1994, that the memory of the first dictatorship might "be allowed to pale under the harsh light cast on this second past" failed to materialize.[155] Indeed, the second past acted as a catalyst to improve, for example, the situation of long-neglected concentration-camp memorials in the West. This positive conclusion, however, should not distract from the many highly problematic elements in both commissions' approaches to Germany's difficult past. Commentators or political actors who cite the inquiry's welcome endorsement of the prohibition on relativizing the Nazi past and trivializing the communist past should overlook neither the vigorous contestation that took place on route to this stance, nor the remaining ambiguities and persistent differences of opinion about the relative weighting of the crimes and legacies of the Third Reich and the GDR.[156]

Notes

1. For partial exceptions, see note 53 in the introduction.
2. Niven, *Facing the Nazi Past*, 61.

3. See Beattie, "A Fifties Revival?"
4. Cf. Niven, *Facing the Nazi Past*, 43f.; Zimmer, *Der Buchenwald-Konflikt*, 7; Leggewie and Meyer, *"Ein Ort, an den man gerne geht,"* 75.
5. Paul Cooke's argument that the first inquiry's report "seemed to be on the verge of re-igniting controversies first sparked during the *Historikerstreit*" overlooks that the debate had begun well before the report's release, and that the latter was in fact an attempt to resolve the dispute, *Representing East Germany*, 43.
6. Müller, "East Germany," 268f.
7. See Bock, "Von der Tribunal-Idee"; McAdams, *Judging the Past*, 105f.; and the discussion of the debate about the bloc parties and the SED's foundation in chapter 3.
8. I: 57–67.
9. I: 89.
10. Ibid.
11. Cf. Bock, "Von der Tribunal-Idee"; Zimmer, *Der Buchenwald-Konflikt*, 32.
12. Author's interview. See also *VI: 274*. Peter Maser expressed similar frustration (author's interview).
13. A. Dirk Moses, "The 'Weimar Syndrome' in the Federal Republic of Germany," in *Leben, Tod und Entscheidung: Studien zur Geistesgeschichte der Weimarer Republik*, eds. Stephan Loos and Holger Zaborowski (Berlin, 2003). Cf. Andrew H. Beattie, "The Past in the Politics of Divided and Unified Germany," in *Partisan Histories: The Past in Contemporary Global Politics*, eds. Max Paul Friedman and Padraic Kenney (New York, 2005).
14. See *Historikerstreit: Die Dokumentation der Kontroverse um die Einzigartigkeit der national-sozialistischen Judenvernichtung* (Munich, 1987). Cf. Maier, *The Unmasterable Past*; Bernd Faulenbach, "Die doppelte 'Vergangenheitsbewältigung': Nationalsozialismus und Stalinismus als Herausforderungen zeithistorischer Forschung und politischer Kultur," in *Die geteilte Vergangenheit*, ed. Danyel, 112; Bernhard Giesen, *Intellectuals and the Nation: Collective Identity in a German Axial Age* (Cambridge, 1998).
15. See Alexander, "On the Social Construction"; Daniel Levy and Natan Sznaider, "Memory Unbound: The Holocaust and the Formation of Cosmopolitan Memory," *European Journal of Social Theory* 5, no. 1 (2002): 87–106.
16. DBPa: Protokoll 2: 26, 21; Protokoll 11: 14. Cf. Mary Fulbrook, "Jenseits der Totalita-rismustheorie? Vorläufige Bemerkungen aus sozialgeschichtlicher Perspektive," in *The GDR and its History*, ed. Barker, 37.
17. For examples of slippage between the two, see Rudolf Wassermann, "Vergangenheits-bewältigung nach 1945 und nach 1989," *Jahrbuch Extremismus und Demokratie* 5 (1993): 29; Jesse, "Vergangenheitsbewältigung," 719f.; Sühl, *Vergangenheitsbewältigung 1945 und 1989*, 8; Wüstenberg, *Die politische Dimension*, 240 (fn. 1), 241 (fn. 8). Cf. Pampel, "Was bedeutet 'Aufarbeitung.'"
18. For instance, historian Manfred Kittel complained about the relative leniency afforded to representatives of the East German regime, IX: 646f. His arguments assumed crimi-nal equivalence. So did the frequent lamentation that, unlike the Nazi Party after 1945, the SED-PDS was not banned. See Wassermann, "Vergangenheitsbewältigung," 38; Vergau, *Aufarbeitung von Vergangenheit*, 102.
19. I: 29.
20. See the views of conservative historian Horst Möller, IX: 577. Cf. Schulte, "Die 'doppelte Vergangenheit'"; Wüstenberg, *Die politische Dimension*, 246 (fn. 28), 293.
21. See I: v, viii, 160f., 340, 485, 708, 738f., 743, 746, 779, 787, 805. Cf. Faulenbach, "Die Arbeit der Enquete-Kommissionen," 31.
22. See, for example, Gerhard Binder, *Die Deutsche Demokratische Republik: Der zweite deutsche Staat* (Paderborn, 1977).

23. IX: 678.

24. Ibid.

25. Cf. Stefan Berger, *The Search for Normality: National Identity and Historical Consciousness in Germany since 1800* (Providence, 1997), 254f. Richard Evans has questioned the appropriateness of such designtions, albeit primarily on the basis of the GDR's un-Germanness, "Zwei deutsche Diktaturen im 20. Jahrhundert?" *Aus Politik und Zeitgeschichte* 55, no. 1–2 (2005): 3–9.

26. I: 53.

27. I: 188, 167.

28. I: 176.

29. I: 108.

30. I: 129. Cf. Hansen, "Noch eine Vergangenheit," 16. For other invocations of totalitarianism, see I: 75, 118, 123, 125, 150f.

31. I: 173. DBPa: Protokoll 2: 21.

32. DBPa: Protokoll 3: 42, 12, 13. Even Keller accepted the proposal, albeit suggesting it should not become a main task for the inquiry.

33. DBPa: Protokoll 5: 5.

34. See DBPa: Protokoll 6: 21, 25, 31.

35. Of the eight areas of historical content listed in the terms of reference, this was the only one which was not allocated to a subcommittee.

36. Schuller, "Bericht der Enquete-Kommission," 739.

37. See "Zur Auseinandersetzung mit den beiden Diktaturen in Deutschland in Vergangenheit und Gegenwart," IX: 574–777. According to the report, it was the "logical concluding point" of the inquiry's activities, I: 743. See Hansen, "Befreiung durch Erinnerung," 75, 77.

38. Horst Möller, "Nationalsozialismus und SED-Diktatur in vergleichender Perspektive," IX: 577, 581.

39. Bernhard Marquardt, "Totalitarismustheorie und die Aufarbeitung der SED-Diktatur," III: 1531, 1537.

40. Jürgen Kocka, "Nationalsozialismus und SED-Diktatur in vergleichender Perspektive," IX: 597, 612.

41. IX: 619.

42. I: 744. Cf. Fulbrook, "Jenseits der Totalitarismustheorie?" 48f.

43. I: 686, 748. Left-liberal historians dissatisfied with the regime centeredness of much postunification research on the GDR—including that produced by the commission—have attempted to move the focus away from the structures of rule, to how these were actually experienced. See Jarausch, *Dictatorship as Experience*. For an early plea for such a development, see Sigrid Meuschel, "Überlegungen zu einer Herrschafts- und Gesellschaftsgeschichte der DDR," *Geschichte und Gesellschaft* 19, no. 1 (1993): 5–14.

44. I: 208, 215.

45. I: 744.

46. For further examples, see Eppelmann's opening statement at the Reichstag hearing, IX: 575; Rainer Eckert, "Zur Rolle der Massenorganisationen im Alltag der DDR-Bevölkerung," II: 1244, 1246, 1249, 1299f.; and the report's discussion of the failure of the SED's totalitarian ambitions in various contexts (the churches, media and cultural policy), but its continuing use of the totalitarian label, I: 499f., 502, 509, 511, 254, 325.

47. IX: 179. For further examples, see the discussion of Wilke's paper on wartime Communist planning (chapter 3) and of the commission's handling of Marxist-Leninist ideology (chapter 4). Cf. Fulbrook, "Jenseits der Totalitarismustheorie?" 39.

48. At other times Möller argued that realization was crucial, IX: 579. Kocka pointed out that several definitions of *totalitarian* were in circulation, 595.
49. IX: 597.
50. Exploring limits to dictatorial ambitions has become a productive avenue of research. See Ralph Jessen and Richard Bessel, *Die Grenzen der Diktatur: Staat und Gesellschaft in der DDR* (Göttingen, 1996); Thomas Lindenberger, ed., *Herrschaft und Eigen-Sinn in der Diktatur: Studien zur Sozialgeschichte der DDR* (Cologne, 1999).
51. IX: 599.
52. Möller conceded that totalitarianism was not a well-rounded theory but a "phenomenology" and that it could not explain origins, but only encompass "structural characteristics," IX: 607, 634. Cf. Fulbrook, "Jenseits der Totalitarismustheorie?" 37, 40f.
53. III: 1537. Cf. Hoffmann, *Stunden Null?* 286.
54. IX: 617.
55. I: 744.
56. IX: 592.
57. On the genesis of public and scholarly debate about totalitarian movements and regimes, see Abbott Gleason, *Totalitarianism: The Inner History of the Cold War* (New York, 1995).
58. I thus disagree with Brigitte Rauschenbach, who argues that even the two dictatorships' comparison obscures their particularities and generally has "denunciatory consequences," "Erbschaft aus Vergessenheit: Zukunft aus Erinnerungsarbeit," *Deutschland Archiv* 25, no. 9 (1992): 934. This is often the case, but that is contingent rather than necessary; a scholarly, genuinely balanced approach is not a priori impossible. Cf. Fulbrook, "Jenseits der Totalitarismustheorie?" 40f.; Jarausch, "Die DDR denken," 12.
59. Differences were acknowledged but were regarded as secondary, relative to the high degree to which the regimes were "basically alike." As Marquardt suggested, "With the notion of totalitarianism *a* definite type of political system is to be characterized," III: 1538, emphasis added.
60. IX: 576, emphasis added.
61. IX: 575, emphasis added. Apart from begging the questions that the hearing was supposed to discuss, here Eppelmann, like Möller after him, argued for comparability on the basis of similarities. Part of the problem was merely a semantic one (shared in English and German): while a comparison should entail consideration of differences and similarities, in colloquial usage "comparable" (*vergleichbar*) often means similar. For example, after listing a series of shared characteristics, Möller said that it was possible to compare the dictatorships on the basis of these criteria, 584. What he most likely meant was that they were basically *alike* on those points. Proponents of dictatorial comparison and totalitarianist approaches frequently point out their opponents' apparent confusion of the notions of comparability and likeness. However, they overlook that such conflation resides on both sides of the debate. See, for instance, Christopher Beckmann, "Die Auseinandersetzung um den Vergleich von 'Dritten Reich' und DDR vor dem Hintergrund der Diskussion um Möglichkeiten und Grenzen vergleichender Geschichtsforschung," *Deutsche Studien* 38, no. 147–48 (2002): 12.
62. IX: 597. Cf. Fulbrook, "Jenseits der Totalitarismustheorie?" 50; Maier, *The Unmasterable Past*, 83.
63. IX: 603.
64. IX: 581. See also Möller's rather convoluted comments on the two dictatorships' preparedness to commit political murder, which he concluded by stating: "Thus I want to emphasize, without at all questioning any quantitative differences—that would of course be quite crazy—that what is important to me here is that the concept of the 'totalitarian system' is a contradiction of the liberal state ruled by law," 637.

65. IX: 579.
66. See also the views of Fischer, IX: 598, and Marquardt, III: 1541–44.
67. IX: 575. For an explicit desire to compare totalitarian structures, irrespective of crimes and numbers of victims, see Hoffmann, "Aufklärung und Ahndung," 45.
68. IX: 580. Marquardt, too, acknowledged differences between the histories and crimes of the regimes, only to put aside the Nazis' exceptional criminality so that the "political system" could be compared and largely equated. One wonders whether the genocide and war of conquest and annihilation are so easily distinguishable from the Third Reich's "structure of rule," III: 1543f.
69. IX: 575.
70. III: 1543.
71. IX: 582.
72. For similar tendencies, see Eckhard Jesse, "'Entnazifizierung' und 'Entstasifizierung' als politisches Problem: Die doppelte Vergangenheitsbewältigung," in *Vergangenheitsbewältigung durch Recht*, ed. Isensee, 17; Hoffmann, *Stunden Null?* 58, 270.
73. See Möller's remarks, IX: 580, 609. Möller referred to work by Wilke, who both within and beyond the commission repeatedly drew parallels between the Nazis' and the Communists' desire to invade their eastern European neighbors especially Czechoslovakia. Such associations failed to do justice to the horror of Nazi racial warfare. Friedrich-Christian Schroeder suggested that the reason for the "omission of such crimes" in the GDR was to be found in the precedent of the Nuremberg Trials and in the GDR's "grace of late birth that saved it from corresponding crimes," 624. This was little more than loose speculation. Meckel objected at the hearing that condemnation of the GDR for its hypothetical part in a war against the West that *might* have been waged by the USSR was not only ahistorical; it also failed to recognize that the FRG would also have gone into battle against the communist foe if the USA had so wished, and that the apparent preparedness to use weapons was a core part of the logic of deterrence in the Cold War, 621.
74. IX: 593.
75. IX: 579. Such views resembled the tendency to seek a cumulative tally of the evils of "communism" evident in Stéphane Courtois et al., *Das Schwarzbuch des Kommunismus: Unterdrückung, Verbrechen und Terror, Mit dem Kapitel "Die Aufarbeitung des Sozialismus in der DDR" von Joachim Gauck und Ehrhard Neubert*, trans. Irmelia Arnsperger et al. (Munich, 1998). Cf. Hansen, "Noch eine Vergangenheit," 16.
76. IX: 623.
77. IX: 588, 593, 611f., 618, 620. Meuschel pleaded for a related distinction between totalitarian and post-totalitarian periods, i.e., post 1956, 599, 617, 641.
78. IX: 629, 626.
79. I: 613.
80. IX: 611, 592. Cf. Jürgen Kocka, "Chance und Herausforderung: Aufgaben der Zeitgeschichte beim Umgang mit der DDR-Vergangenheit," in *Die Partei hatte immer recht*, eds. Faulenbach, Meckel, and Weber, 247ff.
81. IX: 592.
82. Ibid.
83. Ibid.
84. IX: 600f. Möller responded—to the applause of Barbe (SPD)—that Meuschel's discussion of victims was too "abstract," 608. Schroeder claimed that Meuschel had said that "the communist ideology of murder was at least more acceptable for the victims than the National Socialist one," to which Meuschel rightly said that she had not, 623, 641. Barbe claimed to be horrified to hear Meuschel state that it was irrelevant for victims by whom they were killed (although it was Möller who had said that), and argued that

this justified the perpetrators by suggesting that "the end justifies the means," 630f. Meuschel insisted that she had only spoken about the different chances victims had of avoiding persecution and destruction, 641.

85. IX: 625.
86. See Kocka's views, IX: 589f. Only rarely has comparison per se been rejected. Famously, Margherita von Brentano argued that the comparison of the GDR and the Third Reich was a "terrible minimization" of the latter, and that mountains of Stasi and SED files could not be compared with mountains of corpses, cited in Jesse, "'Entnazifizierung' und 'Entstasifizierung,'" 15.
87. IX: 589.
88. Proponents of comparison are quite right to insist that comparison does not necessarily lead to equations or relativization, but they often overlook the facts that in reality it sometimes does so, and that in the commission of inquiry it frequently did so. See for instance Beckmann, "Die Auseinandersetzung um den Vergleich," 10, 13; Schroeder, *Die veränderte Republik*, 310f.
89. IX: 589, 597. See the views of Weber, Faulenbach, and Wolf, 622, 618, 624. Cf. Bernd Faulenbach, "Probleme einer Neukonzeption von Gedenkstätten in Brandenburg," in *Brandenburgische Gedenkstätten für die Verfolgten des NS-Regimes: Perspektiven, Kontroversen und internationale Vergleiche*, ed. Ministerium für Wissenschaft, Forschung und Kultur des Landes Brandenburg (Berlin, 1992), 14; Faulenbach, "Die Verfolgungssysteme des Nationalsozialismus und des Stalinismus: Zur Frage ihrer Vergleichbarkeit," and Hans-Ulrich Wehler, "Diktaturenvergleich, Totalitarismustheorie und DDR-Geschichte," both in *Doppelte Zeitgeschichte*, eds. Bauerkämper, Sabrow, and Stöver; Lozek, "Zum Diktaturvergleich."
90. IX: 595, 600. On the notion of "modern" dictatorships, see Kocka, "The GDR."
91. Indeed, for all her reservations about conservatives' equationism and their use of totalitarianism, Meuschel argued that in some respects the GDR and SED were more totalitarian than the Third Reich and the NSDAP, IX: 602, 617. Möller agreed that regimes could be more or less totalitarian according to differing criteria, 614. For others who see the GDR as more totalitarian, see Hoffmann, *Stunden Null?* 304; Meuschel, "Überlegungen"; Maier, *Dissolution*, 314.
92. IX: 613, 633, 640.
93. IX: 609, 611.
94. IX: 632, 641.
95. See IX: 588f., 625, 628f., 638.
96. Alexander Fischer, in his capacity as facilitator of the discussion at the hearing, perceived basic agreement on the question of the legitimacy of the comparison and on structural parallels and differences, IX: 607.
97. I: 221, 275, 286.
98. I: 743.
99. I: 743f.
100. I: 744.
101. I: 744f.
102. I: 745.
103. Ibid.
104. Ibid.
105. IX: 690.
106. Sa'adah, *Germany's Second Chance*, 103. Cf. Dennis, *The Rise and Fall*, xv.
107. I: 749.
108. I: 709.

109. Author's interviews with Wilke, Eppelmann, Faulenbach, Hansen, Mitter, Weber, and Dietmar Keller (Bonn, 20 June 2001). For the views of the hardliners, see Elm, *Das verordnete Feindbild.*

110. IX: 781.

111. IX: 781f.

112. I: 783. To focus on and assess the inquiry's work largely on the basis of this political summary as some critics have done is misleading. See, for instance, Klaus Körner, *"Die rote Gefahr": Antikommunistische Propaganda in der Bundesrepublik 1950–2000* (Hamburg, 2003), 179f.

113. I: 182, vii.

114. Zimmer, *Der Buchenwald-Konflikt,* 7f. Some commentators incorrectly attribute such discoveries and debates to unification. See Mark A. Wolfgram, "The Legacies of Memory: The Third Reich in Unified Germany," *German Politics and Society* 21, no. 3 (2003): 89–100.

115. Zimmer, *Der Buchenwald-Konflikt,* 14.

116. Ibid., 33.

117. See Reichel, *Politik mit der Erinnerung,* 196–209; Siobhan Kattago, *Ambiguous Memory: The Nazi Past and German National Identity* (Westport, 2001), 129–41; Beattie, "The Victims of Totalitarianism."

118. Ministerium für Wissenschaft, Forschung und Kultur des Landes Brandenburg, *Brandenburgische Gedenkstätten,* 230, 256, 263, 237.

119. Ibid., 231f. Cf. Haustein, *Geschichte im Dissens,* 378.

120. Zimmer, *Der Buchenwald-Konflikt,* 100f.; Niven, *Facing the Nazi Past,* 46.

121. Cf. Bernd Pampel, "Bagatellisierung durch Gedenken? Gedenkstättenarbeit an Orten aufeinanderfolgenden nationalsozialistischen und kommunistischen Unrechts," *Deutschland Archiv* 31, no. 3 (1998): 445; Beattie, "The Victims of Totalitarianism"; Haustein, *Geschichte im Dissens.*

122. See Deutscher Bundestag, "Bericht der Bundesregierung über die Beteiligung des Bundes an Gedenkstätten in der Bundesrepublik Deutschland," *Drucksache* 13/8486 (5 September 1997).

123. However, several commissioners sat on the Bundestag Internal Affairs Committee that deliberated on such matters and held a joint public hearing with the commission at the Sachsenhausen memorial in 1994, mentioned above. The report did recommend that the Central Remand Center in Berlin-Hohenschönhausen be turned into a memorial and that memorials of national significance receive funding from the relevant state and the federal government, I: 647.

124. See Deutscher Bundestag, "Bericht der Bundesregierung über die Beteiligung des Bundes"; Deutscher Bundestag, "Beschlußempfehlung und Bericht des Innenausschusses," *Drucksache* 12/7884 (15 June 1994). Cf. Meyer, "Erinnerungskultur als Politikfeld."

125. I: 6.

126. Niven, *Facing the Nazi Past,* 45. This view is somewhat counterbalanced by the fact that the government was funding a number of Berlin memorials related only to the Nazi past.

127. VI: 50.

128. Haustein, *Geschichte im Dissens,* 182, 284, 289ff., 468; Meyer, "Erinnerungskultur als Politikfeld," 124.

129. See expression of regret about this by Siegfried Vergin (SPD), the second inquiry's deputy chairperson who was chair of the subcommittee on memorials and commemoration, VI: 34. Cf. Haustein, *Geschichte im Dissens,* 39.

130. "Gedenkstättenarbeit für Nachgeborene," VI: 45. Cf. Haustein, *Geschichte im Dissens,* 173ff.

131. *VI: 39.*
132. See Gerhard Finn, "Bericht zur neueren Literatur (ab 1990) über Zahl, Verbleib und Zusammensetzung der Häftlinge nach Internierungsgründen in den sowjetischen Speziallagern der Jahre 1945 bis 1950," *VI: 206–46;* Achim Kilian "Die Häftlinge in den sowjetischen Speziallagern der Jahre 1945–1950," *373–440;* Jan Lipinsky, "Gefängnisse und Lager in der SBZ/DDR als Stätten des Terrors im kommunistischen Herrschaftssystem," *490–566;* Irina Scherbakowa, "Gefängnisse und Lager im sowjetischen Herrschaftssystem," *567–622;* Gedenkstätte Buchenwald, "Konzentrationslager Buchenwald 1937–1945, Speziallager Nr. 2 1945–1950: Zwei Lager an einem Ort—Geschichte und Erinnerungskonstruktion," *247–372;* Annette Leo, "Überlegungen zu einem Vergleich des nationalsozialistischen Konzentrationslagers Sachsenhausen 1937 bis 1945 mit dem sowjetischen Speziallager Sachsenhausen 1945 bis 1950," *441–89.* For a contemporaneous comparative study of Allied internment camps, of which the inquiry was aware, see Lutz Niethammer, "Alliierte Internierungslager in Deutschland nach 1945: Vergleich und offene Fragen," in *Von der Aufgabe der Freiheit: Politische Verantwortung und bürgerliche Gesellschaft im 19. und 20. Jahrhundert, Festschrift für Hans Mommsen zum 5. November 1995,* eds. Christian Jansen, Niethammer, and Bernd Weisbrod (Berlin, 1995).
133. *I: 614.* For a discussion of the latter, see Joël Kotek and Pierre Rigoulot, *Das Jahrhundert der Lager: Gefangenschaft, Zwangsarbeit, Vernichtung,* trans. Enrico Heinemann, Elsbeth Ranke, Ursel Schäfter, and Reiner Pfleiderer (Munich, 2001).
134. *I: 606.*
135. See the caveats of Reinhard Rürup, IX: 246, 354, and Leo 342.
136. Elm insisted on the distinction, *VI: 67.* Cf. Haustein, *Geschichte im Dissens,* 384.
137. See, for example, the views of Fischer and Maser, IX: 321, 14, and Werner Nöckel, *VI: 59.*
138. See statements by Wilke, IX: 242, and Maser, *VI: 14.* Cf. Haustein, *Geschichte im Dissens,* 176.
139. Vergin insisted on seeing whole biographies, *VI: 10.* See also *31f.;* IX: 338, 367, 361, 262, 354. This argument resembled conservatives' arguments against the commemoration of Communists' anti-Nazi resistance; they insisted that one should not honor people who—whatever the strength of their anti-Nazi credentials—went on to support another dictatorship. Cf. Haustein, *Geschichte im Dissens,* 97, 137f., 433 and passim.
140. See IX: 362, 334, 357, 240. Bubis said he was in favor of working through the communist past and honoring the victims of Stalinist denazification; commemoration, he said, had to be conducted in parallel, rather than jointly, which would confuse cause and effect, *VI: 35, 37.* Cf. Haustein, *Geschichte im Dissens,* 179.
141. See *VI: 16f., 22, 27.* Cf. Haustein, *Geschichte im Dissens,* 435.
142. *I: 614.*
143. *I: 617;* see also *615.*
144. *I: 617.*
145. *I: 623.*
146. See Cooke, *Representing East Germany,* 44; Haustein, *Geschichte im Dissens,* 144f., 184, 371, 458, 460; 337ff., 395; Anne Kaminsky, "Die Diskussion über die Opfer des Stalinismus in der gegenwärtigen deutschen Erinnerungskultur," in *"Transformationen" der Erinnerungskulturen in Europa nach 1989,* eds. Bernd Faulenbach and Franz-Josef Jelich (Essen, 2006), 394.
147. *I: 631f.* As mentioned in chapter 4, 17 June was already a National Day of Commemoration, although in 1990 it lost its designation as the Day of German Unity and its public holiday status. The commission was thus not suggesting a formal change—as the PDS

incorrectly suggested, *627*—but merely that 17 June "be again increasingly raised in the public consciousness" to something approximating 27 January, *631.*

148. *I: 615.*
149. *I: 614.*
150. Ibid.
151. *I: 627.*
152. *I: 628.*
153. *I: 633.*
154. Cf. Jürgen Kocka, "Nach dem Ende des Sonderwegs: Zur Tragfähigkeit eines Konzepts," in *Doppelte Zeitgeschichte,* eds. Bauerkämper, Sabrow, and Stöver, 372.
155. *IX: 688.*
156. See Beattie, "The Victims of Totalitarianism," 160ff. On continuing disagreements among victims' groups, see Haustein, *Geschichte im Dissens,* 32, 449, 470.

CONCLUSION

This book has examined the handling of Germany's multiple pasts by the Bundestag's commissions of inquiry. The commissions' main focus and significance lay not in helping the victims of the East German regime, or developing other policies for the past, or pursuing either reconciliation between perpetrators and their victims or understanding between easterners and westerners (chapter 2). Instead, they constituted sites for the contestation of political legitimacy with reference to history. The party-political nature of disagreements, rather than East-West differences, was salient. The major differences over fundamental matters such as the GDR's dictatorial nature, the legitimacy of its foundation, the existence of its putative democratic beginning, and responsibility for the dictatorship existed between Democratic Socialists on the one hand and all the other parties on the other (chapter 3).[1] While the former clung to the GDR's legitimacy as an antifascist response to Germany's fascist past and maintained their hope for a socialist future, the other parties saw that response as fundamentally flawed, if not outright criminal, and saw little or no future for socialism (chapters 4 and 5). The same division applied roughly to the question of the GDR's totalitarian similarity with Nazi Germany (chapter 6). This division between the Democratic Socialists and everyone else can be reduced to that between condemnation and defense of the GDR.

On many other questions, the argumentative topography was more complex. PDS concerns about the totalitarian paradigm and possible relativization of the Nazi past, for example, were shared to some extent by Social Democrats (chapter 6). These two groups also objected to the methodologically questionable aspects of the conservatives' approaches to a range of issues, including the role of Marxist and Marxist-Leninist ideology, and the elision of communist aspirations and their realization in the GDR (chapter 4). Moreover, Social Democrats and Democratic Socialists assumed similar positions on basic questions such as the removal of West Germany from the reappraisal of postwar history, the reduction of East German history to that of the SED regime, and the effective exclusion of society from the picture. These critical left-wing voices were joined by former eastern dissidents in Alliance 90 on other issues, such as the existence of an anti-fascism above and beyond the official regime-sponsored version (chapter 5), and the role a commitment to socialism, or at least to an alternative to the Federal Republic, had played in motivating opposition to the SED (chapter 4). A division between the conservative coalition on the one hand, and the SPD, the PDS, and Alliance 90 on the other, was also evident over the relative success or failure of eastern and western efforts to face up to the Nazi past. Conservatives' rather blinkered condemnation of eastern antifascism and their defense not only of western policies of restitution for the Nazis' Jewish victims, but also of western commemoration of both the Nazis' victims and the anti-Nazi resistance, were juxtaposed with the Left's more even-handed critical appraisal of achievements and deficits on both sides of the divided nation (chapter 5).

There is some truth to Konrad H. Jarausch's and Bernd Faulenbach's depictions of three competing approaches to GDR history: a condemnatory approach adopted by western conservatives, Cold War liberals, and eastern dissidents; an apologetic stance assumed by the PDS; and a mediating, differentiating discourse, found largely among Social Democrats and liberals.[2] However, this constellation requires some qualification in the context of the commissions of inquiry. As the foregoing discussion has highlighted, the mediating discourse included members of the PDS and dissidents in the Alliance 90 on certain issues, while Social Democrats joined the chorus of anticommunist condemnation on others.

Moreover, straightforward acceptance of the relative methodological purity of the mediating approach plays down its ideological nature.[3] In the foregoing chapters, the methodological flaws, blind spots, and inconsistencies of fervent anticommunists' positions have been exposed, and the validity of much of their opponents' criticisms endorsed. Social Democrats sought to modify the zealous anticommunist tendencies of many Christian Democrats. Yet they also conducted politics with history as actively as their rivals to the right and left. Like Christian Democrats, Free Democrats, and members of Alliance 90, they sought to draw legitimacy from their predecessors' struggles against communist dictatorship and from the strength of their democratic commitment, for instance in relation to the "forced unification" of the SPD and KPD (chapter 3). The relative complexity and plausibility of Social Democrats' historical arguments were not merely the result of methodological sophistication, but reflected the difficulties inherent in supporting conservatives' condemnation of communist human-rights abuses without abandoning their own ideological heritage and their critical positions on the western past, for example on the limitations of western *Vergangenheitsbewältigung*. In this situation, calls for differentiation were at least in part a defensive response to conservative attempts to condemn social democracy by association with communism and to impugn the western Left for its excessive accommodation of the GDR and its alleged gelatinization of the fundamental difference between dictatorship and democracy. Differentiation and historicization—however virtuous per se—were strategies adopted by the moderate Left to break the shackles of the dichotomous nature of debates that reflected the continuation of the bipolar logic of the Cold War. No party was exempt from attempts to postulate the validity of its own past and to legitimize its current positions with reference to history.

The confrontation with the East German past did not constitute western victor's justice over the East, because there were winners and losers of the Cold War on both sides of the East-West divide. Debate began in the GDR and was not the result of unification. This applied in particular to the search for responsibility for the dictatorial past and regime abuses, to the rehabilitation of victims and opposition figures, and to debates about antifascism, the Soviet special camps, and memorialization. Moreover, even after unification, easterners actively provoked discussion and led the drive for a thorough reckoning with communism. The commissions of inquiry were themselves proposed by easterners, who were among their most active and prominent members. These activists, now scholars and parliamentarians, were the eastern victors of the Cold War. There were also western losers, and a further argument against the notion of western victor's justice was the important role of intra-western disputes. Western conservatives did not just seek to condemn the GDR and its supporters and defenders in the East, but were keen to excoriate their western left-liberal opponents for forsaking the pursuit of unification, being too soft on communism, and abandoning the totalitarian paradigm. At the same time as rejecting the Left's anti-anticommunism, the Right insisted on its own moral rectitude in maintaining its strident anticommunism and national orientation. Rather than western victor's justice, then, the reckoning with communism as pursued in the commissions amounted to the pursuit of historical, political, and moral validation for anticommunists, whether of eastern or western provenance.

Nevertheless, the common impression of western victor's justice should not simply be corrected; it must also be explained. Here I agree with Paul Cooke's assessment that claims about the colonization of the East German past, while problematic, "cannot simply be dismissed."[4] In part, such perceptions were the result of the western origins of many of the institutions involved in working through the East German past after unification.

With the exception of the Federal Commissioner for the Stasi Records, the institutions responsible for addressing the legacy of the GDR—particularly the courts, but also the commissions of inquiry—all originated in the West, even if they merely continued the efforts of East German prosecutors and judges who had began the process in 1989–90. Moreover, many postunification institutions—but not the commissions of inquiry—were often staffed almost exclusively by westerners, which only helped to reinforce the PDS's self-serving depictions of the condemnation of the GDR as emanating from "Bonn." Constitutionally of course, federal institutions now represented both westerners and easterners, as did the major political parties, but they were still associated with the West in the popular imagination, and that is where the PDS sought to keep them.[5] However, it is inaccurate and misleading for scholars to uncritically perpetuate such depictions.

The commissions sought to counter such views by stressing their "all-German" membership, but they could not overcome four far-reaching problems that were responsible for the persistence of the notion that the West was sitting in judgment over the East. The first was the simple fact that westerners were conspicuously involved. Indeed, they dominated much of the discussion, particularly on prominent occasions such as the first inquiry's two-day final public hearing in the Reichstag in May 1994. It was hardly surprising that East German dissident and author Jürgen Fuchs expressed his profound sense of estrangement both from the proceedings at that hearing specifically and from much public debate about the East German (and Nazi) past and the postunification present more generally. He was, after all, one of very few eastern speakers at the hearing, and the prevailing discourse was largely foreign to him.[6] His provocative, highly critical comments quoted in the introduction amounted to a charge of western expropriation of the eastern past, but for Fuchs the main problem was insufficient rather than excessive rigor displayed toward the collaborators and accomplices of the East German dictatorship.

The second problem was the unrepresentative nature of many of those easterners who did participate actively. The most prominent eastern voices on and before the inquiries were those of opponents of the regime, like Fuchs himself, and, to a lesser extent, its victims. The dissidents represented a minority of the population, and their views on many issues hardly differed from those of western conservatives, such that numerous other easterners felt they lacked a voice.[7] Rather ironically, the unrepresentative nature of the eastern participants in the development of a semi-official history of German division exhibited certain parallels with official antifascism in the GDR. Catherine Epstein perceptively speaks of official East German memory of the Nazi period being based on the "countermemories" of a tiny, antifascist minority of the population, in contrast with the memories of the majority that were more positive about Nazism.[8] This structure is also found in discussions about the East German past after unification. The extent to which the wider population in either instance could identify with such a narrative founded on the experiences and views of the victims and opponents of the regime is open to question. Similarly debatable is the extent to which the moral righteousness of the few could foster critical discussion of the compromises of the many, rather than a defensive apologia or a misleading insistence on their own oppositional credentials. A frequent objection from easterners—and a concern shared by sympathetic westerners—was their inability to recognize or find themselves (*sich wiederfinden*) in the dominant anticommunist discourse.[9]

Thirdly, the commissions adopted a regime-centered approach that focused overwhelmingly on GDR history qua the SED dictatorship. While they insisted that their condemnation of the regime not be interpreted as condemnation of East Germans, the inquiries paid little attention to the experiences of ordinary easterners and largely reduced their history to that of the regime. As expert witness and western professor of education Heinz-Elmar Tenorth said at the Reichstag hearing in May 1994, a gap existed between people's perceptions of their own past experiences and how these were depicted in ideological condemnations or historical accounts of the regime.[10] There was considerable legitimacy to the complaint registered by Arnd Bauerkämper, Martin Sabrow, and Bernd Stöver of insufficient awareness that "lived reality" was not commensurate with the history of dictatorship. Moreover, demanding recognition of such a distinction came "quickly under suspicion of 'ostalgic' distortion," as nostalgia for the East has been designated.[11] Furthermore, as Christoph Kleßmann argues, the dominant regime-centered view and the insistence on the notion of totalitarianism produced "a blockade and rejection rather than insight and agreement."[12] At the first commission's final hearing, Karl Wilhelm Fricke asked expert witness Hans Misselwitz from the Federal Office for Political Education whether he thought it was accurate to suggest, as Jürgen Kocka had reported, that many East Germans were offended by comparisons between the GDR and the Third Reich, and if so, why.[13] Misselwitz clearly thought it was accurate, and he suggested that easterners' continuing antifascist identification was largely responsible.[14] But he went even further, suggesting that there was a certain justification in objecting to having one's own past measured against the Nazi past, because the burdens of the Nazi past were so weighty in terms of personal and moral responsibility.[15] The inquiry had failed to consider such perspectives.

The fourth problem was the highly unbalanced nature of the discussion of the history of German division. The inquiries' subject matter was overwhelmingly a critical discussion of the East, while the West was addressed only tangentially. For all their rhetoric about the shared past of division, western conservatives in particular displayed an almost total refusal to tolerate critical discussion of the FRG and sought in some instances—such as the handling of the Nazi past—to contrast it positively and tendentiously with the negative example of the GDR. Their continuing critique of the western Left notwithstanding, their approach amounted to a black and white view of the East and West respectively. They perceived the contestation of the divided past as a zero-sum game, in which nothing could be conceded about the western past for fear of granting legitimacy to the GDR, or at least credibility to its defenders in the PDS. Such an approach was by no means limited to the commissions; indeed, the institutions and political culture of the old Federal Republic underwent considerable positive reevaluation through the demise of the GDR and the unification process.[16] While everything from the East appeared disposable, everything from the West suddenly became an unquestioned norm.[17] As Marc Howard argues, rather than attempting to reconceptualize the divided past or create a joint narrative for the postwar period, the dominant mode of discussion was "evaluative."[18] Crucially, the outcome of the evaluation was predetermined.

Cumulatively, these tendencies do not merely explain the power of the notion of western victor's justice. They also help to explain the commissions' failure to contribute to the project of inner unity as initially conceived. The lingering "wall in the heads" between easterners and westerners had many causes. Any explanation must include both the persistence of differing values and communication problems that were the result of forty years of divergent socialization processes, as well as the socioeconomic problems of the postunification period and the cultural and political asymmetries of the unification process itself. The collective devaluation of eastern skills and experience was often perceived as entailing the denigration of eastern "biographies," and the vastly differing statuses of the eastern and western pasts during and subsequent to unification exacerbated this.[19] Changes to street names and the demise of other public and physical symbols of the East—such as the Palace of the Republic that had housed the Volkskammer—provided graphic examples which met with considerable resistance by the mid 1990s, when a resurgence of identification as easterners (not with the regime) became evident.[20]

Commentators agree that, of all things that continue to divide easterners and westerners, their views of history are among the most prominent.[21] While the inquiries' public impact is difficult to gauge, there is therefore little evidence to suggest that they achieved their goal of fostering a common view of the German past, and much to suggest that they did not.[22] To be sure, compared with forty years of division and the massive upheaval that accompanied and followed its end, the commissions were a rather insignificant factor.[23] Indeed, compared with the lengthy and better known efforts to prosecute East German officials, or the continuing scandals emanating from the Stasi legacy, the public impact of the Bundestag inquiries was slight.[24] It was certainly smaller than suggested by some commentators who, uninhibited by their equally exaggerated and largely unsubstantiated claims about how little public attention the inquiries attracted, argue that "the East German public" reacted with skepticism at best and hostility at worst to the commissions' handling of East German history, which therefore exacerbated the inner-German divide.[25] The inquiries' public reception must be seen in more differentiated terms. One should not ignore the diversity of their audiences (chapter 2), or the diversity of easterners' views on the GDR or on how it should be addressed in the present. Anyone who took a closer look at the inquiries' work would have seen its efforts at differentiation and particularly its repeated insistence that condemnation of the regime did not entail condemnation of East Germans, but precisely the opposite. Inevitably, however, as discussed in chapter 6, the degree of subtleness and differentiation that the public could register varied, ranging from nuanced scholarly analyses in the published expertise papers, to the more selective and politicized depiction of the reports, to the more sloganistic Bundestag resolutions, and inevitably brief media reports.

Yet one should not just focus on limited lines of communication or potentially mistaken perceptions. On the crucial question of the comparison of dictatorships, for example, it is by no means sufficient to attribute the popular belief that comparison of the GDR and Third Reich entailed their equation to the public's inability to think abstractly or logically, or to the difficulties of translating (presumably rigorous) elite discourse into (fuzzier) popular discourse.[26] As demonstrated in chapter 6, the problem lay very much at the production end, that is, with conservative commissioners' and experts' own practice of dictatorial comparison. For all of the commissions' pretensions to differentiation and methodological soundness, their complete delegitimization of the East German state, their condemnation of socialism and antifascism, their search for repression in everyday life, and their diverse efforts to highlight parallels between the GDR and the Third Reich appeared tantamount to the criminalization of the East German state and the collective denigration of easterners. Simplistic western anticommunism combined with the former dissidents' moral rigor did little to foster a truly inclusive or pluralistic understanding of the divided past. The inquiries may not necessarily have magnified the East-West cleavage or eastern resentment at perceived victor's justice, or contributed directly to PDS electoral success as some authors suggest.[27] But they did little to counter such public perceptions or PDS posturing. Rather than seeing the Bundestag commissions as causative of eastern alienation, it is more accurate to understand them as failing to counteract and perhaps slightly exacerbating already existing problems, not least due to their own antagonistic goals.

In subsequent years, commissioners became rather dismissive of the centrality to the inquiries of the project of inner unity, and more sanguine about its failure to materialize thus far.[28] Comparing such later views with the early rhetoric about fostering national unity through developing a common understanding of recent history suggests an increased acceptance of the limitations of parliamentary processes to reach the wider population, as well as a greater acknowledgement of the durability of mentalities. Only rarely, however, did commissioners consider the possibility that the inquiries themselves may have militated against the achievement of the central goal of inner unity, or reflect critically on their earlier desire for uniformity of historical and political consciousness.[29]

Yet as I have argued throughout, one should not focus on East-West issues to the neglect of others. Unified Germany's developing relationship with its tumultuous twentieth-century history was an equally important matter. The commissions' majority and minority reports indicated that the political parties could not agree on a common understanding of history, but—with the exception of the PDS—they at least agreed on a political-historical position: the antitotalitarian consensus. Participants hailed its endorsement as a major achievement and a significant advance on the starkly diverging positions that had been evident in the Historians' Dispute of the 1980s. In contrast with their diffidence on the question of inner unity, in the author's interviews commissioners highlighted this consensus as the inquiries' most important outcome.[30] Yet questions remain about what the consensus actually meant, and how new or genuine it was. The parties agreed that both the Nazi and communist pasts were important, that the victims of both regimes had to be remembered, and that both regimes had to remain discredited. Only the PDS differed on the last point. Beyond this minimal consensus, the crucial question remained that of the pasts' *relative* significance in Germany's commemorative politics and historical consciousness.[31] For Jürgen Habermas, the only antitotalitarian consensus that would "deserve its name" would not be selective: "The Left must not deceive itself about the specific commonalities of totalitarian regimes and must use the same standard on both sides. The Right on the other hand must not level out or play down differences."[32] Such a position indeed represented an advance on the Historians' Dispute.

The commissions suggested that such a consensus had been reached, but considerable differences remained, limiting its effectiveness and significance. Despite the efforts of individuals such as Dietmar Keller, the PDS as a whole remained outside the consensus, rejecting the notion of totalitarianism and the comparison of the GDR with the Third Reich. Indeed, particularly for the Christian Democrats, the antitotalitarian consensus was aimed precisely at the PDS, which they cast as an extremist party hostile to the democratic order of the Federal Republic and sympathetic to totalitarian alternatives.[33] In contrast, the consensus enjoyed considerable support from left-liberal intellectuals, the SPD, and Alliance 90. While some still had concerns about the usefulness of the totalitarian paradigm for understanding and explaining the GDR, they sought to differentiate its questionable scholarly value from the politically desirable antitotalitarian consensus.[34] This was a tenuous position given the centrality to the consensus of agreement on what constituted a "totalitarian temptation" or a "form of totalitarian ideology, program, party, and movement," from which the consensus was supposed to protect democracy.[35] If agreement was impossible on whether "real existing" socialism had constituted a form of totalitarianism, or whether antifascism or socialism were totalitarian ideologies, the prospects for political agreement on the acceptability of their adherents were slim.[36] Moreover, it was also rather inconsistent to criticize the vagueness or absence of positive notions behind antifascism, as conservatives and Social Democrats did, and then subscribe to another "anti-" consensus, whose positive connotations themselves were less than self-evident.[37]

Such questions highlight the difficulties Germans encountered in defining a positive identity and set of political goals after unification. During the period of division, West and East Germany had defined themselves primarily in negative opposition to the Nazi or fascist past and to the purportedly totalitarian or proto-fascist rival across the border. The endorsement of the antitotalitarian consensus indicated that, after all the vigorous contestation discussed throughout this book, unified Germany adopted the anticommunist West German approach, distancing itself from what was now the double totalitarian past.[38] Some commentators argue that Germany's continuing self-definition ex negativo suggested that the Germans knew better what they did not want to be than what they did.[39] Others argue that it was and remains possible to generate a general respect for the values of democracy from an understanding of "democracy's defeats."[40] The establishment of the first commission of inquiry indicated that both views contain a degree of truth: all the parties agreed on the need to do something to work through the GDR past and to learn from the apparent failure to face up self-critically to Nazism, but it was by no means self-evident what that lesson positively entailed. Nevertheless, the continuity with, indeed the relative strengthening of West German antitotalitarianism was clear. The mid 1980s had seen the cohabitation of conservative adherents of antitotalitarianism in government in the Federal Republic with the cultural-intellectual dominance of the liberal Left that rejected antitotalitarianism. The 1990s witnessed conservatives—buoyed by the support of eastern dissidents—achieve considerable success in delegitimizing eastern and western antifascism and reasserting the totalitarian paradigm. Even if they shied away from direct equation, they endorsed modes of remembering the German past that lumped together communism and Nazism. Conservative positions suggested that Ian Kershaw's 1992 prediction that unified Germany would not witness outright denial of Nazi crimes, but their relativization, was not far off the mark.[41]

The very continuity with western antitotalitarianism indicated a significant change: Germany now sought to draw strength from a positive historical legacy: the West German success story. This positive past motivated and justified the modality of unification via the eastern states' accession to the Federal Republic. It led to the ultimate refusal to consider seriously the development of a new constitution or substantial changes to the Basic Law subsequent to unification. An uncritical approach to western history was also the source of considerable hypocrisy, double standards, and blind spots particularly among conservatives, as highlighted throughout this book. The western success story was one constitutive element of the fundamental asymmetry of the unification process and the postunification standing of the eastern and western pasts, the other being the condemned East German totalitarian past.[42]

A frequent if rather unsuccessful attempt to overcome or at least ameliorate that basic asymmetry and to provide unified Germany with a further positive inheritance was the promotion of the democratic achievements of the East German population and the opposition in particular. As discussed in chapter 3, the first commission sought to highlight the opposition's role and the fact that easterners had taken to the streets in 1989 and wrested power from the SED and the Stasi. The second inquiry continued these efforts in its deliberations on commemoration and memorialization. Reflecting the earnestness with which this positive eastern legacy was embraced, Bernd Faulenbach subsequently suggested that the identity of the "Berlin Republic" has three historical foundations: the success of the old Federal Republic, opposition to Nazism, and the legacy of the East German opposition.[43] This is a rather optimistic view, because the meaning of "1989" has been vigorously contested, as has the opposition's role in it.[44] Perhaps even more importantly, as the celebrations of the tenth-anniversary of the breaching of the Berlin Wall suggested, all too often East German contributions have simply been overlooked. The memory marathon in 2003 associated with the fiftieth anniversary of the 1953 uprising suggested that perhaps greater interest could be engendered for remembering East German democratic movements and desire for national unity.[45] The rather modest attention paid to the fifteenth anniversary of 1989, however, indicated that in fact little had changed.[46] East German history was still regarded predominantly as a dictatorial past that is to be condemned, and whose victims are to be commemorated. It was not held to contain anything worth celebrating, although recent years have seen growing support for and a Bundestag resolution to erect a central memorial to the "liberty and unity of Germany" achieved in 1989–90.[47]

Other developments since the end of the second commission's term have similarly suggested more continuity with the pre-unification period than change. Importantly, after the defeat of the Christian and Free Democrat coalition at the 1998 federal elections, it was left to the new government of the SPD and Alliance 90/The Greens to develop a federal policy on memorials. The new coalition largely endorsed the second commission's recommendations, undertaking, for example, to continue institutional and project funding beyond the end of the initially planned ten-year period. It also opened federal funding to memorials in western states, a move consistent with the moderate Left's greater awareness of the needs of (western) concentration-camp memorial sites as opposed to the conservative parties' preference for funding (eastern) sites with a double past.[48] Such a step had been supported by the commissions, whose conservative members did not dispute the desirability and necessity of commemorating Nazi persecution and its victims, above and beyond the confines of the double past.

Yet subtle but noteworthy differences remained between the moderate Right and the moderate Left, signifying the precariousness of the anti-totalitarian consensus. As Habermas perceived accurately in 1994 and as chapter 6 demonstrated also to be true for subsequent years, despite the commissions' best efforts the left-right division of the political spectrum continued to play a critical role in determining attitudes toward the two pasts: "Where those on the Right tend toward similarity, those on the Left want above all to see differences."[49] The brittleness of the consensus was made abundantly clear in 2004. In January, the Central Council of Jews in Germany suspended its participation in the Foundation of Saxon Memorial Sites, a newly established public body in the eastern state of Saxony charged with the administration of memorials to the victims of Nazi and communist persecution.[50] The Central Council's withdrawal was a reaction to what it saw as a tendency within the foundation to equate the crimes of the Nazi and communist regimes, and it was followed by the withdrawal of other organizations dedicated to the memory of the victims of Nazism. This furor was entangled in a larger controversy over a CDU motion in the

Bundestag that objected to the allegedly insufficient attention paid to communist repression and called for the commemoration of the victims of both "totalitarian dictatorships." The motion suggested that the federal government was failing to implement the recommendations of the second commission of inquiry.[51] In response, liberal-left critics suggested that the CDU and the Saxon foundation had themselves abandoned the inquiry's consensus and were equating the two regimes and their crimes in an unacceptable fashion, even though the conservative positions were in fact no different from those represented by the commissions of inquiry. Thus, far from constituting a genuine consensus, the apparent agreement reached between Left and Right in the mid 1990s represented little more than the temporary result of the victory of anticommunism in the Cold War. In its aftermath, the moderate Left felt compelled to support the rigorous working through of the communist past, but fought an uphill battle against continuing equationist tendencies of the Right.

Such leveling tendencies are by no means unrelated to the more recent explosion of discussion about German suffering during and after the Second World War. Indeed, the debate about the double totalitarian past was an important precursor for the rediscovery of German victimhood. For all of their attacks on the PDS, the commissions' activities did not focus on perpetrators, their punishment, or integration. Indeed, the perpetrators were remarkably absent from the discussion about totalitarianism and the comparability of the two dictatorships. In contrast, as chapters 1 and 2 demonstrated, the at least rhetorical focus was on the victims, while the opposition was also central. In particular, the inquiries' deliberations on commemorative practices—in the East, the West, and unified Germany—concentrated on victims and resistors. Sites of persecution were included, and "perpetrator sites" such as the Stasi headquarters in Normannenstraße in Berlin were supported, but most of the discussion focused on victims and resistance. The relevant section of the second commission's report was accurately entitled "All-German Forms of Memory of the Two German Dictatorships and their *Victims*."[52] The frequently invoked victims often seemed to have suffered at the hands of abstract institutional forces rather than real people.[53] The crimes themselves were not clearly designated; indeed, they almost disappeared through repeated references to "the Nazi dictatorship and its consequences" that avoided actually mentioning what had happened, let alone by whose hand. Moreover, such references were open to interpretation, since the consequences could perhaps also have referred to those for the Germans, such as defeat, occupation, and division.[54] Not too much should be read into these rather limited tendencies, but the success of the proponents of memory of communist crimes and Germans' suffering at the hands of Communists paved the way for those who seek to place German suffering alongside German guilt and the suffering of the Nazis' victims. Not infrequently, conservatives support both projects simultaneously, which is hardly surprising given that they have in common a tendency to play down the specificity of German crimes and to challenge the centrality of memory of those crimes and their victims for contemporary German identity.[55]

Of course, the commissions of inquiry cannot be held accountable for subsequent developments such as the renewed focus on German suffering. Yet they were at least in part responsible for the fracturing of the antitotalitarian consensus they sought to propagate. The ambivalence of the second commission's position, for instance—in rejecting simultaneously both the relativization of Nazi crimes and hierarchies of victims—allowed competing groups representing divergent positions to justify themselves with reference to the commission and to invoke its antitotalitarian consensus. The consensus existed only on paper, and deep divisions remained. Nevertheless, the commissions must be credited with leading and provoking public discussion of Germany's divided past. They made considerable inroads into the media's exclusive concentration on the Stasi. Their contribution to research into, and understanding of, the GDR was considerable, and they served as a catalyst for academic research and political debate.[56] Their contribution to Germany's commemorative politics and thus its memorial landscape was also positive, and the Foundation for Working through the SED Dictatorship continues to support the public confrontation with the past.

Ultimately, however, their greatest significance was twofold: first, that they existed at all and, secondly, that they provided a forum for the political contestation of the history and the legitimacy of the two German states, their various ideologies, political movements, and parties. The central motivations for the first inquiry were a vague sense that something had to be done and a more specific desire to avoid future suggestions of a repetition of the failure to take sufficient measures to face up to Nazism (chapter 1). Retrospectively, commissioners seemed to suggest in highly circular fashion that the inquiries' main achievement lay precisely in having left a lasting record of unified Germany's handling of its divided past, so that they would be discussed and analyzed in studies like this one.[57] Jürgen Fuchs made a similar point at the first inquiry's final hearing. Although he objected to the premature historicization of the East German past, he displayed a keen awareness of the historicity of the events in which he was participating and of his and their own inevitable historicization, an awareness that was shared by the commissions themselves.[58] Such self-consciousness pointed to both the significance and the limitations of the inquiries. The self-satisfaction that emanated from the fact that they were, to a large extent, ends in themselves paradoxically produced a remarkable lack of reflection that in turn limited the inquiries' potential significance, the soundness of their methods and judgments, and their ability to reach a wider audience (chapter 2).

At the same time, however, Fuchs missed the point of the hearing of which he was part. His criticism of western left-liberal intellectuals (including Habermas) and historians (including Faulenbach) who he perceived as dominating the public discourse on the East German past was precisely what the inquiry wanted to hear, especially as it was supported by the moral authority he possessed as a prominent eastern dissident.[59] While he may have felt "lost" in the scholarly and intellectual discourse, the mere fact that he was participating in a panel on the East German past and its postunification treatment indicated precisely that contemporaries like Fuchs were not allowed to be lost. Fuchs's very participation indicated that they, too, would play a central role in the formation of the antitotalitarian consensus he implicitly endorsed and thus in the ongoing politicization, rather than historicization of the recent German past.

Notes

1. Cf. Welsh, "When Discourse Trumps Policy," 148.
2. Cf. Jarausch, "The German Democratic Republic as History," 38–41; Faulenbach, "Die Arbeit der Enquete-Kommissionen," 27.
3. Faulenbach depicts the moderating discourse as apolitical, "Die Arbeit der Enquete-Kommissionen," 27; Jarausch notes more accurately that the middling position, like the others, was at least in part politically motivated, "The German Democratic Republic as History," 41, 43f.
4. Cooke, *Representing East Germany*, 29.
5. Herbert Wolf, "Sine ira et studio??? Standpunkt zum Abschluß der Arbeit der Enquete-Kommission," in *Ansichten* IV, eds. Keller, Modrow, and Wolf, 363; Günter Benser, "Bundestagsdrucksache 12/7820: Auch methodisch ein Dokument voller Widersprüche," and Jürgen Hoffmann, "Deutschlandpolitik als bundesdeutsche Einbahnstraße: Nachtrag zu einem defizitären Kapitel des Abschlußberichtes," both in *Ansichten* V, eds. Černý, Lehmann, and Neuhaus.
6. IX: 695f.
7. Cf. Andrews, "Grand National Narratives," 60; Kamali, "Accountability for Human Rights Violations," 109, 132; Yoder, "Truth without Reconciliation," 65.
8. Catherine Epstein, "The Production of 'Official Memory' in East Germany: Old Communists and the Dilemmas of Memoir-Writing," *Central European History* 32, no. 2 (1999): 200.
9. Jürgen Kocka, IX: 612. Author's interviews with Ilko-Sascha Kowalczuk and Markus Meckel.
10. IX: 649.
11. Bauerkämper, Sabrow, and Stöver, *Doppelte Zeitgeschichte*, 13. Generally, see Cooke, *Representing East Germany*.

12. Kleßmann, *Zeitgeschichte in Deutschland,* 14.
13. IX: 672.
14. Cf. Schroeder, *Die veränderte Republik,* 310.
15. IX: 674.
16. On the positive reevaluation of the FRG's Basic Law in the unification process, see Gregg O. Kvistad, "Parties and Citizens in the Western German Unification Debate," *German Politics and Society* 30 (1993): 34–48. More generally, see Tobias Dürr, "On 'Westalgia': Why West German Mentalities and Habits Persist in the Berlin Republic," in *The Spirit of the Berlin Republic,* ed. Dettke.
17. See M. Rainer Lepsius, "The Legacy of Two Dictatorships and Democratic Culture in United Germany," *Schweizerische Zeitschrift für Soziologie* 21, no. 3 (1995): 765–76; Imanuell Geiss, *The Question of German Unification* (London, 1997). Apart from the far Left and some eastern dissidents, neoconservatives were the only exception, seeing in the FRG an unacceptable abandonment of proper aspirations to national power. See Jacob Heilbrunn, "Germany's New Right," *Foreign Affairs* 75, no. 6 (1996): 80–98; Jerry Z. Muller, "German Neoconservatism and the History of the Bonn Republic, 1968–1985," *German Politics and Society* 18, no. 1 (2000): 1–32.
18. Marc Howard, "Unique, but not beyond Comparison: Comments on Konrad Jarausch's 'The German Democratic Republic as History in United Germany,'" *German Politics and Society* 15, no. 2 (1997): 49.
19. Dürr speaks of the failure of inner unity and blames the lack of western self-criticism, "On 'Westalgia.'"
20. Jennifer A. Yoder, *From East Germans to Germans? The New Postcommunist Elites* (Durham, 1999), 13; Wolfgang Thierse, in Jürgen Kocka and Martin Sabrow, eds., *Die DDR als Geschichte: Fragen, Hypothesen, Perspektiven* (Berlin, 1994), 204f.; Pampel, "Bagatellisierung durch Gedenken?" 443; Helwig, "Aufarbeitung ist Zukunftsgestaltung," 705. See also Paul Betts, "The Twilight of the Idols: East German Memory and Material Culture," *Journal of Modern History* 72, no. 3 (2000): 731–65; Susanne Ledanff, "The Palace of the Republic versus the Stadtschloss: The Dilemmas of Planning in the Heart of Berlin," *German Politics and Society* 21, no. 4 (2003): 30–44.
21. See Felix Philipp Lutz, "Historical Consciousness and the Changing of German Political Culture," in *The Berlin Republic: German Unification and a Decade of Change,* eds. Winand Gellner and John D. Robertson (London, 2003); Annette Leo, "Nicht vereinigt: Studien zum Geschichtsbewusstsein Ost- und Westdeutscher," in *Deutsche Teilung, Repression und Alltagsleben: Erinnerungsorte der DDR-Geschichte,* eds. Heidi Behrens and Andreas Wagner (Leipzig, 2004). Even those commentators who are reasonably positive about easterners' integration in the FRG, who see their very emphasis on inequality and their demands for recognition as a sign of their acceptance of the (western) system, and who argue that East and West are growing together point to "the exception, of course, of their historical memories," McFalls, "Political Culture and Political Change," 90. Cf. Brady and Wiliarty, "How Culture Matters," 4; Sabrow, *Grenzen der Vereinigung.* For a differentiated analysis of survey data, see Schroeder, *Die veränderte Republik,* 320–39.
22. Cf. McAdams, *Judging the Past,* 13.
23. As Jan-Werner Müller argues, easterners' crash course in free-market capitalism was surely more significant than transitional justice, "East Germany," 273.
24. Helga Welsh's thoughtful juxtaposition of the modest actual outcomes of trials and purges, with the, in her view, more influential discursive field that included the inquiries, overlooks that the impact of the former cannot just be measured in terms of numbers of successful prosecutions, etc., "When Discourse Trumps Policy."

25. Kamali, "Accountability for Human Rights Violations," 108ff.; Andrews, "Grand National Narratives," 51, 60.
26. See Beckmann, "Die Auseinandersetzung mit dem Vergleich," 10; Cooke, *Representing East Germany*, 43.
27. Cf. Cooke, *Representing East Germany*, 50f.; McAdams, *Judging the Past*, 114ff.
28. Author's interviews with Wilke, Kowalczuk, Faulenbach, Hansen, Mitter, von Renesse, Weber, and Eppelmann.
29. Cf. Mary Fulbrook, who poses the question of whether working through the past is inimical to inner unity, but concludes that it is not, "Aufarbeitung der DDR-Vergangenheit und 'innere Einheit'—ein Widerspruch?" in *Deutsche Vergangenheiten*, eds. Kleßmann, Misselwitz, and Wichert. The present author's contention is that the two are not necessarily incompatible, but that the style and focus adopted in working through the East German past was indeed inimical to inner unity.
30. Author's interviews with Gutzeit, Kowalczuk, Faulenbach, Hansen, Jacobsen, Weisskirchen, and Eppelmann.
31. Cf. Schroeder, *Die veränderte Republik*, 313.
32. IX: 689.
33. See Koschyk, "Die Beseitigung der Folgen," 477. Cf. Jesse, "'Entnazifizierung' und 'Entstasifizierung,'" 35.
34. Author's interview with Faulenbach.
35. I: 745, 783. Cf. Pampel, "Bagatellisierung durch Gedenken?" 452f.
36. Indeed, as Mary Fulbrook argues, totalitarianism is an "essentially contested concept," "Retheorising 'State' and 'Society' in the German Democratic Republic," in *The Workers' and Peasants' State: Communism and Society in East Germany under Ulbricht 1945–71*, eds. Patrick Major and Jonathon Osmond (Manchester, 2002), 283. It thus serves with difficulty as the basis for a political consensus or identity creation.
37. The commissions' faith in a negatively formulated "anti-" consensus was of course inconsistent with their criticism of Dietmar Keller over GDR antifascism's merely negative focus, discussed in chapter 5.
38. Pampel, "Was bedeutet 'Aufarbeitung,'" 33.
39. See Dettke, *The Spirit of the Berlin Republic*, 3. Cf. Sandner, who suggests that history generally can only teach what should be avoided, "Hegemonie und Erinnerung," 9.
40. Lepsius, "The Legacy of Two Dictatorships," 775. Lepsius insists, "Democracy cannot derive positive confirmation from these dictatorships," ibid., 769. In contrast, Gesine Schwan, among others, argues that acknowledging and accepting historical guilt is by no means incompatible with a positive collective identity, *Politik und Schuld: Die zerstörerische Macht des Schweigens* (Frankfurt am Main, 1997), 49.
41. Kershaw, *Germany's Present, Germany's Past*, 15f.
42. See Beattie, "The Past in the Politics."
43. Faulenbach, "Historical Foundations." Cf. Jan-Werner Müller, "Preparing for the Political: German Intellectuals Confront the Berlin Republic," in *Political Thought and German Reunification*, eds. Williams, Wight, and Kapferer, 222f.
44. See Bernd Okun, "Inwieweit ist der Herbst 1989 'identitätsstiftend' für das vereinte Deutschland? Einige Überlegungen," in *Ansichten* V, eds. Černý, Lehmann, and Neuhaus. While the mainstream parties have difficulties with the distinction between "1989" and "1990," the PDS continues to see the former as a missed opportunity for a democratic GDR. See Historische Kommission beim Vorstand der PDS, "Herbst 1989: Für eine andere DDR—Chancen und Grenzen" (5 October 2004).
45. See Jonathan Sperber, "17 June 1953: Revisiting a German Revolution," *German History* 22, no. 4 (2004): 619–43; Wolfrum, "Neue Erinnerungskultur?"

46. See Tobias Hollitzer, "15 Jahre friedliche Revolution," *Aus Politik und Zeitgeschichte* 54, no. 41–42 (2004): 3–6.

47. See Richard Schröder, "Brauchen wir ein nationales Freiheits- und Einheitsdenkmal?" *Deutschland Archiv* 40, no. 1 (2007): 131-36; Dorothee Wilms, "Was sollte ein Freiheits- und Einheitsdenkmal versinnbildlichen?" *Deutschland Archiv* 40, no. 5 (2007): 868-72; Deutscher Bundestag, "Beschlussempfehlung und Bericht des Ausschusses für Kultur und Medien," *Drucksache* 16/6974 (7 November 2007); Deutscher Bundestag, *Plenarprotokoll* 16/124 (9 November 2007), 12969.

48. Deutscher Bundestag, "Konzeption der künftigen Gedenkstättenförderung des Bundes und Bericht der Bundesregierung über die Beteiligung des Bundes an Gedenkstätten in der Bundesrepublik Deutschland," *Drucksache* 14/1569 (27 July 1999).

49. IX: 689.

50. See the foundation's website, <http://www.stsg.de/> (22 April 2008).

51. Deutscher Bundestag, "Förderung von Gedenkstätten zur Diktaturgeschichte in Deutschland: Gesamtkonzept für ein würdiges Gedenken aller Opfer der beiden deutschen Diktaturen," *Drucksache* 15/1874 (4 November 2003), 1. On the controversy, see Beattie, "The Victims of Totalitarianism."

52. *I: 589*, emphasis added.

53. *I: 591f.*

54. *I: 591.*

55. On the expellees' debate and the broader rediscovery of German suffering, see Langenbacher, "Changing Memory Regimes." On conservative dissatisfaction with the (relative) level of commemoration of the SED dictatorship, see Beattie, "The Victims of Totalitarianism."

56. Cf. Bernhard Wördehoff, "Ein Steinbruch für die Forschung," *Die Zeit*, 29 December 1995; Kleßmann, *Zeitgeschichte in Deutschland*, 13, 36f.; Christoph Kleßmann, "Eine Enquete-Kommission als historisches Gewissen der Nation? Das Parlament stimuliert die Aufarbeitung der jüngsten deutschen Geschichte," *Das Parlament*, 13 November 1998, 1; Gerhard Hirscher, "Materialien der Enquete-Kommission 'Überwindung der Folgen der SED-Diktatur im Prozess der deutschen Einheit,'" *Politische Studien* 373 (2000): 131.

57. Author's interviews with Gutzeit, Jacobsen, Weber, Maser, Wilke, and Weisskirchen. See also the statement in the second inquiry's mandate such that the first inquiry "will remain an important testament to how the German Bundestag and the political public took up this challenge in the early years after unification," *I: 4.*

58. IX: 695–701.

59. IX: 698ff., 696.

Appendices

The appendices reproduce the author's translation of the terms of reference for each of the two commissions of inquiry. Ideally, readers would also be able to consult other significant documents, especially the inquiries' reports. At several hundred pages each, however, they are much too long to include. The terms of reference nevertheless give a sense of the tone of the inquiries' official pronouncements. Moreover, given the repeated references made in this book to the goals and methods of the inquiries, it is perhaps useful for the reader to be able to check my analysis against the original documents.

THE TERMS OF REFERENCE OF THE COMMISSION OF INQUIRY, "WORKING THROUGH THE HISTORY AND CONSEQUENCES OF THE SED DICTATORSHIP IN GERMANY"

(I: 188–91)

I.

To work through politically the history and consequences of the SED dictatorship in Germany is the common task of all Germans. It assumes particular importance on the path to Germany's inner unification.

The legacy of the SED dictatorship still burdens the coming together of people in Germany. The experiences of injustice and persecution, humiliation and incapacitation are still alive. Many people search for enlightenment and struggle for orientation in dealing with their own responsibility and guilt, and that of others. They pose questions about the roots of the dictatorial system erected in the SBZ/GDR, about the political, mental, and psychological consequences of the dictatorship, about the possibilities of political and moral rehabilitation of the victims.

The commission of inquiry established by the decision of the German Bundestag on 12 March 1992 (*Drucksache* 12/2330 of 11 March 1992) is especially called upon to work through these questions. It is committed to the people in all of Germany, but above all to the Germans in the new federal states, who were subjected to dictatorial forms of government for almost six decades. The German Bundestag regards offering them assistance in the examination of the past and in the evaluation of personal responsibility as a fundamental concern of the commission.

The German Bundestag is aware of the limits of a political working through according to the rule of law. Efforts to serve an injured sense of justice by laying bare abuses and naming responsibilities are all the more important. At the same time, it is necessary to contribute to reconciliation in society.

The commission of inquiry is not to preempt or replace the necessary historical research. The goal of its work is to contribute—in dialogue with the public—to the strengthening of democratic self-confidence and the further development of a common political culture in Germany.

II.

The commission thus has the task of working on contributions to political-historical analysis and political-moral evaluation, including:

1. to analyze the structures, strategies, and instruments of the SED dictatorship, especially the question of responsibility for the abuse of human and civil rights and for the destruction of nature and the environment, including:
   - decision-making processes in the SED,
   - the relationship of the SED and the state apparatus, especially that between the various levels of the SED and the Ministry for State Security,
   - the structure and methods of the State Security, the police, and the judiciary,
   - the role of the bloc parties, the mass organizations, and the media,
   - the militarization of society and the role of the "armed organs,"
   - the transformation and instrumentalization of the economy (expropriation; forced collectivization; central command economy),
   - the inconsiderate treatment of nature and the environment;

2. to depict and evaluate the significance of ideology, integrative factors, and disciplinary practices, including:
   - the function and instrumentalization of Marxism-Leninism and antifascism,
   - the status and misuse of education, science, literature, culture, and art as well as sport,
   - the handling as well as the effects and role of career opportunities and privileges;

3. to investigate the abuse of international human-rights conventions and norms as well as the forms of repression in different periods, identify groups of victims, and consider the possibilities for material and moral compensation, including:

- political oppression through the criminal law, the criminal justice and correction systems (conditions of imprisonment; mistreatment; detention; deprivation of citizenship and the like),
- political, mental, and psychological mechanisms of oppression in people's everyday lives and the consequences since 1945–46;

4. to establish the possibilities and forms of deviant and resistant behavior and oppositional action in different areas, along with the factors which influenced them;

5. to depict the role of the churches and their conceptions of themselves in different phases of the SED dictatorship;

6. to assess the significance of the international circumstances, especially the influence of Soviet policy in the SBZ and the GDR;

7. to investigate the significance of the relationship between the Federal Republic of Germany and the GDR, including:

- the German-political [*deutschlandpolitische*] goals, leading ideas, and prospects for action in both states,
- intra-German political, economic, social, and cultural connections and their impacts on the development of the GDR,
- the significance of personal contacts for the consciousness of belonging together,
- the influence of the media of the Federal Republic of Germany in the GDR,
- the activities of the SED and the GDR in the Federal Republic of Germany and internationally;

8. to include the question of continuities and analogies in the thought, behavior, and structures of German history in the twentieth century, especially the time of the National Socialist dictatorship.

III.

Working through the history of the SED dictatorship is—among other things—to be clarified by way of examples with the following historical dates and periods:

- the establishment of the dictatorship and its circumstances 1945–1949 (e.g. the Potsdam Agreement, land reform, forced unification of SPD and KPD to become the SED, political and societal *Gleichschaltung*, etc.)

- the revolt of 17 June 1953
- forced collectivization and the building of the Berlin Wall
- the invasion of the CSSR by Warsaw Pact troops in 1968
- the changeover from Ulbricht to Honecker in 1971
- the peaceful revolution in autumn 1989 and German unification

IV.

The commission is primarily to pursue the following practical consequences:

- to contribute to the political and moral rehabilitation of the victims and overcome the damage caused by the dictatorship
- to list the possibilities for overcoming ongoing disadvantages in education and career
- to contribute to the clarification of the question of governmental criminality in the GDR
- to maintain, preserve, and open the relevant archives
- to improve conditions for the scholarly process of working through the SBZ/GDR past
- to provide recommendations to the German Bundestag in relation to legislative measures and other political initiatives
- to provide indications for the educational-psychological processing of the GDR past

V.

The commission's methods will include the following elements, among others:

- talks with persons affected and citizens' groups at the coal face, dialogue with scholars and initiatives dealing with the history of the GDR
- public hearings and forums
- the commissioning of expertise papers and research projects

THE TERMS OF REFERENCE OF THE COMMISSION OF INQUIRY, "OVERCOMING THE CONSEQUENCES OF THE SED DICTATORSHIP IN THE PROCESS OF GERMANY UNITY"

(I: 4–8)

In the twelfth legislative period of the German Bundestag, the commission of inquiry "Working through the History and Consequences of the SED Dictatorship in Germany" made fundamental contributions to the political, historical, and moral evaluation of the second dictatorship on German soil. It made a major contribution to the societal working through of four decades of the GDR past and will remain an important testament to how the German Bundestag and the political public took up this challenge in the early years after unification. The contribution of the commission of inquiry to the process of Germany's inner unification received considerable public attention and produced a diverse response here and abroad.

The following are to be maintained as fundamental findings of the commission of inquiry:

- The completion of Germany's inner unity and coming to terms with the material and immaterial consequential damage of the SED dictatorship remain central tasks for the coming years. The history of the GDR with all its burdens is part of Germany's common history.

- The SED state was a dictatorship. It was such as a result not only of political aberrations and the abuse of power, but from its very historical and ideological foundations. The abuse of individual and political human rights was systemic and was only exacerbated by individual arbitrariness.

- The SED—which claimed and pushed through with every possible means a "leading role" in the state, the judiciary, the economy, society, education, culture, and science—bears the main responsibility for the injustice committed by this system. The human suffering that emanated from oppression, denial of human rights, and the forced abandonment of personal fulfillment is above all to be attributed to the SED leadership. Those responsible in the other bloc parties and mass organizations bear co-responsibility.

- The political-moral condemnation of the SED dictatorship does not amount to the condemnation of the people who were subjected to it; quite the opposite. The Germans in the GDR had to bear the heavier part of Germany's postwar history.

- With the overthrow of the SED dictatorship in autumn 1989, the East Germans made a fundamental contribution to the achievement today in all of Germany of a widely recognized antitotalitarian consensus, which is among democracy's most important mental foundations. The credo of democratic politics after 1945 "Never again war from German soil, never again a dictatorship on German soil!" remains. This entails the rejection of every form of totalitarian ideologies, programs, parties, and movements.

On the basis of these insights and findings, the further working through of the history, consequences, and current repercussions of the SED dictatorship is of particular political importance. The transformation process must face up to the problems the SED dictatorship created. The German Bundestag therefore sees it as necessary to connect with the work of the previous commission of inquiry and continue it with new emphasis. Working through the SED dictatorship is a process for the entire society. The commission of inquiry "Overcoming the Consequences of the SED Dictatorship in the Process of German Unity" — which is to be established — has the task of giving the parliament and government political recommendations for action to address the consequences and legacy of this history.

The commission of inquiry has the following tasks:

1. Building on the results of the prior commission, it shall make contributions to a political-historical analysis and political-moral evaluation of the SED dictatorship, promote the societal process of working through, and make suggestions for its continuation. Thereby, it will consider whether additional institutional means, e.g. in the form of a foundation, are also to be created. The interest of the commission is directed especially at the external and internal consequences and repercussions of the SED dictatorship and the problems for the process of inner unification that arose from them.

2. The commission of inquiry shall contribute to the consolidation of democratic consciousness, a liberal sense of justice, and the antitotali-

tarian consensus in Germany and countervail any tendency toward the minimization and justification of dictatorships. To that end, the development of all-German forms of memory of the two German dictatorships and their victims is important. Memory of the victims of injustice and violence, of resistance and courage in the dictatorships, as well as the process of the dissolution of SED rule in 1989 shall be kept alive for public consciousness and the national culture. Simultaneously, the forms and contents of honoring the resistance against National Socialism that developed in both German states as well as the instrumentalization of antifascism as an ideology of legitimation in the SBZ/GDR must be considered. In this context and in consideration of the existing federal-state talks, the commission shall prepare recommendations for an encompassing conception for memorials.

3. The commission of inquiry shall help people with their different biographies to find themselves in the unification process. It will thus contribute to reconciliation in society, based on the desire for openness, for historical truth, and for mutual understanding.

   The personal dignity of those affected by injustice and suffering must be restored. That entails publicly honoring the victims as well as the necessity of receiving justice retrospectively, wherever possible. Thus it will be the task of the commission of inquiry to review the extent to which — from the perspective of the victims — deficits exist today and how these can be remedied through legislation.

   Further, it shall review how and to what extent the need exists for political action on the question of how those responsible for the system and their helpers should be dealt with. In this context, the commission will also consider the problems of working through the SED dictatorship with judicial means.

4. The commission of inquiry shall take up topical, relevant questions and develop political recommendations. It will have to develop emphases in its activities. It shall address those sets of societal problems in exemplary fashion in which concrete political action today appears particularly necessary against the background of forty years of SED dictatorship and German division. Recognition of the achievements of people under the repressive conditions in the GDR belongs here, as well as the adjustment of disadvantages and the creation of equal opportunity in united Germany.

The commission will devote itself especially to the following topic areas, in which the ideological bases and the repressive structures are to receive particular attention:

A. Education, Science, Culture

- The goals and methods of the ideological influence of the SED
- The militarization of society and the significance of images of the enemy
- The consequences of the permeation of these areas by the Ministry for State Security
- The possibilities for creating living spaces under and despite this influence
- The ongoing effects of the structures and content of the education system, youth policy, and of science, arts, and culture in the GDR and their evaluation in the transformation process
- Which challenges arise from this appraisal for policy in these areas today?

B. Economic, Social, and Environmental Policy

- The structures of the socialist planned economy and an appraisal at the end of the 1980s
- Social policy and the social situation in the GDR: claim and reality
- Environmental appraisal of the SED dictatorship
- The external economic relations of the GDR
- The consequences for the economic transformation process

C. Divided Germany in Divided Europe

- The integration of the two German states in the two blocs and the question of the possibilities for independent political decisions in the GDR and in the Federal Republic of Germany
- The western work of the SED and the Ministry for State Security
- The policy toward the East of the Federal Government and the parties
- East-West economic and financial relations
- East-West societal, economic, and cultural contacts
- The persecution of those who thought differently in the SBZ/GDR
- The significance of human rights for international politics
- Which consequences arise for the policy of unified Germany in relation to all of Europe and in the handling of dictatorial regimes?

On the Methods of the Commission

The commission of inquiry utilizes predominantly the same instruments as the prior commission (expertise papers, presentations, hearings).

The German Bundestag expects the Federal Government—represented by the relevant ministries including especially the Federal Ministry for the Interior—to accompany and support the work of the commission of inquiry.

The commission will present its report punctually before the end of the legislative period and ensure that relevant sections of the report or corresponding interim report can be considered in the work of the standing committees.

The German Bundestag will ensure that the materials of the commission (report, expertise papers, hearing protocols) will be made available to a broad public in an appropriate form before the end of the legislative period.

BIBLIOGRAPHY

Adorno, Theodor W. "Was bedeutet: Aufarbeitung der Vergangenheit." *Gesammelte Schriften.* Vol. 10:2, 555–72. Frankfurt am Main, 1977.

Agethen, Manfred, Eckhard Jesse, and Ehrhard Neubert, eds. *Der missbrauchte Antifaschismus: DDR-Staatsdoktrin und Lebenslüge der deutschen Linken.* Freiburg, 2002.

Albon, Mary. "Project on Justice in Times of Transition: Report of the Project's Inaugural Meeting." In *Transitional Justice: How Emerging Democracies Reckon with Former Regimes,* ed. Neil J. Kritz. Vol. I, 42–54. Washington, 1995.

Alexander, Jeffrey C. "On the Social Construction of Moral Universals: The 'Holocaust' from War Crime to Trauma Drama." *European Journal of Social Theory* 5, no. 1 (2002): 5–85.

Alter, Reinhard, and Peter Monteath, eds. *Rewriting the German Past: History and Identity in the New Germany.* Atlantic Highlands, 1997.

Andrews, Molly. "Grand National Narratives and the Project of Truth Commissions: A Comparative Analysis." *Media, Culture and Society* 25 (2003): 45–65.

———. "The Politics of Forgiveness." *International Journal of Politics, Culture and Society* 13, no. 1 (1999): 107–24.

Anz, Thomas, ed. *Es geht nicht um Christa Wolf: Der Literaturstreit im vereinigten Deutschland.* Munich, 1991.

Ash, Mitchell G. "Geschichtswissenschaft, Geschichtskultur und der ostdeutsche Historikerstreit." *Geschichte und Gesellschaft* 24, no. 2 (1998): 283–304.

Assmann, Aleida, and Ute Frevert. *Geschichtsvergessenheit—Geschichtsversessenheit: Vom Umgang mit deutschen Vergangenheiten nach 1945.* Stuttgart, 1999.

Badstübner, Rolf. "DDR: zeitgeschichtlich erforschen oder 'aufarbeiten'?" In *Ansichten zur Geschichte der DDR IV,* eds. Dietmar Keller, Hans Modrow, and Herbert Wolf, 87–108. Bonn, 1994.

Barbe, Angelika, Bärbel Bohley, Ulf Fink, Jürgen Fuchs, Martin Gutzeit, Katja Havemann, Roland Jahn, Uwe Lehmann-Brauns, Reinhard Schult, and Manfred Wilke, "Thesen zur Aufklärung der Vergangenheit." *Deutschland Archiv* 25, no. 4 (1992): 446–47.

Barker, Peter. "'Geschichtsaufarbeitung' within the PDS and the Enquete-Kommissionen." In *The GDR and its History: Rückblick und Revision, Die DDR im Spiegel der Enquete-Kommissionen (German Monitor* 49), ed. Barker, 81–95. Amsterdam, 2000.

Baron, Udo "Wege zur Aufarbeitung der SED-Diktatur: Unabhängige Aufarbeitungsinitiativen zur Geschichtsdebatte über die DDR." In *The GDR and its History: Rückblick und Revision, Die DDR im Spiegel der Enquete-Kommissionen (German Monitor* 49), ed. Peter Barker, 67–79. Amsterdam, 2000.

Bauerkämper, Arnd. "DDR-Vergangenheit zwischen Theologie, Strafjustiz und Geschichtswissenschaft: Umgang mit Schuld und Verantwortung im vereinten Deutschland." In *Verantwortung—Schuld—Vergebung (Loccumer Protokolle* 54:98), ed. Wolfgang Vögele, 146–62. Rehburg-Loccum, 1999.

Bauerkämper, Arnd, Martin Sabrow, and Bernd Stöver, eds. *Doppelte Zeitgeschichte: Deutsch-deutsche Beziehungen 1945–1990.* Bonn, 1999.

Bayliss, Thomas A. "The *Wende* in GDR Research." *German Politics and Society* 21, no. 3 (2003): 109–19.

Beattie, Andrew H. "Die Delegitimierung von '1968' nach 1989/90: Das Beispiel der Enquete-Kommissionen des Deutschen Bundestages." In *Erinnerungsort 1968*, eds. Claudia Fröhlich and Andrea Genest. Berlin, forthcoming.

———. "A Fifties Revival? Cold War Culture in Re-unified Germany." In *European Cold War Cultures: Perspectives on Societies in the East and the West*, eds. Thomas Lindenberger, Marcus M. Payk, Bernd Stöver, and Annette Vowinckel. Providence, forthcoming.

———. "The Past in the Politics of Divided and Unified Germany." In *Partisan Histories: The Past in Contemporary Global Politics*, eds. Max Paul Friedman and Padraic Kenney, 17–38. New York, 2005.

———. "The Victims of Totalitarianism and the Centrality of Nazi Genocide: Continuity and Change in German Commemorative Politics." In *Germans as Victims: Contemporary Germany and the Third Reich*, ed. Bill Niven, 147–63. Basingstoke, 2006.

Beckmann, Christopher. "Die Auseinandersetzung um den Vergleich von 'Dritten Reich' und DDR vor dem Hintergrund der Diskussion um Möglichkeiten und Grenzen vergleichender Geschichtsforschung." *Deutsche Studien* 38, no. 147–148 (2002): 9–26.

Behrendt, Lutz-Dieter. "Mittel und Methoden der Vergangenheitsbewältigung." In *Auf den Kehrrichthaufen der Geschichte? Der Umgang mit der sozialistischen Vergangenheit*, eds. Isabelle de Keghel and Robert Maier, 27–34. Hannover, 1999.

Benser, Günter, "Bundestagsdrucksache 12/7820: Auch methodisch ein Dokument voller Widersprüche." In *Ansichten zur Geschichte der DDR* V, eds. Jochen Černý, Dieter Lehmann, and Manfred Neuhaus, 29–39. Bonn, 1994.

———."Möglichkeiten und Grenzen einer antifaschistisch-demokratischen Erneuerung in Deutschland nach dem zweiten Weltkrieg." In *Ansichten zur Geschichte der DDR* IV eds. Dietmar Keller, Hans Modrow, and Herbert Wolf, 137–52. Bonn, 1994.

Berdahl, Daphne. *Where the World Ended: Re-unification and Identity in the German Borderland.* Berkeley, 1999.

Berger, Stefan. *The Search for Normality: National Identity and Historical Consciousness in Germany since 1800.* Providence, 1997.

Bergmann, Werner. "Kommunikationslatenz und Vergangenheitsbewältigung." In *Vergangenheitsbewältigung am Ende des zwanzigsten Jahrhunderts (Leviathan 18)*, eds. Helmut König, Michael Kohlstruck, and Andreas Wöll, 393–408. Opladen, 1998.

Betts, Paul. "Germany, International Justice and the Twentieth Century." *History and Memory* 17 (2005): 45–86.

———. "The Twilight of the Idols: East German Memory and Material Culture." *Journal of Modern History* 72, no. 3 (2000): 731–65.

Biess, Frank. *Homecomings: Returning POWs and the Legacies of Defeat in Postwar Germany*. Princeton, 2006.

Binder, Gerhard. *Die Deutsche Demokratische Republik: Der zweite deutsche Staat*. Paderborn, 1977.

Blankenburg, Erhard. "The Purge of Lawyers after the Breakdown of the East German Communist Regime." *Law and Social Inquiry* 20, no. 1 (1995): 223–43.

Bobach, Reinhard. "Mentale Konversion? Kulturelle Aspekte der deutschen Vereinigung." *Deutschland Archiv* 26, no. 1 (1993): 7–20.

Bock, Petra. *Vergangenheitspolitik im Systemwechsel: Die Politik der Aufklärung, Strafverfolgung, Disqualifizierung und Wiedergutmachung im letzten Jahr der DDR*. Berlin, 2000.

———. "Von der Tribunal-Idee zur Enquete-Kommission: Zur Vorgeschichte der Enquete-Kommission des Bundestages 'Aufarbeitung von Geschichte und Folgen der SED-Diktatur in Deutschland.'" *Deutschland Archiv* 28, no. 1 (1995): 1171–83.

Bock, Petra, and Edgar Wolfrum, eds. *Umkämpfte Vergangenheit: Geschichtsbilder, Erinnerung und Vergangenheitspolitik im internationalen Vergleich*. Göttingen, 1999.

Boll, Friedhelm. *Sprechen als Last und Befreiung: Holocaust-Überlebende und politisch Verfolgte zweier Diktaturen, Ein Beitrag zur deutsch-deutschen Erinnerungskultur*. Bonn, 2003.

Bollinger, Stefan. "'Geschichtsaufarbeitung': Machtinstrument oder Erkenntnishilfe? Einige Anmerkungen." In *Ansichten zur Geschichte der DDR V*, eds. Jochen Černý, Dieter Lehmann, and Manfred Neuhaus, 19–28. Bonn, 1994.

Bouvier, Beatrix W. and Horst-Peter Schulz, eds. *"… die SPD aber aufgehört hat zu existieren": Sozialdemokraten unter sowjetischer Besatzung*. Bonn, 1991.

Bracher, Karl Dietrich. *The Age of Ideologies: A History of Political Thought in the Twentieth Century*. London, 1984.

———. "Vierzig Jahre Diktatur (SED-Unrecht): Herausforderung an den Rechtsstaat." *Recht und Politik* 27, no. 3 (1991): 137–41.

Brady, John S., and Sarah Elise Wiliarty. "How Culture Matters: Culture and Social Change in the Federal Republic of Germany." *German Politics and Society* 20, no. 2 (2002): 1–13.

Bramke, Werner. "Das Bild vom deutschen Widerstand gegen den Nationalsozialismus im Lichte unterschiedlicher Erfahrungen von Teilung und Umbruch." *Zeitschrift für Geschichtswissenschaft* 42, no. 7 (1994): 597–604.

Buchholz, Matthias. "Zur Problematik der 'DDR-Archive.'" In *Bilanz und Perspektiven der DDR-Forschung*, eds. Rainer Eppelmann, Bernd Faulenbach, and Ulrich Mählert, 383–90. Paderborn, 2003.

Calhoun, Noel. *Dilemmas of Justice in Eastern Europe's Democratic Transitions.* New York, 2004.

Case, J. David. "The Politics of Memorial Representation: The Controversy over the German Resistance Museum in 1994." *German Politics and Society* 16, no. 1 (1998): 58–81.

Cooke, Paul. *Representing East Germany since Unification: From Colonization to Nostalgia.* Oxford, 2005.

Courtois, Stéphane, Nicolas Werth, Jean-Louis Panné, Andrzej Paczkowski, Karel Bartosek, and Jean-Lousi Margolin. *Das Schwarzbuch des Kommunismus: Unterdrückung, Verbrechen und Terror, Mit dem Kapitel "Die Aufarbeitung des Sozialismus in der DDR" von Joachim Gauck und Ehrhard Neubert,* trans. Irmelia Arnsperger et al.. Munich, 1998.

Danyel, Jürgen. "Bilder vom 'anderen Deutschland': Frühe Widerstandsrezeption nach 1945." *Zeitschrift für Geschichtswissenschaft* 42, no. 7 (1994): 611–21.

———. "DDR-Antifaschismus: Rückblick auf zehn Jahre Diskussion, offene Fragen und Forschungsperspektiven." In *Vielstimmiges Schweigen: Neue Studien zum DDR-Antifaschismus,* eds. Annette Leo and Peter Reif-Spirek, 7–19. Berlin, 2001.

———. "Die Historiker und die Moral: Anmerkungen zur Debatte über die Autorenrechte an der DDR-Geschichte." *Geschichte und Gesellschaft* 21 (1995): 290–303.

———, ed. *Die geteilte Vergangenheit: Zum Umgang mit Nationalsozialismus und Widerstand in beiden deutschen Staaten.* Berlin, 1995.

Dennis, Mike. *The Rise and Fall of the German Democratic Republic, 1945–1990.* Harlow, 2000.

Dettke, Dieter, ed. *The Spirit of the Berlin Republic.* New York, 2003.

Deutscher Bundesrat. "Ehrenerklärung für die Opfer der kommunistischen Gewaltherrschaft." *Drucksache* 431/92 (1992).

Deutscher Bundestag. "Bericht der Bundesregierung über die Beteiligung des Bundes an Gedenkstätten in der Bundesrepublik Deutschland." *Drucksache* 13/8486 (5 September 1997).

———. "Beschlußempfehlung und Bericht des Innenausschusses." *Drucksache* 12/7884 (15 June 1994).

———. "Beschlussempfehlung und Bericht des Ausschusses für Kultur und Medien." *Drucksache* 16/6974 (7 November 2007).

———. "Förderung von Gedenkstätten zur Diktaturgeschichte in Deutschland: Gesamtkonzept für ein würdiges Gedenken aller Opfer der beiden deutschen Diktaturen." *Drucksache* 15/1874 (4 November 2003).

———. "Konzeption der künftigen Gedenkstättenförderung des Bundes und Bericht der Bundesregierung über die Beteiligung des Bundes an Gedenkstätten in der Bundesrepublik Deutschland." *Drucksache* 14/1569 (27 July 1999).

———. *Plenarprotokoll* 16/124 (9 November 2007).

———, ed. *Materialien der Enquete-Kommission "Aufarbeitung von Geschichte und Folgen der SED-Diktatur in Deutschland"* (12. Wahlperiode des Deutschen Bundestages). IX vols. Frankfurt am Main, 1995.

———, ed. *Materialien der Enquete-Kommission "Überwindung der Folgen der SED-Diktatur im Prozess der deutschen Einheit"* (13. Wahlperiode des Deutschen Bundestages). VIII vols. Frankfurt am Main, 1999.

Doernberg, Stefan. "Zur Legitimität der beiden deutschen Wege nach 1945." In *Ansichten zur Geschichte der DDR* IV, eds. Dietmar Keller, Hans Modrow, and Herbert Wolf, 123–35. Bonn, 1994.

Dorpalen, Andreas. *German History in Marxist Perspective: The East German Approach.* London, 1986.

Dubiel, Helmut. *Niemand ist frei von der Geschichte: Die nationalsozialistische Herrschaft in den Debatten des Deutschen Bundestages.* Munich, 1999.

Dudek, Peter. "'Vergangenheitsbewältigung' Zur Problematik eines umstrittenen Begriffs." *Aus Politik und Zeitgeschichte* 42, no. 1–2 (1992): 44–53.

Dümcke, Wolfgang, and Fritz Vilmar, eds. *Kolonialisierung der DDR: Kritische Analysen und Alternativen des Einigungsprozesses.* Münster, 1996.

Dürr, Tobias. "On 'Westalgia': Why West German Mentalities and Habits Persist in the Berlin Republic." In *The Spirit of the Berlin Republic,* ed. Dieter Dettke, 37–47. New York, 2003.

Eckert, Rainer. "Straßenumbenennung und Revolution in Deutschland: Über die Beseitigung der Symbole und Benennungen der SED-Diktatur." In *Vergangenheitsbewältigung,* ed. Eckhard Jesse, 45–52. Berlin, 1997.

Eley, Geoff. *Forging Democracy: The History of the Left in Europe, 1850–2000.* Oxford, 2002.

———. "The Unease of History: Settling Accounts with the East German Past." *History Workshop Journal* 57 (2004): 175–201.

Elm, Ludwig. *Nach Hitler, Nach Honecker: Zum Streit der Deutschen um die eigene Vergangenheit.* Berlin, 1991.

———. *Das verordnete Feindbild: Neue deutsche Geschichtsideologie und "antitotalitärer Konsens."* Cologne, 2001.

———. "'Zwei Diktaturen'—'zwei totalitäre Regimes': Die Enquete-Kommissionen des Bundestages und der konservative Geschichtsrevisionismus der neunziger Jahre." In *Die selbstbewußte Nation und ihr Geschichtsbild: Geschichtslegenden der Neuen Rechten,* eds. Johannes Klotz and Ulrich Schneider, 205–20. Cologne, 1997.

———. "Zweierlei Vergangenheitsbewältigung: Damals und heute." *Deutschland Archiv* 24, no. 7 (1991): 737–43.

Engler, Wolfgang. "'Kommode Diktatur' oder 'totalitäres System'? Die DDR im Kreuzverhör der Enquete-Kommission." *Soziologische Revue* 19 (1996): 443–49.

Eppelmann, Rainer. "Fünf Jahre deutsche Einheit." *Deutschland Archiv* 28, no. 9 (1995): 897–98.

———. "Die Stiftung zur Aufarbeitung der SED-Diktatur." In *Zehn Jahre Deutsche Einheit: Eine Bilanz,* eds. Wolfgang Thierse, Ilse Spittmann-Rühle, and Johannes L. Kuppe, 229–36. Opladen, 2000.

Eppelmann, Rainer, and Dietmar Keller. *Zwei deutsche Sichten: Ein Dialog auf gleicher Augenhöhe.* Bad Honnef, 2000.

Eppelmann, Rainer, Bernd Faulenbach, and Ulrich Mählert, eds. *Bilanz und Perspektiven der DDR-Forschung.* Paderborn, 2003.

Epstein, Catherine. "The Production of 'Official Memory' in East Germany: Old Communists and the Dilemmas of Memoir-Writing." *Central European History* 32, no. 2 (1999): 181–201.

Erlinghagen, Robert. *Die Diskussion um den Begriff des Antifaschismus seit 1989/90.* Berlin, 1997.

Ernst, Anna-Sabine. "Zwischen eilfertiger Enthüllungshistorie und solider Quellenkritik: Die zeitgeschichtliche DDR-Forschung im Prozeß der Neuordnung." *Zeitgeschichte* 22, no. 7–8 (1995): 249–64.

Evans, Richard J. "Zwei deutsche Diktaturen im 20. Jahrhundert?" *Aus Politik und Zeitgeschichte* 55, no. 1–2 (2005): 3–9.

Faulenbach, Bernd. "Die Arbeit der Enquete-Kommissionen und die Geschichtsdebatte in Deutschland seit 1989." In *The GDR and its History: Rückblick und Revision, Die DDR im Spiegel der Enquete-Kommissionen (German Monitor* 49), ed. Peter Barker, 21–33. Amsterdam, 2000.

———. "Auf dem Weg zu einer gemeinsamen Erinnerung? Das Bild vom deutschen Widerstand gegen den Nationalsozialismus nach den Erfahrungen von Teilung und Umbruch." *Zeitschrift für Geschichtswissenschaft* 42, no. 7 (1994): 589–96.

———. "Die Auseinandersetzung mit der doppelten Vergangenheit im Deutschen Bundestag." In *Grenzen der Vereinigung: Die geteilte Vergangenheit im geeinten Deutschland,* ed. Martin Sabrow, 35–54. Leipzig, 1999.

———. "Die Auseinandersetzung mit der kommunistischen Vergangenheit in vergleichender Perspektive." In *Auf den Kehrichthaufen der Geschichte? Der Umgang mit der sozialistischen Vergangenheit,* eds. Isabelle de Keghel and Robert Maier, 13–26. Hannover, 1999.

———. "Bewahrung der Erinnerung: Bedeutung und Probleme der 'Aufarbeitung' von Vergangenheit heute." In *Die Partei hatte immer recht: Aufarbeitung von Geschichte und Folgen der SED-Diktatur,* eds. Bernd Faulenbach, Markus Meckel, and Hermann Weber, 8–27. Essen, 1994.

———. "Die doppelte 'Vergangenheitsbewältigung': Nationalsozialismus und Stalinismus als Herausforderungen zeithistorischer Forschung und politischer Kultur." In *Die geteilte Vergangenheit: Zum Umgang mit Nationalsozialismus und Widerstand in beiden deutschen Staaten,* ed. Jürgen Danyel, 107–24. Berlin, 1995.

———. "Historical Foundations of the Berlin Republic." In *The Spirit of the Berlin Republic,* ed. Dieter Dettke, 9–23. New York, 2003.

———. "Probleme einer Neukonzeption von Gedenkstätten in Brandenburg." In *Brandenburgische Gedenkstätten für die Verfolgten des NS-Regimes: Perspektiven, Kontroversen und internationale Vergleiche,* ed. Ministerium für Wissenschaft, Forschung und Kultur des Landes Brandenburg, 12–20. Berlin, 1992.

———. "Die Verfolgungssysteme des Nationalsozialismus und des Stalinismus: Zur Frage ihrer Vergleichbarkeit." In *Doppelte Zeitgeschichte: Deutsch-deutsche Beziehungen 1945–1990,* eds. Arnd Bauerkämper, Martin Sabrow, and Bernd Stöver, 268–82. Bonn, 1999.

Faulenbach, Bernd, and Heinrich Pothoff, eds. *Sozialdemokraten und Kommunisten nach Nationalsozialismus und Krieg: Zur historischen Einordnung der Zwangsvereinigung.* Essen, 1998.

Fehr, Helmut. "Öffentlicher Sprachwandel und Eliten-Konkurrenz: Zur Rolle politischer Semantik in den Dekommunisierungskampagnen post-kommunistischer Gesellschaften (Tschechische Republik, Polen und Ostdeutschland)."

In *Eliten, politische Kultur und Privatisierung in Ostdeutschland, Tschechien und Mittelosteuropa,* ed. Ilja Srubar, 65–96. Konstanz, 1998.

Finker, Kurt. "Faschismus, Antifaschismus und 'verordneter Antifaschismus.'" In *Ansichten zur Geschichte der DDR* XI, eds. Ludwig Elm, Dietmar Keller, and Reinhard Mocek, 142–200. Bonn, 1998.

Fippel, Günter. *Antifaschisten in "antifaschistischer" Gewalt: Mittel- und ostdeutsche Schicksale in den Auseinandersetzungen zwischen Demokratie und Diktatur 1945 bis 1961.* Guben, 2003.

———. "Der Mißbrauch des Faschismus-Begriffs in der SBZ/DDR." *Deutschland Archiv* 25, no. 10 (1992): 1055–65.

Fox, Thomas C. *Stated Memory: East Germany and the Holocaust.* Rochester, 1999.

Fraude, Andreas. "'Impulsgeber im Prozeß um Aufarbeitung und Versöhnung': Tätigkeitsbericht der Enquete-Kommission in Mecklenburg-Vorpommern." *Deutschland Archiv* 31, no. 1 (1998): 9–12.

———. "'Leben in der DDR, Leben nach 1989—Aufarbeitung und Versöhnung': Enquete-Kommission in Mecklenburg-Vorpommern." *Deutschland Archiv* 28, no. 7 (1995): 681–82.

———. "Vergangenheitsaufarbeitung in Mecklenburg-Vorpommern: Zur bisherigen Tätigkeit der Enquete-Kommission." *Deutschland Archiv* 29, no. 5 (1996): 676–80.

Freeden, Michael. "Ideology and Political Theory." *Journal of Political Ideologies* 11, no. 1 (2006): 3–22.

Freeman, Mark. *Truth Commissions and Procedural Fairness.* Cambridge, 2006.

Frei, Norbert. *Adenauer's Germany and the Nazi Past: The Politics of Amnesty and Integration,* trans. Joel Golb. New York, 2002.

———. *Vergangenheitspolitik: Die Anfänge der Bundesrepublik und die NS-Vergangenheit.* Munich, 1996.

Fricke, Karl Wilhelm. *Der Wahrheit verpflichtet: Texte aus fünf Jahrzehnten zur Geschichte der DDR.* Berlin, 2000.

Fricke, Karl Wilhelm, Peter Steinbach, and Johannes Tuchel, eds. *Opposition und Widerstand in der DDR: Politische Lebensbilder.* Munich, 2002.

Friederici, Hans Jürgen. "Das Thema 'Antifaschismus' im Enquete-Bericht: Kritische Anmerkungen." In *Ansichten zur Geschichte der DDR* V, eds. Jochen Černý, Dieter Lehmann, and Manfred Neuhaus, 69–75. Bonn, 1994.

Friedrich, Walter. "Regierte die SED ständig gegen die Mehrheit des Volkes?" In *Ansichten zur Geschichte der DDR* V, eds. Jochen Černý, Dieter Lehmann, and Manfred Neuhaus, 123–47. Bonn, 1994.

Fritze, Lothar. *Die Gegenwart des Vergangenen: Über das Weiterleben der DDR nach ihrem Ende.* Weimar, 1997.

Fuchs, Ruth, and Detlef Nolte. "Politikfeld Vergangenheitspolitik: Zur Analyse der Aufarbeitung von Menschenrechtsverletzungen in Lateinamerika." *Lateinamerika Analysen* 9 (2004): 59–92.

Fukuyama, Francis. *The End of History and the Last Man.* New York, 1992.

Fulbrook, Mary. "Aufarbeitung der DDR-Vergangenheit und 'innere Einheit'— ein Widerspruch?" In *Deutsche Vergangenheiten—eine gemeinsame Herausforderung: Der schwierige Umgang mit der doppelten Nachkriegsgeschichte,* eds.

Christoph Kleßmann, Hans Misselwitz, and Günter Wichert, 286–98. Berlin, 1999.

———. "Heroes, Victims and Villains in the History of the GDR." In *Rewriting the German Past: History and Identity in the New Germany,* eds. Reinhard Alter and Peter Monteath, 175–96. Atlantic Highlands, 1997.

———. "Jenseits der Totalitarismustheorie? Vorläufige Bemerkungen aus sozialgeschichtlicher Perspektive." In *The GDR and its History: Rückblick und Revision, Die DDR im Spiegel der Enquete-Kommissionen (German Monitor 49),* ed. Peter Barker, 35–53. Amsterdam, 2000.

———. "Retheorising 'State' and 'Society' in the German Democratic Republic." In *The Workers' and Peasants' State: Communism and Society in East Germany under Ulbricht 1945–71,* eds. Patrick Major and Jonathon Osmond, 280–98. Manchester, 2002.

———. *The Two Germanies, 1945–1990: Problems of Interpretation.* Basingstoke, 1992.

Gajdukowa, Katharina. "Opfer-Täter-Gesprächskreise nach dem Ende der DDR." *Aus Politik und Zeitgeschichte* 54, no. 41–42 (2004): 23–27.

Garton Ash, Timothy. *The File: A Personal History.* London, 1997.

———. *History of the Present: Essays, Sketches and Despatches from Europe in the 1990s.* London, 2000.

Gauck, Joachim, Friedrich Schorlemmer, Wolfgang Thierse, Wolfgang Ullmann, Gerd Poppe, Ulrike Poppe, Hans Misselwitz, Marianne Birthler, Reinhard Höppner, and Burghard Brinksmeier. "'Tribunal' als Forum der Aufklärung." *Deutschland Archiv* 25, no. 2 (1992): 222–24.

Geiss, Imanuel. *The Question of German Unification.* London, 1997.

"Gesetz über Entschädigungen für Opfer des Nationalsozialismus im Beitrittsgebiet." *Bundesgesetzblatt* I (1992), 906.

Geyer, Michael. "Germany, or, The Twentieth Century as History." *South Atlantic Quarterly* 96, no. 4 (1997): 663–702.

Giesen, Bernhard. *Intellectuals and the Nation: Collective Identity in a German Axial Age.* Cambridge, 1998.

Giordano, Ralph. *Die zweite Schuld, oder Von der Last Deutscher zu sein,* new ed. Cologne, 2000.

Gleason, Abbott. *Totalitarianism: The Inner History of the Cold War.* New York, 1995.

Goschler, Constantin. *Wiedergutmachung: Westdeutschland und die Verfolgten des Nationalsozialismus 1945–1954.* Munich, 1992.

Grix, Jonathan. "1989 Revisited: Getting to the Bottom of the GDR's Demise." *German Politics* 6, no. 2 (1997): 190–98.

———. "The Enquete-Kommission's Contribution to Research on State-Society Relations in the GDR." In *The GDR and its History: Rückblick und Revision, Die DDR im Spiegel der Enquete-Kommissionen (German Monitor 49),* ed. Peter Barker, 55–65. Amsterdam, 2000.

Groehler, Olaf. "Der Holocaust in der Geschichtsschreibung der DDR." In *Zweierlei Bewältigung: Vier Beiträge über den Umgang mit der NS-Vergangenheit in den beiden deutschen Staaten,* Ulrich Herbert and Olaf Groehler, 41–66. Hamburg, 1992.

Grünbaum, Robert. "Die Enquete-Kommission des Deutschen Bundestages zwischen Politik und Wissenschaft." *Deutsche Studien* 130 (1996): 111–22.

Grunenberg, Antonia. "Antitotalitarianism versus Antifascism: Two Legacies of the Past in Germany." *German Politics and Society* 15, no. 2 (1997): 76–90.

———, ed. *Welche Geschichte wählen wir?* Hamburg, 1992.

Habermas, Jürgen. "Vom öffentlichen Gebrauch der Historie: Warum ein 'Demokratiepreis' für Daniel Goldhagen." *Blätter für deutsche und internationale Politik* 42 (1997): 408–16.

Hahn, Erich. "Zur Rolle der Ideologie." In *Ansichten zur Geschichte der DDR* I, eds. Dietmar Keller, Hans Modrow, and Herbert Wolf, 211–35. Bonn, 1993.

Hampel, Frank. "Politikberatung in der Bundesrespublik: Überlegungen am Beispiel von Enquete-Kommissionen." *Zeitschrift für Parlamentsfragen* 22, no. 1 (1991): 111–33.

Hansen, Dirk. "Befreiung durch Erinnerung: Zur Arbeit der Enquete-Kommission 'Aufarbeitung von Geschichte und Folgen der SED-Diktatur in Deutschland' des Deutschen Bundestages." *Deutsche Studien* 125 (1995): 71–81.

———. "Gemeinsame Aufarbeitung zweier Vergangenheiten in einem Land?" *Deutsche Studien* 141 (1999): 39–46.

———. "Noch eine Vergangenheit, die nicht vergehen will." *Liberal* 35, no. 3 (1993): 15–18.

———. "Zur Arbeit der Enquetekommission des Deutschen Bundestages 'Überwindung der Folgen der SED-Diktatur im Prozess der deutschen Einheit.'" *Deutsche Studien* 139–40 (1998): 380–402.

Hayner, Priscilla B. *Unspeakable Truths: Confronting State Terror and Atrocity.* New York, 2001.

Heilbrunn, Jacob. "Germany's New Right." *Foreign Affairs* 75, no. 6 (1996): 80–98.

Heinemann, Ulrich. *Die verdrängte Niederlage: Politische Öffentlichkeit und Kriegsschuldfrage in der Weimarer Republik.* Göttingen, 1983.

Heinrich, Horst-Alfred. "Geschichtspolitische Akteure im Umgang mit der Stasi: Eine Einleitung." In *Geschichtspolitik: Wer sind ihre Akteure, wer ihre Rezipienten?* eds. Claudia Fröhlich and Horst-Alfred Heinrich, 9–32. Wiesbaden, 2004.

Helwig, Gisela. "Aufarbeitung ist Zukunftsgestaltung: Enquete-Kommission und Bundesstiftung." *Deutschland Archiv* 31, no. 5 (1998): 705–8.

Herbert, Ulrich. "Drei deutsche Vergangenheiten: Über den Umgang mit der deutschen Zeitgeschichte." In *Doppelte Zeitgeschichte: Deutsch-deutsche Beziehungen 1945–1990*, eds. Arnd Bauerkämper, Martin Sabrow, and Bernd Stover, 376–90. Bonn, 1999.

Herf, Jeffrey. *Divided Memory: The Nazi Past in the Two Germanys.* Cambridge, MA, 1997.

Heydemann, Günter, and Christopher Beckmann. "Zwei Diktaturen in Deutschland: Möglichkeiten und Grenzen des historischen Diktaturenvergleichs." *Deutschland Archiv* 30, no. 1 (1997): 12–40.

Heyer, Christian, and Stephan Liening. *Enquete-Kommissionen des Deutschen Bundestages: Schnittstellen zwischen Politik und Wissenschaft.* Berlin, n.d.

Hilsberg, Stephan. "Identitätsmuster in Ost und West: Zur Überwindung der inneren Teilung durch ihre Aufarbeitung." *Deutschland Archiv* 27, no. 3 (1994): 291–93.

————. "Die innere Einheit Deutschlands: Eine brauchbare Vision?" *Deutschland Archiv* 29, no. 4 (1996): 607–12.

————. "Rolle und Funktion der Blockparteien und Massenorganisationen in der DDR." In *Die Partei hatte immer recht: Aufarbeitung von Geschichte und Folgen der SED-Diktatur*, eds. Bernd Faulenbach, Markus Meckel, and Hermann Weber, 78–91. Essen, 1994.

Hirscher, Gerhard. "Materialien der Enquete-Kommission 'Überwindung der Folgen der SED-Diktatur im Prozess der deutschen Einheit.'" *Politische Studien* 373 (2000): 130–31.

Hirschmann, Albert O. "Exit, Voice, and the Fate of the German Democratic Republic: An Essay in Conceptual History." *World Politics* 45, no. 2 (1993): 173–202.

Historikerstreit: Die Dokumentation der Kontroverse um die Einzigartigkeit der nationalsozialistischen Judenvernichtung. Munich, 1987.

Historische Kommission beim Vorstand der PDS. "Herbst 1989: Für eine andere DDR — Chancen und Grenzen." 5 October 2004. Available online: <http://archiv2007.sozialisten.de/partei/geschichte/view_html?zid=24040> accessed 22 April 2008.

Historische Kommission der PDS. "Zum Zusammenschluß von KPD und SPD 1946: Erklärung der Historischen Kommission vom Dezember 1995." 13 November 1995. Available online: <http://archiv2007.sozialisten.de/partei/strukturen/historische_kommission/dokumente/view_html?zid=18203> accessed 22 April 2008.

Hockerts, Hans Günter. "Wiedergutmachung in Deutschland: Eine historische Bilanz." *Vierteljahreshefte für Zeitgeschichte* 49, no. 2 (2001): 167–214.

Hoffmann, Christa. "Aufklärung und Ahndung totalitären Unrechts: Die Zentralen Stellen in Ludwigsburg und in Salzgitter." *Aus Politik und Zeitgeschichte* 43, no. 4 (1993): 35–45.

————. "Deutsche Vergangenheitsbewältigung." *Jahrbuch Extremismus und Demokratie* 5 (1993): 193–218.

————. *Stunden Null? Vergangenheitsbewältigung in Deutschland 1945 und 1989.* Bonn, 1992.

Hoffmann, Christa, and Eckhard Jesse. "Die 'doppelte Vergangenheitsbewältigung' in Deutschland: Unterschiede und Gemeinsamkeiten." In *Deutschland: Eine Nation — doppelte Geschichte*, ed. Werner Weidenfeld, 209–34. Cologne, 1993.

Hoffmann, Christhard. "One Nation — Which Past? Historiography and German Identities in the 1990s." *German Politics and Society* 15, no. 2 (1997): 1–7.

Hoffmann, Jürgen. "Deutschlandpolitik als bundesdeutsche Einbahnstraße: Nachtrag zu einem defizitären Kapitel des Abschlußberichtes." In *Ansichten zur Geschichte der DDR* V, eds. Jochen Černý, Dieter Lehmann, and Manfred Neuhaus, 49–67. Bonn, 1994.

Hollitzer, Tobias. "15 Jahre friedliche Revolution." *Aus Politik und Zeitgeschichte* 54, no. 41–42 (2004): 3–6.

————."Die gesellschaftliche Aufarbeitung der SED-Diktatur." In *Bilanz und Perspektiven der DDR-Forschung*, eds. Rainer Eppelmann, Bernd Faulenbach, and Ulrich Mählert, 391–400. Paderborn, 2003.

Howard, Marc. "Unique, but not beyond Comparison: Comments on Konrad Jarausch's 'The German Democratic Republic as History in United Germany.'" *German Politics and Society* 15, no. 2 (1997): 49–52.

Huyssen, Andreas. *Twilight Memories: Marking Time in a Culture of Amnesia.* New York, 1995.

Ihme-Tuchel, Beate. *Die DDR.* Darmstadt, 2002.

———. "Marxistische Ideologie: Herrschaftsinstrument und politische Heilslehre." In *Bilanz und Perspektiven der DDR-Forschung,* eds. Rainer Eppelmann, Bernd Faulenbach, and Ulrich Mählert, 107–12. Paderborn, 2003.

Institut für Marxismus-Leninismus beim Zentralkomitee der SED, ed. *Die Vereinigung von KPD und SPD zur Sozialistischen Einheitspartei Deutschlands in Bildern und Dokumenten.* (East) Berlin, 1976.

Isensee, Josef. *Vergangenheitsbewältigung durch Recht: Drei Abhandlungen zu einem deutschen Problem.* Berlin, 1992.

Ismayr, Wolfgang. *Der Deutsche Bundestag: Funktionen, Willensbildung, Reformansätze.* Opladen, 1992.

———. "Enquete-Kommissionen des Deutschen Bundestages." *Aus Politik und Zeitgeschichte* 46, no. 27 (1996): 29–41.

Jacoby, Wade. *Imitation and Politics: Redesigning Modern Germany.* Ithaca, 2000.

Jansen, Marlies. "Enquete-Kommission." In *Handbuch zur deutschen Einheit,* eds. Werner Weidenfeld and Karl-Rudolf Korte, 264–75. Frankfurt am Main, 1996.

———. "Enquete-Kommission." In *Handbuch zur deutschen Einheit 1949–1989–1999,* eds. Werner Weidenfeld and Karl-Rudolf Korte, 330–42. Frankfurt am Main, 1999.

Jarausch, Konrad H. "Beyond Uniformity: The Challenge of Historicizing the GDR," in *Dictatorship as Experience: Towards a Socio-Cultural History of the GDR,* ed. Konrad H. Jarausch, trans. Eve Duffy, 3–14. New York, 1999.

———. "Care and Coercion: The GDR as Welfare Dictatorship." In *Dictatorship as Experience: Toward a Socio-Cultural History of the GDR,* ed. Konrad H. Jarausch, trans. Eve Duffy, 47–69. New York, 1999.

———. "Die DDR denken: Narrative Strukturen und analytische Strategien." *Berliner Debatte Initial* 4–5 (1995): 9–15.

———. "A Double Burden: The Politics of the Past and German Identity." In *Ten Years of German Unification: Transfer, Transformation, Incorporation?* eds. Jörn Leonhard and Lothar Funk, 98–114. Birmingham, 2002.

———. "The Failure of East German Antifascism: Some Ironies of History as Politics." *German Studies Review* 14, no. 1 (1991): 85–101.

———. "The German Democratic Republic as History in United Germany: Reflections on Public Debate and Academic Controversy." *German Politics and Society* 15, no. 2 (1997): 33–48.

———. "Normalisierung oder Re-Nationalisierung? Zur Umdeutung der deutschen Vergangenheit." *Geschichte und Gesellschaft* 21 (1995): 571–84.

———. *The Rush to German Unity.* Oxford, 1994.

———. "Zehn Jahre danach: Die Revolution von 1989/90 in vergleichender Perspektive." *Zeitschrift für Zeitgeschichte* 48, no. 10 (2000): 909–24.

———, ed. *After Unity: Reconfiguring German Identities.* Providence, 1997.

————, ed. *Dictatorship as Experience: Towards a Socio-Cultural History of the GDR,*
trans. Eve Duffy. New York, 1999.

Jarausch, Konrad H., and Martin Sabrow, eds. *Weg in den Untergang: Der innere
Zerfall der DDR.* Göttingen, 1999.

Jasper, Gotthard. "'Vergangenheitsbewältigung': Historische Erfahrungen und
politische Voraussetzungen," in *"Ohne Erinnerung keine Zukunft!" Zur Aufarbeitung von Vergangenheit in einigen europäischen Gesellschaften unserer Tage,* eds.
Clemens Burrichter and Günter Schödl, 17–31. Cologne, 1992.

Jesse, Eckhard. "Doppelte Vergangenheitsbewältigung in Deutschland: Ein
Problem der Vergangenheit, Gegenwart und Zukunft." In *Vergangenheitsbewältigung,* ed. Jesse, 11–26. Berlin, 1996.

————. "'Entnazifizierung' und 'Entstasifizierung' als politisches Problem: Die
doppelte Vergangenheitsbewältigung." In *Vergangenheitsbewältigung durch
Recht: Drei Abhandlungen zu einem deutschen Problem,* ed. Josef Isesee, 9–36.
Berlin, 1992.

————. "Oppositionelle Bestrebungen in der DDR der achtziger Jahre: Dominanz
des dritten Weges?" In *Wiedervereinigung Deutschlands: Festschrift zum 20jäh-
rigen Bestehen der Gesellschaft für Deutschlandforschung,* eds. Karl Eckart, Jens
Hacker, and Siegfried Mampel, 89–101. Berlin, 1998.

————. "Vergangenheitsbewältigung." In *Handwörterbuch zur deutschen Einheit,*
eds. Werner Weidenfeld and Karl-Rudolf Korte, 715–22. Frankfurt am Main,
1992.

————. "Vergangenheitsbewältigung im internationalen Vergleich: Die Reaktionen auf den Zusammenbruch des Nationalsozialismus/Faschismus und des
Kommunismus." In *Dem Zeitgeist geopfert: Die DDR in Wissenschaft, Publizistik
und politischer Bildung,* eds. Peter Eisenmann and Gerhard Hirscher, 19–36.
Munich, 1992.

————. "War die DDR totalitär?" *Aus Politik und Zeitgeschichte* 44, no. 40 (1994):
12–23.

————. "Die zweite deutsche Diktatur auf dem Prüfstand: Materialien der Enquete-Kommission 'Aufarbeitung von Geschichte und Folgen der SED-Diktatur in Deutschland.'" *Jahrbuch Extremismus und Demokratie* 8 (1996): 230–41.

————, ed. *Vergangenheitsbewältigung.* Berlin, 1997.

Jessen, Ralph, and Richard Bessel, eds. *Die Grenzen der Diktatur: Staat und Gesellschaft in der DDR.* Göttingen, 1996.

Joppke, Christian. *East German Dissidents and the Revolution of 1989: Social Movement in a Leninist Regime.* New York, 1995.

Joseph, Detlef. *Nazis in der DDR: Die deutschen Staatsdiener nach 1945 — Woher
kamen sie?* Berlin, 2002.

Kamali, Maryam. "Accountability for Human Rights Violations: A Comparison
of Transitional Justice in East Germany and South Africa." *Columbia Journal of
Transnational Law* 40 (2001): 89–141.

Kaminsky, Anne. "Die Diskussion über die Opfer des Stalinismus in der gegenwärtigen deutschen Erinnerungskultur." In *"Transformationen" der Erinnerungskulturen in Europa nach 1989,* eds. Bernd Faulenbach and Franz-Josef
Jelich, 381–97. Essen, 2006.

Kappelt, Olaf. *Braunbuch DDR: Nazis in der DDR*. (West) Berlin, 1981.

Käppner, Joachim. *Erstarrte Geschichte: Faschismus und Holocaust im Spiegel der Geschichtswissenschaft und Geschichtspropaganda der DDR*. Hamburg, 1999.

Karstedt, Susanne. "Coming to Terms with the Past in Germany after 1945 and 1989: Public Judgments on Procedures and Justice." *Law and Policy* 20, no. 1 (1998): 15–56.

Kattago, Siobhan. *Ambiguous Memory: The Nazi Past and German National Identity*. Westport, 2001.

Keil, Lars-Broder, and Sven Feliz Kellerhoff. *Deutsche Legenden: Vom "Dolchstoß" und anderen Mythen der Geschichte*. Berlin, 2002.

Keller, Dietmar, and Matthias Kirchner, eds. *Zwischen den Stühlen: Pro und Kontra SED*. Berlin, 1993.

Kershaw, Ian. *Germany's Present, Germany's Past*. London, 1992.

Kittel, Manfed. *Die Legende von der "zweiten Schuld": Vergangenheitsbewältigung in der Ära Adenauer*. Berlin, 1993.

Klein, Thomas. "Alternatives und oppositionelles Denken in der SED seit Mitte der 80er Jahre: Chance und Ausgang innerparteilicher Alternativenbildung in der Endphase der DDR." In *Ansichten zur Geschichte der DDR IV*, eds. Dietmar Keller, Hans Modrow, and Herbert Wolf, 213–23. Bonn, 1994.

Kleßmann, Christoph. "Opposition und Resistenz in zwei Diktaturen in Deutschland." *Historische Zeitschrift* 262 (1996): 453–79.

———. "Das Problem der doppelten 'Vergangenheitsbewältigung.'" *Die neue Gesellschaft/Frankfurter Hefte* 38, no. 12 (1993): 1099–105.

———. "Der schwierige gesamtdeutsche Umgang mit der DDR-Geschichte." *Aus Politik und Zeitgeschichte* 51, no. 30–31 (2001): 3–5.

———. *Zeitgeschichte in Deutschland nach dem Ende des Ost-West-Konflikts*. Essen, 1998.

———. "Zwei Diktaturen in Deutschland: Was kann die künftige DDR-Forschung aus der Geschichtsschreibung zum Nationalsozialismus lernen?" *Deutschland Archiv* 25, no. 6 (1992): 601–6.

Kleßmann, Christoph, Hans Misselwitz, and Günter Wichert, eds. *Deutsche Vergangenheiten—eine gemeinsame Herausforderung: Der schwierige Umgang mit der doppelten Nachkriegsgeschichte*. Berlin, 1999.

Kloth, Hans Michael. "'Versorgungsfall' Vergangenheit? Stiftung zur Aufarbeitung der SED-Vergangenheit gegründet." *Deutschland Archiv* 31, no. 5 (1998): 861–65.

Knütter, Hans-Helmuth. "Antifaschismus und politische Kultur in Deutschland nach der Wiedervereinigung." *Aus Politik und Zeitgeschichte* 43, no. 9 (1991): 17–28.

Kocka, Jürgen. "Chance und Herausforderung: Aufgaben der Zeitgeschichte beim Umgang mit der DDR-Vergangenheit." In *Die Partei hatte immer recht: Aufarbeitung von Geschichte und Folgen der SED-Diktatur*, eds. Bernd Faulenbach, Markus Meckel, and Hermann Weber, 239–49. Essen, 1994.

———. "The GDR: A Special Kind of Modern Dictatorship." In *Dictatorship as Experience: Towards a Socio-Cultural History of the GDR*, ed. Konrad H. Jarausch, trans. Eve Duffy, 17–26. New York, 1999.

————. "Nach dem Ende des Sonderwegs: Zur Tragfähigkeit eines Konzepts." In *Doppelte Zeitgeschichte: Deutsch-deutsche Beziehungen 1945–1990*, eds. Arnd Bauerkämper, Martin Sabrow, and Bernd Stöver, 364–75. Bonn, 1999.

————. *Vereinigungskrise: Zur Geschichte der Gegenwart*. Göttingen, 1995.

Kocka, Jürgen, and Martin Sabrow, eds. *Die DDR als Geschichte: Fragen, Hypothesen, Perspektiven*. Berlin, 1994.

König, Helmut. "Von der Diktatur zur Demokratie oder Was ist Vergangenheitsbewältigung." In *Vergangenheitsbewältigung am Ende des zwanzigsten Jahrhunderts (Leviathan 18)*, eds. Helmut König, Michael Kohlstruck, and Andreas Wöll, 371–92. Opladen, 1998.

König, Helmut, Michael Kohlstruck, and Andreas Wöll, eds. *Vergangenheitsbewältigung am Ende des zwanzigsten Jahrhunderts (Leviathan 18)*. Opladen, 1998.

Körner, Klaus. *"Die rote Gefahr": Antikommunistische Propaganda in der Bundesrepublik 1950–2000*. Hamburg, 2003.

Koschyk, Hartmut. "Die Beseitigung der Folgen der SED-Diktatur und die Frage der inneren Einheit." In *Wiedervereinigung Deutschlands: Festschrift zum 20jährigen Bestehen der Gesellschaft für Deutschlandforschung*, eds. Karl Eckart, Jens Hacker, and Siegfried Mampel, 473–84. Berlin, 1998.

Kotek, Joël, and Pierre Rigoulot. *Das Jahrhundert der Lager: Gefangenschaft, Zwangsarbeit, Vernichtung*, trans. Enrico Heinemann, Elsbeth Ranke, Ursel Schäfter, and Reiner Pfleiderer. Munich, 2001.

Kritz, Neil J., ed. *Transitional Justice: How Emerging Democracies Reckon with Former Regimes*. 3 vols. Washington, 1995.

Kühnhardt, Ludger. "Umbruch—Wende—Revolution: Deutungsmuster des deutschen Herbstes 1989." *Aus Politik und Zeitgeschichte* 47, no. 40–41 (1997): 12–18.

Kühnrich, Heinz. "'Verordnet'—und nichts weiter? Nachdenken über Antifaschismus in der DDR." *Zeitschrift für Geschichtswissenschaft* 40, no. 9 (1992): 819–33.

Kuppe, Joahnnes L. "Was bei der Aufarbeitung der Vergangenheit zu bedenken ist." *Deutschland Archiv* 25, no. 9 (1992): 978–81.

Kutter, Amelie. "Geschichtspolitische Ausgrenzungen in der Vereinigungspolitik: Das Beispiel der Enquete-Kommission." In *Die DDR war anders: Eine kritische Würdigung ihrer sozialkulturellen Einrichtungen*, eds. Stefan Bollinger and Fritz Villmar, 25–59. Berlin, 2002.

Kvistad, Gregg O. "Parties and Citizens in the Western German Unification Debate." *German Politics and Society* 30 (1993): 34–48.

Landtag Mecklenburg-Vorpommern, ed. *Leben in der DDR, Leben nach 1989: Aufarbeitung und Versöhnung, zur Arbeit der Enquete-Kommission*. X vols. Schwerin, 1996–1998.

Langenbacher, Eric. "Changing Memory Regimes in Contemporary Germany?" *German Politics and Society* 21, no. 2 (2003): 46–68.

Ledanff, Susanne. "The Palace of the Republic versus the Stadtschloss: The Dilemmas of Planning in the Heart of Berlin." *German Politics and Society* 21, no. 4 (2003): 30–44.

Leggewie, Claus, and Erik Meyer. *"Ein Ort, an den man gerne geht": Das Holocaust-Mahnmal und die deutsche Geschichtspolitik nach 1989*. Munich 2005.

Le Gloannec, Anne-Marie. "On German Identity." *Daedalus* 123, no. 1 (1994): 129–48.

Leo, Annette. "Keine gemeinsame Erinnerung: Geschichtsbewusstsein in Ost und West." *Aus Politik und Zeitgeschichte* 53, no. 40–41 (2003): 27–32.

———. "Nicht vereinigt: Studien zum Geschichtsbewusstsein Ost- und Westdeutscher." In *Deutsche Teilung, Repression und Alltagsleben: Erinnerungsorte der DDR-Geschichte*, eds. Heidi Behrens and Andreas Wagner, 58–68. Leipzig, 2004.

Leonhard, Jörn, and Lothar Funk, eds. *Ten Years of German Unification: Transfer, Transformation, Incorporation?* Birmingham, 2002.

Leonhard, Wolfgang. *Die Revolution entläßt ihre Kinder.* Cologne, 1955.

Lepsius, M. Rainer. "Das Erbe des Nationalsozialismus und die politische Kultur der Nachfolgestaaten des 'Großdeutschen Reiches.'" In *Demokratie in Deutschland: Soziologisch-historische Konstellationsanalysen*, 229–45. Göttingen, 1993.

———. "The Legacy of Two Dictatorships and Democratic Culture in United Germany." *Schweizerische Zeitschrift für Soziologie* 21, no. 3 (1995): 765–76.

Levy, Daniel, and Natan Sznaider. "Memory Unbound: The Holocaust and the Formation of Cosmopolitan Memory." *European Journal of Social Theory* 5, no. 1 (2002): 87–106.

Lindenberger, Thomas. "Everyday History: New Approaches to the History of the Post-War Germanies." In *The Divided Past: Rewriting Post-War German History*, ed. Christoph Kleßmann, 43–67. Oxford, 2001.

———, ed. *Herrschaft und Eigen-Sinn in der Diktatur: Studien zur Sozialgeschichte der DDR.* Cologne, 1999.

Lozek, Gerhard. "Zum Diktaturvergleich von NS-Regime und SED-Staat: Zum Wesen der DDR im Spannungsfeld von autoritären und totalitären, aber auch demokratischen Strukturen und Praktiken." In *Ansichten zur Geschichte der DDR IV*, eds. Dietmar Keller, Hans Modrow, and Herbert Wolf, 109–21. Bonn, 1994.

Lübbe, Hermann. "Der Nationalsozialismus im deutschen Nachkriegsbewußtsein." *Historische Zeitschrift* 236, no. 3 (1983): 579–99.

Lutz, Felix Philipp. "Historical Consciousness and the Changing of German Political Culture." In *The Berlin Republic: German Unification and a Decade of Change*, eds. Winand Gellner and John D. Robertson, 19–34. London, 2003.

Mählert, Ulrich, and Manfred Wilke. "Die DDR-Forschung: Ein Auslaufmodell? Die Auseinandersetzung mit der SED-Diktatur seit 1989." *Deutschland Archiv* 37, no. 3 (2004): 465–74.

Maier, Charles S. *Dissolution: The Crisis of Communism and the End of East Germany.* Princeton, 1997.

———. "Geschichtswissenschaft und Ansteckungsstaat." *Geschichte und Gesellschaft* 20 (1994): 616–24.

———. "Overcoming the Past? Narrative and Negotiation, Remembering and Reparation: Issues at the Interface of History and Law." In *Politics and the Past: On Repairing Historical Injustices*, ed. John Torpey, 295–304. Lanham, 2003.

———. *The Unmasterable Past: History, Holocaust and German National Identity.* Cambridge, MA, 1988.

Major, Patrick. *The Death of the KPD: Communism and Anti-Communism in West Germany, 1945–1956.* Oxford, 1997.

Markovits, Andrei S., and Philip S. Gorski, *The German Left: Red, Green and Beyond.* Cambridge, 1993.

Markovits, Inge. *Imperfect Justice: An East-West German Diary.* Oxford, 1995.

Maser, Peter. "Auf dem Weg zur deutschen Einheit: Anmerkungen zur neuen Enquete-Kommission des Deutschen Bundestages." In *Unrecht überwinden: SED-Diktatur und Widerstand,* Gerhard Finn, Frank Hagemann, Peter Maser, Helmut Müller-Embeys, Günther Wagenlehrer, and Hermann Wentker, 69–77. Sankt Augustin, 1996.

McAdams, A. James. "Germany after Unification: Normal at Last?" *World Politics* 49, no. 2 (1997): 282–308.

———. *Germany Divided: From the Wall to Reunification.* Princeton, 1993.

———. *Judging the Past in Unified Germany.* Cambridge, 2001.

———. "Revisiting the *Ostpolitik* in the 1990s." *German Politics and Society* 30 (1993): 49–60.

———. "Vergangenheitsaufarbeitung nach 1989: Ein deutscher Sonderweg?" *Deutschland Archiv* 36, no. 5 (2003): 851–60.

McAdams, A. James, and John Torpey, "The Political Arsenal of the German Past." *German Politics and Society* 30 (1993): 1–6.

McFalls, Laurence H., *Communism's Collapse, Democracy's Demise? The Cultural Context and Consequences of the East German Revolution.* New York, 1995.

———. "Political Culture and Political Change in Eastern Germany." *German Politics and Society* 20, no. 2 (2002): 75–92.

Meckel, Markus. "Aufarbeitung der DDR-Geschichte als Aufgabe des Bundestages." In *Rück-Sicht auf Deutschland: Beiträge zur Geschichte der DDR und zur Deutschlandpolitik der SPD,* ed. SPD-Bundestagsfraktion, 53–61. Bonn, 1993.

———. "Demokratische Selbstbestimmung als Prozeß: Die Aufgabe der Politik bei der Aufarbeitung der DDR-Vergangenheit." In *Die Partei hatte immer recht: Aufarbeitung von Geschichte und Folgen der SED-Diktatur,* eds. Bernd Faulenbach, Markus Meckel, and Hermann Weber, 250–78. Essen, 1994.

———. "Hilfe beim Verständnis der eigenen Vergangenheit: Hermann Weber zum Fünfundsiebzigsten." In *Bilanz und Perspektiven der DDR-Forschung,* eds. Rainer Eppelmann, Bernd Faulenbach, and Ulrich Mählert, 428–34. Paderborn, 2003.

———. *Selbstbewußt in die deutsche Einheit: Rückblicke und Reflexionen.* Berlin, 2001.

Mehringer, Harmut. "Sozialdemokratisches Exil und Nachkriegs-Sozialdemokratie: Lernprozesse auf dem Weg zum Godesberger Programm." In *"Ohne Erinnerung keine Zukunft!" Zur Aufarbeitung von Vergangenheit in einigen europäischen Gesellschaften unserer Tage,* eds. Clemens Burrichter and Günter Schödl, 109–23. Cologne, 1992.

Meuschel, Sigrid. "Überlegungen zu einer Herrschafts- und Gesellschaftsgeschichte der DDR." *Geschichte und Gesellschaft* 19, no. 1 (1993): 5–14.

Meyer, Erik. "Erinnerungskultur als Politikfeld: Geschichtspolitische Deliberation und Dezision in der Berliner Republik." In *Die NS-Diktatur im deutschen Erinnerungsdiskurs,* ed. Wolfgang Bergem, 121–36. Opladen, 2003.

Milfull, John. "What was Different about the German Democratic Republic?" *Australian Journal of Politics and History* 48, no. 1 (2002): 65–71.

Miller, Barbara. *Narratives of Guilt and Conformity in Unified Germany: Stasi Informers and their Impact on Society*. London, 1999.

Ministerium für Wissenschaft, Forschung und Kultur des Landes Brandenburg, ed. *Brandenburgische Gedenkstätten für die Verfolgten des NS-Regimes: Perspektiven, Kontroversen und internationale Vergleiche*. Berlin, 1992.

Mitter, Armin. "Angst und Hilflosigkeit in den Köpfen: Die DDR-Vergangenheit wird zum Problem der Zukunft." In *Krise—Umbruch—Neubeginn: Eine kritische und selbstkritische Dokumentation der DDR-Geschichtswissenschaft 1989/90*, eds. Rainer Eckert, Wolfgang Küttler, and Gustav Seeber, 107–10. Stuttgart, 1992.

Moeller, Robert G. "Sinking Ships, the Lost *Heimat* and Broken Taboos: Günter Grass and the Politics of Memory in Contemporary Germany." *Contemporary European History* 12, no. 2 (2003): 147–81.

———. *War Stories: The Search for a Usable Past in the Federal Republic of Germany*. Berkeley, 2001.

———. "What Has 'Coming to Terms with the Past' Meant in Post-World War II Germany?" *Central European History* 35, no. 2 (2002): 223–56.

Monteath, Peter. "The German Democratic Republic and the Jews." *German History* 22, no. 3 (2004): 448–68.

Moreau, Patrick. "Mit Lenin im Bauch… ? Die PDS auf der Suche nach einer Berliner Republik von Links." *Politische Studien* 349 (1996): 27–42.

Moses, A. Dirk. "Coming to Terms with the Past in Comparative Perspective: Germany and Australia." *Aboriginal History* 25 (2001): 91–115.

———. "The Non-German German and the German German: Dilemmas of Identity after the Holocaust." *New German Critique* 34, no. 2 (2007): 45–94.

———. "The 'Weimar Syndrome' in the Federal Republic of Germany." In *Leben, Tod und Entscheidung: Studien zur Geistesgeschichte der Weimarer Republik*, eds. Stephan Loos and Holger Zaborowski, 187–201. Berlin, 2003.

Mühlberg, Dietrich. "Vom langsamen Wandel der Erinnerung an die DDR." In *Verletztes Gedächtnis: Erinnerungskultur und Zeitgeschichte im Konflikt*, eds. Konrad H. Jarausch and Martin Sabrow, 217–51. Frankfurt am Main, 2002.

Muller, Jerry Z. "German Neoconservatism and the History of the Bonn Republic, 1968–1985." *German Politics and Society* 18, no. 1 (2000): 1–32.

Müller, Jan-Werner. "East Germany: Incorporation, Tainted Truth, and the Double Division." In *The Politics of Memory and Democratization: Transitional Justice in Democratizing Societies*, eds. Alexandra Barahona De Brito, Carmen Gonzalez Enriquez, and Paloma Aguilar, 248–74. Oxford, 2001.

———. "Preparing for the Political: German Intellectuals Confront the Berlin Republic." In *Political Thought and German Reunification: The New German Ideology?* eds. Howard Williams, Colin Wight, and Norbert Kapferer, 209–35. Basingstoke, 2000.

Müller, Werner. "SED-Gründung unter Zwang: Ein Streit ohne Ende? Plädoyer für den Begriff 'Zwangsvereinigung.'" *Deutschland Archiv* 42 (1991): 52–58.

Naimark, Norman N. *The Russians in Germany: A History of the Soviet Zone of Occupation, 1945–1949*. Cambridge, MA, 1995.

Nationalrat der Nationalen Front des demokratischen Deutschland, ed. *Braun-buch: Kriegs- und Naziverbrecher in der Bundesrepublik: Staat, Wirtschaft, Armee, Verwaltung, Justiz, Wissenschaft*. (East) Berlin, 1965.

Naumann, Klaus. "Die geteilte Vergangenheit: Geschichte als Politik." *Blätter für deutsche und internationale Politik* 36, no. 11 (1991): 1392–401.

Neubert, Erhard. *Geschichte der Opposition in der DDR 1949–1989*. Bonn, 1997.

Neubert, Harald. "Die Vorgeschichte der deutschen Zweistaatlichkeit im internationalen Bedingungsgefüge (Thesen)." In *Ansichten zur Geschichte der DDR V*, eds. Jochen Černý, Dieter Lehmann, and Manfred Neuhaus, 41–48. Bonn, 1994.

Neuhäußer-Wespy, Ulrich. "Aspekte und Probleme der Umorientierung in der Geschichtswissenschaft der DDR von 1971/72." In *Geschichtswissenschaft in der DDR I*, eds. Alexander Fischer and Günther Heydemann, 77–102. (West) Berlin, 1988.

Niethammer, Lutz. "Alliierte Internierungslager in Deutschland nach 1945: Vergleich und offene Fragen." In *Von der Aufgabe der Freiheit: Politische Verantwortung und bürgerliche Gesellschaft im 19. und 20. Jahrhundert, Festschrift für Hans Mommsen zum 5. November 1995*, eds. Christian Jansen, Lutz Niethammer, and Bernd Weisbrod, 469–92. Berlin, 1995.

Niven, Bill. *Facing the Nazi Past, United Germany and the Legacy of the Third Reich*. London, 2002.

Nora, Pierre. "Between Memory and History: *Les Lieux de Mémoire*." *Representations* 26 (1989): 7–25.

Nothnagle, Alan. *Building the East German Myth: Historical Mythology and Youth Propaganda in the German Democratic Republic, 1945–1989*. Ann Arbor, 1999.

O'Dochartaigh, Pol. *Germany since 1945*. Basingstoke, 2004.

Offe, Claus. *Varieties of Transition: The East European and East German Experience*. Cambridge, 1996.

Okun, Bernd. "Inwieweit ist der Herbst 1989 'identitätsstiftend' für das vereinte Deutschland? Einige Überlegungen." In *Ansichten zur Geschichte der DDR V*, eds. Jochen Černý, Dieter Lehmann, and Manfred Neuhaus, 163–68. Bonn, 1994.

Olick, Jeffrey K. *In the House of the Hangman: The Agonies of German Defeat, 1943–49*. Chicago, 2005.

Olsen, Jonathan. "Germany's PDS and Varieties of 'Post-Communist' Socialism." *Problems of Post-Communism* 45, no. 6 (1998): 42–52.

Ommler, Norbert. "Zweierlei 'Vergangenheitsbewältigung' ohne Tangieren des gemeinsamen Kerns?" *Geschichte — Erziehung — Politik* 4, no. 7–8 (1993): 433–40.

Oswald, Franz. "Negotiating Identities: The Party of Democratic Socialism between East German Regionalism, German National Identity and European Integration." *Australian Journal of Politics and History* 50, no. 1 (2004): 75–85.

Otto, Wilfried. "Opposition und Widerstand zwischen Hoffnung und Enttäuschung." In *Ansichten zur Geschichte der DDR III*, eds. Dietmar Keller, Hans Modrow, and Herbert Wolf, 227–56. Bonn, 1994.

———. "Widerspruch und Widerstand in der SED." In *Ansichten zur Geschichte der DDR I*, eds. Dietmar Keller, Hans Modrow, and Herbert Wolf, 129–48. Bonn, 1993.

Pampel, Bernd. "Bagatellisierung durch Gedenken? Gedenkstättenarbeit an Orten aufeinanderfolgenden nationalsozialistischen und kommunistischen Unrechts." *Deutschland Archiv* 31, no. 3 (1998): 438–53.

———. "Was bedeutet 'Aufarbeitung der Vergangenheit'? Kann man aus der 'Vergangenheitsbewältigung' nach 1945 für die 'Aufarbeitung' nach 1989 Lehren ziehen?" *Aus Politik und Zeitgeschichte* 45, no. 1–2 (1995): 27–38.

Pätzold, Kurt. "Die Legende vom 'verordneten Antifaschismus.'" In *Ansichten zur Geschichte der DDR* III, eds. Dietmar Keller, Hans Modrow, and Herbert Wolf, 111–30. Bonn, 1994.

Pfaff, Steven, and Hyojoung Kim. "Exit-Voice Dynamics in Collective Action: An Analysis of Emigration and Protest in the East German Revolution." *American Journal of Sociology* 109, no. 2 (2003): 401–44.

Pingel, Falk. "Vom Paradigma der Weltrevolution zur Unbestimmtheit der Postmoderne: Was heisst 'Zeitgeschichte' im Ost-West-Vergleich heute?" In *Doppelte Zeitgeschichte: Deutsch-deutsche Beziehungen 1945–1990*, eds. Arnd Bauerkämper, Martin Sabrow, and Bernd Stöver, 330–45. Bonn, 1999.

Pollack, Detlef. "Die konstitutive Widersprüchlichkeit der DDR, Oder: War die DDR-Gesellschaft homogen?" *Geschichte und Gesellschaft* 24, no. 1 (1997): 110–31.

Pommerin, Reiner. "Die Zwangsvereinigung von KPD und SPD zur SED: Eine britische Analyse vom April 1946." *Vierteljahreshefte für Zeitgeschichte* 36, no. 2 (1988): 319–25.

Poppe, Ulrike, Rainer Eckert, and Ilko-Sascha Kowalczuk, eds. *Zwischen Selbstbehauptung und Anpassung: Formen des Widerstands und der Opposition in der DDR.* Berlin, 1995.

Poutrus, Patrice G., Jan C. Behrends, and Dennis Kuck, "Historische Ursachen der Fremdenfeindlichkeit in den neuen Bundesländern." *Aus Politik und Zeitgeschichte* 50, no. 39 (2000), 15–21.

Pritchard, Gareth. *The Making of the GDR 1945–1953: From Antifascism to Stalinism.* Manchester, 2000.

Probst, Lothar. "Germany's Past, Germany's Future: Intellectual Controversies since Reunification." *German Politics and Society* 30 (1993): 21–33.

Pross, Christian. *Paying for the Past: The Struggle over Reparations for Surviving Victims of the Nazi Terror,* trans. Belinda Cooper. Baltimore, 1998.

Quaritsch, Helmut. "Theorie der Vergangenheitsbewältigung." *Der Staat* 31 (1992): 519–51.

Rauschenbach, Brigitte. "Erbschaft aus Vergessenheit: Zukunft aus Erinnerungsarbeit." *Deutschland Archiv* 25, no. 9 (1992): 929–42.

Reich, Ines. "Geteilter Widerstand: Die Tradierung des deutschen Widerstands in der Bundesrepublik und der DDR." *Zeitschrift für Geschichtswissenschaft* 42, no. 7 (1994): 635–43.

Reichel, Peter. *Politik mit der Erinnerung: Gedächtnisorte im Streit um die nationalsozialistische Vergangenheit,* revised ed. Frankfurt am Main, 1999.

Roberts, Geoffrey K. *Party Politics in the New Germany.* London, 1997.

Rosenberg, Tina. *The Haunted Land: Facing Europe's Ghosts after Communism.* New York, 1995.

————. "Overcoming the Legacies of Dictatorship." *Foreign Affairs* 74, no. 3 (1995): 134–52.

Ross, Corey. *The East German Dictatorship: Problems and Perspectives in the Interpretation of the GDR.* London, 2002.

Sa'adah, Anne. *Germany's Second Chance: Trust, Justice and Democratization.* Cambridge, MA, 1998.

Sabrow, Martin, ed. *Grenzen der Vereinigung: Die geteilte Vergangenheit im geeinten Deutschland.* Leipzig, 1999.

Sandner, Günther. "Hegemonie und Erinnerung: Zur Konzeption von Geschichts- und Vergangenheitspolitik." *Österreichische Zeitschrift für Politikwissenschaft* 30, no. 1 (2001): 5–17.

Schätzler, Johann-Georg. "Staatenfusion und Abrechnungsmentalität." *Deutschland Archiv* 30, no. 1 (1997): 105–15.

Schildt, Axel. *Ankunft im Westen: Ein Essay zur Erfolgsgeschichte der Bundesrepublik.* Frankfurt am Main, 1999.

Schiller, Kay. "The Presence of the Nazi Past in the Early Decades of the Bonn Republic." *Journal of Contemporary History* 39, no. 2 (2004): 285–94.

Schönherr, Albrecht, ed. *Ein Volk am Pranger? Die Deutschen auf der Suche nach einer neuen politischen Kultur.* Berlin, n.d.

Schroeder, Friedrich-Christian. "Die Enquetekommission des Deutschen Bundestages 'Aufarbeitung von Geschichte und von Folgen der SED-Diktatur in Deutschland.'" *Politische Studien* 324 (1992): 23–27.

Schroeder, Klaus. *Der SED-Staat: Partei, Staat und Gesellschaft 1949–1990.* Munich, 1998.

————. *Die veränderte Republik: Deutschland nach der Wiedervereinigung.* Stamsried, 2006.

Schröder, Richard. "Brauchen wir ein nationales Freiheits- und Einheitsdenkmal?" *Deutschland Archiv* 40, no. 1 (2007): 131-36.

Schubarth, Wilfried, Ronald Pschierer, and Thomas Schmidt. "Verordneter Antifaschismus und die Folgen: Das Dilemma antifaschistischer Erziehung am Ende der DDR." *Aus Politik und Zeitgeschichte* 41, no. 9 (1991): 3–16.

Schuller, Wolfgang. "Bericht der Enquete-Kommission 'Aufarbeitung von Geschichte und Folgen der SED-Diktatur in Deutschland.'" *Geschichte in Wissenschaft und Unterricht* 46, no. 12 (1995): 738–45.

Schulte, Marc. "Die 'doppelte Vergangenheit' in der politischen Diskussion im Bundestag." *Geschichte—Erziehung—Politik* 4, no. 6 (1993): 361–68.

Schulz, Wilfried. "Die PDS und der SED/DDR-Antifaschismus: Historischer Klärungsbedarf oder nur Nostalgie und neue Feindbilder." *Deutschland Archiv* 27, no. 4 (1994): 408–13.

Schütrumpf, Jörn. "Stalinismus und gescheiterte Entstalinisierung in der DDR." In *Wendezeiten—Zeitenwände: Zur "Entnazifizierung" und "Entstalinisierung,"* eds. Rainer Eckert, Alexander von Plato, and Jörn Schütrumpf, 77–83. Hamburg, 1991.

Schwabe, Uwe, and Rainer Eckert, eds. *Von Deutschland Ost nach Deutschland West: Oppositionelle oder Verräter? "Haben die Ausreisewilligen der 80er Jahre den*

Prozess der friedlichen Revolution und das Ende der DDR eher beschleunigt oder gefährdet?" Leipzig, 2003.

Schwan, Gesine. *Politik und Schuld: Die zerstörerische Macht des Schweigens.* Frankfurt am Main, 1997.

Schweitzer, Carl-Christoph, Detlev Karsten, Robert Spencer, R. Taylor Cole, Donald P. Kommers, and Anthony J. Nicholls, eds. *Politics and Government in Germany, 1944–1994: Basic Documents.* Providence, 1995.

Siegmund, Jörg. *Opfer ohne Lobby? Ziele, Strukturen und Arbeitsweise der Verbände der Opfer des DDR-Unrechts.* Berlin, 2003.

———. "Die Opferverbände des SBZ/DDR-Unrechts." In *Bilanz und Perspektiven der DDR-Forschung,* eds. Rainer Eppelmann, Bernd Faulenbach, and Ulrich Mählert, 413–19. Paderborn, 2003.

Simon, Annette. *Versuch, mir und anderen die ostdeutsche Moral zu erklären.* Giessen, 1995.

Sperber, Jonathan. "17 June 1953: Revisiting a German Revolution." *German History* 22, no. 4 (2004): 619–43.

Staritz, Dietrich. *Geschichte der DDR 1949–1985.* Frankfurt am Main, 1985.

Steinbach, Peter. "Darf der pluralistische Staat 'Geschichtspolitik' betreiben? Zu einer Kontroverse der jüngsten Vergangenheit." In *Vergangenheitsbewältigung,* ed. Eckhard Jesse, 79–87. Berlin, 1997.

———. "Die Erfahrungen der Arbeiterbewegung in Verfolgung, Widerstand und Exil." In *Sozialdemokraten und Kommunisten nach Nationalsozialismus und Krieg: Zur historischen Einordnung der Zwangsvereinigung,* eds. Bernd Faulenbach and Heinrich Pothoff, 23–52. Essen, 1998.

———. *Nationalsozialistische Gewaltverbrechen in der deutschen Öffentlichkeit: Die Diskussion nach 1945.* (West) Berlin, 1981.

———. "Postdiktatorische Geschichtspolitik: Nationalsozialismus und Widerstand im deutschen Geschichtsbild nach 1945." In *Umkämpfte Vergangenheit: Geschichtsbilder, Erinnerung und Vergangenheitspolitik im internationalen Vergleich,* eds. Petra Bock and Edgar Wolfrum, 17–40. Göttingen, 1999.

———. "Vergangenheitsbewältigung in vergleichender Perspektive: Politische Säuberung, Wiedergutmachung, Integration." In *Geschichte und Transformation des SED-Staates: Beiträge und Analysen,* ed. Klaus Schroeder, 394–423. Berlin, 1994.

Stephan, Cora, ed. *Wir Kollaborateure: Der Westen und die deutschen Vergangenheiten.* Reinbek bei Hamburg, 1992.

Sühl, Klaus, ed. *Vergangenheitsbewältigung 1945 und 1989: Ein unmöglicher Vergleich? Eine Diskussion.* Berlin, 1994.

Süssmuth, Rita. "Auf dem Weg zur inneren Einheit Deutschlands—der Beitrag des Deutschen Bundestages." In *Eine deutsche Zwischenbilanz: Standpunkte zum Umgang mit unserer Vergangenheit,* eds. Süssmuth and Bernward Baule, 21–40. Munich, 1997.

Teitel, Rudi G. *Transitional Justice.* Oxford, 2000.

Thierse, Wolfgang. "Oktober 1917—November 1989: Sozialismus zwischen Diktatur und Emanzipation." In *Diktatur und Emanzipation: Zur russischen und deutschen Entwicklung 1917–1991*, eds. Bernd Faulenbach and Martin Stadelmaier, 204–13. Essen, 1993.

———. "Schuld sind immer die anderen: Ein Plädoyer für die selbstkritische Bewältigung der eigenen Geschichte." In *Ein Volk am Pranger? Die Deutschen auf der Suche nach einer neuen politischen Kultur*, ed. Albrecht Schönherr, 13–18. Berlin, n.d.

Thomaneck, Jürgen K.A., and Bill Niven. *Dividing and Uniting Germany.* London, 2000.

Thompson, Mark. "Reluctant Revolutionaries: Anti-Fascism and the East German Opposition." *German Politics* 8, no. 1 (1999): 40–65.

Thompson, Peter. "The PDS: Marx's Baby or Stalin's Bathwater? or Vom Nutzen und Nachteil der Historie für das Leben der PDS." In *The GDR and its History: Rückblick und Revision, Die DDR im Spiegel der Enquete-Kommissionen (German Monitor 49)*, ed. Peter Barker, 97–112. Amsterdam, 2000.

Thumfart, Alexander. *Die politische Integration Ostdeutschlands.* Frankfurt am Main, 2002.

Timm, Angelika. *Jewish Claims against East Germany: Moral Obligations and Pragmatic Policy.* Budapest, 1997.

Torpey, John. "Coming to Terms with the Communist Past: East Germany in Comparative Perspective." *German Politics* 2, no. 3 (1993): 415–35.

———, ed. *Politics and the Past: On Repairing Historical Injustices.* Lanham, 2003.

Vergau, Jutta. *Aufarbeitung von Vergangenheit vor und nach 1989: Eine Analyse des Umgangs mit den historischen Hypotheken totalitärer Diktaturen in Deutschland.* Marburg, 2000.

Von Ditfurth, Christian. *Blockflöten: Wie die CDU ihre realsozialistische Vergangenheit verdrängt.* Cologne, 1991.

Von Plato, Alexander. "Eine zweite 'Entnazifizierung'? Zur Verarbeitung politischer Umwälzungen in Deutschland 1945 und 1989." *Gewerkschaftliche Monatshefte* 42, no. 7 (1991): 415–28.

Wassermann, Rudolf. "Vergangenheitsbewältigung nach 1945 und nach 1989." *Jahrbuch Extremismus und Demokratie* 5 (1993): 29–50.

Weber, Hermann. "Die Aufarbeitung der DDR-Geschichte und die Rolle der Archive." In *Die Partei hatte immer recht: Aufarbeitung von Geschichte und Folgen der SED-Diktatur*, eds. Bernd Faulenbach, Markus Meckel, and Weber, 42–56. Essen, 1994.

———. *Die DDR 1945–1990*, revised, expanded ed. Munich, 1999.

———. "Gab es eine demokratische Vorgeschichte der DDR?" *Gewerkschaftliche Monatshefte* 43, no. 4–5 (1992): 272–80.

———. *Geschichte der DDR*, revised ed. Munich, 1999.

———. "'Hauptfeind Sozialdemokratie': Zur Politik der deutschen Kommunisten gegenüber den Sozialdemokraten zwischen 1930 und 1950." In *Halbherziger Revisionismus: Zum post-kommunistischen Geschichtsbild*, eds. Rainer Eckert and Bernd Faulenbach, 25–46. Munich, 1996.

———. "Rewriting the History of the German Democratic Republic: The Work of the Commission of Inquiry." In *Rewriting the German Past: History and Identity in the New Germany*, eds. Reinhard Alter and Peter Monteath, 197–207. Atlantic Highlands, 1997.

Weber, Hermann, with Gerda Weber. *Damals, als ich Wunderlich hiess: Vom Parteihochschüler zum kritischen Sozialisten, Die SED-Parteihochschule Karl Marx bis 1949*. Berlin, 2002.

Wehler, Hans-Ulrich. "Diktaturenvergleich, Totalitarismustheorie und DDR-Geschichte." In *Doppelte Zeitgeschichte: Deutsch-deutsche Beziehungen 1945–1990*, eds. Arnd Bauerkämper, Martin Sabrow, and Bernd Stöver, 346–52. Bonn, 1999.

Weinke, Annette. "Der Umgang mit der Stasi und ihren Mitarbeitern." In *Vergangenheitsbewältigung am Ende des zwanzigsten Jahrhunderts (Leviathan 18)*, eds. Helmut König, Michael Kohlstruck, and Andreas Wöll, 167–91. Opladen, 1998.

Welsh, Helga A. "Entnazifizierung in der DDR und die 'Wende.'" In *Wendezeiten – Zeitenwände: Zur "Entnazifizierung" und "Entstalinisierung*," eds. Rainer Eckert, Alexander von Plato, and Jörn Schütrumpf, 65–76. Hamburg, 1991.

———. "When Discourse Trumps Policy: Transitional Justice in Unified Germany." *German Politics* 15, no. 2 (2006): 137–52.

Wielenga, Friso. "Schatten der deutschen Geschichte: Der Umgang mit der Nazi- und DDR-Vergangenheit in der Bundesrepublik Deutschland." *Deutschland Archiv* 27, no. 10 (1994): 1058–73.

———. *Schatten deutscher Geschichte: Der Umgang mit dem Nationalsozialismus und der DDR-Vergangenheit in der Bundesrepublik*. Vierow bei Greifswald, 1995.

Wilke, Manfred. "Die deutsche Einheit und die Geschichtspolitik des Bundestages." *Deutschland Archiv* 30, no. 4 (1997): 607–13.

———. "Die deutsche Einheit und die Geschichtspolitik des Bundestages." In *Wiedervereinigung Deutschlands: Festschrift zum 20jährigen Bestehen der Gesellschaft für Deutschlandforschung*, eds. Karl Eckart, Jens Hacker, and Siegfried Mampel, 449–72. Berlin, 1998.

———. "Der Historiker und die Politik: Alexander Fischer als Sachverständiges Mitglied der Bundestags-Enquete-Kommission 'Aufarbeitung von Geschichte und Folgen der SED-Diktatur in Deutschland.'" In *Wandel durch Beständigkeit: Studien zur deutschen und internationalen Politik: Jens Hacker zum 65. Geburtstag*, eds. Karl G. Kick, Stephan Weingarz, and Ulrich Bartosch, 79–99. Berlin, 1998.

Wilms, Dorothee. "Begründung, Entstehung und Zielsetzung der Enquete-Kommission 1992–1994 im Deutschen Bundestag." In *The GDR and its History: Rückblick und Revision, Die DDR im Spiegel der Enquete-Kommissionen (German Monitor 49)*, ed. Peter Barker, 9–20. Amsterdam, 2000.

———. "Was sollte ein Freiheits- und Einheitsdenkmal versinnbildlichen?" *Deutschland Archiv* 40, no. 5 (2007): 868–72.

Winkler, Heinrich August, "Kein Bruch mit Lenin: Die Weimarer Republik aus der Sicht von SED und PDS." In *Halbherziger Revisionismus: Zum post-kommunistischen Geschichtsbild*, eds. Rainer Eckert and Bernd Faulenbach, 11–23. Munich, 1996.

———, ed. *Griff nach der Deutungsmacht: Zur Geschichte der Geschichtspolitik in Deutschland*. Göttingen, 2004.

Wisniewski, Roswitha. "Das Bildungssystem der DDR und sein Vermächtnis." In *The GDR and its History: Rückblick und Revision, Die DDR im Spiegel der Enquete-Kommissionen (German Monitor 49)*, ed. Peter Barker, 129–43. Amsterdam, 2000.

Wittek, Bernd. *Der Literaturstreit im sich vereinigenden Deutschland: Eine Analyse des Streits um Christa Wolf und die deutsch-deutsche Gegenwartsliteratur in Zeitungen und Zeitschriften*. Marburg, 1997.

Wittich, Bernd. "Betrifft: Ludwig Elm, Zweierlei Vergangenheitsbewältigung: Damals und heute—DA 7/1991." *Deutschland Archiv* 25, no. 6 (1992): 625–29.

Wolf, Herbert. "Einfluß und Elend der marxistischen Theorie im DDR-Sozialismus oder auch: Starb der Sozialismus an Marx oder Marx am 'realen Sozialismus.'" In *Ansichten zur Geschichte der DDR* III, eds. Dietmar Keller, Hans Modrow, and Herbert Wolf, 9–69. Bonn, 1994.

———. "Sine ira et studio??? Standpunkt zum Abschluß der Arbeit der Enquete-Kommission." In *Ansichten zur Geschichte der DDR* IV, eds. Dietmar Keller, Hans Modrow, and Herbert Wolf, 357–78. Bonn, 1994.

Wolffsohn, Michael. "Doppelte Vergangenheitsbewältigung." In *Vergangenheitsbewältigung 1945 und 1989: Ein unmöglicher Vergleich? Eine Diskussion*, ed. Klaus Sühl, 37–43. Berlin, 1994.

Wolfgram, Mark A. "The Legacies of Memory: The Third Reich in Unified Germany." *German Politics and Society* 21, no. 3 (2003): 89–100.

Wolfrum, Edgar. *Geschichte als Waffe: Vom Kaiserreich bis zur Wiedervereinigung*. Göttingen, 2002.

———. *Geschichtspolitik in der Bundesrepublik Deutschland: Der Weg zur bundesrepublikanischen Erinnerung 1948–1990*. Darmstadt, 1999.

———. "Geschichtspolitik in der Bundesrepublik Deutschland 1949–1989: Phasen und Kontroversen." In *Umkämpfte Vergangenheit: Geschichtsbilder, Erinnerung und Vergangenheitspolitik im internationalen Vergleich*, eds. Petra Bock and Edgar Wolfrum, 55–81. Göttingen, 1999.

———. "Neue Erinnerungskultur? Die Massenmedialisierung des 17. Juni 1953." *Aus Politik und Zeitgeschichte* 53, no. 40–41 (2003): 33–39.

Wolle, Stefan. "Herrschaft und Alltag: Die Zeitgeschichtsforschung auf der Suche nach der wahren DDR." *Aus Politik und Zeitgeschichte* 47, no. 26 (1997): 30–38.

———. "Im Kleinhirn der Krake: Der Beginn der Stasi-Auflösung in Berlin im Januar 1990." In *Dem Zeitgeist geopfert: Die DDR in Wissenschaft, Publizistik und politischer Bildung*, eds. Peter Eisenmann and Gerhard Hirscher, 103–12. Munich, 1992.

Wurl, Ernst. "Die 'SED-Diktatur': Überlegungen im Kontext einer Kritik des Begriffs aus dem Bericht der Enquete-Kommission des Deutschen Bundestages." In *Ansichten zur Geschichte der DDR* V, eds. Jochen Černý, Dieter Lehmann, and Manfred Neuhaus, 99–121. Bonn, 1994.

Wüstenberg, Ralf K. *Die politische Dimension der Versöhnung: Eine theologische Studie zum Umgang mit Schuld nach den Systemumbrüchen in Südafrika und Deutschland*. Gütersloh, 2004.

Yoder, Jennifer A. "Culprits, Culpability, and Corrective Justice." *Problems of Post-Communism* 45, no. 4 (1998): 14–21.

———. *From East Germans to Germans? The New Postcommunist Elites.* Durham, 1999.

———. "Truth without Reconciliation: An Appraisal of the Enquete Commission on the SED Dictatorship in Germany." *German Politics* 8, no. 3 (1999): 59–80.

Zens, Maria. "Truism and Taboo: The Rhetoric of the Berlin Republic." In *Political Thought and German Reunification: The New German Ideology?* eds. Howard Williams, Colin Wight, and Norbert Kapferer, 64–95. Basingstoke, 2000.

Zimmer, Hasko, in collaboration with Katja Flesser and Julia Volmer, *Der Buchenwald-Konflikt: Zum Streit um Geschichte und Erinnerung im Kontext der deutschen Vereinigung.* Münster, 1999.

Zimmering, Raina. *Mythen in der Politik der DDR: Ein Beitrag zur Erforschung politischer Mythen.* Opladen, 2000.

Zimmermann, Moshe. "Die Erinnerung an Nationalsozialismus und Widerstand im Spannungsfeld deutscher Zweistaatlichkeit." In *Die geteilte Vergangenheit: Zum Umgang mit Nationalsozialismus und Widerstand in beiden deutschen Staaten,* ed. Jürgen Danyel, 133–38. Berlin, 1995.

INDEX